S0-CKS-175

Economic Liberalism and Its Rivals

The Formation of International Institutions among the Post-Soviet States

This book examines the critical role that the economic ideas of state leaders play in the creation and maintenance of the international economic order. Drawing on a detailed study of the 15 post-Soviet states in their first decade of independence, interviews with key decision makers, and the use of closed ministerial archives, the book explores how the changing ideas of state officials led countries to follow one of three institutional paths: rapid entry into the World Trade Organization, participation in a regional Customs Union based on their prior Soviet ties, or autarky and economic closure. In doing so, the book traces the decisions that shaped the entry of these strategically important countries into the world economy and provides a novel theory of the role of ideas in international politics. As a dynamic study of ideas and institutions based on a relatively large number of countries in a period of crisis, this book is the first of its kind.

Keith A. Darden is Associate Professor of Political Science, Director of the Yale Central Asia Initiative, and recipient of the Lex Hixon '63 Prize for Teaching Excellence in the Social Sciences at Yale University. His extensive fieldwork has carried him to Russia, Ukraine, Belarus, the Baltic states, the states of Central Asia, and the Caucasus. After receiving his Ph.D. from the University of California, Berkeley, and prior to taking his appointment at Yale, Professor Darden was an Academy Scholar at Harvard University and a visiting Fellow at the Davis Center for Russian Studies. Professor Darden's work has been published in *World Politics*, *Politics and Society*, the *Journal of Common Market Studies*, and other journals.

Economic Liberalism and Its Rivals

The Formation of International Institutions among the Post-Soviet States

KEITH A. DARDEN
Yale University

CAMBRIDGE
UNIVERSITY PRESS

HF
1557
. D37
2009

CAMBRIDGE UNIVERSITY PRESS
Cambridge, New York, Melbourne, Madrid, Cape Town, Singapore, São Paulo, Delhi

Cambridge University Press
32 Avenue of the Americas, New York, NY 10013-2473, USA

www.cambridge.org
Information on this title: www.cambridge.org/9780521866538

© Keith A. Darden 2009

This publication is in copyright. Subject to statutory exception
and to the provisions of relevant collective licensing agreements,
no reproduction of any part may take place without the written
permission of Cambridge University Press.

First published 2009

Printed in the United States of America

A catalog record for this publication is available from the British Library.

Library of Congress Cataloging in Publication Data

Darden, Keith A., 1970–
Economic liberalism and its rivals : the formation of international institutions among the
post-Soviet states / Keith A. Darden.
   p.   cm.
Includes bibliographical references and index.
ISBN 978-0-521-86653-8 (hardback)
1. Former Soviet republics – Foreign economic relations.   2. Former Soviet republics –
Economic policy.   3. Liberalism – Former Soviet republics.   I. Title.
HF1557.D37   2008
337.47 – dc22   2007033518

ISBN   978-0-521-86653-8 hardback

Cambridge University Press has no responsibility for the persistence
or accuracy of URLs for external or third-party Internet Web sites
referred to in this publication and does not guarantee that any
content on such Web sites is, or will remain, accurate or appropriate.
Information regarding prices, travel timetables, and other factual
information given in this work are correct at the time of first printing,
but Cambridge University Press does not guarantee the accuracy
of such information thereafter.

Contents

University Libraries
Carnegie Mellon University
Pittsburgh, PA 15213-3890

v

Figures and Tables

Acknowledgments

Some projects have a way of holding on longer than others, and this book has managed to keep me in its grasp for some time now. In the process, however, it has had the benefit of many great minds and repeated acts of genuine kindness. I can only briefly acknowledge some of those contributions here.

The project began at the University of California at Berkeley and was shaped by the committee that advised the original dissertation. The ideas grew out of an intellectual friendship with my chair, Ernie Haas, whose generosity of time and spirit has left its mark on this work as well as all of my others. George Breslauer not only imparted to me the knowledge of Russia and the Soviet Union that I lacked when this project was in its infancy, but his sage advice shepherded me through the many struggles that I encountered during the writing and rewriting of the book. Steve Weber has never been shy about forcing me to ground theory in fact, and he gave me the courage to abandon many of my original formulations when research revealed other processes to be at work. The book could not have been completed without his many years of friendship and support. Victoria Bonnell gave generously of her time and advice and cautioned me wisely against a larger project that surely would have overwhelmed me.

The manuscript was rewritten entirely after my arrival at Yale University and benefited tremendously from my colleagues there and at Harvard. In my first years at Yale, I had the luxury of the constant advice and companionship of an exceptional cohort of colleagues. Two great scholars of post-Communism, Anna Grzymala-Busse and Pauline Jones Luong, both gave their insight to the manuscript. Anna, in particular, read every word, fixed many errors, told me what was good (and what wasn't), and hefted

me across the finish line when times got tough. Don Green, David May-
hew, Victoria Murillo, Bruce Russett, Nicholas Sambanis, Ken Scheve, and
Jim Vreeland all gave freely of their time and advice on chapters of the
manuscript. Ken directed my reading in the quantitative methods needed
to complete Chapter 9 and brought his clarity of mind to the theoretical
side of the project. Jeffrey Sandberg and Victoria Frolova provided me with
excellent research assistance.

The work was also shaped substantially by time at Harvard University,
both as a visitor at the Davis Center for Russian Studies during the writing
of the dissertation and as a postdoctoral scholar at the Harvard Academy
for International and Area Studies. Tim Colton showed great kindness in
welcoming me as a graduate student to participate in the intellectual life
of the Davis Center, and the book has benefited greatly from the community of scholars that I discovered in Cambridge. I would particularly like to
thank Rawi Abdelal, Grzegorz Ekiert, Henry Hale, Steve Hanson, Yoshiko
Herrera, Oleg Kharkhordin, Mark Kramer, Oxana Shevel, Joshua Tucker,
Cory Welt, Jason Wittenberg, and David Woodruff for their contributions
to different parts of the manuscript. I am particularly grateful to Rory Mac-
Farquhar, who read and commented on several chapters of this manuscript
in ways that significantly improved the project as a whole.

This manuscript owes a great debt to several generous institutions. The
primary research was funded by a MacArthur Foundation Regional Relations Fellowship from the Institute of Governmental Cooperation and Conflict. Essential support for aspects of the research and writing was provided
by the Social Science Research Council, the Institute for the Study of World
Politics, the Academy for Educational Development (NSEP), the Berkeley
Program in Post-Soviet Studies (BPS), the Harvard Academy for International and Area Studies, Yale's Department of Political Science, the Mac-
Millan Center for International and Area Studies at Yale, and the Institution
for Social and Policy Studies at Yale.

A great many other people have contributed to this dissertation and,
unfortunately, only a small number of them can be acknowledged here.
Many individuals in the post-Soviet states played a critical role in this project.
I owe a deep and abiding debt to the people who brought me into their homes
as a guest, fed me, housed me, and spoke frankly to me about the world as
they saw it. I would especially like to thank those government officials who
took time out of their very busy schedules to meet with me and to discuss
their thoughts on the economic crisis that confronted them. Were it not
for the cooperation of the Interstate Economic Commission, the Integration

Commission, and the Executive Secretariat of the Commonwealth of Independent States, and numerous national ministries, there would be very little of substance in this book. I would particularly like to thank Boris G. Vladimirov, formerly of the IEC, for giving his staff the authority to meet with the citizen of a Cold War enemy and for providing me with my first interview and introduction to the post-Soviet universe.

Nikita Lomakin of St. Petersburg State University gave critical advice at the very earliest stage of my research. Andrei Zagorskii of the Moscow State Institute for International Relations (MGIMO), through both his published work and the time he devoted to meeting with me, helped to orient my initial investigation of the CIS institutions. Ken Jowitt provided insight and inspiration at the beginning of the project and at critical points along the way. Lynnley Browning, Gavin Helf, Teresa Sabonis-Helf, Lise Howard, Marc Howard, Maranatha Ivanova, Nicolas Jabko, Beth Kier, Bob Powell, Galina Vasilieva, Ned Walker, Omar Wasow, and Lucan Way all made their mark on the project in critical ways that cannot be acknowledged appropriately here. I am particularly grateful to Lew Bateman at Cambridge University Press for his constant support and to Helen Wheeler for carrying the book through the production process.

In this endeavor, as in all others, I have enjoyed the support and encouragement of my family. I have always discussed my work and ideas with my father, my mother, and my sister Elena. They share in this product in the deepest and most profound ways. I dedicate the book to them, and to my son, Caleb, who has provided the joy to my life and the inspiration to write many, many books. I can only hope that they are pleased with the result and can see some of themselves in what I have written.

Economic Liberalism and Its Rivals

The Formation of International Institutions among the Post-Soviet States

PART ONE

THEORY AND METHODOLOGY

I

A Natural Experiment

In 1921, after the Bolshevik forces defeated the White Armies of the Russian Empire and completed their reconquest of tsarist territories, they found themselves in control of a vast and heterogeneous swath of Eurasia. The inhabitants of their new dominion were overwhelmingly rural – primarily peasants or nomads – the vast majority of whom were unschooled, illiterate, and devoid of national identity, instead identifying themselves by their family, tribe, or village, or simply as "people from here." Aside from the fact that they were all now subject to Soviet control, the peoples of Eurasia had very little in common with one another. They spoke more than 150 different languages and countless dialects. Most were linked to their countrymen by neither road nor rail. Heterogeneity, insularity, and isolation were the order of the day.

Seventy years of Soviet control changed all of that. Over the subsequent decades, the peasants and nomads were systematically collectivized, educated, electrified, urbanized, industrialized, nationalized, organized, terrorized, surveilled, and ruled in much the same way across the vast territory of the Union of Soviet Socialist Republics (USSR). The result of this methodically imposed project in social and political engineering was that by 1991, whether one lived in Tashkent or Tula, one was governed by identical political institutions, participated in the same centrally planned economy, and studied similar types of texts in similar schools. As famously dramatized in *The Irony of Fate*, a Brezhnev-era comedy, one even walked streets with the same layout and the same names, lived in the same apartments, sat on the same furniture, and ate off the same dishes. In short, by 1991, both the formal structures of the state and the informal organization of everyday life had become standardized throughout Soviet territory in a way that is historically unprecedented.

It is precisely because of the peculiarity of the region's history that it provides an excellent opportunity to explore the underlying sources of international order. As a result of the high level of Soviet standardization, the collapse of the Soviet Union into 15 independent states initiated a unique natural experiment in the formation of international institutions. As new states, the 15 former Soviet republics had no prior international institutional membership; all were starting from scratch. Moreover, the legacy of Stalinist planning created what statistical methods typically cannot: a level of control akin to laboratory conditions. In short, the collapse of the USSR left 15 states with remarkable historical and institutional commonalities, facing very similar economic choices and at the same moment in history.

A careful examination of the results of this experiment will provide the core theme of this book. In particular, I will examine why, despite all of their political, economic, and institutional commonalities, the post-Soviet states followed different courses with respect to membership in international economic institutions. Since achieving independence in 1991, the post-Soviet states have chosen three distinct institutional arrangements for governing their trade relations with other countries, and the divergence is quite stark. By the end of their first decade of independence, Kyrgyzstan, Estonia, Latvia, Georgia, and Lithuania adopted free trade policies and secured rapid entry into the World Trade Organization (WTO). Russia, Belarus, Kazakhstan, and Tajikistan had formed a regional economic union and a customs union (CU) with a protectionist common external tariff. Uzbekistan, Turkmenistan, and for much of the decade Ukraine and Azerbaijan pursued autarkic strategies, erecting barriers to trade and eschewing membership in international trade institutions. In sum, with the freedom of political independence, the new states forged three different paths during the 1990s: rapid entry into Western multilateral institutions, the formation of a regional bloc, and the pursuit of national autarky. Similar states made very different choices (Figure 1.1). Why?

The predominant theories in international relations have clear arguments about why states form, join, and comply with international institutions and should, in principle, have sufficient explanations for why the various post-Soviet republics would proceed along different paths. *Realists* maintain that international institutions are formed by powerful states to serve their own interests and to force weaker states into compliance with their demands. *Liberals* suggest that states join international institutions to reduce transaction costs or to enable a winning coalition of commercial interests to profit from them materially. More recently, *constructivist* scholars have taken the position that states join institutions and select policies that are consistent

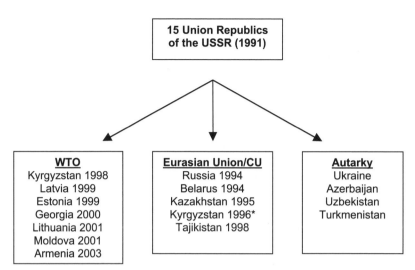

FIGURE 1.1. International economic institutions of the post-Soviet states. *Note:* Kyrgyzstan formally signed the Customs Union agreement but never adopted the common external tariff. See Chapter 8.

with their identity; in other words, a state's self-conception will determine what it wants and the institutions to which it wishes to belong. Each of these schools of thought makes attractive claims that I will examine later in detail, but a few comparisons make clear the need to look beyond traditional theory for our explanation.

Take, for example, the cases of Moldova and Estonia. Aside from membership in the Soviet Union, these two small countries hold in common many of the factors that traditional theories would draw on to explain a country's choice of international institutions. Constructivists would note that both countries were late additions to the Soviet Union; neither country's present-day territory was fully subsumed into the USSR until after World War II. In both countries, strong anti-Russian and anti-Soviet nationalist organizations mobilized popular sentiment for independence during the waning years of the USSR, and both governments boycotted the 1991 referendum on the preservation of the Soviet Union. Realists would note that upon becoming independent, both Estonia and Moldova were small, militarily feeble countries with significant Russian minorities. Moreover, the economic profiles of the two countries were quite similar: both countries relied heavily on agriculture, depended on subsidized energy imports from Russia, and traded almost exclusively with other Soviet republics. On the basis of the similarities outlined previously, conventional theories would predict that these two countries would follow analogous routes with respect to their membership in international institutions.

Indeed, in the early 1990s, both countries behaved much the same way. Both rejected membership in the Commonwealth of Independent States (CIS), and both cut their major economic ties with Russia and turned to Western partners for their energy supply. And, unfortunately, both countries suffered several years of sharp decline in gross domestic product (GDP) following the breakup of the Soviet Union. Yet in 1994, the paths of these two countries radically diverged. Estonia began to pursue rapid entry into the WTO and the European Union, while Moldova reversed course by joining the CIS. Moldova, in fact, began to privilege trade with its former Soviet partners and even sold its national energy network to the state-owned Russian firm, Gazprom. Given these two countries' strong nationalist pasts, analogous production profiles, and similar weaknesses with respect to their neighbors, the emerging differences in their institutional trajectories have been puzzling.

The story of Belarus and Ukraine is similar. These two countries, like Estonia and Moldova, held in common most factors that conventional theories consider to be important in explaining states' motivations to join international institutions. Neither country predated the Soviet Union or had a significant history of self-rule; in fact, both were essentially administrative units created by Soviet bureaucrats. Both countries' economies were constructed according to an identical plan, producing the same highly industrialized workforce and the same distribution of production across different sectors. In both countries, anti-Russian or anti-Soviet nationalism was, at best, a "minority faith"; consequently, in the 1991 referendum, both countries voted overwhelmingly to remain in the Soviet Union.[1] When the USSR disintegrated, both countries also inherited large, advanced military forces and nuclear weapons. Yet despite these historical, economic, and strategic commonalities, Belarus has ardently advocated the formation of a customs union while Ukraine has shunned its neighbors by establishing a protectionist tariff and rejected membership in both regional and international trade institutions.

We need not restrict our view to Eastern Europe; similar comparisons exist between Kazakhstan and Uzbekistan, Kyrgyzstan and Tajikistan, and

---

[1] Andrew Wilson, *Ukrainian Nationalism in the 1990s: A Minority Faith* (Cambridge: Cambridge University Press, 1997); Keith A. Darden, "The Origins of Economic Interests: Explaining Variation in Support for Regional Institutions among the Post-Soviet States" (Ph.D. Dissertation, University of California, Berkeley 2000).

Georgia, Armenia, and Azerbaijan. Throughout the former Soviet Union, we find countries in similar strategic circumstances, with similar economic structures, and similar forms of national identity making different institutional choices. Why?

The argument of this book is that the root of these different institutional trajectories lies in the idea-driven choices of state leaders. What differentiates the post-Soviet states have not been their economic circumstances or their inherited institutional structures, but rather the particular economic ideas of the new governing elites in each state since 1991. Amidst the corruption, violence, and impoverishment of the region after the collapse of the Soviet Union lay a political battle among groups that differ fundamentally in their economic ideas, their ideas about the way that economies function and the best means of ordering social and economic life. This book is about the nature and outcomes of this political struggle, and about how economic ideas shaped the way that governing elites of the post-Soviet countries have defined national economic interests and charted a course in international affairs.

In identifying economic ideas as a critical variable, I seek to draw on, and contribute to, a broad collective endeavor spanning several decades of research in international and comparative politics that has sought to demonstrate, in the succinct phrase coined by Peter Hall, the "political power of economic ideas."[2] In doing so, I have been fortunate to enter a literature where some of the fundamental claims have been ably demonstrated. Peter Hall's landmark studies of Keynesianism and monetarism made a compelling case for the role of economic paradigms in shaping domestic economic policy. John Ruggie, in a seminal 1983 article in *International Organization*, detailed how the emergence of an Anglo-American economic consensus on Keynesian "embedded liberalism" underpinned the formation of the principal postwar international economic order.[3] This book contributes to these landmark studies, and the rich literatures they have spawned, with new cases, new methods for identifying and testing for the effects of economic ideas, and new theory.[4]

---

[2] Peter A. Hall, ed., *The Political Power of Economic Ideas: Keynesianism across Nations* (Princeton, N.J.: Princeton University Press, 1989); Peter A. Hall, "Policy Paradigms, Social Learning, and the State: The Case of Economic Policy-Making in Britain," *Comparative Politics* 25, no. 3 (April 1993): 275–296.

[3] John Gerard Ruggie, "International Regimes, Transactions and Change: Embedded Liberalism in the Postwar Economic Order," *International Organization* 36 (1982): 195–231.

[4] Indeed, the study of economic ideas is one of the few areas of the social sciences where a case can be made that the work of scholars has been cumulative, in terms of both the steady addition of new cases and the refinement of theory. Some of the richest empirical and theoretical

The post-Soviet states also provide a challenge to these earlier accounts, as the primary explanatory factors that existing ideational arguments draw on to explain change or variation were constant across the 15 post-Soviet states. The prior political–economic institutions identified by Hall, Sikkink, Dobbin, and others as important to the selection of ideas were common to all 15 post-Soviet states. The formative experience of economic hardship, a factor

studies of role of economic ideas in shaping policy have been of the Latin American countries. Following Albert Hirschman's seminal work, *National Power and the Structure of Foreign Trade*s (Berkeley: University of California Press, 1945), Emmanuel Adler, *The Power of Ideology: The Quest for Technological Autonomy in Argentina and Brazil* (Berkeley: University of California Press, 1987), Kathryn Sikkink, *Ideas and Institutions: Developmentalism in Brazil and Argentina* (Ithaca, N.Y.: Cornell University Press, 1991), and more recently Victoria M. Murillo, "Political Bias in Policy Convergence: Privatization Choices in Latin America," *World Politics* 54 (2002): 462–493, have shown that economic ideas shaped the formation of economic institutions, industrial strategy, and the role of the state in the economy. Focusing on Russia's regions, Yoshiko Herrera, *Imagined Economies: The Sources of Russian Regionalism* (New York: Cambridge University Press, 2005) has made a very compelling case that attitudes towards the central government were based more on economic ideas of the provinces than the elusive reality of their financial relations. Studies of Europe and the United States have similarly shown the relevance of specific sets of economic ideas or cultures to broad institutional changes in the relationship of the state to the market and the formation of economic institutions. Hall and Mark Blyth, *Great Transformations: Economic Ideas and Institutional Change in the Twentieth Century* (Cambridge: Cambridge University Press, 2002), have identified the role of "policy paradigms" such as Keynesian economics and monetarism in shaping the institutions and *political* economies of Western Europe. Frank Dobbin, *Forging Industrial Policy: The United States, Britain, and France in the Railway Age* (Cambridge: Cambridge University Press, 1994), points to the distinct economic cultures that determined different institutions that evolved for the management of railways in France, Britain, and the United States. And Kathleen R. McNamara, *The Currency of Ideas: Monetary Politics in the European Union* (Ithaca, N.Y.: Cornell University Press, 1998), has made the case for the role of shared economic ideas in the convergence on monetary union in the European Union in the 1990s. In international relations, in addition to Ruggie's work, we have Ikenberry's careful demonstration of the emergence of a consensus of Anglo-American economic experts on the ideas that underpinned postwar international monetary and trade institutions. The work of John S. Odell, *U.S. International Monetary Policy: Markets, Power, and Ideas as Sources of Change* (Princeton, N.J.: Princeton University Press, 1982), and Judith Goldstein, *Ideas, Interests, and American Trade Policy* (Ithaca, N.Y.: Cornell University Press, 1993), showed that U.S. international monetary and trade policy could not be explained without reference to an evolving set of economic ideas. Ernst Haas, *When Knowledge Is Power: Three Models of Change in International Organizations*. (Berkeley: University of California Press, 1990) has demonstrated how the evolution of the institutions and policies of the World Bank reflected the emergence of a scientific consensus among its economists about the goals and causes of development. This book also finds its roots in Keohane and Goldstein's initial theoretical formulation of the role of "causal ideas" in Judith Goldsten and Robert O. Keohane, "Ideas and Foreign Policy: An Analytical Framework," *Ideas and Foreign Policy: Beliefs, Institutions and Political Change*, ed. Judith Goldstein and Robert O. Keohane (Ithaca, N.Y.: Cornell University Press, 1993), pp. 3–30.

highlighted by Ruggie, was endured by each of the former Soviet republics. Similarly, the factors pointed to by some contemporary constructivist scholarship – the norms borne by representatives of the Western international institutions and transnational civil groups,[5] or the dictates of "world culture"[6] or "international society"[7] in the late 20th century – were common to all. Thus, although the approach here shares much with the existing ideas literature, it necessarily develops an alternative because the key variables of those studies are constants in the post-Soviet cases; they cannot explain the variation.

WHY AND HOW IDEAS MATTER: THEORETICAL FOUNDATIONS

The full explication of the theory informing this book's explanation of the institutional choices of the post-Soviet states will be the primary task of the next chapter, but its commonalities with and differences from the existing literature can be summarized by answering four basic questions central to the theory of economic ideas: Why do economic ideas matter? How do economic ideas matter? What is the relationship between ideas and interests? And why are some ideas selected rather than others?

Consistent with much of the constructivist literature, I argue that the main reason why ideas matter is that knowledge of causation is inherently imperfect. In the academic discipline of international relations, this point is not only epistemological – i.e. there are inherent limits on the capacity of the researcher to infer causal relationships – but more importantly, it is also ontological: imperfect knowledge is an elemental attribute of the actors and interactions that we study. Actors inherently lack objective knowledge of the relationship between cause and effect in economics and other matters in the world. Because of these limitations, we should not characterize

[5] Martha Finnemore and Kathryn Sikkink, "International Norm Dynamics and Political Change," *International Organization* 52 (1998): 887–917; Margaret E. Keck and Kathryn Sikkink, *Activists beyond Borders: Advocacy Networks in International Politics* (Ithaca, N.Y.: Cornell University Press, 1998); Thomas Risse and Kathryn Sikkink, "The Socialization of International Human Rights Norms into Domestic Practices: Introduction," in *The Power of Human Rights: International Norms and Domestic Change*, ed. Thomas Risse, Stephen C. Ropp, and Kathryn Sikkink (Cambridge: Cambridge University Press, 1999).

[6] John W. Meyer and Brian Rowan, "Institutionalized Organizations: Formal Structure as Myth and Ceremony," in *The New Institutionalism In Organizational Analysis*, ed. Walter W. Powell and Paul J. DiMaggio (Chicago: University of Chicago Press, 1991).

[7] Alexander Wendt, *Social Theory of International Politics* (Cambridge: Cambridge University Press, 1999); Hedley Bull, *The Anarchical Society: A Study of Order in World Politics* (London: Macmillan, 1977); Barry Buzan, "The English School: An Underexploited Resource in IR," *Review of International Studies* 27, no. 3 (2001): pp. 471–488.

any state's actions as responding directly to the "objective" structural factors highlighted in materialist theories and models. Instead, political actors rely on inference, "paradigms," informed conjecture, and imagination – in short, on their ideas – to identify relevant causal relationships and determine appropriate policy. Actors use their ideas about causation (quite literally) to make sense of the world; not only do states use their ideas to characterize the problems they face, but these ideas also expound the range of options available for dealing with these problems. More than simply "road maps,"[8] these ideas constitute the building blocks of our understanding of the world.

This is not to suggest that actors' ideas matter only under conditions of uncertainty, as many of the best studies of the role of ideas have assumed, or that ideas are more likely to have a bearing in situations that are novel[9] or especially complex,[10] or where cost–benefit analyses of different courses of action are especially difficult to calculate. By most accounts, the greater is the uncertainty, the less that actors can rely on the objective situation, and the greater the effect of their ideas.

However, the claim that I will make is somewhat different and ultimately much stronger. Because uncertainty is a constant feature of human understanding, rather than merely an occasional or variable condition, actors' ideas play just as much of a role when actors are "certain" or highly confident of the costs, benefits, and probable outcomes of a given set of circumstances as when they experience new or ambiguous situations. Actors' feelings of certainty, I argue, do not imply objective knowledge, but rather only reflect the degree of confidence that actors have in their ideas, and the extent to which those ideas have come to be taken for granted. Novel situations might make the contingency and fragility of mental constructs more apparent, but their subjectivity is nonetheless ever-present. In other words, it is not the case that actors sometimes calculate their interests on the basis of objective conditions and at other times resort to their ideas, but rather that actors' reasoning *always* rests on a set of ideas about causation that are inherently and inescapably subjective, even when they are grounded in and consistent with known experience. For this reason, it is only meaningful to speak of actors' economic ideas, not their objective understanding of economic causation.

[8] Goldstein and Keohane, "Ideas and Foreign Policy."

[9] Mark Blyth, *Great Transformations: Economic Ideas and Institutional Change in the Twentieth Century* (Cambridge: Cambridge University Press, 2002), pp. 31–32.

[10] Peter M. Haas, "Introduction: Epistemic Communities and International Policy Coordination," in "Knowledge, Power, and International Policy Coordination," ed. Peter Haas, *International Organization* 46 (special issue 1992): 1–35.

The question of *how* ideas matter clearly affords multiple answers. In this book I focus primarily on one: the fact that economic ideas determine economic and institutional preferences. The logic behind the argument that economic ideas – actors' ideas about how the economy works – determine or "induce" actors' preferences regarding different institutional arrangements is straightforward. Political actors do not bear any natural predisposition toward certain economic institutions; for example, they do not naturally prefer customs unions to free trade in the way that a person might prefer apples to pears. Rather, governments may have a more basic preference for wealth or economic growth and might then believe (to continue the example) that a customs union is a better means to secure wealth than is free trade. Our preferences for political and economic institutions are less like tastes, i.e. fixed and exogenous, than they are like our preferences for tools; they are endogenous to our beliefs about how things work. What links a preference for growth to support for institutions such as a customs union is a set of economic ideas that establish a causal link between the institutional means and the economic ends.

If we assume that actors form international institutions because they believe they can derive benefit from them, it then follows naturally from this reasoning that shared economic ideas form the basis of international economic institutions. This does not mean that institutions are always consensual, or that some participants do not benefit from a given arrangement more than others, but rather that underpinning any institution is a core set of economic ideas and beliefs by which a state judges an institution's utility, merit, and function. Ruggie labels this ideational bedrock an institution's "social purpose."[11] And while it is often the case that different actors support institutions for different reasons – that is to say, on the basis of different sets of ideas – institutions must be grounded in a set of shared ideas that lead most participants to believe in the institution's effectiveness. When such beliefs are undermined – as in Western Europe during the Great Depression, or in the Soviet Union in the late 1980s – it is remarkable how quickly institutions that once seemed to be permanent fixtures can dissolve.[12]

On the question of how interests and ideas relate, I will suggest that economic and institutional preferences are not only induced by ideas about causation – of which economic ideas are one type – as I have suggested

---

[11] John Gerard Ruggie, "Territoriality and Beyond: Problematizing Modernity in International Relations," *International Organization* 47 (1983): 139–174.

[12] Mark R. Beissinger, *Nationalist Mobilization and the Collapse of the Soviet State* (Cambridge: Cambridge University Press, 2002), pp. 2–3.

earlier, but are themselves a kind of idea. Much of the existing constructivist literature has erroneously structured itself on a dichotomy between
interests and ideas and mistakenly understood interests or preferences as
exogenous, objective, and material in provenance. By identifying all economic motivations with structuralism or materialism, and by attempting to
deny or subordinate economic motivations to other aspects of culture or
identity, the literature squanders much of the explanatory power and plausibility of ideational arguments. By identifying economic interests as a type
of idea, it is possible to subsume economic motivations into a more coherent
ideational framework.

Finally, I argue that economic ideas and other ideas about causation, or
what Kant referred as *pragmatic beliefs*,[13] are chosen on the basis of an
individual's determination of the ideas' utility in achieving desired ends. In
other words, an actor's perception of an idea's efficacy determines whether
that idea is embraced or rejected. Economic ideas and the preferences they
induce, far from being imposed on states by an international authority or
social structure, instead form a system of beliefs that actors consciously
adopt or reject. While actors often resist conceptual change and interpret
experiences in light of existing beliefs that provide them with a sense of order
and security in the world, they retain the capacity to judge the merits of those
beliefs. Because actors remain intuitively cognizant of the fragility and contingency of their causal understanding of the world, they will continue to
assess their ideas in light of evidence, experience, and perceived plausibility
in the eyes of others. That is, actors maintain a pragmatic relationship to
the ideas that guide their actions, no matter how deeply held they might
seem; indeed, actors will often abandon a given way of thinking if it seems
to produce undesirable or contradictory results.[14] Hence, periods of economic crisis tend also to be periods of conceptual crisis and rapid ideational
change.

Moreover, I depart from much of the existing literature about ideas by
asserting that although individuals have a pragmatic relationship to their
ideas – they select and reject them according to their perceived plausibility
and utility – ultimately there are no systematic explanations of the selection of ideas. The freedom that inheres in individual minds means that the
selection of new ideas is contingent, is undetermined, and can be described

---

[13] Immanuel Kant, *Critique of Pure Reason*, trans. Norman Kemp Smith (New York: St.
Martins Press, 1965), A824/B852.
[14] On the social nature of this process of "disappointment," see Hirschman, *Shifting Involvements: Private Interest and Public Action* (Princeton, N.J.: Princeton University Press, 1982).

but not systematically explained. Considerable progress can be made if we recognize the contingent, if not stochastic, elements of idea selection, and if we cease the attempt to locate/embed the idea selection process systematically in other deep holistic structures – be they material,[15] institutional,[16] or cultural.[17] As shown in Chapter 2, this ontological position provides considerable leverage in explaining the heterogeneity and dynamism that are intrinsic to the international political order. Such variation is inexplicable within a holist or strictly idealist ontology.[18]

In sum, I offer a theory, out of a pragmatist tradition, that suggests that actors do not simply choose strategies of action on the basis of immutable, exogenous, and predetermined preferences. Instead, they choose a framework of economic reasoning out of a dynamic cultural reservoir. Once adopted, this set of ideas then constitutes the way that actors characterize their options and induces preferences over the imagined possible outcomes. When shared among a country's decision-making elite, a given set of economic ideas will favor a certain definition of the national interest and produce a certain set of beliefs about the international and domestic institutions needed for economic growth. When a set of economic ideas is shared across many countries, it can provide the basis for the creation of international institutions and the establishment of a particular form of international economic order.

The empirical implications of this approach are straightforward.[19] To explain the choice of international economic institutions by the post-Soviet states, we must turn to the economic ideas that decision makers in these countries have drawn on in defining their national economic interests and the international institutions that can best serve them.

---

[15] Karl Marx and Friedrich Engels, *The German Ideology*, ed. C. J. Arthur (New York: International, 1970).

[16] Peter A. Hall, ed., *The Political Power of Economic Ideas: Keynesianism across Nations* (Princeton, N.J.: Princeton University Press, 1989); Kathryn Sikkink, *Ideas and Institutions: Developmentalism in Brazil and Argentina* (Ithaca, N.Y.: Cornell University Press, 1991).

[17] Frank Dobbin, *Forging Industrial Policy: The United States, Britain, and France in the Railway Age* (Cambridge: Cambridge University Press, 1994); Wendt, *Social Theory*.

[18] The primary example of a constructivist account that combines idealism and holism is Wendt (*Social Theory*). The approach shares assumptions about human nature and knowledge with the philosophical tradition of pragmatism (cf. Dewey, Peirce, Laudan) – the basic tenet of which is that objective truth is not knowable, and the truth of a proposition is determined by its utility in achieving practical ends. The general theory is laid out in greater detail and compared with constructivist approaches in Chapter 2.

[19] The method of explanation follows closely that suggested by Ngaire Woods, "Economic Ideas and International Relations: Beyond Rational Neglect," *International Studies Quarterly* 39, no. 2 (1995): 161–180.

IDEATIONAL VARIATION AMONG POST-SOVIET ELITES

The first step toward explaining the choices made by the post-Soviet states is to identify the different economic ideas that have informed their policy-making. On the basis of ethnographic fieldwork, personal interviews with officials, and detailed study of internal government documents, I have found that the governing elites of post-Soviet states employ one of three distinct frameworks for understanding the economy.[20] I have labeled these frameworks "liberalism," "Soviet integralism," and "mercantilism." Each mode of thinking rests on a different set of ideas about how economies function, and thus each leads its practitioners to hold different beliefs about how to cope with the economic crisis that has faced the region and the proper institutions for governing economic activity. The tenets underlying these modes are provided in detail in Chapter 4, but I will briefly sketch them here.

Soviet integralists are the descendants of Soviet economic theory and draw heavily on its concepts and causal principles. They consider monopolistic cooperation rather than market competition as the key to growth and view the regional economy as an interdependent, specialized whole that gained efficiency under Soviet leadership through specialization and economies of scale.[21] To the integralist, the disintegration of this economic whole into separate parts, and the atomization and fragmentation inherent to the market, have proved catastrophic. They deem the ensuing economic crisis to be the natural result of the breaking of ties among Soviet enterprises, an event that eliminated the benefits derived from specialization and scale. Soviet integralists believe that the 15 national components of the former Soviet economy, including Russia itself, are unable to resolve their problems on their own, and that the preservation and maintenance of the common economic system would be in the best interest of all of the post-Soviet states. Thus, the Soviet integralist favors the regional integration of quasi-monopolistic production complexes, or "financial–industrial groups," over the market "fragmentation" that results from competition. Integralism leads its practitioners to view regional cooperation as a vital interest.

[20] The typology is drawn from interviews with more than 200 officials in eight of the post-Soviet countries in the mid-1990s designed to elicit their economic views. For further details on the method, see Chapter 4.
[21] Put in abstract terms, integralists posit that economic effectiveness requires that the needs of the social whole be placed above the freedom and idiosyncratic orientations of its constituent parts, and that both individuals and society as a whole will benefit from the rational organization and management of the economic totality based on a division of labor designed to achieve preset goals.

Liberals believe that the independent decisions of rational individuals with financial stakes in ensuring efficiency will, in a competitive environment, produce the best individual and social returns. The liberal believes that the state should not intervene directly in economic activity, and that balanced budgets, stable currencies, market competition, and free trade will provide the conditions under which individual actions will lead to efficiency and economic growth. In the post-Soviet context, economic liberals claim that the specialized sectoral industrial monopolies favored by integralists need to be destroyed or restructured as competitive markets, and that enterprises should be deprived of state support. Liberals will support regional cooperation so long as it facilitates competition but are opposed to any attempts to insulate the regional market or reconstitute Soviet-era production chains.

Finally, the *mercantilists* of the region believe that economic growth can only be gained at another country's expense. The mercantilist rejects the supposed virtues of regional specialization and strives to develop the nation's capacity for closed-cycle production of as many goods as possible (the specifics of the doctrine differ slightly from the pre-nineteenth-century European variant). Governments advance this goal by instituting high protective tariffs, promoting value-added exports, and maintaining a heavy level of state intervention in the economy. Mercantilists reject regional cooperation as a threat to their interests and view regional institutions as attempts at imperialism.

The argument of this book is straightforward. Where integralist ideas prevail among government officials, we will see efforts to bolster regional economic institutions. Where liberal ideas are dominant among government officials, we will see those governments endeavor to pursue rapid entry into the WTO. Where mercantilist views reign among officialdom, we will see unilateralism and autarky. Each set of officials will believe that they are promoting growth and acting in their country's best interests by serving the objective needs of their economy. Each will believe that officials in those countries that choose differently do so because of political pressures, or because they are in some way deluded or confused. But in each case, a government's institutional and policy choices will rest on a particular view of the economy that induces those preferences, and that is inherently and irreducibly subjective.

A METHODOLOGY FOR THE STUDY OF IDEAS

Given the institutional similarity of the post-Soviet states, where did these three different schools of thought come from, and why did they vary? The question is a critical one, as the most compelling critique of my argument is that these three ideational frameworks (mercantilism, integralism, and liberalism) are simply ideological masks worn to justify or rationalize actors' "genuine" interests, interests that are exogenously determined.[22] According to this critique, it is not the economic ideas that induce the institutional preferences, but prior preferences that lead actors to select the ideas.[23]

Realists, for example, could contend that the integralist ideational framework adopted by Russia in 1995 simply served its hegemonic designs in the region, and that it is Russia's desire to exercise its power, rather than any particular way of thinking about economic interests, that drives its support for a regional customs union. Liberals might argue, in contrast, that the integralist rhetoric of the Russian government in 1995 was no more than a socially palatable justification for protectionist policies that favor inefficient producers while forcing consumers to pay the price. In each of these cases, the true causes of state action would be motivations that officials would be loath to admit publicly, but not the ideas themselves. The apparent correspondence between the economic ideas that actors express and their subsequent behavior may simply mask an alternative, hidden motivation or drive that constitutes the true causal explanation. The problem is simple, yet affords no easy empirical solution: as we are unable to read actors' minds, how can one distinguish an ideology selected to rationalize or justify a preformed preference from an idea that genuinely induces a preference?

Such concerns are not to be dismissed lightly. They highlight a methodological problem faced by all ideational arguments, and indeed by all observational approaches in the social sciences.[24] And while these potential problems – known in the statistical literature as omitted variable bias and

[22] Gary King, Robert O. Keohane, and Sidney Verba, *Designing Social Inquiry* (Princeton, N.J.: Princeton University Press, 1994), p. 191.
[23] The main thrust of this critique is most easily traced to Marx's critique of the German ideology.
[24] As King, Keohane and Verba note: "Insofar as ideas reflect the conditions under which political actors operate – for instance, their material circumstances, which generate their material interests – analysis of the ideas' impact on policy is subject to omitted variable bias: actors' ideas are correlated with a causally prior omitted variable – material interests – which affects the dependent variable.... And insofar as ideas serve as rationalizations of policies pursued on other grounds, the ideas can be mere consequences rather than causes of policy. Under these circumstances, ideas are endogenous: they may appear to explain actors' strategies, but in fact they result from these strategies" (King, Keohane, and Verba, *Designing Social Inquiry*, p. 191). The authors see this as a problem specific to ideational arguments, but the problem is just as acute for material explanations. The material "structure" could have been determined by some other underlying set of ideas, and there is no reason to privilege material explanations as the null hypothesis.

endogeneity – cannot be eliminated completely without resort to random-ized experimentation, this book tackles the problem in three ways.[25] First, I use historical methods to demonstrate that circumstantial and idiosyn-cratic factors were behind the emergence of different economic ideas across post-Soviet countries. By making the case that the factors leading to the adoption of economic ideas in each country were highly circumstantial and idiosyncratic, and thus not systematically related to any set of factors that could constitute the "true" explanation of why countries chose a certain route, we gain greater confidence that the economic ideas are themselves driving institutional choice. By detailing, for example, how the pervasive-ness of liberal ideas among Estonian elites finds its source in the economic experiments that Moscow chose to conduct in the republic in the 1970s (a chance historical event), and that the economic liberalism of the Estonian Communist Party predates the collapse of the USSR, we gain confidence that those ideas were not simply selected for instrumental reasons in 1992 when free trade and membership in the World Trade Organization became an option. Thus, even though economic ideas were not distributed randomly across the post-Soviet region as they would be in a genuine experiment, the fact that different ideas were adopted in different countries for reasons that were demonstrably idiosyncratic or contingent on unique events means that their distribution is akin to one that was stochastic. By explicitly arguing that economic ideas *lack systematic causes* and by using qualitative meth-ods to demonstrate the contingent processes that lead to the adoption of ideas, the project to identify the systematic *effect* of ideas gains an impor-tant methodological foothold.[26] Ironically, the absence (or impossibility) of a systematic theory of the selection of ideas enhances our ability to test for their effects.

Second, to support the claim for the exogeneity of idea-selection further, I demonstrate that cross-national and temporal variation in economic ideas is not systematically related to the conditions identified as causal in existing explanations, such as a country's production profile, the way its domestic

---

[25] Donald P. Green and Alan S. Gerber, "Reclaiming the Experimental Tradition in Political Science," in *Political Science: The State of the Discipline*, ed. Helen V. Milner and Ira Katznelson, 3rd ed. (New York, New York: W. W. Norton and Co., 2002), pp. 805–832.

[26] In effect, I use qualitative methods to "prove the null" – i.e. to demonstrate that the causes of ideational selection are contingent and idiosyncratic rather than systematic. Because the demonstration of contingency is also a demonstration that the distribution of ideas is exogenous to our other variables, then this serves to buttress the systematic analysis (both quantitative and qualitative) of the effects of ideas. Demonstrable contingency, in this sense, substitutes for randomization as a way of ensuring exogeneity of the explanatory variable.

political institutions are ordered, the extent to which it depends on Russia for its energy supply, or how vulnerable it is to military attack. As noted previously, this task is easier in the former Soviet Union because the countries are, ex ante, quite similar. To evaluate or eliminate the possibility that these factors are causing the institutional outcomes as well as the ideas, I test the existing explanations using qualitative and methods and, because case comparison can be difficult to follow for 15 countries over 10 years, I also construct a cross-sectional time series dataset for the period and employ a variety of statistical tools to show that existing explanations do not hold and that a robust relationship exists between the economic ideas of a government and the choice of international institutions. With 15 countries over a 10-year period, we have sufficient observations to determine whether existing explanations can account for the changes in institutional commitment.

Third, I trace historically the formation of the international institutions and the decisions of individual states to join. Here, the causal demonstration follows more along the lines of Holmes than Hume, as I use interviews with participants, autobiographical accounts, and internal documents to demonstrate how economic ideas were employed in critical decisions. In addition to serving as a more direct demonstration of the argument, the process-tracing makes it possible to identify causation in a way more sophisticated than the quasi-experimental design and statistical analysis would allow.

By ruling out rival explanations, by demonstrating the contingent and unsystematic process by which certain economic ideas came to be employed by the government in each country, and by demonstrating a strong link between the economic ideas and the policy choices through both statistical methods and traditional qualitative case methods, we gain confidence that economic ideas are genuinely driving institutional choice among the post-Soviet states.

MEASURING IDEAS

Of course, each of these methodological steps is predicated on the ability to identify, or "measure," the economic ideas employed in policymaking. To do this, I employed the method of content analysis using multiple data sources, and further verified the measure using a set of policy indicators to identify additional observable implications of the ideas.

First, to develop the basis for the typology and coding measures, I used interviews with economic officials in Armenia, Georgia, Russia, Belarus, Ukraine, Kazakhstan, Uzbekistan, and Kyrgyzstan to draw out their ideas about how economies function. I conducted more than 200 interviews with decision makers in each country's presidential administration; the Ministries of Finance, Economy, Trade, Industry, Foreign Affairs, Foreign Economic Relations, Fuel and Energy, Electricity, and CIS Affairs; and the Customs Commission between May 1996 and December 1997.[27] These interviews were also used to glean factual information about the development of national policy.

Using this typology and set of coding indicators, I constructed two measures, both based on the content analysis of public statements by officials. The most comprehensive is an index coding each of the 15 governments for every six months between 1991 and the end of 2000 based on statements by the president, the prime minister, and the first deputy prime minister in presidential regimes and on the ideational positions of the ruling coalition in the three parliamentary regimes – Estonia, Latvia, and Moldova. This measure is supplemented by a content analysis of all public statements by officials for 1992, 1994, 1996, and 1998. Both measures are detailed in Chapter 9.

The classification of actors' causal ideas using written sources and interviews inevitably relies on a qualitative assessment of the mode of reasoning employed by a particular actor and by the majority of actors within each government. The clear differences between the economic ideas in the region made errors of interpretation less likely, but actors' ideas are always muddier than ideal-typical formulations, and a risk of error or bias is inherent in the interpretive enterprise.

To verify the content coding further, I also examined the 15 countries' record in key economic policy areas, with the expectation that the economic ideas employed by the government will impact more than just the state's willingness to participate in international institutions. It should affect the ways in which governments define their interests and make policy in all economic spheres, and in ways not anticipated by other theoretical approaches. By examining other areas of policy we may derive further indication that a government employs a particular set of economic ideas. For this reason, I examine the governments' key choices on energy policy, privatization policy, and macroeconomic and industrial policy across the 10-year period. While these policy measures are not indicators of economic ideas, per se, as that would assume the relationship between economic ideas and policy that the book is trying to prove, the extent to which economic ideas also

---

[27] Not all ministries were available for interview in all nine states. Interviews also included the president or vice president of the National Association of Industrialists and Entrepreneurs, and the IMF and World Bank mission representatives.

manifest in predicted patterns of economic policymaking in other spheres builds confidence in both our coding and our findings.

Finally, this book draws on internal government documents and memos in which the logic behind different policies taken by the government was laid out or discussed. While not available for all states, this body of data provided the most valuable resource for coding economic ideas because actors are less inclined to misrepresent their motivations when crafting mundane official documents that are never intended to be seen by the public. These sources were particularly important for tracing the role of economic ideas in the decisions to join institutions and primarily appear in Chapter 10.

To measure the dependent variable, this book develops an original set of measures for institutional membership and participation. To get a broad picture, I chart each country's institutional membership over the decade, as well as its foreign economic regime to determine the extent to which those institutional obligations were met. To measure each country's annual effort to secure entry into the WTO, I construct a new measure based on a count of the working group meetings, document submissions, and other WTO accession-related events that a country pursues within a given year. To track each country's participation in the regional economic institutions of the Commonwealth of Independent States, this book uses several sources and measures. For the statistical analysis, it draws on a dataset of signing, ratification, and implementation rates of the CIS countries using sources not publicly available. Using government archives, I also chart the specific policies taken by several states to form and develop the regional institutions.

So that the references to multiple data sources and indicators do not lead to confusion, the logic of the argument and indicators used for testing it are diagrammed in Figure 1.2.

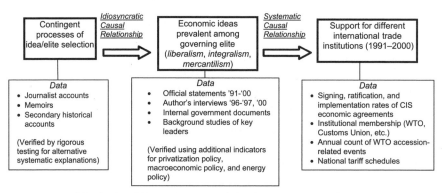

FIGURE 1.2. The logic of the argument and the data sources used.

In sum, several methods are employed to test the book's empirical claim that actors' ideas about economic causation determine whether they support cooperation in regional economic institutions. The first method is a broad comparison of 15 countries across 10 years, using carefully crafted indicators to evaluate the merits of competing causal claims. The second provides detailed case studies, both of the countries and of the institutions, to provide more direct evidence of causation in the timing, sequence, and process of events. The combination of the two provides an explanation of the degree of cooperation among post-Soviet states that is both rich and rigorous.

AN OUTLINE OF THE CHAPTERS

The organization of the book follows the logic of explanation. Chapter 2 makes the general theoretical case regarding the role of ideas in international politics that informs the empirical argument of the book. In particular, it develops the argument that political preferences are not like tastes and explains in greater detail why actors' ideas about causation – of which their economic ideas are one subtype – induce their preferences. Extending this argument to international relations, the chapter goes on to develop a theory of international order that is "ideas all the way up," i.e. that shared ideas are the basis of international order, but that we must examine the microlevel selection of ideas to explain the variation in international institutions across time and space – both the broad historical shifts such as the broader worldwide turns toward liberalism in the late nineteenth and late twentieth centuries, as well as the variation and change among the post-Soviet states in the contemporary period. To do this, the chapter then discusses basic mechanisms by which ideas spread across polities, as well as how we determine whose ideas matter within polities.

Chapter 3 returns to the central empirical problem addressed by the book by describing the three institutional trajectories, and detailing the institutions and their members and participants over the 1990s. With the theoretical importance of economic ideas established, Chapter 4 then turns to the more substantive task of identifying the ideas relevant in the region. The chapter begins with a broad conceptual distinction between liberalism and integralism, traces the history of those ideas and their impact on economic order, and develops a set of indicators and methods for identifying and coding the ideas as they are encountered in contemporary post-Soviet politics.

Part Two of the book comprises 15 country studies, divided by region into four chapters. The chapters document the changes in the economic ideas of each government over time, detail the contingent and idiosyncratic nature of the processes by which ideas and the elites who harbor them come to hold sway, and demonstrate the systematic effects of those ideas on economic policy and institutional choice. The purpose of these chapters is twofold. These chapters, on the one hand, make the case for contingency of idea and elite selection to show that idea selection was not driven by some other systematic factor that would render our focus on them irrelevant. Second, the chapters draw on subtle changes in timing and sequence to demonstrate causation within countries over time. These chapters make the case that ideas were unsystematically selected in the post-Soviet states but have systematic and significant effects on institutional choice.

Part Three of the book compares across cases and over time to test for alternative explanations and to isolate and identify the role of economic ideas. Chapter 9 is primarily statistical and presents a formal test of the explanation against alternatives. The chapter presents the realist, liberal, and nationalist arguments; derives hypotheses from them; and tests them using a cross-sectional time-series dataset comprising the 15 countries over 10 years. The role of economic ideas is also tested and found to have a substantively and statistically impact on both participation in the CIS institutions and progress toward membership in the WTO. Chapter 10 uses both cross-sectional comparisons of support for key agreements and detailed historical analysis using internal government documents, interviews, and autobiographical accounts to provide a clear demonstration of the causal role of ideas in the key institutional decisions during the period. In particular, it shows how integralist ideas about how the regional economy should be governed provided the basis for the creation of the most significant regional economic institutions, the Interstate Economic Commission, the Customs Union, and ultimately the Eurasian Economic Union. Chapter 11 addresses the implications of the study and draws conclusions based on the findings.

2

A Theory of International Order

As discussed in the previous chapter, the primary empirical finding of this book is that a country's choice to pursue membership in the World Trade Organization, to focus primarily on regional trade institutions, or to take an autarkic path stems from the economic ideas of those who govern it. Why should we expect this to be the case? To what extent should the relationship between ideas and institutional choice hold more generally? To answer these questions, this chapter lays out a broader theoretical case for the relationships among ideas about causation, government choice, and international order. Applying this framework to the question of international economic order, I suggest that changes in international economic order, such as the rise of free trade at the end of the nineteenth century, the move toward autarky in the interwar period in Europe, the rapid increase in the liberalization of trade at the end of the twentieth century, or the creation of regional institutions in Europe and the post-Soviet states, are the aggregation of choices by individual governments, taken relatively independently of the decisions of other states, and based on their economic ideas.

The critiques of this position from liberal and realist theories are to be expected and are dealt with later in the book (Chapter 9). But in principle, one would expect that this argument could find easy theoretical grounding in constructivism, the large and growing branch of International Relations (IR) theory that privileges ideas in its explanation of international order. But an effort to apply contemporary constructivist theory to the question of why states choose different international institutions rapidly runs into a fairly significant problem. Not only is constructivist IR theory not designed to deal with such variation in state behavior, but according to most current constructivist theories the empirical problem identified in this book should not exist.

The problem lies not with constructivism, per se, which (following John Searle) I identify as the position that norms, institutions, and even the basic actors of international politics exist solely because some individuals share a belief in their existence.[1] Indeed, this book shares that position along with many elements of the "individualistic" or "Weberian" tradition of constructivism associated with the work of Ernst Haas, Peter Haas, Emmanuel Adler, and John Ruggie. Rather, the problem lies with the turn of many constructivists to holism – the notion that the world has a social structure that cannot be reduced to the attributes, qualities, and interactions of states or individuals.[2] If the potential insights that constructivist theories can offer to an explanation of the variation in state behavior or of changes in international order over time are to be realized, then the holistic assumptions must be shed. Toward this end, this chapter offers an alternative (individualist) constructivist theory of the origins of international institutions, one better suited to the explanation of change in general and in post-Soviet Eurasia particularly. In the first part of the chapter, I demonstrate that the holistic assumption that there is a prior intersubjective international society that constitutes national identities and interests is empirically unsustainable. I argue that the variation that we find empirically in the rules, norms, and principles that order international politics in different historical periods and in different regions of the contemporary world would simply be impossible if state behavior were determined by a common social structure. To the extent that one can speak of international societies, they both are partial (i.e. not system-wide) and are constituted by state actors. Insofar as they exist, the norms and principles of international societies are subject to change as the ideas of individual actors change.

In place of a holistic constructivism, I offer a theory that stresses the individual microfoundations of a shared or intersubjective social order – an argument that is "ideas all the way up" rather than "ideas all the way down."[3] Given the "bottom-up" approach, I start with the problem of individual preference-formation, arguing that individuals' political preferences are an idea – a product of their general goals and their beliefs about causation. I then discuss generally how shared ideas about causation – such as the economic ideas that are the main explananda in this book – provide the basis for international institutions and how variation in such ideas

---

[1] John R. Searle, *Intentionality: An Essay in the Philosophy of Mind* (Cambridge: Cambridge University Press, 1983), p. 2.
[2] Wendt, *Social Theory*, p. 26.
[3] Wendt, *Social Theory*, p. 20.

is an underexplored component of variation in support for international institutions. Finally, I move to the problem of aggregation, or how ideas come to be shared at the national and international levels and whose ideas ultimately matter in international politics. Here I argue that critical differences in how states control the development and dissemination of ideas, as well as regime type, must be taken into account to explain the development of national preferences for different international institutional forms and membership in international institutions. Without taking such "unit-level" features into account, we cannot hope to explain the variation in support for different institutional orders historically, or among the post-Soviet states in the contemporary period.

PROBLEMS WITH HOLISM

According to many constructivists, one of the primary distinguishing characteristics of the theory is its holism. Indeed, the holistic notion of an international society of states is a central tenet of a large and growing body of constructivist work in international relations – and one with a long and distinguished history. Martin Wight, Hedley Bull, and their "English school" followers have suggested that states exist in an international society governed by rules that states adhere to because of the utility that social order provides.[4] Alexander Wendt has suggested that the culture of this international society constitutes the relations between states and the nature of their interests.[5] Martha Finnemore has argued that international organizations establish the norms in this international society or culture and that these norms define the interests and behavior of states.[6] Michael Barnett argues, in turn, that the structure of this international society is a set of intersubjective roles that states play out in their interactions with one another.[7] John Meyer claims that the very units of international politics are the products of a common "world culture" and that their wants and intentions can be read off this prior cultural script.[8] Although these accounts differ in some significant respects, they are united by an assumption that states behave in

---

[4] Martin Wight, *Systems of States* (Bristol, England: Leicester University Press, 1977); Bull, *The Anarchical Society*; Barry Buzan, "The English School," pp. 471–488.

[5] Wendt, *Social Theory*.

[6] Martha Finnemore, *National Interests in International Society* (Ithaca, N.Y.: Cornell University Press, 1996).

[7] Michael Barnett, "Institutions, Roles, and Disorder: The Case of the Arab States System," *International Studies Quarterly* 37, 3 (1993): 271–296; Michael Barett, *Dialogues in Arab Politics: Negotiations in Regional Order* (New York: Columbia University Press, 1998).

[8] Meyer et al., "Institutionalized Organizations."

a way that is deemed socially appropriate – i.e. in a way consistent with the identities, roles, norms, and/or interests defined by an intersubjective international social structure. It is this "holistic" focus on the constitutive role of society or social structure that many authors have defined as one of the key distinguishing features of constructivism.[9]

Holism, of course, is not unique to constructivism; Kenneth Waltz's neo-realism also put forward a holistic notion of the international system. What distinguishes constructivism is the link between holism and idealism – the belief that the social structure of the international system is an ideational one, a set of collective ideas that includes the identities that constitute actors and the norms that govern their behavior. It is assumed by constructivists that the structure of the international system is intersubjective and constructed socially. Put simply, this means that all actors share a common understanding of the world of international politics: the identities and interests of each actor are known by all other actors and all actors share an understanding of the norms that govern their interactions. This collective view of the world, moreover, is not a view that has been created by an actor or a group of actors. Rather, it emerges "socially," is a separate theoretical entity from the actors, and, according to some constructivists, endows agents with their core properties – their identities and their interests.[10] As Jeffrey Legro writes about collective ideas:

These ideas are social and holistic – they are not simply individual conceptions that are shared or added together. Collective ideas have an intersubjective existence *that stands above individual minds* and is typically embodied in symbols, discourse, and institutions . . . Collective ideas, therefore cannot be reduced to individual ideas, belief systems, cognition, or psychology, even if such phenomena related to the human mind may often be a critical part of collective change.[11]

In sum, a holistic constructivism (1) assumes the existence of an international society; (2) assumes that this society is structured by an understanding of roles, identities and norms that is common to all members; and (3) assumes that this common understanding is an entity ontologically distinct from and separate from the actors themselves, one that "constitutes" who they are and what they want.

This type of holistic constructivism is both theoretically and empirically problematic. On the theoretical side, the notion of an intersubjective

---

[9] Wendt, *Social Theory*.
[10] Wendt, *Social Theory*, p. 26.
[11] Jeffrey W. Legro, "The Transformation of Policy Ideas," *American Journal of Political Science*, 44, 3 (2000): 419–432. Emphasis added.

social structure that is both distinct from and ontologically prior to the ideas of individuals is difficult to square with the commonsense notion that ideas exist in minds. If collective ideas could truly "stand above individual minds,"[12] then it would be possible to have collective ideas that were not held in the mind of any individual – an empirical impossibility. Where would such ideas be found, and by what possible mechanism could they influence individual behavior if they are not held by individuals? Very simply, without a collective mind or brain there can be no collective ideas that cannot in principle be reduced to the shared or aggregated ideas of individuals.

There are certainly intersubjective beliefs that structure state behavior, and some roles, identities, and norms are only meaningful or sustainable in a social context, i.e. if they are shared by others. Wendt is right to note that roles are only meaningful in a social context,[13] but this in no way validates the tenets of holism. The fact that a friendship or alliance only exists socially means only that two or more actors must conceive of themselves as friends, married, or allied in order for the relationship to exist. It is the beliefs of the agents that constitute the "structure." If either individual alters his conception of the relationship – regardless of what the other actor thinks or does – the friendship or alliance is not preserved. Whether in world politics or social relations between individuals, the shared ideas that structure behavior ultimately rest on and can be reduced (if desired) to the beliefs of individuals. To arrive at the conclusion that social ideas are ontologically distinct from the ideas held in the minds of individuals one would have to assume a social brain.

Because holistic constructivist approaches have taken an intersubjective social order as their starting point, the microfoundations needed to explain how elements of an intersubjective order emerge in world politics are missing. With no focus on the individual, a holistic constructivism lacks any plausible account of where shared ideas come from or how an international order based on them might possibly change over time or vary across regions.[14] If we take a "top-down"[15] structuralist approach, in which the social structure is prior and shapes the agents, change can only be exogenous or inconsistent with the theory, as endogenous change would imply

---

[12] *Ibid.*, p. 420.

[13] Wendt, *Social Theory*, p. 26.

[14] Finnemore attempts to solve this problem by positing that the intersubjective norms of the international system are generated by international organizations and subsequently taught to states. Finnemore does not explain how international organizations come to acquire this authoritative role (Finnemore, *National Interests*).

[15] Wendt, *Social Theory*, p. 26.

that agents have the independent capacity to alter the system's structure and are therefore not constituted by it.[16] At an even more basic level, the reliance on holism leaves no account of how, or whether, such an international ideational structure comes to insinuate itself into the heads of a world full of human actors, and to constitute their interests and behavior. The existence of an international structure of intersubjective meaning spanning all of international society, and indeed the existence of an international society itself, must simply be taken as an assumption.

There is, of course, reason to question this assumption empirically, for the world of international relations, despite some diplomatic conventions, is not normatively or ideationally homogeneous – a fact reflected in the variation in forms of international order that we encounter in post-Soviet Eurasia alone. People in different parts of the world obviously view the world differently and act on the basis of different principles. Many of the more significant rules, norms, and forms of governance are not global in scope, and thus the proposition that international society exists a priori and constitutes (all) states and (all) the relations between them is questionable. In some cases, such as those among the post-Soviet states, the principles underlying regional arrangements can be inconsistent with or even antithetical to those that scholars have identified as the norms of international society. The significant differences in the types of international order deemed legitimate by each of the post-Soviet states is but one anomaly; there is no shortage of such instances. Indeed, the keystone of the international society claims – the argument that sovereignty is a constitutive norm of international society[17] – cannot be sustained empirically, as world politics has always been characterized by heterogeneity of institutions, practices, and organizing principles.[18]

---

[16] Wendt devotes a chapter of his book to the issue of change, but all of his mechanisms are social processes that ultimately affect the ideas and preferences of the units and therefore seem to be inconsistent with the original holistic assumptions of the theory. Wendt, *Social Theory*, chap. 7.

[17] Bull, *The Anarchial Society*, pp. 8–9; Wendt, *Social Theory*, pp. 272–297; John Gerard Ruggie, "Continuity and Transformation in the World Polity: Toward a Neorealist Synthesis," in *Neorealism and Its Critics*, ed. Robert O. Keohane (New York: Columbia University Press, 1986), pp. 131–157; Ruggie, "Territoriality and Beyond," pp. 139–174.

[18] Stephen D. Krasner, "Westphalia and All That," in *Ideas and Foreign Policy: Beliefs, Institutions, and Political Change*, ed. Judith Goldstein and Robert O. Keohane (Ithaca, N.Y.: Cornell University Press, 1993), pp. 235–264; David A. Lake, "Anarchy, Hierarchy, and the Variety of International Relations," *International Organization* 50, no. 1 (1996): 33; Daniel H. Deudney, "The Philadelphian System: Sovereignty, Arms Control, and Balance of Power in the American States-Union, Circa 1787–1861," *International Organization* 49 (1995): 191–228; Hendrik Spruyt, *The Sovereign State and Its Competitors: An Analysis of Systems Change* (Princeton, N.J.: Princeton University Press, 1994).

And such anomalies all speak to a very deep and insurmountable problem: a theory that claims that international society constitutes states and their patterns of behavior cannot account for the contradictory organizing principles and general variation in international politics.

This variation does not mean that international norms are not important or pervasive, or that they do not affect the behavior of some states. It simply means that international society or an international social structure does not encompass all states and is not, therefore, constitutive or ontologically prior.[19] States (and individuals) are clearly able to define their own courses of action and govern their relations in a variety of ways. And if norms and institutions exist only insofar as states (and individuals) comply with them, then a microexplanation of why states comply is an integral part of an explanation of those norms and institutions. The question of why an international institution exists cannot be separated from the question of why some states join or comply with a norm or institution and others do not.

In sum, this book shares the constructivist position that shared ideas, norms, and institutions exist or are important but differs in the way it makes sense of them theoretically. The international society and constructivist literatures take an intersubjective international social space for granted and suggest that states and their interests are constructed by this social space – an extreme form of methodological holism. By not incorporating another locus, or source, for ideas other than an all-encompassing international social space (society), individual agency drops out of the theory, and the capacity to explain the variation in national preferences and variation in support for international norms and institutions disappears along with it. Unless we recognize that adherence to international norms and institutions is conditional on the intentions of states and that those intentions are subject to unit-level change, we will be unable to account for the fact that sovereignty, human rights, free trade, and other norms and institutions have been selected as organizing principles by some collectivities and not by others.[20] Indeed, from a holistic perspective, the empirical problem presented in this book, of why states choose different international trajectories, should not exist. Each of the post-Soviet states would be expected to follow the liberal script established by leading states and international institutions. The fact that

---

[19] For in this case it would be universal, just as the constitutive rules of chess apply to all parts of the chess board and constitute the game as such. Chess would no longer be chess if the pieces chose not to obey the rules in certain parts of the board.

[20] See also Jeffrey W, Legro, "Which Norms Matter? Revisiting the 'Failure' of Internationalism," *International Organization* 51 (1997): 31–63.

states have taken different institutional trajectories, trajectories that are not unique to this region, begs explanation.

IDEATIONAL INDIVIDUALISM: THE ROLE OF CAUSAL IDEAS IN PREFERENCE-FORMATION

To remedy this problem requires that we redirect constructivist theory, that we rebuild it upon more individualist foundations. We need a more micro-foundational approach to explain many of the intersubjective institutional features of the world to which constructivist theory has rightly called our attention, one that allows us to account for evident variation. At the core of this approach is the argument that preferences, or interests, are a type of idea and that the dichotomy between interests and ideas that has structured much of social science debate is false. Starting with basic assumptions about how individuals think, the argument proceeds deductively. I start by showing that preference-formation is an ideational process that cannot logically be rooted in objective structures (or brute facts). I then discuss how these ideas and preferences are aggregated up – first to the state level, and ultimately to the international level – to form the basis for international institutions. The result is an argument that is "ideas all the way up," from individual preferences to international order.

IDEAS AND INDIVIDUAL PREFERENCE-FORMATION

An argument that is "ideas all the way up" requires a clear definition of ideas. Put most simply, ideas are mental content – those things that are exclusively in the domain of the mind and cannot be directly observed with the senses. While this definition is certainly broad, it is not all-inclusive. The fact that an idea cannot be verified ostensively or perceived directly by the senses means that it can be distinguished easily from other phenomena. "Brute facts" like tanks, missile silos, and factories are not ideas.[21] On the other hand, the causal principles and other categorical or relational concepts by which we "process" information, exercise judgment, and give mental order to the world are all ideas. Unlike the former, the latter cannot be directly observed, which has led some philosophers and social scientists to treat them as artifacts of a prescientific era and to deny that they exist.[22]

---

[21] Although the categories "tank," "missile silo," "factory," etc., are ideas, the observable physical entities that they refer to are not. That is the point being made here.

[22] For a discussion of this development in the philosophy of mind, see Searle 1992, chap. 1. Searle correctly points out that even if mental content cannot be observed by a third party (i.e. is not objective), it is directly experienced by every conscious individual and that this is sufficient grounds for dismissing arguments that it does not exist.

A set of preferences is one way of representing what an actor wants; it is an ordering of different possible states of the world, or "outcomes," ranked according to their desirability. The first clue that preferences are ideas is that one cannot point to, touch, or otherwise directly measure the preferences of an actor.[23] Even if they have observable effects – on what actors choose, for example – the preferences of actors are inherently and exclusively mental. But the preferences, particularly political preferences, are ideational in a much more fundamental sense as well. Actors' causal ideas – their beliefs about how the world works – are necessarily employed in the ranking of outcomes, i.e. in the formation of preferences.

To understand this process, we can think of the formation of a preference ranking as involving two separate ideational elements. The first element is a set of abstract goals, such as justice, spiritual salvation, or material gain. Such goals are clearly subjective; they exist in the mind of the actor and we cannot see them or touch them. Even if certain wants, such as the desire for health, material comfort, and physical survival, are fairly common and appear to have a strong evolutionary/biological basis, they are nonetheless articulated as ideas in the mind.[24] The second element is a set of causal beliefs about how a given outcome or condition will satisfy those goals. Without such beliefs, different outcomes could not be ranked according to their desirability. In some cases, the beliefs will be quite simple, such as the belief that my prospects of survival are enhanced if I am outside rather than inside a burning building. In others instances, such as my belief that my material welfare will be enhanced if my government adopts a lower grain tariff, the set of beliefs may be quite complex.

Regardless of whether they are simple or complex, such beliefs about how a given outcome might serve our goals, and the ranked ordering of possible outcomes based on those beliefs, rest on ideas about causation. Like our goals, causal beliefs are inherently subjective because any causal connection that we make is necessarily an idea. As Hume noted, "Beyond the constant conjunction of similar objects, and the consequent inference from one to the other, we have no notion of any [causal] necessity or connexion."[25] In

---

[23] On how the problem of the unobservability of preferences is elided by behavioralists see Amartya Sen, "Rational Fools: A Critique of the Behavioural Foundations of Economic Theory," *Philosophy and Public Affairs* 6 (1977): 317–344.

[24] And one can easily think of examples where actors are willing to sacrifice any one of these in the service of another goal. Although we tend to think of survival as some type of primitive and basic goal, individuals (soldiers, for example) have sacrificed their lives for religious salvation, national glory, or simply the welfare of others.

[25] David Hume, *An Enquiry Concerning Human Understanding*, 2nd ed. (Indianapolis: Hackett, 1993), p. 55.

other words, one cannot (literally) point *directly* to relationships of cause and effect any more than to abstract principles like liberty and justice. A causal relationship is always inferred, primarily on the basis of the "constant conjunction" of a sequence of phenomena.[26] Ideas about causal relationships are thus ideational constructs, albeit very useful ones, that link phenomena.[27] It is for this reason that it makes sense to say that an actor's interest, if we define it as the preference for an outcome based on the belief that it will serve the actor's basic goals, is an idea – an idea that is derived from an actor's ideas about causation and about desirable ends.

When it comes to political preferences, the link between our causal ideas (an integral element of our worldview) and the formation of preferences over outcomes is particularly clear. Political preferences are obviously not something that we are born with, like a taste for apples over pears.[28] Rather, as noted in Chapter 1, the designs or wants of actors are necessarily "informed" or "induced" preferences. A preference for a law, policy, or institution derives from an understanding that such acts will provide benefit.[29] In this sense, our political preferences are more like our preference for owning a screwdriver rather than a hammer – the preference is not natural or inherent but stems from our understanding of the problems we expect to face and how we expect the tool to resolve them. Similarly, any preference over political outcomes – the passage of a law or decree, the creation of an international trade institution, a declaration of war – is inseparable from our basic understanding of how our goals can best be achieved by such an outcome. Hence, it is meaningless to speak of preferences as if they were something separate from, or prior to, ideas. Causal ideas tell us why we

[26] I say "primarily" inferred because Searle's argument that we can identify events that have never before occurred in conjunction as causal is compelling. Searle identifies *intentional causality*, where we intend to do something and then "make it happen," as the basis for an understanding of cause and effect that does not rely on the observation of repeatedly conjoined events. See Searle, *Intentionality*, chap. 4.

[27] The nonobservability of causal relationships had led philosophers from Nietzsche to Bertrand Russell to treat causality as a fiction. Nietzsche went so far as to describe "interpretation by causality" as "a deception," noting that "the supposed instinct for causality is only fear of the unfamiliar and the attempt to discover something familiar in it – a search, not for causes, but for the familiar," Friedrich Nietzsche, *The Will to Power*, trans. Walter Kaufmann and R. J. Hollingdale (New York: Vintage Books, 1968, section 551). Nietzsche's and Russell's criticisms have become one of the primary bases for the postmodern rejection of science. It does not necessarily follow that because causality is not directly observable it does not exist, nor that the inherent subjectivity of causal notions makes them all equally (im)plausible.

[28] Political preferences are not exogenous.

[29] Benefit to whatever goals an *individual* might have, including the public welfare or the "common good."

want something, what reward we can expect it to provide for us; without causal beliefs, we would have no preferences.

Causal ideas not only tell us why we want something, but how we can get it; they inform our choice of means as well as our valuation of ends.[30] To act in a way desired to bring about a specific end implies that the actor conceives of a causal relationship or chain of causal relationships that links the means and the end, regardless of what the end might be.[31] Raising interest rates to slow inflation, for example, rests on the assumption of a causal relationship, as does the sacrifice of a lamb to secure a good harvest. Likewise, one's participation in a riot, public demonstration, or war may rest on one's causal assumptions about how one thinks others are likely to behave. It is this use of ideas as "road maps" to select means for satisfying our interests, rather than the valuation of ends, that has been the primary focus of the ideas literature.[32]

When examining the role of ideas in the valuation of ends and the selection of means, the distinction between rationalism and constructivism becomes irrelevant. Rationality is based on causation, and our understanding of causation is necessarily an idea. Thus, even if we assume that all actors are rational, any instance in which rational faculties are employed draws on beliefs about causes and effects that are not universal. Put more precisely, since the reasoning upon which actors form their preferences and choose courses of action can ultimately be broken down into chains of causal relationships, the variability in notions of causation means that people reason differently. Rationality, by this logic, is a universal human faculty, but an actor's reasoning always has a specific content, a content that depends on his/her assumptions about cause and effect relations in the world. Thus, from

[30] In this sense, they influence both our preferences over outcomes, and our preference for a given strategy for attaining it. On the distinction between preferences over outcomes and preferences over strategies, see Robert Powell, "Anarchy in International Relations Theory: The Neorealist-Neoliberal Debate," *International Organization* 48 (1994): 313–344.

[31] The person may not be able to articulate the causal relationships that he assumes in acting (and people may have different ways of articulating the same set of causal relationships), but this does not prevent the interpretive researcher from discerning the underlying principles upon which the actions and thoughts rest. For the implicit or nonarticulated assumptions that go into action see Searle's discussion of the background. Searle, *Intentionality*, chap. 5; John R. Searle, *The Construction of Social Reality* (New York: The Free Press, 1995), chap. 6.

[32] Goldstein and Keohane, "Ideas and Foreign Policy," p. 13. As noted by Keohane and Goldstein, "causal beliefs imply strategies" (10) and the reverse is clearly true as well (i.e. that strategies rest on causal beliefs). Strategic rationality also incorporates perceptions about the other actors and how they are likely to choose. On "perceptions of power" in strategic interaction, see Pauline Jones Luong, *Institutional Change and Political Continuity in Post-Soviet Central Asia: Perceptions and Pacts* (Cambridge: Cambridge University Pres, 2002).

our assumptions, it follows logically that preferences are ordered and strategies of action are chosen on the presumption of a set of causal relationships that vary across individuals and may vary systematically.

INDIVIDUAL ACTORS AND PRACTICAL REASON

It is this understanding of the role of causal ideas – the ideas we hold about how the world works – in the formation of preferences and in the selection of strategies that lies at the theoretical core of this book. It is what justifies the focus on the economic ideas of political actors in the post-Soviet states as something critical to an explanation of their institutional choices rather than as nothing more than an ex post justification for their actions. It is because ideas about causation are not objectively given and not derived automatically from the context or environment in which a person acts that understanding actors' ideas about causation is essential to an explanation of how they define their preferences and choose courses of action. Empirically, this means that it will prove necessary to understand actors' ideas about causal relationships in order to explain their behavior.

How generalizable is this explanation about the relationship between causal ideas and individual choice? For the argument to hold, we need to make only three basic and plausible assumptions about the human actor. First, we must assume that human beings think about the world in terms of causal relationships.[33] That is, our ideas about causation are a critical if not foundational part of how we think about the world. Empirically, this is plausible: in all times and all places human beings appear to have thought about the world in terms of causal relationships, and contemporary psychology and neuroscience suggest that the propensity to think causally is a natural feature of the human brain.[34]

Second, if we are to use this argument to explain variation in choice, we must assume that actors' causal beliefs have varied, and varied systematically. Given that causation is inferred, it seems reasonable to assume that actors throughout history have inferred or conceived of causal relationships differently and that understanding of causation is often regionally and

---

[33] The philosophical foundations are found in David Hume, *An Enquiry Concerning Human Understanding*. Hume's ideas about causality remain the dominant understanding of causation in the philosophical tradition.

[34] H. Zullow, G. Oettingen, C. Peterson, and M.E.P. Seligman, "Pessimistic Explanatory Style in the Historical Record: Caving LBJ, Presidential Candidates and East versus West Berlin," *American Psychologist* 43 (1988): 673–682; Allison Gopnik, Andrew N. Meltzoff, and Patricia K. Kuhl, *The Scientist in the Crib: What Early Learning Tells Us about the Mind* (New York: Perennial, 2001), pp. 73–79; Richard Bentall, *Madness Explained* (London: Allen Lane, 2003).

historically specific.[35] One of the hallmarks of a common culture, for example, is a common understanding of mechanisms of cause and effect.

Finally, we must assume that human action is largely intentional, as opposed to being driven primarily by emotional impulse, unconscious habit, or genetically determined behavioral patterns. At least in the forms of human action of most interest to politics, it is likely that people deliberate about their options and have conscious reasons for making the choices that they do.

From these assumptions, the rest of the argument follows logically and necessarily. And we can see plenty of empirical evidence to support it. Different causal ideas, and not just different information, clearly impact the way actors order their preferences and select courses of action. The Puritans, for example, practiced worldly asceticism based on a religious causal belief that asceticism was required in order to achieve eternal heavenly bliss. Without understanding the Puritan mode of thinking, it is not possible to make sense of the Puritan preference for an ascetic life.[36] Similarly, for centuries various tribes took their choicest livestock and burned them on altars in the hope that this would gain them victory in battle, good harvests, and safe journeys. These actions, too, are only comprehensible on the basis of an understanding of these actors' modes of thinking.

Such religious examples are useful because they allow us to see relations between cause and effect as features of the mind rather than as simply objective statements of fact about the world. They also reveal how otherwise counterintuitive preference orderings can be made comprehensible with a better understanding of actors' modes of thinking. But we need not limit ourselves to nonsecular views of the world. Economic ideas, the primary focus in the subsequent chapters, have been some of the most prevalent and consequential of all causal beliefs in determining government policy. In Russia in the 1990s, for example, the elimination of social supports, the freeing of prices, and the nonpayment of wages and pensions, the combination of which amounted to precipitous economic decline and suffering of the population, were all undertaken on the grounds that these actions would ensure the stabilization of the currency and bring about an influx of foreign investment and rapid growth. These policy preferences were ultimately based on a constellation of interlinked causal axioms (monetarism) that suggested that the sacrifices would be duly rewarded.

---

[35] Nonsecular causal principles (involving the actions of spirits and gods, etc.) are nonetheless causal principles. Most magical rituals involve an assumed logic of cause and effect.

[36] Max Weber Max, *The Protestant Ethic and the Spirit of Capitalism*, trans. Talcott Parsons (New York: Charles Scribner's Sons, 1958).

In none of these examples can the actors' preferences be explained without reference to the causal ideas that lay behind them. All of the actors in these examples wanted to maximize their utility. But the facts crucial to explaining why actors associate a higher utility with one outcome rather than another, or with one course of action rather than another, lie in understanding the ideas by which the actors relate causes and effects: an understanding of the particular ways in which actors think. The simple assumption that actors are rational, coupled with an examination of the exogenous factors that are assumed by the theorist to be the basis for an actor's preferences, does not suffice as an explanation – even if we use causal ideas to account for how those preferences are translated into strategies and outcomes. Preferences must be accounted for and preferences are structured by causal ideas.

Note the clear contrast between this view (C) and alternatives (A and B) as shown in Figure 2.1. (A) shows the traditional materialist view, where

A. Ideas as epiphenomena, used to justify actions taken according to predetermined interests

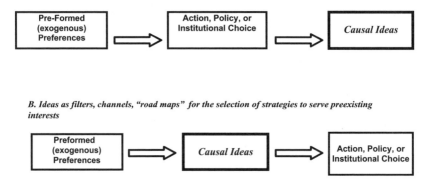

B. Ideas as filters, channels, "road maps" for the selection of strategies to serve preexisting interests

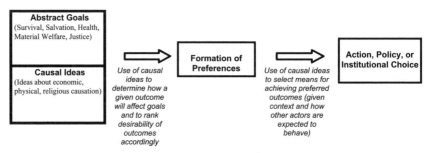

C. Causal ideas as "inducers" of both preferences and strategies

FIGURE 2.1. Alternative views of the role of causal ideas.

preferences are defined by an objective material structure assumed by the theorist, and causal ideas are treated as epiphenomenal, as rhetoric used to justify actions to oneself or others in more palatable terms. (B) shows the more conventional ideational view, which takes interests for granted but sees ideas having an important role both in interpreting objective interests and in selecting strategies for attaining them under conditions of uncertainty. (C), in contrast, identifies the goals and causal ideas that both induce preferences and are employed in the selection of means (strategies) to achieve those ends.

INDUCED INSTITUTIONAL PREFERENCES

The role of causal ideas in structuring actors' preferences is particularly pronounced when we are talking about preferences over possible institutional arrangements. Institutional preferences are always "induced" preferences. They are determined by a set of causal beliefs that suggest an institution will have desirable effects. Individuals hold those beliefs, but institutions are inherently social outcomes; they can only be created in concert with others. As a result, it is only when causal ideas are shared that we see collective support for an institution.

To see how this works, let us first take an example not directly related to international relations. Imagine that three groups of actors are trying to develop institutions that will reduce the automobile casualty rate. One group of actors might think that the casualty rate is due to the fact that cars are unsafe, and that the legislation of new safety measures such as seat belts and airbags will increase the safety of the car and thus reduce the casualty rate. On the other hand, another group of actors, all neoclassical economists, might suggest that cars are, in fact, *too* safe. They might argue that the safer the car, the fewer incentives there are for drivers to be careful and responsible, and the more likely it is that accidents will occur. Hence, it is the removal of safety features that will lower the overall casualty rate; indeed the existing casualty rate may not even be conceived of as a problem at all: i.e. the true problem is one of moral hazard. A third group of actors, all Soviet economists, might suggest that the problem lies in the fact that the aggregation of self-directed individual actions *inherently* leads to undesirable outcomes, in this case automobile accidents.[37] They might advocate replacement of a system of private automobiles with a larger system of public transport manned by trained professionals. Each of these groups of actors employs a different logic of causation.

[37] See Chapter 4.

TABLE 2.1. *Ranked Order of Preferences over Institutional Arrangements for Limiting Automobile Casualty Rates*

Group 1	Group 2 (Neoclassical Economists)	Group 3 (Soviet Economists)
Safety measures	No safety measures	Public transit
Public transit	Safety measures	Safety measures
No safety measures	Public transit	No safety measures

In this case, different causal ideas lead to radically different sets of preferences over possible institutional arrangements to resolve the same problem. For our purposes, the question of which one of these characterizations of the problem is accurate is not as important as the fact that actors with different ideas about cause and effect will come to characterize problems in different ways. Most importantly, the utility that each actor associates with the three different institutional outcomes (no change or even a ban on safety measures, a legislated system of safety regulation, a system of public transport) is a function of the way that actor conceives of the causes of the problem, or the actor's causal ideas (see Table 2.1).

Thus we can see how different causal ideas will lead to different preferences over outcomes. Causal ideas shared across states or other international entities can lead to a *common* sense of a problem and its specific terms, and a common preference ranking over institutional forms, which facilitates the development of a common institutional solution.[38] Indeed, in the chapters to come, I show that it is a similar variation in modes of thinking that is responsible for the different regional economic institutions among the post-Soviet states.

The analogy to national or international economic arrangements is not difficult to see. In fact, if we take three main schools of economic thought and derive preferences over institutional arrangements for dealing with economic crises or market failures, then the preference orderings in Table 2.2 might obtain. Members of any one of these groups could most likely arrive at a common set of institutional arrangements among themselves, but it is distinctly unlikely that institutional arrangements could be established between actors in different groups. In this way, common modes of economic thinking among states can facilitate the development of common international

---

[38] The insight that shared causal beliefs are the basis for stable international institutions is one of the central contributions of Ernst Haas to the field. The nascent idea appears in Haas's *Beyond the Nation-State: Functionalism and International Organization* (Stanford, Calif.: Stanford University Press, 1964), esp. pp. 105–106, and is developed further in Haas's subsequent work.

TABLE 2.2. *Ranked Order of Preferences over Institutional Arrangements for Preventing/Managing International Economic Crises*

Group 1 (Keynesian Economists)	Group 2 (Neoclassical Economists)	Group 3 (Soviet Economists)
Embedded liberalism	Laissez-faire	State control
Laissez-faire	Embedded liberalism	Embedded liberalism
State control	State control	Laissez-faire

institutional arrangements by generating a common set of preferences over such arrangements and a shared perception of their necessity. Indeed, Ruggie, Ikenberry, and others suggest that Keynesian ideas played such a role in the development of the postwar international economic order.[39]

The example of the World Trade Organization (WTO) may help illustrate how international economic institutions rest on and incorporate shared causal ideas of their members. The WTO is interesting in that countries with uncompetitive industries and minimal domestic capacity for innovation agreed to "lock in" the removal of trade barriers and establish international intellectual property rights. Both of these features clearly carry important distributional consequences and were the subject of protracted negotiation. One cannot say that the Uruguay Round exhibited a happy consensus in which distributional issues were not in the foreground. Nonetheless, the institutional provisions of the WTO are inconceivable without some degree of common understanding of basic liberal economic tenets that leads actors to believe that free trade provides benefits to all sides, or that property rights are needed to create proper incentives to innovate and thus are a benefit even to those who are unpropertied. On an even more basic level, we could say that these provisions rest on consensus on a set of liberal ideas about how market competition provides for the greatest social and individual returns.[40]

---

[39] John A. Ruggie, "Territoriality and Beyond: Problematizing Modernity in International Relations," *International Organization* 47 (1993): 139–174; John G. Ikenberry, "Creating Yesterday's New World Order: Keynesian 'New Thinking' and the Anglo-American Postwar Settlement," in *Ideas and Foreign Policy: Beliefs, Institutions, and Political Change*, ed. Judith Goldstein and Robert Keohane (Ithaca, N.Y.: Cornell University Press, 1993), pp. 57–86.

[40] Likewise, John Ruggie posited that the rise of a consensus on the principles of "embedded liberalism" accounted for particular institutional features of the international postwar order in a way that sheer power considerations could not. So long as this "social purpose" continued, Ruggie presciently argued, we would expect the institutions to remain, even as the power relations present at the time of their formation underwent significant changes. The consensus version of liberalism has become increasingly less "embedded" and far more monetarist in recent years (Blyth, *Great Transformations*), but the basic logic of the argument holds.

Without this consensus, it is unlikely that most states would have a preference for free trade.

To focus on the underlying consensus is not to trivialize the distributional consequences of the institution or to suggest that their formation was a simple consensual matter. We may simply note that liberal economic ideas have increasingly come to dominate decision-making elites' thinking about how economies work, and that this has a significant effect on states' preferences over institutional outcomes. This point will be demonstrated on the basis of concrete cases in the chapters that follow.

TOWARD A SHARED INTERNATIONAL ORDER: THE DIFFUSION, AGGREGATION, AND SELECTION OF IDEAS

Thus far we have only established how individually held ideas about causation shape individuals' preferences and how, by extension, shared ideas lead to a common preference for specific institutions. But because our goal is to explain international affairs, these qualities of the individual need to be linked to different international institutions and to the process by which national interests are defined.

I establish the analytical link between individual beliefs and international institutional order in two steps. First, I identify three basic mechanisms for the spread or diffusion of ideas – i.e. I clarify how ideas come to be shared within and across collectivities. Second, given that these mechanisms never lead ideas to be fully shared or intersubjective even within a given polity, I examine the role of political institutions in selecting the ideas that determine state behavior, i.e. how political institutions determine whose ideas matter.

STEP I: BASIC MECHANISMS DRIVING THE SPREAD OF IDEAS

The initial leap from the individual to collective preference-formation is accomplished in part by recognizing that while ideas must be held individually, as there is no social mind, they are also shared among collectivities. Hence, insofar as causal ideas play a central role in ordering preferences, when a set of ideas is shared across a group of individuals those individuals will order their preferences similarly.[41] We know empirically that both the size of collectivities and the range of ideas shared among them have expanded dramatically over time. Thus, the empirical recognition that ideas

---

[41] This is only conditionally true and is generally more applicable with regard to institutional preferences.

are shared among (and across) collectivities further begs the question of how and why individuals have selected these ideas. By what processes have ideas spread?

To explain how ideas come to be shared across individuals or polities, I offer three basic mechanisms: deliberate selection, ecological selection, and imposition.

In cases of *deliberate selection*, individuals willingly change their beliefs by selecting and retaining ideas that they perceive to be useful or "true." Shared ideas are the product of the fact that many individuals have voluntarily deemed them plausible; the net effect of the microlevel selection of ideas by individuals are the macrocultural patterns constructivists have typically identified.

The process by which this takes place is described in Kuhnian terms by most scholars: a crisis/anomaly is followed by the development, selection, and diffusion of an idea or paradigm that resolves the initial crisis.[42] The initial crisis occurs when important events are found to be inconsistent with expectations based on existing ideas about causation. In the case of economic ideas, the pervasive sense of doubt is generally sparked by an economic crisis that prescribed remedies fail to alleviate.[43] But the anomalous event need not be painful, as it is perceived failure rather than material hardship that shakes the foundations of causal beliefs.[44]

Once prior ideas are questioned, individuals search for alternatives. The selection process, as noted in Chapter 1, is one that is highly contingent. Individuals may innovate, select known alternatives from within their cultural environment, or expand their knowledge. Most commonly, individuals emulate – i.e. they adopt the ideas of their more successful peers in the hope

---

[42] See Thomas S. Kuhn, *The Structure of Scientific Revolutions*, 2nd ed. (Chicago: University of Chicago Press, 1970), chap. 6. Some version of this pattern – with the crisis typically a major policy failure – is found in most theoretical discussions of ideational change: Legro, "The Transformation"; Jack Levy, "Learning and Foreign Policy: Sweeping a Conceptual Minefield," *International Organization* 48 (1994): 305; Blyth, *Great Transformations*; Javier Corrales and Richard Feinberg, "Unilateral versus Multilateral International Sanctions: A Public Choice Perspective," *International Studies Quarterly* 43 (1998/1999): 1–36; Kathleen R. McNamara, *The Currency of Ideas: Monetary Politics in the European Union* (Ithaca, N.Y.: Cornell University Press, 1998); Ruggie, "International Regimes."

[43] Ruggie (depression and war), Blyth (Great Depression, stagflation of the 1970s), Peter Hall (stagflation), Sikkink (economic crises of 1930s, 1960s).

[44] The appearance, for example, of a collectivity with a new and apparently more successful model can lead to the perception of one's own approach as a failure, even if one's performance has not actually changed in any objective sense. On the destabilizing effects of the rise of a successful alternative, see Corrales and Feinberg.

that they may achieve the same results.[45] Because actors lack good abstract criteria for selecting among sets of ideas, they are particularly susceptible to such demonstration effects. This process of idea-selection – the choice of a set of beliefs based on a logical and empirical assessment of their plausibility or utility – is a more informal version of scientific induction.[46] Insofar as a set of ideas continues to be effective in achieving desired ends, the belief is consolidated and comes to be generally perceived as true.[47]

A second mechanism leading to the spread of ideas, albeit limited to competitive environments, is *natural or ecological selection*: i.e. the ideas of the more effective or more violent competitors spread as those groups expand and other groups are eliminated. In this case, even if it is not the utility of the content of the ideas that is responsible for the success of the more competitive group, if one society eliminates another through warfare the ideas of the more competitive group will spread at the expense of alternatives. It is quite clear that this has been one of the dominant mechanisms behind the reduction in the diversity of shared ideas: In 1000 B.C. the world had an estimated 600,000 independent political units. In the contemporary period, the number of independent political units is close to 200. While it is not the case that these political units are ideationally homogeneous, there is little doubt that much ideational or cultural heterogeneity has been eliminated through the eradication of groups or societies through some combination of "guns, germs, and steel."[48] Hence, as a result of the Second World War, societies based on Nazism or Fascism were eliminated as they were defeated in warfare by societies organized on the principles of Communism and liberalism.

Finally, ideas can spread through *imposition*.[49] This can be achieved by indoctrination, forced conversion, and/or elimination of alternatives through

---

[45] Peter M. Haas, "Introduction: Epistemic Communities and International Policy," "Knowledge, Power, and International Policy Coordination," ed. Peter Haas *International Organization* 46 (special issue 1992): 5–6.

[46] And although selection of ideas is individual, as only individuals have ideas, the deliberative process inevitably has a significant social component. The adoption of ideas by members of a community or polity rests on persuasion, the availability of information, and other inherently social processes. Thomas Risse, "'Let's Argue!': Communicative Action in International Politics," *International Organization* 54, no. 1 (Winter 2000): 1–39.

[47] Legro, "Transformation."

[48] Jared Diamond, *Guns, Germs, and Steel: The Fates of Human Societies* (New York: W. W Norton, 1997).

[49] John G. Ikenberry and Charles Kupchan, "Socialization and Hegemonic Power," *International Organization* 44, no. 3 (1990): 283–315; John G. Ikenberry, *After Victory: Institutions, Strategic Restraint, and the Rebuilding of Order after Major Wars* (Princeton, N.J.: Princeton University Press, 2003).

the control of schools, religious institutions, or other media for transmitting ideas. Imposition is the primary method for attaining shared beliefs *within* a polity and is particularly common for spreading religious or nationalist ideas that do not lend themselves to external validation or "testing." Imposition means denying to the supporters of alternative ideologies the capacity to organize or to disseminate or pass on their ideas and thus militates toward the adoption of an orthodoxy. In the modern period, the rise of mass schooling and centrally controlled curricula have provided an effective means for imposing shared beliefs among large, geographically dispersed populations.[50]

STEP 2: WHOSE IDEAS MATTER? THE ROLE OF UNIT-LEVEL INSTITUTIONS

The combination of these selection and imposition mechanisms has led to a high degree of homogeneity of ideas both within and across modern states, especially among the schooled governmental elites that take decisions.[51] Yet while certain core beliefs are often held in common within modern polities, it is unreasonable to assume that the ideas within states or other political units are fully intersubjective – i.e. that there is a coherent political culture contained within the boundaries of a given political unit. In some polities the "common core" of shared beliefs may be quite limited. Given this diversity of ideas, whose ideas matter?

To answer this question some additional assumptions are required. For the sake of convenience, we can assume that the political units of concern are states – although the logic of analysis would work for nonterritorial units as well. Second, we can assume that these units have some set of institutions in place for taking decisions on behalf of the collectivity. The central question then becomes how those institutions affect what, or whose, ideas matter in determining state preferences.

IR theories have typically answered this question by a universal assumption. Following the holistic societal analogy, constructivists, like realists, have typically adopted a statist position; they assume that states are like individuals – thinking corporate beings. Statists take for granted that the constraints imposed by societal actors are relatively minor or that preferences

---

[50] Keith A. Darden, "The Origins of Economic Interests: Explaining Variation in Support for Regional Institutions among the Post-Soviet States" (Ph.D. Dissertation, University of California, Berkeley, 2000).

[51] Few U.S. citizens, for example, question the fundamental importance of preserving private property or competitive markets.

are derived from consensual state or national identities.[52] In contrast, liberal or societal approaches to IR gravitate to the other extreme. They generally assume that state leaders are so constrained that they have no alternative but to pursue some aggregation of societal preferences (the preferences of the median voter of an electorate or selectorate, or the winning commercial coalition).[53] Because states are not unitary they are not meaningfully understood as actors and are generally disaggregated into executives, legislatures, and electorates.[54] Strikingly, the dominant theories of international relations do not deal systematically with institutional variation among the units.

It is unreasonable to assume, however, that the question of whose ideas matter in determining state policy can be answered in the same way across all polities. Both the "statist" position that it is only the beliefs of the top leadership that are relevant, or that all share a common identity that renders the question of who decides moot, and the "societal" position that the preferences of societal actors necessarily aggregate up to become state policy,

---

[52] Typically, the theoretical treatment of these concerns has been encapsulated in the discussion of the extent of state "autonomy," but the notion of autonomy lends itself too easily to anthropomorphism and clusters together different concepts that it will prove useful to keep separate. The notion of autonomy is central to the work of all of those writing in the statist tradition, including Nettl, "The State as a Conceptual Variable," pp. 569–570; Krasner, *Defending the National Interest*; Nordlinger, *On the Autonomy of the Democratic State*; and Mansfield and Busch, "The Political Economy." Peter J. Katzenstein, *Small States in World Markets* (Ithaca, N.Y.: Cornell University, 1978), traces the use of the concept to Hegel's theory of the state, and it seems that Hegel likely drew his notion of state autonomy from the Kantian doctrine of the autonomy of the human will (the will that gives itself its own law apart from external constraint). In this respect, the anthropomorphism was present from the very incorporation of the concept into the study of politics and has thus understandably been difficult to extract. For accounts championing such anthropomorphism, see Wendt, *Social Theory*, chap. 5, and Mlada Bukovansky, "The Altered State and the State of Nature: The French Revolution and International Politics," *Review of International Studies* 25 (1999): 197–216.

[53] The literature here falls into two general categories. (1) those who focus primarily on electoral pressures and force state leaders to press the interests of societal actors in international affairs (e.g. Rogowski, *Commerce and Coalitions*; Milner, "Resisting Protectionism"; Mattli, *Logic of Regional Integration*, p. 51; and (2) those who argue that commercial coalitions influence the formulation of state policy both by supporting the election of and by lobbying state officials. State preferences, from this perspective, can be accurately deduced on the basis of an assessment of the interests of the country's commercial organizations, sectors, or factors of production, e.g. Frieden, "Invested Interests"; Milner, *Resisting Protectionism*; Andrew Moravcsik, "Taking Preferences Seriously: A Liberal Theory of International Politics," *International Organization* 51 (1997): 513–553, and *The Choice for Europe: Social Purpose and State Power from Messina to Maastricht* (Ithaca, N.Y.: Cornell University Press, 1998), p. 3.

[54] Helen V. Milner, *Interests, Institutions, and Information: Domestic Politics and International Relations* (Princeton, N.J.: Princeton: Princeton University Press, 1997a), pp. 4, 9–14.

can find cases where they appear to fit. But as universal assumptions they run sharply against the empirical variation that we find in the way that ideas and foreign policy preferences are actually aggregated or selected in different countries.[55] It is more profitable to answer the question of whose ideas matter differently for different types of states.

As the basis for theoretical parsimony, I would suggest that the central issue in determining whose ideas matter in the formation of state preferences is the extent to which key decision makers are constrained or influenced by societal (nonstate) actors and that one may usefully think of these constraints as the product of three basic parameters: leaders' *accountability*, *accessibility*, and *control*.

The question of how accountable a country's leadership is to the society it governs is a primarily a question of the ease with which decision makers can be removed from office if their actions are inconsistent with the ideas of the societies they govern. We can always expect leaders to exercise a degree of independence or autonomy in foreign policy matters. Even in highly democratic societies, elections occur infrequently, choice of candidates is limited, and voters make choices along multiple dimensions – of which foreign policy is arguably one of the least salient. Nonetheless, those decision makers who hold elected office are more likely to be responsive to the preferences of their constituents and to factor societal concerns into the formulation of policy or bargaining positions in international negotiations. We should certainly expect it to matter whether or not countries hold regular competitive elections, and the degree of leadership accountability should partially determine the extent to which public opinion or mass ideas play a role in the formation of state preferences when it acts internationally.

Even in countries that hold no elections, the leadership may be heavily influenced by nonstate actors so long as the policy process is made *accessible*. To measure the degree to which the policy process is accessible to involvement from societal actors, we are concerned with several questions: To what extent are organized interests or lobbying organizations involved directly in the policymaking process? Are positions drafted by state officials working in isolation within government departments or state ministries, or do societal actors such as policy lobbies, nongovernmental organizations (NGOs), epistemic communities, large firms, business associations, and labor and consumer groups play an important role by providing information, assistance,

---

[55] It is not clear, for example, how one would apply a theory (Milner, *Interests*) that assumed a dynamic among an executive, legislature, and electorate for a country that lacked these institutions.

and pressure in the formulation of national policy agendas in international negotiations?[56] Are channels of access to the policy process open to all those organized groups who take an interest in the process, as in pluralist systems, or restricted to a few state-sanctioned interest organizations, as in corporatist systems? Or are there no regularized channels of access at all? These questions, too, are important for determining whether and/or how the preferences of societal actors are aggregated into the international politics of the state. Where the policymaking process is more accessible to domestic or transnational societal actors, state preferences are more likely to reflect the ideas of some subset of those actors involved in the process.

The third institutional variable concerns the extent to which the state controls the range of ideas available to individuals and has the capacity to manipulate the initial process by which ideas are selected within a population. By manipulating the development and spread of ideas, some state organizations are able to privilege certain ideas and the preferences induced by them. In this case, the primary concern is the extent to which societal actors are able to develop and disseminate ideas independently of the state, in particular: whether there are independent media organizations or whether the means of articulating and transmitting ideas is publicly controlled by the state; whether state-controlled schools with centralized control over curricula limit the range of available knowledge; whether the state permits an independent expert or scientific community. Moreover, to the extent that ideas are shared or circulated primarily within organized groups, we must also ask whether individuals are able to organize into groups (religious institutions, political organizations, labor unions, business lobbies) without securing the approval of the state or whether the coercive apparatus of the state is capable of preventing organized dissent. States that are able to control public dissent and to prevent independent organizations from forming or engaging in political activity, and that also have an important role in shaping the preferences of society through control of media, schools, and other social institutions are much more likely to formulate national policy and preferences internally, i.e. within the apparatus of the state, and to be generally unconstrained in doing so by societal actors.

With these basic variables, we can identify a range of polity types according to whose ideas might be most significant in explaining the development of national foreign policy preferences. For the purpose of simplifying visual

---

[56] Again, the international relations literature that focuses on nonstate or transnational actors appears to assume that these actors universally carry some influence. It does not account for variation across states in the extent to which these actors have a role in policymaking.

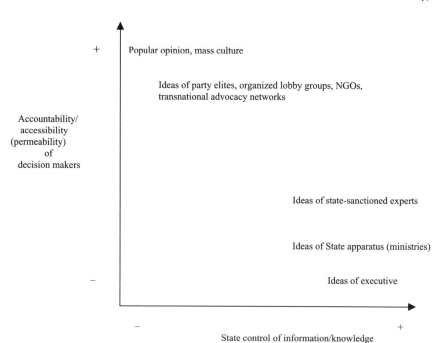

FIGURE 2.2. Whose ideas matter – variation across polity types.

presentation, I assume that accountability and accessibility tend to be closely correlated and plot them on a single axis (Figure 2.2).[57]

Those countries that fall into the upper left corner, what we would consider *liberal democratic* states, would be the most constrained by the ideas and concerns of societal actors. With leaders made accountable through established democratic institutions and a low level of state restriction and repression of societal organization and activity, one would expect that the ideas/preferences of societal actors would significantly shape or at least constrain the formation of national policy preferences by elites. Commercial organizations, labor unions, transnational advocacy networks, foreign lobbies, and other organized interest groups would be expected to have a significant impact on policy.[58] Moreover, the stock of popularly held ideas and

[57] Given that accountability and accessibility are tightly linked, insofar as those leaders who are accountable to societal actors will be more likely to include them in the policymaking process, I use only one of them here.

[58] Indeed, several important studies of regional institutions formed among countries in this category have substantiated this: Moravcsik, "Taking Preferences Seriously"; Milner, *Interests*; Mattli, *Logic*, pp. 48–50, 70–77; Sandholtz and Zysman, "1992: Recasting the European Bargain," *World Politics* 42, no. 1 (October 1989): 95–128. Similar findings emerge from

myths about identity, history, and so on, can also be expected to play a role in the formulation of policy. Greater societal constraint simply means that the ideas of societal actors will be important to the international activities of the state, regardless of what those ideas might be.

In the lower right corner we find the opposite extreme, cases where the state wields extensive control over information and ideas, where there are few institutionalized channels to hold leaders accountable, and where societal groups are generally not given access to policymaking. In such cases of *state domination*, independent societal institutions are eliminated or subject to severe constraints. It is often the case that membership is compulsory in certain state-sanctioned societal institutions, such as labor organizations or officially recognized religious organizations, and that the leadership of these organizations is then coopted by or subordinated to the state apparatus.[59] State control of the media means that societal actors may lack information or receive false information about the nature of international initiatives – making it particularly difficult for them to develop a set of preferences different from those of the government. In state-dominated cases, it is unlikely that societal groups will play an important role in the formation of state preferences and the ideas that play a role in the formation of policy preferences will be those held by the top leadership of the state. The majority of post-Soviet states fall into this category under our period of study.

In sum, whose ideas matter depends on the structure of unit-level institutions. Where the state's leadership is held accountable by elections, where the policymaking process is accessible to nonstate actors, and where the state does not control the extent to which societal actors organize themselves or express their ideas, one can expect that broadly held popular beliefs will play a more significant role in the formation of national preferences. In those cases where the leadership is held accountable only to a much narrower circle, where nonstate actors are not privy to the policymaking process, and where the state wields extensive powers over the dissemination of ideas, the ideas that matter are those held by top elites or state officials.

The upshot of this discussion of unit-level institutions is that the shared ideas that are the foundations of international order – the rules, norms, and

---

the literature on the effectiveness of transnational advocacy networks and the spread of human rights regimes: Keck and Sikkink, *Activists beyond Borders*; Thomas Risse and Kathryn Sikkink. "The Socialization of International Human Rights Norms into Domestic Practices: Introduction," *The Power of Human Rights: International Norms and Domestic Change*, ed. Thomas Risse, Stephen C. Ropp, and Kathryn Sikkink (New York: Cambridge University Press, 1999).

59 See Schmitter, "Still the Century of Corporatism," for a discussion of state corporatism under authoritarianism.

institutions that structure the relations among the units of international politics – need not be consensual within states. Nor, as pointed out previously, do ideas need to be consensual across the international system as a whole. The minimal condition for establishing international order is that a set of causal ideas must be shared by the relevant actors across each of the units. Where such "islands of common understanding" emerge within and across states, they provide the basis for establishing institutional arrangements – regardless of whether those ideas are considered heterodox or heretical by significant portions of their own population or by other states in the international system. As a result, the international norms and institutions that we identify empirically are always partial in their scope – incorporating only a subset of states in the system – and contingent insofar as they rest on the support from the states or units that constitute them and, ultimately, on the beliefs of groups who hold sway within the units. As those groups governing the units change, or as their beliefs change, or as the institutional order within the units changes to privilege new groups and beliefs, the cultural landscape of the international system is altered – undermining the prior institutional arrangements. Thus, rather than acting as a structural determinant of actors' identities and beliefs, the norms and principles of international societies are subject to change as the ideas that hold sway in their constitutive units change and evolve.

CONCLUSION: FROM INDIVIDUAL IDEAS
TO INTERNATIONAL ORDER

We are now in a position to state in concise terms the tenets of the theory of international order and institutional choice that we will use to explain institutional choice in post-Soviet Eurasia.

The theory offered here suggests that international actors do not simply choose strategies of action based on fixed preferences; nor do they simply act according to socially or systemically defined rules that determine appropriate behavior. Actors first select a set of causal ideas, ideas about how the world works, out of their "cultural reservoir," a body of salient beliefs that become shared through imposition, emulation, or ecological selection. This set of ideas then shapes the way actors characterize their options and induces preferences over the perceived possible outcomes. When shared among the relevant decision makers within a country, different causal ideas lead to different definitions of the national interest and radically different views on the desirability of different international institutions and normative arrangements. Ideas shared internationally provide the basis for the creation of international institutions and the islands of common understanding that transcend state boundaries provide the foundations for the nonuniversal, contingent forms of international social order evident in world politics.

An examination of the causal ideas employed by national governments is therefore essential to an explanation of how state actors define national interests and choose strategies of action. In particular, we cannot explain why states choose to adhere to the norms and institutions identified by other constructivist theories without an understanding of the systematic distribution of ideas across countries. Where causal ideas are shared among states, cooperation is facilitated by the harmonization of state preferences over possible institutional arrangements. To the extent that the causal ideas employed by decision makers vary across states, cooperation between those states is impeded. More generally, one can expect that variation in modes of reasoning leads to variation in the support for different international institutional forms.

In sum, variation in support for different international norms and institutions across different countries and regions can partially be explained by the use of different causal ideas by different governments. Changes in international or regional institutions can occur as people revise or replace their ideas about causation and refashion international institutions to make them consistent with new modes of thinking and the preferences induced by them. To the extent that actors' ideas converge as a result of voluntary choice, ecological/natural selection, or imposition, they provide the foundations for a common set of institutions. But variation in ideas leads inevitably to variation in institutional forms or institutional failure. Shared understanding is a prerequisite of a common international order – however partial and fleeting it may be.

Empirically, we find this to be the case with respect to the economic ideas and international institutional choices among the 15 post-Soviet states. To make this argument, let us first turn to the task of identifying the variation in institutional choices made by the 15 states. We can then characterize the various economic ideas prevalent among decision makers in the 15 post-Soviet states and, finally, examine their effects on support for international institutions of different types.

3

Three International Trajectories

The first step is to identify precisely what happened in the 10 years after the post-Soviet states became independent, i.e. to identify the variation in institutional choice. As discussed briefly in Chapter 1, the first post-Soviet decade brought marked differences in the institutions countries selected or created to manage their economic relations with other states, leading to three distinct international trajectories among countries in the region. One course was oriented to the pursuit of global multilateral liberalism – or nondiscriminatory and freer trade – exemplified by membership in the World Trade Organization. A second path led toward regionalism, or the active participation in economic institutions that privileged trade and economic ties among the former Soviet republics and sustained barriers to exchange with the rest of the world. The third road was toward autarky, or the reliance on national rather than international institutions for managing international economic exchange and the general closure of the economy through high tariffs, inconvertible currencies, or other restrictions.

Each of these institutional alternatives – the WTO, the CIS, and national autarky – entailed the adoption of a set of rules that significantly influenced international economic interaction and exchange, including rules governing the treatment of foreign enterprises, currency convertibility, the use of subsidiesm, and other aspects of the relationship between business and the state. Moreover, each alternative required that authority be allocated to a different set of decision-making institutions for establishing new sets of rules and standards related to international economic relations. Each constituted a distinct international trajectory.

The purpose of this chapter is to identify precisely which international trade institutions each of the post-Soviet states joined, established, or participated in between 1991 and 2000 – to provide a clear characterization of the empirical puzzle. This chapter does not, however, make any moves to explain those choices. Indeed, it studiously avoids any discussion of causation and is devoted strictly to a description of the variation on the dependent variable and the methods used to measure it. Although this can make for rather dry reading at times, the firewall that this section of the book constructs between its measurement of economic ideas (the independent variable) and institutional choice (the dependent variable) is methodologically critical. It is designed to ameliorate one of the central problems with the empirical application of ideational or constructivist arguments: a failure to draw clear distinctions between the ideas and the outcomes that they are trying to explain, which often drifts into endogeneity or, worse, tautology.[1] For this reason, this book tries, in this chapter and the next, to parse causes and effects both with new methods for measuring ideas and with new measures of institutional choice. The ideas are then rejoined with the actions as we examine actors' motivations in the explanatory chapters of the book, but for now they must be treated separately and I have divided the discussion into separate chapters: The next chapter discusses the measurement of ideas;[2] this one measures institutional choice.

To do this, I begin by describing the global, regional, and national institutions that countries have selected to govern their international economic affairs. I devote particular attention to the regional institutions of the Commonwealth of Independent States because there is such a dearth of reliable published work on the region. I then propose a new set of standardized measures for institutional choice and participation in the region and use these to chart both cross-sectional variation across all 15 countries in the region and changes in individual countries over time. By charting the variation across time as well as across the region, we gain a fuller understanding of the empirical puzzle, and a new cross-sectional time-series dataset

---

[1] I recognize that the inseparability of intentions (meaning) from outcomes is not considered a problem to be solved by many who write in this literature. And while I respect this position, Clifford E. Geertz (*The Interpretation of Cultures* [New York: Basic Books, 1973], p. 6), for example, is clearly correct that the difference between a wink and a blink rests on the intentions and meaning attached to the action by the actor, not on the objective description of the movements of the eye. I also find that "reasons" and "actions" can usually be separated analytically in matters of concern to social scientists. And without clearly separating out the ideas/motivations, measuring them independently, and testing them against alternative explanations, I find it hard to have confidence in an argument that a given set of ideas is causal – rather than simply justificatory, something imagined by the observer, or descriptive of the action itself (as with the wink).

[2] See also the methodological appendix of this book.

(with considerably more observations) to use in testing rival claims. Finally, I outline the progress of each state over the 10-year period.

WTO

Let us start with the World Trade Organization. Although I have referred to the WTO as a body associated with the principles of free trade and competition, the institution is formally organized on the principle of nondiscrimination – i.e. members must agree to grant all other members Most Favored Nation (MFN) status – not free trade. Indeed, there is no organizational restriction on the level of protection allowed to new members. In practice, however, the WTO has become a liberal institution that both promotes and enforces liberalization. Each successive round of negotiations (previously under the General Agreement on Tariffs and Trade, or GATT) has led its members to bind themselves to lower tariffs, to eliminate quotas and other legal restrictions on trade, and to adhere to rules designed to preserve fair market competition.

The liberal thrust of the WTO is felt especially strongly by new members because of the weak position of the applicant in the accession process, a procedure that involves two distinct elements. First, applicants must adopt a common set of international standards and rules for managing foreign economic relations, preserving property rights, and adjudicating disputes – an *acquis* that all members share in common and that is designed to facilitate transparency and fair competition. This includes matters such as rules for determining the country of origin of goods, measurement and certification standards, sanitary rules, and antidumping rules. The second and generally more protracted process is the negotiation of an agreement with existing members that fixes maximal limits on the level of protection that a country may impose on trade with other WTO members and the extent to which it may subsidize or aid certain exports. These agreements are idiosyncratic and a product of the specific entry negotiations for each country.

It is the one-sided nature of the negotiation with prospective members that leads to a liberal bias among entrants. Because countries can only be admitted to the organization by a *consensus* of current members (146 countries as of April 2003), the "negotiation" phase of accession primarily involves unilateral tariff or market-access concessions by the prospective member in an effort to secure support for entry. This liberalizing tendency was particularly acute for the post-Soviet countries, as the United States took an aggressive role in demanding that aspiring members bind themselves to a low level of trade protection. As a result, as far as post-Soviet countries were concerned, the WTO only admitted states that agreed to a liberal trade policy. Progress toward WTO membership of a post-Soviet state is thus an indication of the acceptance of a multilateral liberal trade order.

MEASUREMENT

Because critical aspects of the accession process are closed to the public and the terms of accession agreements vary, there is no simple way to measure progress toward membership in the WTO on an annual basis, but I have developed two indicators – one of which is useful for cross-sectional time-series analysis. The first indicator, which is a useful descriptive statistic but virtually ensures serial correlation in quantitative analysis, measures overall progress toward WTO membership by charting each state's progress according to when it completed certain necessary steps, comprising:

1. The submission of an application
2. The submission of the Memorandum on Foreign Trade (a detailed description of the country's trade regime)
3. The onset of tariff negotiations
4. The approval of the Text of the Protocol of Accession by the General Council of the WTO

The WTO provides precise information on the date that an application and the Foreign Trade Memorandum are received, as well as the date that the Protocol of Accession is approved, but not on the timing or content of the tariff negotiations. They do, however, provide the dates for each meeting of the Working Group associated with each country's accession process, and we can assume that three meetings of the working group is a basic sign that the negotiations have progressed. Using this as a guide, we can note clear differences in the rate of progress along this trajectory across the 15 states.

The progress of each state toward WTO membership between 1993 and 2001 is shown in Table 3.1.

The second indicator measures the rate of activity oriented toward membership with an annual count of the number of WTO "events" leading to membership, such as document submissions or Working Party meetings. The second measure is important because progress toward WTO accession is unidirectional, i.e. once documents are submitted they are not withdrawn, and in all cases the accession process is protracted. In principle, it would be preferable to measure progress in the negotiations rather than simply the number of meetings, but such information is confidential. As a measure of a country's support for the WTO process in a given year, annual activity will

TABLE 3.1. *Progress toward WTO Membership, 1993–2001*[a]

	1993	1994	1995	1996	1997	1998	1999	2000	2001
Kyrgyzstan	0	0	0	2	2	4	4	4	4
Latvia	1	2	2	3	3	4	4	4	4
Estonia	0	1	3	3	3	3	4	4	4
Georgia	0	0	0	1	2	2	4	4	4
Lithuania	0	2	2	3	3	3	3	4	4
Moldova	1	1	1	2	2	2	3	3	4
Armenia[b]	1	1	2	2	3	3	3	3	3
Russia	1	2	2	3	3	3	3	3	3
Ukraine	1	2	2	3	3	3	3	3	3
Kazakhstan	0	0	0	2	2	3	3	3	3
Belarus	1	1	1	2	2	2	2	2	3
Uzbekistan	0	1	1	1	1	2	2	2	2
Azerbaijan	0	0	0	0	1	1	1	2	2
Tajikistan	0	0	0	0	0	0	0	0	0
Turkmenistan	0	0	0	0	0	0	0	0	0

[a] Stages: 1 = application received, 2 = Foreign Trade Memorandum sent, 3 = Working Party has held third meeting, 4 = Approval of Accession by General Council of the WTO.
[b] Armenia secured membership in 2003, but that is beyond the temporal scope of this analysis.

serve as an adequate proxy. These findings are shown in Table 3.2 (data cease once a country has secured membership).

Using these data in combination with other sources, we can glean a general picture of progress toward WTO membership across the region. As seen in the first table, several countries took the first steps toward entry into the WTO shortly after attaining independence. By the end of 1993 six states had applied for membership, and three more had submitted applications by the end of 1994. Russia was the first to submit an application, in June 1993, but was immediately followed by Belarus, Latvia, Moldova, Armenia, and Ukraine. Already in 1992, Estonia had eliminated all import tariffs and sent an observer mission to what was then the GATT, but its formal application was not received until March 1994. Similarly, Lithuania had liberalized its trade regime but only formally applied to the WTO in January 1994. Uzbekistan was the final member of this "first wave" of applications – submitting its application in December 1994. A second wave of applications appeared in the late 1990s. In 1996, Kyrgyzstan, Kazakhstan, and Georgia all submitted applications. These were followed by Azerbaijan's application in June 1997. Tajikistan submitted an application in May 2001 and Turkmenistan has never submitted an application.

TABLE 3.2. *Annual Count of WTO Accession–Related Events,[a] 1992–2000*

	1992	1993	1994	1995	1996	1997	1998	1999	2000
Kyrgyzstan	0	0	0	0	2	2	5		
Latvia	0	1	1	2	2	1	2		
Estonia	0	0	2	5	2	1	0	3	
Georgia	0	0	0	0	1	1	3	2	
Lithuania	0	0	2	1	2	1	0	0	1
Moldova	0	1	0	0	1	1	1	2	1
Armenia	0	1	0	1	2	1	0	1	0
Russia	0	1	1	2	2	2	2	0	1
Ukraine	0	1	1	2	1	2	1	0	1
Kazakhstan	0	0	0	0	2	2	1	0	0
Belarus	0	1	0	0	1	1	1	0	0
Uzbekistan	0	0	1	0	0	0	1	0	0
Azerbaijan	0	0	0	0	0	1	0	1	0
Tajikistan	0	0	0	0	0	0	0	0	0
Turkmenistan	0	0	0	0	0	0	0	0	0

[a] Events = document submissions or meetings of the Working Group.

For many countries in the first wave, the submission of the application marked the beginning of several years of nonactivity in the WTO process without moving on to the next stage of submitting a Foreign Trade Memorandum. Of the first wave of applicants, Belarus did not submit its Foreign Trade Memorandum until January 1996 (2.5 years), Moldova until September 1996 (3 years), and Uzbekistan did not move to the next (nonbinding) stage until October 1998 (4 years) and has made no further progress toward entry. As the second stage was merely the act of providing the information that would allow the multilateral and bilateral negotiation processes to begin and accession to commence in earnest, it is clear that these countries showed no strong interest in pursuing WTO membership in the intervening years. All of these countries were actively involved in CIS integration during this time and Belarus held off on its WTO accession pending joint decisions by the Customs Union members regarding the conditions of their membership.

In contrast, several countries submitted their Memoranda and began negotiations almost immediately. Russia was again the first to submit its Memorandum in March 1994 (9 months after applying), followed by Latvia, Estonia (11 months), Lithuania (11 months), Armenia (17 months), and Ukraine (20 months). Latvia attained membership in 1998, Estonia in 1999, and Lithuania, after protracted negotiations about agricultural protection, became the fifth post-Soviet state to be approved for membership in December 2000.

For Russia, Ukraine, and Armenia, progress toward accession slowed markedly after they submitted their trade Memoranda. Armenia, which many observers believed to be on the cusp of membership in summer 1997, finalized its accession only in 2003 and the Working Party met only once between 1998 and 2002. In the case of both Russia and Ukraine, the Working Party continued to meet regularly until 1998, but the meetings became nothing more than a formality during the mid-1990s, with both governments unwilling to reduce their high tariffs or make movement toward the concessions that would gain them entry.[3] Ukraine continued to resist trade liberalization or reform, despite the fact that the United States and the European Union devoted considerable resources and political pressure to the task of securing Ukraine's WTO entry and made participation in WTO negotiations a condition for receiving aid.

Russia followed a similar trajectory until 2000, when its moves toward the WTO stepped up considerably after the election of Vladimir Putin. Remarking on the shift, General Secretary of the WTO Mike Moore noted in 2001 that "the recent delivery of Russia's revised market access offers in goods and services marked a major change in the tone of the negotiations.... From this new spirit of cooperative negotiation we now see actual engagement between Russia and its trading partners in the negotiations on market access in both goods and services.... The multilateral work also continues to develop. It is not secret that this work has not progressed as quickly as we all hoped.... The big breakthrough has come in the last year, with the Russian side demonstrating its clear commitment to legislative and administrative reform." The genuine push for WTO entry beginning in 2000 was also noted by several Russian trade officials in interviews I conducted in Moscow in November 2000.

Of the second wave of applicants, Georgia, Kazakhstan, and the Kyrgyz Republic all moved rapidly, submitting their Memoranda within less than nine months after application. The Kyrgyz Republic moved with extreme rapidity in its WTO negotiations and in 1998, just under three years after submitting its application, became the first of the post-Soviet states to secure membership. Georgia also pursued membership aggressively and gained WTO approval for accession in October 1999 after a flurry of negotiations and Working Party meetings in 1998 and 1999. In contrast, Kazakhstan, like Belarus, slowed the negotiation process and took no steps that would prevent the establishment of the Customs Union (see Chapter 10). Beginning in

---

[3] Both countries continued to hold regular meetings until 1998, and hence the stalemate in negotiations is not reflected in the "activity" measure.

2000, Kazakhstan began to move more actively toward membership, making three distinct tariff offers in negotiations in 2000 and 2001, but here, too, the accession process has followed Russia's lead closely (and is outside the period of our analysis). The reasons for this will be explored in Chapter 10.

REGIONALISM

When it comes to the regional economic institutions, the problems of data collection and interpretation are Herculean. The officials who work in the regional institutions, unlike those of the WTO, are generally inclined to view the basic operation of joint institutions as a matter of secrecy. This tendency makes access to basic primary sources about the workings of these institutions needlessly difficult. Perhaps because of these difficulties, the secondary literature on the regional economic institutions is spare and often unreliable, a problem compounded by the profound lack of neutral discussion of the CIS. (It is revealing that the most comprehensive Western academic account of the CIS institutions to date is entitled *Getting It Wrong*.)[4] Faced with both opacity and bias, I have done my best to rely primarily on hard-won documentary evidence and my own experiences as a researcher within these organizations in the 1990s to chart their development.

As with the WTO, I will first describe the CIS institutions and then discuss the system of indicators that I have developed to measure each country's support for them. Because it has become commonplace for Western scholarship to assume that the regional institutions were of no significance, I make a considerable effort to show whether, and in what ways, the different regional institutions "mattered." In particular, I devote a great deal of attention to the Customs Union and the Economic Union that succeeded it – which I consider to be the most significant and sorely misunderstood of the regional institutions. Given that even such knowledgeable commentators as Anders Aslund have recently claimed that "a CIS customs union failed...and will fail again in the future. It delivered no freer trade than the CIS free-trade zone [which Aslund rightly discredits]. No participant harmonized its customs with anybody else,"[5] it is clear that considerably more work needs to be done to set the record straight. This occasionally makes for dry discussion,

---

[4] Martha Brill Olcott, Anders Aslund, and Sherman W. Garnett, *Getting It Wrong: Regional Cooperation and the Commonwealth of Independent States* (Washington, D.C.: The Carnegie Endowment for International Peace, 2000).

[5] Anders Aslund, "Post Soviet Free Trade," The Carnegie Endowment for International Peace, http://www.ceip.org/files/Publications/aslund_postsoviettrade.asp?from=pubdate, 2003.

but in an effort to be merciful to the reader much of this evidence has been relegated to the footnotes.

THE COMMONWEALTH OF INDEPENDENT STATES

For the purposes of convenient discussion, I have divided the regional economic institutions into three categories. The first category is what we might call the general framework of the Commonwealth of Independent States – an organization that currently includes all of the former Soviet republics with the exception of the three Baltic states. Within this framework, the most important role is played by two intergovernmental bodies, the Council of Heads of State (CHS), which comprised the presidents of the member-states, and the Council of Heads of Government (CHG), which assembled the prime ministers of each country. The two councils hold meetings biannually, and their decisions are officially taken by "consensus," which in practice meant that agreements were only binding on signatories and states could opt out of any agreements they chose.

In addition to the Councils of Heads of State and Government, several other general CIS institutions were created in the first two years after the Soviet collapse. In 1992, agreements were signed to create a Joint Parliamentary Assembly, which carried no decision-making authority and served as a means for parliamentarians to share legislation and create "draft" legislation for individual implementation by CIS members, and an Economic Court, whose decisions have consistently been ignored.[6] In January 1993, an Interstate Bank was established, although its role has been limited because the new ruble zone it was designed to manage never materialized. The most significant of these secondary institutions is the Executive Secretariat of the CIS, created in May 1993 (and renamed the Executive Council in 2000). The Executive Secretariat, which was designed to facilitate the meetings of the councils, had a body of permanent member-state representatives and an independent staff to draft new proposals for further cooperation and integration.

Did these institutions matter? Only in some cases. According to a confidential internal audit conducted by the Executive Secretariat in July 1997, out of the 856 documents passed by the CIS Heads of State and Heads of Government from the organization's inception in 1991 until July 1997, 471

---

[6] The agreement to create the Interparliamentary Assembly was signed in March 1992, but the first meetings did not take place until 1993. The Economic Court was created on 6 July 1992. Not a single one of the court's decisions has been implemented.

could be considered effective.[7] Thus, about half of the CIS agreements technically went into effect. Of these, about 102 agreements were singled out for either ratification or some additional form of legal implementation by national parliaments and are much more likely to have been effective. But as most analysts acknowledge, compliance with the law cannot be taken for granted among the post-Soviet states. But even if we assume a relatively low level of compliance with national legislation, which is probably impossible to measure in the post-Soviet space, it would still mean that a small, yet significant, portion of the agreements was effective.

CIS ECONOMIC UNION AND THE IEC

A second set of CIS regional institutions, more specifically economic in nature, are those associated with the Treaty on Economic Union, signed by 11 countries in September 1993 and subsequently ratified by 9. The treaty called for the full-scale economic reintegration of the post-Soviet states with the free movement of goods, services, capital, and labor; and a common policy on monetary, fiscal, tax, pricing, industrial support, foreign economic relations, customs, and currency issues; and the harmonization of commercial legislation and a common statistical base. The first step in the agreement was the establishment of a free trade area among the post-Soviet states, to be followed by a customs union, and economic and monetary union.

In addition to the general Treaty on Economic Union, the CIS members established several subsidiary sector- and issue-specific institutions to manage regional economic matters. Such intergovernmental sectoral councils were created to manage or discuss jointly the production and transit of oil and gas, foreign economic relations, customs, hydrometeorology, and a wide range of other joint concerns. These councils and commissions were groups of experts and ministry officials, usually deputy ministers, who met regularly to resolve common problems, share information, and make proposals for integration or collaboration.[8]

This surge in institutional development following the Treaty on Economic Union culminated in the formation of the Interstate Economic Commission

---

[7] I informally obtained this audit in August 1997 from the Executive Secretariat offices in Minsk.

[8] The number of such councils continued to grow in number until 1997, when they peaked at approximately 50 organizations – a number that had remained constant as of 2007. Some of these councils, such as the Council of Heads of the Customs Services, which has called the heads of the customs services together four times per year each year since it was founded in 1994, were quite active and important.

of the Economic Union (IEC),[9] established by agreement of the Council of Heads of State in October 1994.[10] The purpose of the IEC was to reintegrate the CIS economies on the basis of their prior Soviet ties, nominally through implementation of the Treaty on the Establishment of the Economic Union. It was also to exercise control over the, by then, rapidly increasing number of councils and commissions.[11] According to its treaties,[12] the IEC was given the authority to make decisions that would be directly implemented in all of the signatory republics, i.e. without ratification by the CHS or CHG or further approval from the national governments. This included the authority to remove or add tariffs, rewrite national standards, implement a proposed payments union, and handle all practical questions pertaining to the Customs Union.[13] The IEC also had control over all of the accounting and budgeting functions of the CIS organs, including all councils and commissions, although the budgetary outlays were ultimately ratified by the CHG and CHS. It had control over the finances and agendas of the councils, with the right to create new councils or eliminate existing ones. To perform these tasks, the organization was given a staff of 200 officials and an administrative budget larger than that of Russia's Ministry of Economy.[14]

---

[9] Mezhgosudarstvennyi Ekonomicheskii Komitet. Hereafter IEC.

[10] Also established was the Interstate Monetary Commission (MVK), which met quarterly and drew all 12 CIS ministers of finance and of economy and the heads of the central banks.

[11] The IEC was the third and most comprehensive manifestation of an institution that was designed to help manage common economic affairs centrally. This began in October 1992 with the formation of the Consultative Economic Working Committee of the Council of Heads of State and Heads of Government, which within less than a year became the Coordinating-Consultative Commission of the CIS (May 1993), which in turn became the Interstate Economic Commission of the Economic Union (October 1994). With each step the authority and staff expanded.

[12] There were two key treaties that established the IEC and defined its authority. The first treaty, "On the Formation of the Interstate Economic Commission of the Economic Union," signed on 21 October 1994, laid out the basic institutional framework and decision-making rules. ("Soglashenie o sozdanii Mezhgosudarstvennogo ekonomicheskogo Komiteta Ekonomicheskogo soiuza," signed 21 October 1994. *MEK Biulleten'*, no. 1, 1996, p. 25). The specific responsibilities of the IEC are detailed in an appendix to the agreement "Polozhenie o Mezhgosudarstvennom Ekonomicheskom Komitete Ekonomicheskogo soiuza." *MEK Biulleten'*, no.1, 1996, pp. 28–33. A second treaty, "On the Activities of Inter-state and Inter-governmental Organs of the CIS Handling Questions of an Economic Nature," signed only a few months later, served to extend the authority of the IEC and to increase the scope of matters under its purview. The IEC did not actually begin operation until July 1995 and Ukraine did not name its representative to the Kollegia of the IEC until 6 March 1996. *MEK Biulleten'*, no. 1, 1996, p. 42.

[13] Agreement on the Creation of the Interstate Economic Commission, *MEK Biulleten'*, no.1, 1996, p, 39.

[14] The WTO Secretariat, in contrast, has a staff of 550 to serve a membership of more than 140 countries.

In addition to its staff, the IEC comprised two decision-making bodies. The lower body, a Kollegia of 11 permanent representatives,[15] each of which held the rank of minister in his home government, met biweekly. It was the Kollegia's responsibility to review the documents generated by the IEC staff and revise them into draft agreements for submission to the upper chamber of the IEC. The upper body, a *Presidium* composed of the first deputy prime ministers[16] of the participant governments, was set to meet quarterly. Decisions taken by the Presidium either went into effect immediately or were submitted to the CHG for further approval.

Depending on the issue under consideration, decisions in the Kollegia and Presidium would be taken according to one of four sets of decision rules.[17] Matters to be decided by consensus included those concerning the shift to a customs union; the common market of goods, services, capital, and labor; currency union; and other "strategic" issues in the development of the Economic Union. Matters to be decided by qualified majority (three-fourths) included the decision to introduce import quotas, the selection of a reserve currency, the creation of joint investment funds, and other concrete issues of economic development, other than those explicitly cited as matters to be decided by consensus. Third, on policies that involved a significant outlay of economic resources or those with deep economic consequences, decisions were to be taken by a system of weighted majority voting according to each state's "economic potential." According to this weighting system, the Russian Federation carried 50 votes; Ukraine 14; Belarus, Kazakhstan, and Uzbekistan 5 votes each; and the remaining states 3 votes each. Finally, procedural questions were decided by simple majority.[18] Any party could opt out of a decision or item of legislation, so the various rules lost much of their significance. It simply meant that individual parties could not block other states from collective decisions to which they were opposed.

Did the IEC matter? Yes, but not in the ways – or to the extent – defined by its treaties. Although the IEC was technically given the right to make immediately operational decisions, over an extremely wide range of issues, in practice, the authority of the IEC was like that of most post-Soviet domestic institutions – a matter of continuous dispute in which legal documents and

---

[15] One from each CIS member except Turkmenistan.
[16] The third-highest ranking official in the country.
[17] *MEK Biulleten'*, no. 1, 1996, p. 32.
[18] "Poriadok raspredeleniia golosov" Prilozhenie 2 k Soglasheniiu o sozdanii Mezhgosu-darstvennogo Ekonomicheskogo Komiteta Ekonomicheskogo soiuza. 21 October 1994. *MEK Biulleten'*, no. 1, 1996, p. 34.

"formal" rights and obligations play a subsidiary role.[19] In the case of the IEC, this meant that less authority was exercised than its charters or subsequent treaties would suggest.[20] Aside from some minor exceptions, proposals generated by the IEC were still sent to the Heads of State and Heads of Government for approval. Nonetheless, a substantial institutional architecture was established for taking joint decisions on a wide range of economic issues in which the IEC played an important role.

What was this role? In addition to developing its own proposals for further integration, the IEC served as a conduit through which ministries of national governments could share information, legislation, and experience with one another. Such outcomes are difficult to measure empirically, but interviews suggested that the IEC played an important role in facilitating the harmonization of regional legislation by diffusing policy innovations, largely from Russia to the other member-states. In interviews conducted in 1996 and 1997 in several of the CIS member-states, national officials demonstrated a strong knowledge of the IEC and its procedures and reported that they often adopted its recommendations or developed their legislation in accordance with IEC models or advice that they received from the IEC staff.[21] Ministry staff read IEC documents carefully, submitted revisions, and implemented a significant number of the IEC documents ratified by the Councils of Heads of State and Government. The IEC provided the ministries with useful

---

[19] Note the complaints registered in the IEC's first annual report to the CHS: "In summing up the results of the IEC's activities in 1995, it is necessary to call attention to the lack of resolution (*nereshennost'*) of certain problems in the definition of the authority of the IEC on the whole, and of the authorized representatives of the states of the CIS in its Kollegia. It presents itself as expedient that states conduct definite work in this direction, so that in the Kollegia of the IEC are not defended this or that country's interests, but primarily worked out and initiated ideas and suggestions for the deepening of economic integration of the CIS." Reprinted in *MEK Biulleten'*, 1'96, 48.

The struggle over the IEC's authority marked the biannual meetings of the CIS Heads of State and Government, and the role and authority of the IEC has been regularly debated in the meetings of its own Kollegia since its creation, but there has been no real change, only new declarations. Anvar Sadykovich Makhmudov, the authorized representative of the republic of Uzbekistan in the Kollegia of the IEC. *Stenograficheskii Otchet* 1996, 21.

[20] The fact that the member-states would not actually give over any elements of their sovereignty to the IEC was established at the first meeting when consensus could not be achieved on this point.

[21] During the interviews respondents were asked questions about CIS procedures to get a sense of how familiar they were with CIS institutions. This was to measure the extent to which these institutions actually existed as something more than a few offices in Moscow. I found that the level of knowledge was remarkably high in general, and particularly strong in those states with the highest levels of implementation of CIS agreements.

models and advice that gave them immediate advantage in the development of national legislation.[22] All of this suggests that the IEC played an important direct role in harmonizing the development of national economic policies, not simply in developing new CIS legislation to be submitted to the Councils of Heads of State and Government.

It is worth noting that even the member-states that demonstrated strong support for CIS institutions on the whole were very selective in choosing the institutions to which they paid their budgetary share on time, and the IEC was among those institutions that were consistently paid.[23] In addition, the actual transfer of cash payments by the central government is only a small part of the resources that active participants devoted to the IEC, the sectoral councils, and other regional economic institutions. A hidden administrative cost was borne separately by the national ministries. Understaffed and underfunded, government ministries devoted a great deal of time and travel resources to generating and analyzing proposals for collective regional projects. While not exclusively devoted to regional institutions, each ministry within a post-Soviet government in the 1990s also generally had an entire department specifically addressed to relations with CIS countries in order to deal with the high volume of multilateral and bilateral issues under discussion and preparation. Most countries also had a separate ministry or agency devoted to CIS affairs. Hence, members devoted considerable resources to the management of regional economic affairs through the CIS institutions.

Regarding the IEC itself, the independence of the organization was eventually pared back as part of a reorganization of the CIS structures that took place in 1999 and 2000. At this time, the IEC was reduced in size, renamed the Economic Council, and given the primary task of implementing agreements signed by the CHS and CHG – in particular the agreement on the creation of a Free Trade Zone. The new Economic Council was effectively subordinated to a reformed Executive Secretariat, itself renamed the "Executive Commission," and was moved from Moscow to Minsk – a fact that reduced some of the IEC's more qualified staff. Nonetheless, between 1994 and 2003, the IEC/Economic Council of the CIS produced hundreds of agreements that were signed by the CIS Heads of State; as noted earlier, many of these were realized in practice.

---

[22] This was noted in virtually all interviews with integralists as well as several liberals.

[23] The overall budgetary outlays of the IEC were small, approximately $10 million per year, but for poor countries barely able to finance their own ministries, this was a significant sum.

THE CUSTOMS UNION/EURASIAN ECONOMIC UNION

A smaller subset of post-Soviet countries, led by Russia, Belarus, and Kazakhstan, supported more rapid implementation of the Treaty on Economic Union and pushed for a much more robust set of regional economic institutions. This self-selected vanguard of regional integration began, in the mid-1990s, to create a new set of trade institutions alongside the CIS that were more comprehensive in scope than the CIS institutions. The first step was the formation of a Customs Union in 1995. Subsequent agreements in 1996 and 1999 ultimately culminated in a Eurasian Economic Union agreement in 2000. As these are the most significant and least understood of the regional institutions, let us examine them carefully.

The Customs Union began as a bilateral agreement between Belarus and Russia.[24] The two countries signed a bilateral customs union agreement on 6 January 1995. Upon hearing of the agreement, however, Kazakh president Nazarbaev immediately traveled to Moscow and by 20 January a new Customs Union agreement had been signed that included Russia, Belarus, and Kazakhstan and was open to further membership.[25] In March 1996, Kyrgyzstan acceded to the agreement, which it subsequently ratified in July 1997. Tajikistan sought membership, but because of objections by Kazakhstan based on concerns about the republic's ongoing civil war was only admitted in February 1999.

The Customs Union agreement incorporated the core elements of a traditional customs union but also called for the formation of a common economic and industrial policy apparatus, defining a "customs union" broadly as "an economic union/amalgamation [*ob"edinenie*] of states."[26] The union was to be based on two principles. The first principle encapsulated the traditional concept of a customs union. It called for the creation of a "single

---

[24] The Customs Union was part of the bilateral unification efforts that began after the ouster of Shushkevich in Belarus and the installment of Victor Chernomyrdin as head of the Russian government.

[25] As in 1991, Kazakhstan forced open a more parochial "Slavic" customs union and laid the groundwork for other CIS states to join. Here we also see the persistent tension between Nazarbaev's approach and Lukashenko's desire to have a particular relationship with Russia and to foster a "Slavic union" of Russia, Belarus, and Ukraine. Nazarbaev was most concerned with the construction of a political-economic bloc, the Eurasian Union, that would replace the USSR and encompass all of the former Soviet republics. Nazarbaev has firmly opposed the creation of smaller unions, particularly the "Slavic union," which he finds ethnic and parochial – and presumably a threat to Kazakhstan's territorial integrity given the dense Slavic settlement in the north of the country.

[26] Article 1: "Goals and Principles of the Customs Union," Soglashenie o Tamozhennom soiuze mezhdu RF i RB. Kazakhstan later added to the treaty.

economic territory" with a "single customs territory" to be realized through
the removal of all barriers to trade between the members, the establishment
of an identical trade regime (both tariff and nontariff barriers), and the
formation of a mechanism for regulating future foreign economic activity.
The second principle was somewhat ambiguous, calling for "a single-type
mechanism for the regulation of the economy" and "unified legislation" –
something we tend to associate more with an economic union.[27]

More specifically, the customs union involved the unification of foreign
economic policy in four key areas.[28] First and foremost, members removed
all tariffs and restrictions on trade with one another and established a common external tariff. Second, in addition to the common tariff, members
harmonized all aspects of the regulation of foreign economic activity, including excise taxes, the collection of value added tax (VAT), nontariff barriers, customs valuation, and relations with third countries and international
organizations. Third, members integrated the management of their Customs Services and established collective efforts for protecting the external
border of the customs union from smuggling or other incursions. Fourth,
the countries provided for the mutual convertibility of their currencies at
central bank rates and made considerable progress to harmonize their tax,
price, and other economic policies for the purpose of creating standardized conditions for enterprises throughout the territory of the union. With a
few exceptions, the formation of the Customs Union involved Belarus and
Kazakhstan's adopting the Russian system for managing foreign economic
relations – although not Russian control. Any changes in the system were to
be decided jointly.

But did the Customs Union agreement matter? Did it ever actually take
effect? Looking at the agreements the members signed, the diplomatic communications between members, internal memos, the ministerial commands
and directives of the governments, and the resultant tariff schedules of the
members, we can see definitively that the Customs Union of Russia, Belarus,
and Kazakhstan was established. Indeed, the Customs Union Agreement

---

[27] Soglashenie o Tamozhennom soiuze mezhdu RF i RB. Kazakhstan later added to the treaty.
[28] The full list of agreements and subagreements, with further details on their implementation,
    can be found in Darden, "The Origins." The list of documents given to prospective members
    at the end of 1995 also provides a good assessment of all that the customs union entailed.
    See 18 January 1996 – Protokol rab. soveshchaniia ruk Bel (Miasnikovich), Kaz (Isingarin),
    and Ros chastei (Bol'shakov) Mezhpravitelstvennoi bel-kaz-ros komissii po koordinatsii
    raboty i kontroliu za vypolneniiem dogovorennostei o dal'neishem rasshirenii i uglublenii
    vzaimnogo sotrud.

was implemented and monitored with great thoroughness and rapidity.[29] The adoption of the Russian tariff was nearly complete, with only a few points subject to compromise.[30] Several of Kazakhstan's export tariffs also remained in place, although these were eliminated in early 1996.[31]

The adoption of the common external tariff and the complete freeing of trade among the countries had deep economic implications for all sides. For Russia, it meant a significant loss of budgetary revenues. The formation of a customs union heavily impacted one of the state's most reliable sources of revenue – the export taxes it earned on trade with CIS countries. The amounts in question are quite significant, and Russia's removal of export taxes in relations with Kazakhstan alone was projected to cost the government $1.2 billion in tax revenues.[32]

For Belarus and Kazakhstan, the adoption of the Russian tariff dramatically increased the tariff on the import of basic commodities. In Belarus, import tariffs increased by an average of 15 percentage points each and Belarus added a list of export tariffs, although the latter were largely on commodities not produced in Belarus. Table 3.3 gives a sense of the effect of the new regime on the duties for basic commodities.

---

[29] See Darden, "The Origins," chap. 11.

[30] In particular, a compromise was reached whereby Kazakhstan and Belarus were allowed to "grandfather" certain tariff levels, or loopholes were written in. Kazakhstan, for example, was allowed to maintain a lower import tariff on automobiles, but Russia retained automobile border checkpoints with Kazakhstan as a way of preventing the use of this loophole to import cars into Russia via Kazakhstan. Belarusian citizens were allowed to import one automobile for personal use at the old (lower) tariff rate, although this arrangement was difficult to monitor and somewhat subject to abuse. Author's interview with IEC Customs, 28 May 1997.

[31] Rare earth metals, cadmium, bismuth, copper, and cotton fiber. In the documents made available to me there is some ambiguity as to whether the Kazakh export tariffs in these areas were not included in the common external tariff, rather than simply allowed as exceptions for Kazakhstan. The protokol of a working meeting on 20 July 1995 in Almaty between delegations of RK and RF "po voprosam Formirovaniia TS" signed by Bol'shakov and Isingarin suggests that export tariffs on rare earth metals, cotton fiber, tantalum, cadmium, and copper were added to the general Customs Union trade regime. This is further reinforced by the 20 July 1995 agreement providing "an inventory of goods which upon export will use the level of tariffs in accordance with Ukaz Prez RK from 24.02.94 #1579," which includes the same goods. The export tariffs were removed by Kazakhstan in March 1996 (Postanovlenie Pravitelstva 12 March 1996 #810).

[32] These would be partly offset by increased revenues from VAT and excise taxes, but tax compliance is lower for these taxes (Russian Ministry of Economy estimate 1995). This information was provided in a confidential World Bank Memo. The source cannot be disclosed.

TABLE 3.3. *Sample Changes in the Belarusian Import Tariff Due to the Formation of a Common External Tariff Regime in 1995*

Commodity[a]	Before	After
Meat and Meat Products	0	15
Butter	0	20
Vegetables	0	15
Potatoes	0	25
Sausages	0	20
Confectionery	0	20
Mineral fuel, oil	1	5
Pharmaceuticals	0	10
Plastics	5	10
Leather clothes	15	30
Timber	15	20
Knitted wear	15	20
Textiles	15	25
Ferrous metal products	5	20
Metal-cutting machine tools	5	20
Lathe machine tools	5	20
Tools	5	15
Calculators	15	30
Electrical equipment	5	10
Tape recorders	5	30
TV sets	25	30
Integrated circuits	5	20
Buses	5	30
Passenger cars	25	40
Trucks	25	40
Motorcycles	5	25
Weapons	15	100

[a] *Source:* World Bank Memo from Sergei Kritchevsky to John Hansen, 8 August 1995, subject: Belarus Customs Union.

Likewise, Kazakhstan's average weighted import tariff increased from 3.0% to 7.5% as a result of the changes in the tariff.[33] The average tax rate before the customs union, as calculated by the Ministry of Industry and Trade and the Ministry of Economy of Kazakhstan, rose from 13.7% to 20.0%. Of this, the average customs tariff increased from 3.0% to 7.5%

[33] Calculation of the World Bank (internal memo). The new tariffs were implemented with Resolution #1125 of the Government of the Republic of Kazakhstan, "On Rates of Customs Duties on Imported Goods," 15 August 1995.

and the excise average increased from 2.1% to 4.4%. Export restrictions, in contrast, were lessened under the customs union, as many of the Kazakh restrictions were removed. The average tax rate on exports dropped from 15.7% to 14.7%. The average weighted tariff for export was reduced from 5.3% to 4.1%.[34]

In addition to a significant increase in import tariffs on goods originating outside the customs union, the decision to adopt Russian legislation meant changing everything from the way that they had been calculating customs values and duties, to verification of delivery, to export controls, to the complete unification of trade policy regimes so that their laws reflected the Russian Federation law "On the Customs Tariff." Because minor distinctions in the way customs duties were formulated and deliveries verified could easily become loopholes for escaping Russian customs duties, the Russians were quite rigid about the thorough implementation of all aspects of the customs code and methods.[35]

Only four months after the signing of the agreement, all internal barriers to trade had been removed.[36] Already by 21 March the State Customs Committee of the Russian Federation signed a law removing all tariffs on goods to and from Belarus and establishing methods for the common registration [*oformlenie*] of goods imported and exported from the common customs space of Russia and Belarus.[37] The Russian Federation removed all tariffs, taxes, and duties on goods in trade with Kazakhstan on 4 April,[38] and Kazakhstan reciprocated with respect to Russia and Belarus one week later.[39] Indeed, the border between Russia and Belarus – including all customs checkpoints and monitoring – was completely removed in late 1995

---

34 World Bank calculation (internal memo). The new export tariffs were implemented with Resolution #1449, "On Rates of Customs Duties on Exported Goods," 6 November 1995.

35 The legal norms, tariffs, and taxes are closely interconnected, and harmonization in one area can be rendered meaningless without harmonization in the others. A member might remove a tariff on alcoholic spirits, for example, but if it initiates an excise tax on the import of vodka, then the effect is essentially the same. Likewise, if one of the Customs Union partners calculates the tariff on the basis of a customs value that includes the original value of the good plus the addition of VAT, the ultimate tariff is going to be greater than if the VAT is not included in the principal value upon which the tariff is calculated.

36 The multilateral protocol where the orders of the national customs administrations were ratified was the "Protokol o vvedenii rezhima svobodnoi torgovli v polnom ob"eme bez iz"iatii I ogranichenii."

37 Prikaz #167 GTK RF "O pervoocherednykh merakh po realizatsii Soglasheniia o TS mezhdu RF i RB."

38 Prikaz #203, GTK RF "O pervoocherednykh merakh po realizatsii Soglasheniia o TS mezhdu RF i RK," 4 April 1995.

39 Prikaz #8, GTK RK, 12 April 1995.

and the external border jointly monitored. The same initially took place on the border between Russia and Kazakhstan, but the Kazakhs failed to reinforce their external borders (with Kyrgyzstan and Uzbekistan) to the satisfaction of the Russians and the customs posts on the border with Kazakhstan were eventually reestablished.[40]

Subsequent tariff changes by Russia and Kazkhstan led to the partial breakdown of the common external tariff. Early in 1996, unable to come to an agreement with Russia and Belarus on proposed changes, Kazakhstan made unilateral changes in its external tariff.[41] Even with the changes, Kazakhstan's tariff remained largely consistent with the common external tariff of the Customs Union (CU).[42] Kazakh customs officials in 1997 indicated that their customs tariff overlapped 85% with Russia's. And Belarussian customs officials reported that they continued to make changes in their tariff that kept it more than 98% in line with the Russian tariff at any given time.

The extent to which the common external tariff was preserved – and the considerable difference it made to be a member of the Customs Union – can be seen in Table 3.4. Table 3.4 shows correlations of the 1997 tariff schedules for the eight post-Soviet countries for which data were available from the United Nations Conference on Trade and Development (UNCTAD).[43]

---

[40] Kazakhstan was clearly unhappy about this and complained that Russia was treating the Customs Union as being of a purely "declarative character" because they retained customs controls at Sheremetevo and Domodedovo and for those arriving by car, generating lines at the border between Russia and Kazakhstan. Spravka "O khode...," 11 November 1995. Note, however, that for "physical persons" there are no borders in the CU, even between Kazakhstan and Russia. The border checkpoints exist only for the transit of goods. MEK Customs; Nurgalieva.

[41] The changes in the Kazakh tariff were technically within the CU agreement, which stipulated that if one country made a proposal for changes in the external tariff that was not addressed by the other members within a period of six weeks, then that government was permitted to take unilateral action. According to an internal Kazakh document, "because within the framework of the CU a single option was not achieved, it was necessary for the Republic of Kazakhstan to temporarily, until the acceptance of a common agreement, introduce partial changes in the level of the import customs tariff." Postanovlenie Pravitelstva, 3 March 1996 #300. June 1996 "Spravka o khode vypolneniia Soglashenii i Dogorov s stranami SNG" (Prepared by the Department of Foreign Economic Relations of the Customs Committee of the Republic of Kazakhstan.

[42] The Kazakh government's decision removed tariffs on those goods that were not produced in the republic, goods purchased with international credits, and goods that were used for production for export, i.e. raw materials for the chemicals and metals industry. It also lowered the tariff on cars to 2% of the customs value and increased tariffs to protect the domestic production of salt, meat preserves, and metal tailings (*otkhody metallov*) to 30%.

[43] Table 3.4 shows pairwise correlations using tariff information detailed at the HS6 (i.e. six-digit) level. I am deeply grateful for the research assistance of Alexandra Guisinger in compiling this table and in general apprising me of the available tariff data and how they are aggregated.

TABLE 3.4. *Correlations among Tariff Schedules (1997)*

	Belarus	Estonia (1996)	Georgia (1999)	Lithuania	Latvia	Moldova (1996)	Russia	Ukraine
Belarus	1.00							
Estonia (1996)	−0.01	1.00						
Georgia (1999)	0.04	0.03	1.00					
Lithuania	0.34	−0.03	0.21	1.00				
Latvia	0.31	−0.01	0.24	0.53	1.00			
Moldova (1996)	0.35	0.09	0.33	0.35	0.41	1.00		
Russia	0.99	−0.01	0.03	0.33	0.31	0.34	1.00	
Ukraine	0.29	0.01	0.14	0.40	0.50	0.58	0.29	1.00

As shown in the table, two years after the formation of the Customs Union the tariff schedules of Russia and Belarus remained virtually identical. As a point of comparison, the tariff schedules of Belarus (or Russia) and Ukraine – which of all these countries have the most similar economic structure – overlap less than 30%.

THE TREATY ON THE DEEPENING OF INTEGRATION

The Customs Union and its institutions continued to evolve and in March 1996, Russia, Belarus, Kazakhstan, and Kyrgyzstan signed the Treaty on the Deepening of Integration in Economic and Humanitarian Spheres – more conventionally known as the *chetverka*, or the "Treaty of the Four." The treaty was designed to establish a set of decision-making institutions for better managing the foreign economic policy of the customs union and to provide a better institutional framework for moving forward on economic union of the four countries.

Two new institutions defined the *chetverka*, the Interstate Council and the Integration Commission. The Interstate Council was a decision-making body made up of the presidents and prime ministers of the four governments. All decisions in the Interstate Council were to be taken by consensus (i.e. unanimity) and all financing was also divided up evenly among the four parties,[44]

---

[44] The equal financing placed a greater burden on the smaller states but was part of an effort to emphasize the equality of the members. The preliminary estimate of expenditures for May–December 1996 alone was 10,730,000,000 Russian rubles (RR) and 310,000 U.S. dollars (USD). (Draft – Preliminary estimate of expenditures for May–December 1996. Attached to draft protocol of first meeting of the Interstate Council, 20 April 1996). The Kyrgyz

although the Russian government provided office space, apartments, and other perquisites for the officials working in Moscow.[45] Once a decision was taken by the Interstate Council, however, it was to "have immediate execution by the governments of the treaty members. When necessary, decisions of the Interstate Council require transformation of the national legislation of the members of the treaty."[46] Thus, the decisions of the Interstate Council had primacy over national legislation, but because each national government still held a veto over collective policy, no decision could be taken without the agreement of all parties.

The Integration Commission (IK) comprised a permanent staff as well as a decision-making board that met four times per year. Unlike the IEC, where the representatives of the Kollegia had the rank of minister but did not hold positions of power within their national governments, the IK assembled the key figures who would be responsible for carrying out any joint decisions on economic matters – giving it the quality of a joint cabinet of ministers for economic affairs.[47] The members of the IK's board were the Ministers of Economy, Finance, and Cooperation with CIS States of the member-states.[48] The IK's board also worked on the principle of unanimity.

Ministry of Economy was unhappy about having to pay this sum. In a letter (3 May 1996) from First Deputy Minister of Economy Moldokulov to the Government of Kyrgyzstan we see that "the Ministry of Economy submits the proposal to reexamine the tentative estimate of expenses and the general number of workers in the IK" and to shrink both. "In the long term, when the IK does something concrete we can reexamine the number and each of its structures. On other matters we have no recommendations. Can recommend them for ratification at the regular meeting of the Interstate Council." And indeed, the Kyrgyz government appears to have paid less at the outset. On 1 July 1996, the Ministry of Finance purchased 150,000,000 RR from the National Bank and paid it to the IK. (As reported in letter from Minister of Finance Nanaev to Prime Minister Dzhumagulov 8 July 1996).

[45] The budget of the Integration Commission in 1997 was only about $3.3 million. It must be kept in mind, however, that the size of the economies involved is small. Moreover, in CIS states, a smaller percentage of GDP was actually collected as tax revenue and each of these states faces a perpetual budgetary crisis that threatens both social unrest and further economic collapse. In 1997, the budget of the Integration Commission stood at 14,670 million Russian rubles (approximately $3 million) and 220,000 U.S. dollars (*Smeta Raskhodov* [Estimate of Expenses] of the Integration Commission [IK] for 1997. Appended to the agenda for the second meeting of the IK, 25 July 1996). Russia paid an additional 3,720 million rubles on top of the regular budget. The budget for May–December of 1996 was 5,694 million RR and 186,000 USD, with Russia spending an additional 1,123 million RR for facilities and perquisites of the staff.

[46] Article 9, Treaty on Interstate Council.

[47] While students of Western European integration have placed a great premium on the fact that international civil servants and representatives were not officeholders in national governments, in the CIS, not holding a government post most often means not being heeded.

[48] "Vremennaia struktura apparata Integratsionnogo Komiteta i skhema ego upravleniia" Bulletin 96/1, p. 27.

The IK's permanent staff, which was directly under the control of the IK chairman, was organized into ministerial subdivisions.[49] It was responsible for drafting new proposals and governing the activities of workgroups of national experts created for almost all areas of economic policy.[50] The large staff reduced the need to rely on the resources of the Russian ministries, as had often been the case with the Customs Union, and increased the autonomous role of the IK. And though the IK was not initially given the authority to take decisions of a "mandatory character," this was added through subsequent decisions of the Interstate Council.[51] In practice, the IK exerted considerable influence over the affairs of the members.[52]

The significance of the IK was reflected in the quality of its staff and the active participation of high-level officials from each of the member-states.

[49] In 1996–1997, the staff were organized into six departments: the General Economic Department, the Trade-Customs Department, the Department of Sectoral Integration, the Department of Cooperation in Social and Humanitarian Spheres, the Legal Department, and the Financial-Economic Department (*Finansovo-khoziaistvennoe upravlenie*). *Biulleten' Razvitiia Integratsii* no. 1, (1996): 30.

[50] According to the treaty, the functions of the IK were to provide a common market with equal rights/conditions for the economic subjects of the member countries; to conduct common economic reforms; to establish equal property and ownership rights for subjects throughout the territory; to take part in the creation of a model body of civil law and laws on the role of the state in the economy (literally "state regulation of the economy"); to conduct a common pricing policy; to complete the formation of the single customs territory and to provide a common system of governance of that territory; to conduct a common structural policy oriented "to the creation of industrial and agrarian economic complexes based on the mutual complementarity of the economies, maximal use of the advantages of a rational division of labor, and effective use of natural resources"; to work out a system of measures for state support for the development of cooperation in production, encouragement of capital investment in production, including subsidizing goal-oriented programs and projects of the parties, the development of goals representing the common interest of the parties; to cooperate in the formation of transnational conglomerates; to work out concrete proposals on financial-budgetary issues for the integration of the parties' policies; to strengthen coordination in on monetary and credit issues and create an effective payments system; to ensure equal access of the parties to each others' currency and securities markets; to create an interbank union to move toward unified standards and practices of regulating banking activity; etc., etc., etc. Polozhenie ob IK, Bulletin 96/1, p. 21.

[51] Treaty, Article 19. Bulletin of the IK, 96/1, p. 11. The authority issue was not clarified in the subsequent *polozhenie* (regulation) on the IK signed by the Interstate Council on 16 May 1996. The Interstate Council's decision included a provision that "consensual [unanimous] decisions of the IK . . . on questions touching on the Agreement on the Customs Union, take on a mandatory character for organs of the executive power of the member-states of the Customs Union." Thus, in areas in which the member-states could agree, the decisions of the IK, like those of the Interstate Council, had priority over national legislation. The "Reshenia Mezhgosudarstvennogo Soveta RB, RK, KR, i Rf ot 31 Dec 1996 #4 'O merakh po realizatsii soglasheniy o TS" and the accompanying "Polozhenie o poriadke priniatiia resheniy po voprosam realizatsii soglasheniy o TS" can be found in Bulletin #1/97, pp. 11–15.

[52] For detailed discussion, see Darden, *The Origins,* chaps. 12 and 13.

Nigmatzhan Isingarin, the second highest ranking figure in the government of Kazakhstan, took on the post of chairman – a permanent position that led him to relocate to Moscow though simultaneously holding the post of first deputy prime minister of Kazakhstan.[53] Isingarin's deputies in the IK were the first deputy prime ministers from the remaining three member countries.[54] The quarterly meetings of the board involved active participation of the top officials in each of the four governments.

The member governments also passed national legislation codifying the authority of the IK. In 1996, the Belarussian government passed a law whereby decisions of the IK, the IEC, and the joint Russian-Belarussian Executive Commission were to be directly implemented within a period of 20 days.[55] On 6 October 1996, Kyrgyzstan passed a nearly identical law, but one that included the criterion of gaining financial approval from the Ministry of Finance.[56] Kyrgyzstan also reorganized the structure of authority of its national ministries in order to improve implementation of the treaties, as Kazakhstan had in 1995 during the formation of the Customs Union.[57] Kazakhstan passed a similar law in 1997.[58]

---

[53] Isingarin simultaneously retained the post of first deputy prime minister of Kazakhstan.

[54] Bol'shakov-Russia, Tagaev-Kyrgyzstan, Ling-Belarus.

[55] The decision established the responsibility of various ministries for drafting national documents to correspond to the decisions of the supranational organs and to secure their passage by the government, after which they would be monitored "just like other Belarusian laws."

[56] Postanovlenie Pravitel'stva Kyrgyzskoy Respubliki #462 "Ob organizatsii rabotu po realizatsii reshenii Mezhgossoveta i Integratsionnyi Komitet RB, RK, KR, i RF, a takzhe MEK, Mezhgossoveta RK, KR, RU." (Other source has October 4.)

[57] The Kyrgyz Republic created the Ministry for Cooperation with CIS Countries (Postanovlenie Prav KR of 3 May 1996 #200) and the Department of Foreign Economic Relations under the Ministry of Industry and Trade (Postanovlenie Pravitelstva KR of 27 May 1996 #241). Following the changes in July 1996, the Ministry of Economy changed the management of foreign economic policy in its ministry, abolishing the section for relations with CIS countries and creating two new sections (*otdel*) for foreign economic activity and international relations. In an internal assessment of the government's effectiveness in implementing common legislation by the Minister of Economy completed in November 1996, it was noted that there was still considerable overlap in the ministries, and that this meant that the orders from the government to implement the request of the IK for information meant that "questions were not answered or were answered at such a low level of quality that they could not be compiled." The minister concluded that "the problem is that there is no coordination on foreign economic activity in the republic, which leads to the unsatisfactory implementation of decisions, protocols and agreements from the IEC, IK, and Mezhgossovet of Kaz, Uzb, Kyr." The minister recommended that issues of analytical compilation for integration projects should be done by MinCoopCIS in conjunction with the Department of Foreign Economic Relations of the Ministry of Trade and Industry. Letter from Minister of Economy Koichumanov to 1st VPM Tagaev of KR, 12 November 1996.

[58] Isingarin stressed that the failure of RK and RF to sign such agreements was leading to violations of the treaty in the regular briefs (*spravki*) sent out by the IK. Ultimately, Isingarin

The Treaty of the Four was expanded, in both membership and substantive scope, by two other treaties before the end of the decade. In February 1999, Tajikistan joined the other four states in signing on to the Treaty on the Customs Union and a Single Economic Space, which included a package of agreements geared to economic integration and the accession of Tajikistan to the Customs Union. And in October 2000, a new agreement was signed by the same five parties establishing the Eurasian Economic Union. The Eurasian Economic Union was only a slight modification of the existing institutions but demonstrated a reaffirmation of the members' commitment to regional institutions after the 1998 financial collapse created economic havoc in their trade relations. In addition to the Interstate Council, the Integration Commission, and the Interstate Parliament, a Community Court was formed with two representatives from each country serving six-year terms. Moreover, the voting rules within the Integration Commission shifted to two-thirds majority and were weighted by country, as was the financing of the union's budget, and a Commission of Permanent Representatives, similar to the Kollegia of the IEC, was added to the staff of the IK. Russia was given 40% of the votes and paid 40% of the budget, Kazakhstan and Belarus each had 20%, and the Kyrgyz Republic and Tajikistan carried 10% each. Aside from these changes, however, the institution remained essentially as before.

Finally, the most deeply institutionalized "regional" arrangement is the bilateral union between Belarus and Russia that began with the creation of the Belarussian-Russian Community in April 1996. In December 1999, the "Community" was reformulated in a new Belarussian-Russian Union treaty, and the union has made the most far-reaching progress in the economic integration of countries in the region and has created a Supreme Council,

---

sent a letter directly to Prime Minister Kazhegeldin (#IK-936 14 August 1997) arguing that "in accordance with the program realizing the first order measures for realizing the treaty of 29 March 1996 the governments of the treaty should have taken decisions on the realization of the treaty and the responsibility of officers of organs of state power for implementing the polozhenii and decisions of the collective organs of integration. In Belarus and Kyrgyzstan corresponding postanovlenie were taken (copies enclosed). I ask you to give the command to prepare such postanovlenie." Kazakhstan ultimately took the decision, but there is no evidence in the documents made available to me of a corresponding decision taken by the Russian government (although the Russian government did implement the IK decisions, as discussed in Darden, "The Origins," chap. 13.) Note also 15 April 1997 "Informatsiia o rabote v I kvartale 1997" (distributed to the member-states) in which the IK states that "a negative effect on the effectiveness and tempo of integration is the nonimplementation of the RK and RF of the decision of the Interstate Council of 16 May 1996, in particular the adoption of... the postanovlenie o poriadke realizatsii Dogovora ot 29 March 1996 and the decision of collective organs of integration."

Joint Parliament, Council of Ministers, Court, and other joint institutions. Over time, political institutions of the two countries are to be merged, and a common currency, i.e. the acceptance by Belarus of the Russian ruble as common currency was slated to take place in 2005 but did not occur.

Several other nominal structures have been established in the region, but they have been of limited effect. In April 1994, Kazakhstan, Kyrgyzstan, and Uzbekistan formed a separate Central Asian Economic Union with a variety of attendant institutions, to which Tajikistan later acceded, but this "union" was primarily a consultative body. Similarly, in October 1997 (in Strasbourg, France), the leaders of Georgia, Azerbaijan, Ukraine, and Moldova signed a joint communiqué. At a meeting in Washington in April 1999, the informal group produced another declaration that also bore the signature of Uzbekistan. The so-called GUUAM group has produced no common economic agreements.

MEASUREMENT

There are several ways to measure countries' support for regional economic institutions over the period from 1992 to 2000. First and foremost, membership in the various institutions is a basic indicator. Since the establishment of the CIS itself in 1991, there were new regional institutions established virtually every year up until the creation of the Eurasian Union in 2000. At the same time, because the level of institutionalization was largely progressive, i.e. institutions established later involved deeper integration than their predecessors, we can also get a sense of the changing level of institutional involvement of each state over time. Indeed, one can think of the institutions as a set of progressive steps that proceeded temporally, from no involvement with the CIS toward full economic union, as shown in Table 3.5. And simply by counting each state's membership in these institutions, we can get one measure of their commitment to regional institutions over the decade:[59]

There are a number of advantages to measuring commitment to regional economic institutions in this way and it fits with what appear to be most observers' intuitions about the variation across states and across time. From Table 3.6 we can clearly discern three different clusters of post-Soviet states. Judging from formal membership, regional economic institutions have been supported most actively by Belarus, Russia, Kazakhstan, Kyrgyzstan, and

[59] Note that the "exposure risk" was equal for all of these states: i.e. any post-Soviet state could have joined these institutions.

TABLE 3.5. *The Most Significant Regional Economic Institutions, 1991–2000*

Year of Appearance[a]	Treaty/Agreement
1991	Commonwealth of Independent States (CIS)
1993	CIS Charter
1993	Treaty on Economic Union
1994	Interstate Economic Commission
1995	Customs Union
1996	Treaty on Deepening Integration in Economic and Humanitarian Spheres ("Treaty of the Four")
1999	Treaty on the Customs Union and a Single Economic Space
2000	Eurasian Union

[a] I note the year in which the agreement first appeared, because for several of these agreements states did not all sign on in the same year.

TABLE 3.6. *Number of Regional Economic Institutions in Which Each Post-Soviet Country Had Membership, 1992–2000*

	1992	1993	1994	1995	1996	1997	1998	1999	2000
Belarus	1	3	4	5	6	6	6	7	8
Kazakhstan	1	3	4	5	6	6	6	7	8
Kyrgyzstan	1	3	4	4	6	6	6	7	8
Russia	1	3	4	5	6	6	6	7	8
Tajikistan	0	3	4	4	4	4	4	7	8
Armenia	1	3	4	4	4	4	4	4	4
Uzbekistan	1	3	4	4	4	4	4	4	4
Moldova	0	0	4	4	4	4	4	4	4
Azerbaijan	0	3	3	3	3	3	3	3	3
Georgia	0	0	2	2	2	2	2	2	2
Turkmenistan	1	1	1	1	1	1	1	1	1
Ukraine	1	1	1	1	1	1	1	1	1
Estonia	0	0	0	0	0	0	0	0	0
Latvia	0	0	0	0	0	0	0	0	0
Lithuania	0	0	0	0	0	0	0	0	0

Tajikistan, with the first two having the highest level of integration because they also signed a bilateral union treaty.

A second group of states has effectively opted out of the entire regional economic framework. Estonia, Latvia, and Lithuania never joined the CIS and never participated in CIS summits in any capacity. Similarly, Turkmenistan and Ukraine joined the Commonwealth but refrained from formal membership in subsequent institutions. Georgia also initially refused membership, ultimately joined the organization in December 1993, but has had limited subsequent participation. Azerbaijan withdrew from the CIS in October 1992 but formally rejoined the organization in September 1993 and has had only limited participation.

A third group of states, which comprises Armenia, Uzbekistan, and Moldova, participated actively in general CIS institutions but did not take subsequent steps to join the Customs Union or the subsequent integration agreements. Moldova is a particularly interesting case, as it did not officially join the CIS until April 1994 and immediately took on membership in all of its economic institutions, and then its participation stalled. Ukraine and Turkmenistan never signed and ratified the CIS charter.[60]

But a simple tally of membership in the main organizations is insufficient for several reasons. The main problem is that formal membership is often an unreliable indicator of the extent to which a country actually participated in an institution. One indicator of this is the fact that countries neither withdraw nor are expelled from any of these institutions; they simply stop participating. Membership has been nothing more than a formality for some countries, e.g. Turkmenistan. Moreover, strange as it may seem, the lack of formal membership appears to be no impediment to active participation. For example, even though neither Azerbaijan, Georgia, nor Ukraine ratified the agreement to form the Interstate Economic Commission, all three states sent permanent representatives to the IEC Kollegia, voted on agreements, and otherwise participated fully in the workings of the institution. Indeed, Ukraine – which neither signed nor ratified the CIS Charter – consistently paid the second largest share of the budget (17%) after Russia and contributed disproportionately to the organization's staff! In sum, there has been considerable variation in the activity or involvement of countries that is not captured by attention to formal membership; we need a means for distinguishing genuine levels of support both over time and across countries.[61]

One alternative would be simply to tally the annual number of agreements signed by each country. This is a poor indicator for support for CIS institutions for two reasons, one substantive and one methodological. The substantive argument against using the number of signed agreements is that this number is not particularly revealing because of the propensity of several members of the CIS to sign agreements with no intention of following them.

[60] It should be noted that a failure to ratify the CIS charter appears to be no impediment to participation in CIS institutions.

[61] Finally, because the measure is effectively cumulative, it is inappropriate for cross-sectional time-series analyses, and it does not allow for accurate measurement of change over time.

Indeed, as noted previously, this is true of all members to a varying extent.[62] The signed agreements are not irrelevant, but because a signed agreement can mean different things for different members, they are not very good as a standard measure. Methodologically, the problem with using signed agreements as a dependent variable in statistical analysis is that they make the country observations dependent on one another. A state can only sign an agreement if another country in the region also signs, a significant violation of the assumption of the independence of observations that is essential to ordinary least squares (OLS) and the other estimation procedures that I use in Chapter 9.

To ameliorate these problems, I look at a special subset of CIS agreements. Of the total corpus of CIS agreements, the majority technically went into effect immediately upon signature and did not require subsequent ratification or the demonstration that internal government procedures were performed for the agreements to go into force. But the most significant agreements generally required that ratification or implementation be demonstrated to the Executive Secretariat, which compiled detailed data from each country from 1991 through the end of 1998. These data allow us to identify the annual rate at which such agreements were implemented or ratified by each country, and it is reasonable to assume that the rate of ratification or implementation within this subset of agreements is a good proximate measure of the extent to which a country adhered to CIS agreements more generally. Moreover, because a country's decision to ratify or implement an agreement does not require the actions of other states, this measure is more consistent with the necessary statistical assumption of independence.

Because the overall number of agreements available for ratification changes over time and we do not wish to mistake an increase or decrease in the overall level of activity in CIS institutions for an increase or decrease in a specific country's level of support relative to other states, we need to control for such general shifts. Following Franzese (1999), who faced a similar problem in efforts to explain individual countries' inflation rates, I control for this general variation over time with a variable for the average number of agreements ratified within each year by all other countries in the sample. This variable, labeled *ratavg*, is calculated specifically for each country and for each year by averaging the number of CIS agreements ratified by the

---

[62] As noted in an interview with a Kazakh government official, the presidents of the CIS countries will often sign agreements and kiss one another with gusto in front of the television cameras but then wipe their mouths, return to their home countries, and ignore the signed agreements.

TABLE 3.7. *Annual Ratification/Implementation Rates of CIS Economic Agreements Requiring Parliamentary Action or Implementation (CISratify/ratavg)*

	1993	1994	1995	1996	1997	1998	Average
Belarus	9.3	2.3	1.9	1.7	4.2	0.5	3.3
Tajikistan	1.6	4.6	0.3	0.4	3.9	3.4	2.4
Uzbekistan	3.5	1.6	3.4	1.7	1.1	0.5	2.0
Kazakhstan	0.0	4.1	1.2	0.7	1.8	2.1	1.6
Azerbaijan	1.6	0.0	0.5	3.1	1.6	2.1	1.5
Russia	3.5	0.3	1.9	0.9	0.9	1.0	1.4
Kyrgyzstan	0.0	0.8	2.7	1.7	0.6	1.5	1.2
Ukraine	0.0	0.0	0.6	3.1	0.9	1.5	1.0
Armenia	0.0	1.1	1.5	1.9	0.6	1.0	1.0
Moldova	0.0	1.1	1.9	0.4	0.6	0.5	0.7
Georgia	0.0	0.3	0.2	0.2	0.0	1.5	0.4
Turkmenistan	0.0	0.8	0.0	0.2	0.2	0.5	0.3
Estonia	0.0	0.0	0.0	0.0	0.0	0.0	0.0
Latvia	0.0	0.0	0.0	0.0	0.0	0.0	0.0
Lithuania	0.0	0.0	0.0	0.0	0.0	0.0	0.0

other 14 countries within that year. Put simply, *ratavg* gives us a benchmark of what would be the "normal" number of agreements for a country to ratify in any year, so that it is easier to determine the level of activity relative to that of the other post-Soviet states. This gives us a standardized measure for the variation both over time and across countries. Table 3.7 shows the ratio of each country's ratified or implemented agreements to the average of all other countries for each year.

UNILATERALISM/AUTARKY

Throughout the 1990s, several states either rejected membership in or had limited participation in international economic institutions. Of these, some also pursued an autarkic path: they closed off their economies to trade and aspired to a higher degree of self-sufficiency. Although the state practices that fall into the category of what we will call "autarky" varied somewhat across countries, limited participation in international institutions and moves toward state control and closure were common threads that characterize many countries in the region at different times throughout the decade.

To a great extent, given that trading through state contracts was the norm in 1991, most countries started out, de facto, with a degree of autarky and closure. Restrictions on trade, or closure of the economy, took a variety of

forms. In the first year of independence all 15 countries were engaging in
trade with one another through state contracts, and one common autarkic
practice was to cease to honor interstate contracts and to keep goods within
the republic. To a certain extent this was seen in all republics in the first
year after the Soviet collapse, but was particularly characteristic for Ukraine,
Georgia, Moldova, and Turkmenistan.[63] Most countries in the region also
placed some controls on exports, using licenses, bans, or high tariffs. This
was done in part because the continued subsidization of prices in most
countries made the export of subsidized goods for sale on international
markets a particularly lucrative venture. In 1992, there was little in the way
of free trade within the region, but several countries sustained relatively
strong interstate trading relationships and thus could not be characterized
as autarkic or closed.

As countries introduced their own currencies and several countries began
to engage in liberalization and privatization, reliance on interstate contracts
diminished and closure took new forms. As a simple means for identifying
"closed" or "autarkic" economies in the region, I draw on a slightly modified
version of the Sachs-Warner criteria for a closed economy:[64]

1. Limited or no participation in regional or international trade institutions
2. Nontariff barriers (NTBs) covering 40 percent or more of trade with FSU as well as non-FSU partners
3. Average tariff rates of more than 15 percent with all partners[65]
4. A black market exchange rate that is depreciated by 20 percent or more relative to the official exchange rate, on average
5. A state monopoly on major exports

Similarly to Sachs-Warner criteria, a country need have only one other characteristic in conjunction with the first to be considered autarkic. Critically, these restrictions must apply to trade with both post-Soviet and Western countries, as several of the countries active in the regional trading institutions have relatively closed economies with respect to the rest of the world. Using these criteria, Table 3.8 indicates the period in which the international trade regime of the 15 countries can be considered to be autarkic. The criteria according to which they are coded as autarkic are listed in parentheses.

[63] Author's interview R7.
[64] Jeffrey D. Sachs and A. Warner, "Economic Reform and the Process of Global Integration," *Brookings Papers on Economic Activity* (1995): 1–118.
[65] Sachs and Warner use 40%, but in the contemporary period that is exceptionally high.

TABLE 3.8. *Periods of Autarky, 1991–2000*

Country	Period of Autarky
Armenia	
Azerbaijan	1991–2000 (1, 5)
Belarus	
Estonia	
Georgia	1991–1995 (1, 2, 5)
Kazakhstan	
Kyrgyzstan	
Latvia	1991–1993 (1, 2, 5)
Lithuania	1991–1993 (1, 2, 5)
Moldova	1991–1994 (1, 2, 5)
Russia	
Tajikistan	
Turkmenistan	1992–2000 (1, 2, 3, 4, 5)
Ukraine	1991–1995 (1995–2000) (1, 2, 3)
Uzbekistan	1994–2000 (1, 2, 3, 4, 5)

OVERVIEW

Charting post-Soviet institutional pathways over the decade, we see a certain consistency in the patterns by the late 1990s. The countries involved most actively in the formation of regional economic institutions were Russia, Belarus, Kazakhstan, Kyrgyzstan, and Tajikistan. All five countries were active participants in CIS institutions and also pushed forward with more intensive efforts at economic integration in the Customs Union, the Treaty of the Four, and the Eurasian Economic Union. At the same time, by the end of the decade, five of the post-Soviet states – Kyrgyzstan, Georgia, and the three Baltic states – secured entry in the WTO, to be joined by Moldova in 2001 and Armenia in 2003. Of the remaining four states, Turkmenistan, Uzbekistan, and Azerbaijan all had extensive state control over trade, especially in the most critical sectors, and had eschewed active participation in either regional or global institutions. This pattern also fit Ukraine for the first part of the 1990s, and Ukraine joined neither the Customs Union nor the WTO during these years. At the same time, toward the end of the 1990s Ukraine was taking some steps toward the liberalization of its trade and was, simultaneously, taking a more active role in the institutions of the CIS proper and, along with Moldova, officially took on observer status in the Eurasian Union in May 2002.

It is important to note that all three trajectories, at least during this period, were mutually exclusive choices. In principle, this need not have been the case for the CIS Customs Union and the WTO. Customs Unions and other preferential trading arrangements are provided for under Article XXIV of the GATT treaty, and provisions were made so that the three Baltic states could both enter the WTO and subsequently join the European customs area with EU membership. In practice, however, the high tariffs of the Customs Union that was formed in the CIS precluded WTO membership. The United States and other negotiating partners made it very clear that they would not admit states into the WTO with a schedule compatible with the high Russian external tariff. Although the Kyrgyz Republic secured membership in both organizations, it never adopted the common external tariff of the CU, choosing instead to meet its obligations to the WTO. Although the necessity of choosing between the Customs Union and the WTO did not become clear to most countries in the region until the mid-1990s, these two options were mutually exclusive institutional paths and will remain so until the Customs Union regime is liberalized.

4

Liberalism and Its Rivals

History, Typology, and Measurement

> We have here a tolerably decided contrast between bodies-politic and indi-
> vidual bodies; and it is one which we should keep constantly in view. For it
> reminds us that while, in individual bodies, the welfare of all other parts is
> rightly subservient to the welfare of the nervous system . . . in bodies-politic
> the same thing does not hold, or holds to but a very slight extent. It is
> well that the lives of all parts of an animal should be merged in the life
> of the whole, because the whole has a corporate consciousness capable of
> happiness or misery. But it is not so with a society; since its living units do
> not and cannot lose individual consciousness, and since the community as
> a whole has not corporate consciousness. This is an everlasting reason why
> the welfare of citizens cannot rightly be sacrificed to some supposed benefit
> of the State, and why, on the other hand, the State is to be maintained solely
> for the benefit of the citizens. *The corporate life must here be subservient
> to the lives of the parts, instead of the lives of the parts being subservient
> to the corporate life.*[1]

Now that we have a good sense of the international institutional choices
made by the states in the region over the first decade of their independence,
let us turn to the ideas. To do so, we take a historical turn, since each of the
ideas found in the region has a long pedigree. By tying the economic ideas of
the post-Soviet period to these historical trends, we can see how post-Soviet
Eurasia serves in many respects as a microcosm, or laboratory, for the effects
of the main economic ideas that dominated the twentieth century.

I begin by drawing a distinction between two broad categories of economic ideas that were prevalent across the world in the twentieth century,
liberalism and integralism. Next, I identify Soviet economic thought as a

---

[1] Herbert Spencer in Tim S. Gray, *The Political Philosophy of Herbert Spencer: Individualism
and Organicism* (Brookfield, Vt.: Avebury, 1996). Emphasis added.

form of integralism and demonstrate how it was employed in the construction of the Soviet Union's historically unique economic institutions, many of which are of continued relevance in the post-Soviet context. With this baseline, I then specify the three sets of economic ideas held by elites in the region after the breakup of the Soviet Union: liberalism, mercantilism, and a revised form of Soviet integralism. Finally, I explain the procedures and indicators used to measure ideas.

LIBERALISM AND INTEGRALISM: CONCEPTUALIZATION AND TYPOLOGY

The twentieth century was characterized by great diversity in economic ideas, programs, and agendas, and no discussion of the era could hope to be exhaustive. But domestic and international politics of these decades were also clearly dominated by a central rivalry between two economic philosophies: liberalism – the primary national manifestation of which was the United States but that also provided the guiding ethos of the main Western international institutions, and a set of ideas that, following Ernst Haas, I will call *integralism*, the most extreme form of which was Soviet Communism.[2] As a prelude to understanding the politics and institutional changes of the post-Soviet period, let us briefly outline the distinction between the two.

First and foremost, liberalism and integralism started from fundamentally different conceptions of the relationship between the individual and society. Liberalism began with the premise of individualism: i.e. the rational, self-interested individual was considered a basic universal fact and liberals did not endow "society" with any collective needs apart from the specific needs of the individuals who constitute it. For the integralist, in contrast, the lives and interests of individuals were subservient to, or rather conflated with, the needs of the "corporate life," i.e. of society as a whole. To the integralist, "the individual" was a liberal fiction. The individual person was nothing more than *ein Teilganzes*, a part of the whole, just one element of a social–economic organism from which it derived its meaning and purpose and to which its needs were subordinate.[3]

---

[2] Ernst Haas, *Nationalism, Liberalism, and Progress: The Rise and Decline of Nationalism* (Ithaca, N.Y.: Cornell University Press, 1997), pp. 46–50.

[3] The expression is from Werner Sombart, *Deutscher Sozialismus* (Berlin: Buchholz and Weisswange, 1934). As expressed by the Austrian economist Othmar Spann, "Society stands on a higher plane than do individuals" (*Types of Economic Theory*, trans. Eden and Cedar Paul [London: George Allen and Unwin, 1930]).

Following from these different assumptions about the nature of society, liberals and integralists took opposed views of the economy. The core idea of liberalism was that with a combination of private property and market competition, individual choices would lead naturally to the most efficient allocation of resources and to the greatest individual and social wealth – an idea captured in Adam Smith's metaphor of the invisible hand. Private property would provide individual incentives to invest and produce, because individuals could reap the benefits of their labors. Competition would lead to the elimination of inferior or overpriced goods from the marketplace and hence improve quality and efficiency in the production of all goods and services. The result would yield the greatest possible benefit for the society as a whole without the need for state intervention.

Integralists, in contrast, saw the market as an artificial form of social atomization and believed that putting critical economic decisions in the hands of individuals would lead to chaos, injustice, and ultimately failure. Property rights, by dividing that which was by its nature whole and collective, were seen as an impediment to proper management of the economy. For the integralist, market competition was, at best, economic "anarchy" with multiple producers producing only the goods that were profitable in an uncoordinated and inefficient way, rather than producing what society needed through cooperative efforts and planning. At their worst, "free markets" and private property put control in the hands of a few seeking to serve their own needs rather than the needs of society.

Liberals and integralists were similarly divided on the role and purpose of the state. For the liberal, the state's role should be limited to the task of maintaining a framework of laws and property rights, reducing the administrative costs of exchange, and ensuring that competition is preserved. Pricing and production decisions would be left to the individual private actors, and competition rather than compulsion would provide incentives to produce. Market prices, rather than commands, would signal to the relevant economic actors where to devote their productive resources.

The integralist argued, in contrast, that since the goal of economic policy was to identify the needs of the social organism and to coordinate, or command, its separate components to behave in a way consistent with those social needs, the state's authority in economic affairs must be supreme. The state, as the embodiment of the social totality, was the only actor capable of serving the needs of the whole and therefore should be given the right to organize economic life, set prices, close off avenues of trade, and control the distribution of land.

TABLE 4.1. *Differences between Liberalism and Integralism*

	Liberalism	Integralism
Basic unit whose needs are served by economic activity	Individual	Society as a whole
Preferred form of property	Private ownership	Collective/state control
Primary source of efficiency	Competition	Specialized cooperation
Primary role of the state	Law and contract enforcement	Direction and organization of production

The differences between the two bodies of economic thought are summarized in Table 4.1.

Liberalism has had many variants, from the laissez-faire liberalism of the nineteenth century to Keynesianism and monetarism, but all are driven by a reliance on market competition as the basis for a dynamic economy and by the belief that the decisions of individuals, taken in aggregate, can produce efficiency and growth rather than chaos. Similarly, integralist ideas have taken a variety of different specific forms. Although Socialism and Communism came to be the dominant strains of integralist economic ideas, the initial advocates of integralist economics were German Catholic theorists caught up in the ideas of the Counter-Enlightenment and romanticism at the dawn of the nineteenth century. The integralist argument for a "rational" planned economy serving social needs first appears after the publication of the *Wealth of Nations* in Johann Gottlieb Fichte's *Der geschlossene Handelsstaat* (The Closed Mercantile State, 1800). Fichte was followed by the German romantics Adam Müller and Friedrich Gentz, and economists of the *Gemeinwirtschaft* (communal economy) school, such as Adolf Wagner and Albert Schäffle, who argued for nationalization of industry and price controls on the grounds that "the rights of society, the economy, the state stand above ... the inferior rights of the individual."[4] By the beginning of the twentieth century, Othmar Spann, Werner Sombart, and other National Socialists had no trouble establishing a distinguished non-Marxist German pedigree for their integralist ideas.[5]

The greatest rise in influence of integralist ideas occurred in the 1920s and 1930s, as the economic failure of the Great Depression did much to discredit

[4] Quoted in Avraham Barkai, *Nazi Economics: Ideology, Theory, and Policy* (New Haven, Conn.: Yale University Press, 1990), p. 85.

[5] Avraham Barkai, *Nazi Economics: Ideology, Theory, and Policy* (New Haven, Conn.: Yale University Press, 1990), p. 85.

liberal economics. Integralist ideas were the favored economic doctrine of Fascist regimes, as integralist economics shared the "view of man as an integral part of an organic whole [that] is the basis of fascism's political philosophy."[6] In the decades prior to the Second World War, integralist ideas gained currency and *etatist* economic institutions were established in Italy, Spain, Portugal, Germany, and throughout much of Eastern Europe and Latin America. In their various forms, integralist doctrines have been adopted as a blueprint for the creation of economic institutions throughout the world, always rivaling liberalism for political influence.

SOVIET INTEGRALISM

But far and away the most enduring manifestation of integralist ideas was Communism, particularly the form that emerged in the Soviet Union and spread to Eastern Europe and much of the Third World in the postwar period. And it is Soviet economic thought that is of primary interest here. Through their dissemination in Soviet institutions of higher education, and their incorporation into the practical handbooks and policy prescriptions of the economic planners, Soviet economic ideas exerted a powerful hold on concepts of economic organization and efficiency in the USSR, a hold that has endured even after the abandonment of state planning and the breakup of the Soviet Union.

The core logic underlying Soviet economic thought is that efficient outcomes are attained when the perceived needs of the whole of society are given primacy and the various social elements are organized into a specialized, cooperative division of labor oriented towards the satisfaction of those needs. I call this body of economic thought *Soviet integralism* rather than Communism or Socialism, for two reasons. The first is that Socialism and Communism are bodies of economic thought typically associated with the works of Karl Marx. And while the Soviets certainly drew on the ideas of Marx and European Marxists like Karl Kautsky, their theories of how a socialist economy should be organized often found little basis in Marx's thought or in the ideas of European Socialism. Second, within the Soviet context the term "Communism" referred to all aspects of Soviet society, and thus the term fails to distinguish between Soviet institutions and the ideas that informed their design. As a label for so many things, "Communism" functions effectively as a label for none. The confusion is only

---

[6] Zeev Sternhell, *Birth of Fascist Ideology: From Cultural Rebellion to Political Revolution* (Princeton, N.J.: Princeton University Press, 1994), p. 345.

increased in the post-Soviet period, when Soviet economic ideas were held by many who did not consider themselves "Communist" and had no association with post-Soviet Communist parties. The term "Soviet integralism" provides a way to identify those who are Soviet in their thinking even if they are no longer Communist in name.

Like other integralisms, the Soviet variant conceived of the socialist economy and society as an organic "unity" or "whole" that was commonly discussed in terms of organic metaphors.[7] Indeed, the metaphor of economy-as-organism captured the central integralist position that the social "whole" exists as a basic irreducible entity and the "parts," while specialized and distinctly recognizable, cannot meaningfully stand on their own – just as the hands and feet are useless without the heart and the head. The socialist economy was considered to be directly analogous to a living organism in which the parts derive their purpose and function only as part of a larger whole, apart from which they cannot function.[8] As stated clearly by one Soviet economist, "In socialist production the interests of a separate area, ministry, firm or enterprise do not run counter to the interests of the national economy as a whole, because each enterprise is an integral part of the whole."[9] Applied to social and economic practice the organic conception of society and economy meant that "individual" authority and choice had to be

---

[7] In extreme cases, the economy was talked about as if it were actually an organism. Note the discussion of two prominent early Soviet economists: "The transitory economy is no mechanical mixture, but is a chemical *synthesis* of elements of the past and future in various compositions. It could hardly be otherwise as we are dealing here with a *socio-economic organism*" (Leontiev and Khmelnitskaia 1927, 96–97, Cited in Isaac Guelfat, *Economic Thought in the Soviet Union, Concepts and Aspects: A Comparative Outline* (The Hague: Martinus Guelfat 1969), 11. In earlier work (Darden, "The Origins"), I employed the term "organicism" rather than "integralism" for this mode of thinking. The logic behind doing so was similar to that of Michael Mann's in *The Dark Side of Democracy: Explaining Ethnic Cleansing* (Cambridge: Cambridge University Press, 2005): "The people was one and indivisible, united, integral. I call their nationalism 'organic,' rather than the competing term 'integral,' because it was influenced by biological metaphors of human development which were sweeping the late 19th century human sciences. The state's main task was thus to maintain the whole organism, not institutionalize conflict between its parts. One movement could represent the nation, since it could ultimately transcend any conflict of interests arising within the people. Class conflict and sectional interests were not to be compromised but transcended. As the 20th century began, the notion that the transcending agent might be the state began to grow."

[8] See also the elegant discussion of the "solidary conception" of Soviet society by Gregory Grossman, "The Solidary Society: A Philosophical Issue in Communist Economic Reforms," in *Essays in Socialism and Planning in Honor of Carl Landauer*, ed. Gregory Grossman (Englewood Cliffs, N.J.: Prentice-Hall, 1970).

[9] Mikhail Bor, *Aims and Methods of Soviet Planning* (London: Lawrence and Wishart, 1967), p. 56.

subordinated to the "needs" of the collectivity.[10] This was a very powerful and pervasive theme in Soviet life.[11]

The perceived need for planning followed directly from this theoretical practice of privileging the notion of collective needs and social organization. As in other integralist doctrines, there was no faith that individuals or economic actors would spontaneously organize themselves in ways that would productively serve society's needs. Hence planning, and the reduction of individual autonomy and authority that it necessarily entailed, would best serve society's interests.[12] Put more concretely, the logic of state economic planning rested on a belief that the conglomeration of individual choices would only lead to chaos and confusion, and that the proper use of resources required central direction and orientation of individuals in a way that conformed to a general plan that would benefit society as a whole. Soviet economic theory assumed that by organizing the totality like a giant machine geared tightly to the performance of set tasks, planning and the social organization of labor could attain an efficiency that would never arise from the cumulation of ad hoc individual efforts. It was only through comprehensive planning that all factors and their interaction with one another could be taken into account and altered to serve the needs of all.[13] In *The*

---

[10] Another way of putting this is that Soviet thought essentially lacked the concept of the individual as an autonomous locus of authority separate from society. For an alternative perspective, see Kharkhordin, *The Collective and the Individual*.

[11] The input–output models used by Soviet economists are effectively diagrammatic and mathematical representations of this single whole, just as aggregate supply and demand curves represent the aggregation of individual choices to the market liberal. As Bor (*Aims and Methods*, pp. 82–83) notes, "It is only by the summary of the input–output table of the national economy that all major national-economic proportions can be computed in their dynamics, mutual relation and inter-dependence." All statistics were seen as integrated and only deriving meaning in relation to one another. "In a socialist community the plan is national-economic and penetrates the whole national economy from top to bottom.... No figure which appears to indicate a quantitative expression of social phenomena... can be taken separately from the system of indices of the national economy." N. Pertsovich and V. Shamash, "Statisticheskii Uchet Sotsialistecheskoi Promyshlennosti" *Narodnoe Khoziaistvo i Uchet* (Kharkov, 1933): 6. Cited in Guelfat, *Economic Thought*. The statistical representations follow from the underlying holistic assumptions.

[12] In this way, Soviet economic theory fit quite nicely with the general Leninist principle of the party's leading role. Only the party could identify the needs of society, and only the party should be endowed with the authority to make decisions (of any kind).

[13] In the words of an early Gosplan official, "[The Revolution] sets against the philosophy of decay a national economic plan, an organized influence of the economic community on its surroundings." I. G. Aleksandrov, "Proizvodstvennie faktory v postroenii ekonomicheskikh raionov," *Planovoe Khoziaistvo*, March 1926, p. 101, cited in Guelfat, *Economic Thought*, p. 52.

ABC of Communism, Preobrazhenskii and Bukharin describe the popular-
ization of the 1919 Communist Party program:

The basis of communist society must be the social ownership of the means of production and exchange. Machinery, locomotives, steamships, factory buildings, ware-
houses, grain elevators, mines, telegraphs and telephones, the land, sheep, horses,
and cattle, must all be at the disposal of society. All these means of production must
be under the control of *society as a whole*, and not as at present under the control
of individual capitalists or capitalist combines... In these circumstances society will
be transformed into a huge working organization for cooperative production. There
will then be neither disintegration of production nor anarchy of production. In such
a social order, production will be organized. No longer will one enterprise compete
with another; the factories, workshops, mines, and other productive institutions will
all be subdivisions, as it were, of one vast people's workshop, which will embrace
the entire national economy of production. It is obvious that so comprehensive an
organization presupposes a general plan of production.[14]

The ordering of the social economy in this totalizing way required that a few
command and the rest must obey, and the enactment of this principle meant
that all economic decision making was made part of a hierarchical command structure.[15] Economic decision-making authority was concentrated
in a single peak body,[16] which was to implement the task of organizing
collective economic life in strict accordance with scientific laws and without
"voluntarism and subjectivism."[17]

But there was more to Soviet economic thought than the notion that
the economy should be planned and organized like a single factory or a
mechanism. The core of Soviet economic theory pertained to the principles
according to which production could be efficiently organized on a societal scale. These laws of Soviet economic theory are interlinked and easily
summarized.[18] All were directed at increasing the productivity of labor,

[14] N. Bukharin and E. Prebrazhensky, *The ABC of Communism: A Popular Explanation of
the Program of the Communist Party of Russia* (Ann Arbor: University of Michigan Press,
1966), p. 70.

[15] While the logic of planning was also supported by the fact that in its early development, the
Soviet Union had limited capital resources and required their efficient utilization, it is also
important to understand the reasoning behind it. Industrial starting conditions mattered,
but the reason that the Soviets believed that the *state* would make the best and most efficient
use of societal resources was clearly not a natural or inevitable conclusion to draw strictly
on the basis of the circumstances (given that this is the polar opposite of the liberal position)
and continued long after initial development concerns were resolved.

[16] For most of Soviet history this was Gosplan of the USSR.

[17] Gosplan 1969, 3. This was more the postwar conception. In the early years of the plan
voluntarism was championed.

[18] The main economic laws of Socialism requiring discussion here are the laws of proportional development, specialization, concentration, cooperationalization, combinization,

considered the key to the expansion of social wealth. The basic causal chain linking adherence to these laws to increased labor productivity is as follows: First, specialization and the division of labor were to create efficiency in production as each social element mastered its particular task, leading to the greater effectiveness of the totality.[19] Full specialization meant the formation of monopolies, since all redundancy or "irrational parallelism" had to be removed, and the concentration of production into larger factories to increase efficiency in the use of capital resources.[20] By combining resources that one would use in two smaller factories to create one large and more technologically advanced one, it would be possible to attain improved efficiency and economies of scale. For the Soviet integralist, the concentration of production in huge factories that produced a high volume of a specialized good would lead to optimal growth in a way that would never be possible if capital resources were dispersed among multiple independent producers. Thus, in contrast to the liberal model, which saw virtue in a market of similar producers in competition, the Soviet integralist believed that "specialization and cooperationalization should provide the fundamental increase in economic efficiency of production due to its concentration, increased volume [*seriinost'*], and the approach of the optimal growth rates in the level of [production] technology and the quality of manufactured products."[21] Herein lies the causal connection between the division of labor, specialization, scale, technology, and the organization of production into a single cooperative whole that is at the heart of the Soviet integralist model.[22]

and division and transformation of labor (*planirovanie, spetsializatsiia, kontsentrirovanie, kooperirovanie, kombinirovanie, razdelenie truda, i proportsional'noe razvitie*). This is not an exhaustive selection. Several other aspects of Soviet economic thought influenced the general drive for industrialization, the pace of economic growth, and the types of goods produced by the planned economy. These matters are important, but we will limit ourselves to the laws that pertain directly to the formation of economic institutions and the proper organization of production, as these are our primary concern. I do not deal with the laws that affect what was produced, e.g. the *Zakon operezhaiushchego (ili preimushchestvennogo) rosta proizvodstva sredstv proizvodstva*, only the organization of production.

[19] In this respect, the Soviet theories do not differ greatly from those of Adam Smith or Frederick Taylor. The priority of specialization and other factors was stressed at the beginning of each subsection of the handbook treating different aspects of the formulation of the plan. Gosplan SSSR, *Metodicheskie Ukazaniya k Sostavleniyu Gosudarstvennogo Plana Razvitiya Narodnogo Khozyaistva SSSR* (Moscow: Ekonomika, 1969), e.g. pp. 261, 22–23.

[20] Gosplan SSSR, *Metodicheskie Ukazaniya*, p. 692.

[21] Gosplan SSSR, *Metodicheskie Ukazaniya*, p. 692.

[22] The law of proportional development, which stressed the "homogenization" (*odnorodnost'*) of all regions through the elimination of socioeconomic differences, also had significant effects on the organization of Soviet economic life. The goal was to raise all regions to the same high level of industrial development, which meant that heavy industry, the symbol of industrial progress, was to be evenly distributed throughout the USSR. This served the

SOCIALIZATION — *OBOBSHCHESTVLENIE*

All of these principles were to be realized through a process the Soviets called "socialization."[23] Socialization was the linchpin of the Soviet economic project, a guiding principle equivalent to the role of market competition in the mind of the liberal. Defined by the Soviets, socialization was "the conversion of individual and fragmented means of production of many producers into socially-concentrated means"[24] entailing the "division, cooperationalization, and concentration of labor."[25] In essence, socialization involved the replacement of the individual, spontaneous, and ad hoc elements of production, as are characteristic in traditional or market economies, with a centralized, organized, integrated, and "cooperative" system of production in which collective goals were paramount. Out of many autonomous parts, socialization created an integrated whole.

To get a sense of how socialization worked in practice, and how extensively it was applied to the organization of even the most basic features of life, let us take the simple examples of hot water and steam heat. In most of the industrialized world, hot water and steam heat are supplied at a person's dwelling by individual water heaters and boilers that they purchase

---

ideal of equity and justice but was also believed to increase efficiency. On the basis of ideas about specialization and the productivity of labor the integralist believed that heavier industry necessarily implied greater efficiency and labor productivity. Hence, efficiency in the economy as a whole would be increased with the spread of industrial production to all its geographic parts, for these nonindustrialized or "backward" parts were holding back the efficiency potential of the totality. An overriding concern with increases in the productivity of labor through specialization as the key to efficiency and growth led to the location of large factories throughout the USSR as a way to modernize and increase the productivity of the population. ENKhK, "Akademiya obshchestvennykh nauk pri Tseka KPSS Kafedra ekonomiki i organizatsii proizvodstva," in *Edinyi Narodno-khozyaistvennyi Kompleks: Soderzhanie i zakonomernosti razvitiya* (Moscow: Mysl', 1985). It was also believed that the production of the means of production (machine-building) was the key to renewed growth, which further fueled heavy industrial production. The link between the need to promote sectors "defining technical progress" (i.e. heavy industry) and productivity is directly drawn in the section of the Gosplan handbook dealing with industrial planning. Gosplan 1969, 22. While many scholars have noted that the USSR was a unique "empire" because the "periphery" was developed at the expense of the "core," none have explained this curious phenomenon. Perhaps this is because the USSR was not constituted as an "empire" at all, but as a multinational state with an economy organized on the basis of the general nondiscriminatory principles laid out here.

[23] The Russian term is *obobshchestvlenie*. The word combines the Russian word for society, "obshchestvo," with the suffix that is the equivalent of "-ization." I have chosen to use the literal translation despite the fact that this risks confusion with the social science term of different meaning.

[24] D. N. Ushakov, ed., *Tolkovyi Slovar' Russkogo Iazyka: Tom II* (Moscow: State Press for Foreign and National Dictionaries, 1938), p. 677.

[25] ENKhK, "Akademiya," 8.

from competing firms. Put somewhat abstractly, this means that one function – heating water – is performed in thousands of different locations,[26] with competition among companies selling the means to perform that function, i.e. water heaters. This is what Soviet economists meant when they referred to "individual and fragmented means of production" or "irrational parallelism." In contrast, in the design of Soviet cities, the production of hot water and steam was "socially concentrated" into a single production complex called a Thermal Energy Center (TETs). The TETs heated all of the hot water and steam for the city, or for a region of the city, in a single plant. A vast system of pipes then distributed hot water and steam to every building. In a true feat of specialization and concentration, the one function of heating water and steam was performed by a single entity in one location. Every hot shower or warm radiator was linked to this system; separated from this system, no part could function independently.

This shift from ad hoc individual means of production and want satisfaction to concentrated, planned social means was the essence of socialization. By replacing the individual with the social in all spheres of life, the individual was deprived of autonomy but a more efficient and technologically advanced system for the organization of collective life was gained. Individual elements became parts in a superior and more efficient whole. Or so it went in theory.[27]

The scale of the TETs pales in comparison to a similar integralist rationalization of industry. The socialization of industrial production entailed the formation of what were known as *complexes*. Analogous to a TETs, but on a scale covering the whole Soviet Union, a complex was created for each major economic function or sector. In ideal-typical form, a complex involved complete functional differentiation among enterprises, with as little redundancy, or "irrational parallelism," in the operation as possible and hence little possibility of competition within the Soviet system.[28] For a staggering number of goods, this meant that the performance of each particular specialized production function would be concentrated in a single, gigantic, monopolistic enterprise. Hence, if the goal was to produce tractors for the collective farms, one factory would produce *all* of the engines, another

---

[26] As many locations as there are households.

[27] With no "irrational parallelism" these vast systems were completely debilitated whenever one of their specialized parts broke down. As most who have had to take cold showers in winter can attest, the failures of this centralized system lead to a simultaneous sense of resentment toward and powerlessness before "the system."

[28] "Competition" only existed in those materials (like steel and grain) that were needed in such vast quantities that they could not be produced in a single specialized factory. However, concentration in steel was still exceptionally high. See Rumer, *Soviet Steel*.

would produce *all* of the tires, yet another would produce *all* of the steering wheels, and so forth. Finally, a single factory would assemble the tractor. Working together, these enterprises, each a specialized monopoly producer of its part, would produce all the tractors for the entire USSR. According to a tally taken at the time of the collapse, in more than 209 of the 344 aggregate industrial product categories, one enterprise accounted for more than half of the total output for the product. Out of these, 109 categories had one producer supplying more than 90% of production.[29] As with the TETs, in a "complex," all of the existing resources would be collectively organized to pursue a larger social vision and the independence of any one part of the complex was undermined by its dependence on the functioning of the whole.

The principle of socialization was implemented with vigor, and we see the formation of complexes or their equivalents in all spheres. In transport, an integrated system of subways and trains was developed rather than individual automobile use. In agriculture, collectivization destroyed the autonomous units of the peasantry through the removal of individually controlled plots in favor of massive collective farms. In the *sovkhoz*, farmers became specialized workers in a grand scheme of agricultural production employing gigantic farm equipment that could only be used collectively. In energy, the formation of a complex meant that "electricity, oil, gas, and other sectors were unified into the fuel and energy complex with a high degree of concentration and centralization of production."[30] A high-wattage electrical grid (*Mir*) that spanned the entire communist bloc was created. In the sphere of oil and gas, a Soviet Union–wide network of pipelines was constructed; it supplied every factory and home with its primary energy source. This effectively created a fuel structure akin to a Soviet Union–wide TETs and built in the energy interdependence that has become so important in the post-Soviet period.

The extent to which integralist principles were employed in the rationalization of the Soviet economy is readily apparent in the instructions found in the handbook used to formulate the five-year plans. Note the following (complete) list of the main tasks the individual Republican plans are to perform:

1. Deepen production specialization of the union republic in the union-wide division of labor, include in production the most economical...natural resources...and their rational use

[29] Krivogorsky and Eichenseher, 1996.
[30] ENKhK, "Akademiya," 14.

2. Improve interrepublican and interregional ties, halt nonrational transportation, and establish new, more effective interregional economic ties, in particular between western and eastern regions of the country[31]

3. Distribute new industrial enterprises with greater capital inputs and valued production[32]

4. Strengthen the complex-oriented development of the economy of the union republics

5. Establish the necessary force of unified specialized enterprises of inter-sectoral production, construction industry, and repair bases

6. Develop the cooperationalization and combinization of production in every possible way[33]

Through the fulfillment of these directives, the actual production structures of the economy were made to conform to Soviet integralist notions of how an economy worked. Because planners' ideas were actually put into practice, specialization, concentration, and a functional and territorial division of labor were more than just a set of abstract "beliefs" about the economy and its functions by the time of the breakup of the USSR. They were, and to a great extent still are, objective features of the Soviet economy.[34]

By 1989, after painful decades of implementation, this theory of the economy had been fully put into practice. Socialization – the simultaneous specialization and concentration of production among enterprises through

---

[31] It is not clear what is meant by nonrational transportation. Other parts of the text seem to suggest that this means the further development of specialized cross-union production, not the limitation of transportation costs.

[32] Notice the key is their even distribution, not cost-effective location.

[33] Gosplan 1969, 672.

[34] Although this was clearly not always the case, particularly with the distribution of resources. I am far less concerned with the unintended consequences of the planned economy typically of concern to economists, e.g. disequilibrium, shortage, "storming," or the rapid increase in production in the lead-up to economic planning deadlines, negative incentives to improve. For a summary, see Grossman *Essays in Socialism*, 192–197. I am concerned, however, with the organization of production – particularly with the geographical location and functional tasks of the enterprises. Unlike other aspects of the Soviet economy, these features were largely the intended consequence of the plan. In taking this line of argument, I do not wish to discount the findings of Berliner and others that enterprises often sought a degree of autonomy by reducing their level of specialization or by providing for their own inputs. While this was clearly the case to a certain extent, there is reason to suspect that it was overstated in the literature on the Soviet economy (personal communication, Barney Schwalberg and Joseph Berliner). At best, the additional production inside plants provided a kind of insurance for an enterprise but were in no way a substitute for the basic structure of the Soviet economy, which was highly specialized.

the formation of complexes – was obtained.[35] By the 1980s, the actual economy of the USSR *was* like an organism, in which the activities of individual parts needed to be subordinated to the priorities of the whole, and no separate part could function independently.[36] The use of specialized production technologies meant that scant few of the factories in this system could function independently and all needed to be employed in concert to produce the end product for sale.[37] In addition, these integral parts were dispersed throughout 15 union republics and more than 20 autonomous regions. Combined with the intrinsic functional specialization of the complexes, this spatial distribution of production across the Soviet Union as a whole created a high degree of interdependence among the republics and regions. As intended by the planners, industrialization of the republics generated "a Union-wide system of planned sectoral and territorial economic dependencies"[38] and "a high level of homogeneity of all structures, each of which [was] dependent on the whole."[39]

Characterizing the development of the Soviet economy on the eve of its collapse, one Soviet economist wrote:

Scientific, industrial, agro-industrial, construction, transport and a series of other complexes function successfully. In the country there number approximately 400 sectors, more than 200 massive territorial production complexes, tens of thousands of enterprises, collective farms, state farms employing wage labor (*sovkhozy*) and other organizations. All of them form a single whole (*edinoe tseloe*).[40]

This concept of the "single whole," the keystone of integralist thinking, continued to be of paramount importance in the discussion of the post-Soviet period. As for the "successful functioning" of the system, let it suffice to say that even as Soviet economists recognized the problems of inefficiency, slow growth, and substandard quality that the USSR faced, the "unified

---

[35] "The formation in the national economy of the scientific-, fuel and energy-, industrial-, construction-, transport-, and agro-industrial-complexes reflected the increased integration of the economy, a qualitatively new level of socialization (*obobshchestvleniia*) of production, and its concentration and specialization." ENKhK, "Akademiya," p. 14.

[36] And when a commitment to the goals of the whole waned, the system ceased to function. The actions of individuals came to undermine the functioning of the economy rather than support it. See "Neotraditionalism," chap. 4 of Jowitt, *New World Disorder*.

[37] To put this condition in Oliver Williamson's terms, virtually *all* production assets of the USSR were "specific assets." Oliver Williamson, *Markets and Hierarchies: Analysis and Antitrust Implications* (New York: Free Press, 1975).

[38] ENKhK, "Akademiya," p. 22. A more fitting translation of *odnorodnost'* here might be something like "of-origin-in-a-single-whole-ness" rather than homogeneity.

[39] ENKhK, "Akademiya," p. 5.

[40] ENKhK, "Akademiya," p. 22.

multi-sectoral national-economic complex" was believed to be endowed with "great productive-technological potential."[41] Few questioned the achievements brought by the "socialization" of production. While many thought there were problems with management and enterprise incentives, few believed the organization of production itself was flawed. Indeed, above all else, it was precisely in this organization that many believed the potential for renewed economic advancement lay.

SOVIET INTEGRALISM REVISED

As the Soviet economy began to fall into discredit under glasnost, integralist thinking began to evolve, but most of the basic logic and causal mechanism remained intact. The basic ideas about specialization and concentration of production leading to efficiency and growth were still believed by post-Soviet integralists to be operative causal principles. As their Soviet predecessors had, the contemporary integralists stressed the importance of a structure of productive relations based on specialization, a regional division of labor, economies of scale, and heavy industrial manufacturing. They continued to believe that the state was required to generate efficient industries and that the proper way to do so was through a "socialized" or "complexlike" form of production. In this way, they shared with the Soviet integralists the idea that the creation of economic efficiency lies in a particular social organizational structure of production rather than a structure of incentives for rational individuals. Unlike the liberals, they do not have faith that competitive private enterprises will simply appear if the state is kept out of economic affairs. Indeed, they believe that, particularly in the transition phase, the state is needed to assist in the creation, organization, and initial support of those enterprises. As one noted liberal expert has explained, "Although these socialist economists overtly embraced the market, they failed to accept the autonomous functioning of market forces."[42]

In post-Soviet integralist thinking, central planning has been converted into "indicative planning" or state industrial policy. Under central planning, prices, production, distribution, and investment were all determined by state fiat. Under indicative planning, the state provides credits, tax breaks, and other subsidies as an incentive to private producers to orient their activities according to a state development plan. Any discussion of direct state

---

[41] ENKhK, "Akademiya," p. 3.
[42] Anders Aslund, *How Russia Became a Market Economy* (Washington, D.C.: The Brookings Institution, 1995), p. 77.

planning, or the egalitarian territorial distribution of assets, a.k.a. "proportional development," or the path to Communism is noticeably absent from the language of most contemporary integralists. It is only specialization, concentration, and the regional division of labor – now believed to be the secular driving forces of the economy untainted by the Communist political agenda – that have been retained.

In the post-Soviet period, integralists call for the reformation of the complexes into financial-industrial groups (FIGs).[43] In integralist thinking, a FIG combines the specialized division of labor of the complexes with the contemporary mandate of private enterprise by turning the complex into an industrial bloc of separate enterprises held together by an international joint stock holding company and financed by a commercial bank, through which state credits can also be channeled.[44] While initial financing for improvements might be from the state, the complexes, now as FIGs, would produce for a protected, but still competitive, regional market until they became competitive enough to survive in the larger world economy.[45] Once competitive, they would become self-financing market entities.

The clearest existing model of such an entity is the Russian FIG Gazprom.[46] After being created out of the Soviet Fuel and Energy Ministry, Gazprom, which in Russian is the short form of "gas industry," has managed to recombine much of the preexisting gas complex throughout the CIS into a single FIG. As in the complex, the entire chain of production is combined into a single monopolistic entity. Indeed, in addition to the production and transport of natural gas and gas condensate, Gazprom engages in its own machine-building, pipeline construction, and "space program" (satellite launches), and still supplies "the employees of gas enterprises located in the Northern areas [of Russia] with all of life's necessities."[47] In the 1990s, it was a private microcosm of the USSR, a Soviet complex now operating as a private firm. It was widely noted as the paradigm by integralists.

---

[43] For a useful discussion of the Russian financial-industrial groups see Juliet Johnson, "Russia's Emerging Financial-Industrial Groups," *Post-Soviet Affairs* 13 (1997): 333–365. The FIGs I speak of here are only what Johnson calls "industry-led FIGs," as these are the ones that the integralists have in mind.

[44] According to the Russian law on FIGs, the banks registered with FIGs will also have lower reserve requirements.

[45] Interviews: R1, R17, R18, R21.

[46] However, see Johnson, "Russia's Emerging Financial."

[47] In 1996, Gazprom provided for 90% of Russian domestic gas consumption and 38.7% of the world's gas trade (Gazprom 1996). According to former first vice premier Boris Nemtsov, it also provides approximately 25% of the state budget of the Russian Federation (personal communication, 28 September 1998).

In sum, despite the acceptance of some private ownership and a recognition of the basic selective powers of the market, post-Soviet integralists still believed in, valued, and sought to retain the basic mechanism of the Soviet economy. Unlike the market liberals, they did not see Soviet production complexes as "negative value added" and did not believe that Soviet factories have value only as scrap metal. In their minds, the elements of the Soviet production complex need to be reintegrated and revitalized as FIGs, not destroyed through market "fragmentation."

Given that the specialized industrial complexes covered the territory of the entire Soviet Union, and the former union is now divided into 15 different republics, the reintegration of the complexes as FIGs also demands the economic integration of the new republics. For this reason economic integration is a central feature of the integralists' vision of progress in the region. In the post-Soviet period, integralists felt strongly that the potential of the integrated economic complex had been squandered in the breakup of the union, and they sought to revive the regional division of labor so dutifully crafted by the Soviet planners after the reckless "voluntarism" and "subjectivism" of political leaders had dismembered the organized economic whole.[48] In its dismembered state, all of the acquired value of 70 years of industrialization was inaccessible to any individual republic or region. What had value when held in common could not function when parsed.

As the demands of managing the whole take precedence over the autonomy of the parts, nationalist concerns over sovereignty are generally viewed by integralists as emotional, irrational, and atavistic. Thus, far more so than liberal market integration, integration under the organic mode of reasoning involves more than just the opening of borders. It requires the creation of regional institutions to manage collective affairs that have the authority to do so effectively.

In sum, for the integralists, the key to growth lies in the reactivation of industrial production through the reestablishment of the specialized system of production developed under the Soviet period. In practical terms, this manifests as a preference for the following:

1. *Regional economic integration and the creation of supranational organs* to manage the collective economic affairs of the region and

---

[48] We will recall that in the formation of the plan, "voluntarism and subjectivism are not permitted" (Gosplan SSSR, *Metodicheskie Ukazaniya*, 3) The integralists refer to anything that does not conform to what they see as objective economic laws as "subjectivism." When asked to characterize the reasons that other states did not behave in the way characterized by them, they would respond that they did so for "subjective reasons" and detail how those states were actually acting *against* their interests.

conduct common structural policy. In particular, collective organs are needed for the supranational enforcement of regional agreements and contracts, both intergovernmental and interfirm.

2. *The transformation of the Soviet production complexes into regional financial-industrial groups* with state support coordinated at a regional level: the acceptance, if not the deliberate creation, of regional monopolies for many goods.

3. *Coordinated subsidy of transport and energy costs throughout the post-Soviet space.* The system of prices upon which the Soviet complexes were based needs to be temporarily restored so that they can continue to function and "compete" with foreign imports.

4. *The formation of a Customs Union.* This involves the liberalization and facilitation of trade within the post-Soviet space via the removal of internal barriers and the creation of a protective tariff around the post-Soviet space in strategic industries. The goal is to secure a protected internal market for high-value-added goods until competitiveness improves.

5. *Currency stability, if not currency union, within the post-Soviet space.* This is so that transactions can be made between economic subjects in all parts of the former Union.

LIBERALISM

Beginning in the mid-1980s, the Soviet economic system and the thinking behind it increasingly came under attack. At the same time, the removal of legal limits on access to Western ideas in the glasnost period, an increased role of Western governments and international institutions as advisers to the Soviet government and its successor states, and a general desire to emulate the successes of the capitalist West led to the spread of liberal economic ideas among the post-Soviet states.

Since 1991, the International Monetary Fund (IMF) has done much to contribute to the expansion of the market liberal mode of reasoning throughout the former Soviet Union – in direct consultation with governing elites via its country missions, through the three-week "boot camp" that it runs in Vienna for training a new generation of economic officials, and simply by exercise of the authority that many governments of the CIS place in it as the purveyor of the world's combined economic wisdom and problem-solving capabilities. But the IMF and World Bank were not the only organizational push in this direction; the United States Agency for International Development (USAID), the European Union's Technical Aid to the Commonwealth of Independent States (TACIS),[49] the Soros Foundation, the Harvard Institute for International Development (HIID), and many other organizations combined to proselytize this way of thinking about economic relationships. There are many indigenous sources as well, and many countries have turned their former Communist Party schools into schools of business management for training a new generation in liberal economics.

The fact that liberal economic ideas largely entered from abroad meant that the form that liberalism took in the region was heavily influenced by the contemporary thinking of the international development community. Several authors have noted that by 1990 something of a consensus had emerged among development economists, particularly those working actively in the IMF and the World Bank, about what was needed for an economy to grow. This shared set of economic principles, known as the "Washington Consensus,"[50] embodied some basic economic propositions about what would create growth in developing countries, summarized here by Schleifer and Treisman:

At the turn of the twenty-first century, there is little dispute among economists about what conditions are conducive to economic growth and prosperity. Markets should be free. Property should be private and secure. Inflation should be low. Trade between countries should not be obstructed. To achieve these goals, a country's government must leave prices alone, avoid owning or subsidizing firms, enforce contracts, regulate responsibly, balance its budget, and remove trade barriers. Any government that does all this can expect national income to grow.[51]

All of these prescriptions were designed to facilitate competition and encourage investment – the liberal engines of economic efficiency and growth. The causal logic linking these institutions to growth was straightforward: the elimination of state ownership and establishment of private property provide individual incentives to invest and produce, because individuals can expect to reap the benefits of the investments they make in their property. The removal of price restrictions allows for competition on

[49] Technical Assistance for the Commonwealth of Independent States is the European Union's aid program.
[50] The term was coined by John Williamson of the World Bank and includes the following 10 propositions: fiscal discipline; a redirection of public expenditure priorities toward fields offering both high economic returns and the potential to improve income distribution, such as primary health care, primary education, and infrastructure; tax reform (to lower marginal rates and broaden the tax base); interest rate liberalization; a competitive exchange rate; trade liberalization; liberalization of inflows of foreign direct investment; privatization; deregulation (to abolish barriers to entry and exit of firms); secure property rights.
[51] Andrei Shleifer and Daniel Treisman, *Without a Map: Political Tactics and Economic Reform in Russia* (Cambridge, Mass.: MIT Press, 2000), p. vii.

the basis of price, leading to improvement in cost efficiency by producers in order to survive and to reorientation of resources toward profitable enterprises. A stable currency is believed necessary so that returns on an investment made at the present moment will not be wiped out by changes in the value of the currency in the future. In short, the liberal economic ideas carried to the region posited that individual ownership and autonomy, and free prices, will spontaneously lead to competition and a superior allocation of resources as producers seek to gain greater profits. This competition will improve quality and efficiency in the production of all goods and services – yielding the greatest possible benefit for the society as a whole.

It is noteworthy that other than a framework to sustain competition, specific forms of economic production are not specified by the liberals. For unlike Soviet integralists, liberals are deliberately agnostic about the specific forms of production that are best. In liberalism, the success of the market rests on the fact that we have no a priori knowledge of which forms of production are superior, but that competition will lead to the "selection" of the best available option by individuals and, through emulation and aggregation, by the market as a whole. Where the knowledge and implementation of new forms of production will originate is not specified.[52] Whereas integralism suggested that superior solutions were scientifically knowable, market liberals suggested that one can only create the conditions conducive for them to appear.

Throughout the 1990s, an ever-expanding cadre of elites in the CIS used some variant of this mode of thinking, although the general principles outlined earlier were adapted by market liberals in the region to the extant economic problems of the post-Soviet countries, which were not so much underdeveloped as "misdeveloped" countries in the liberals' view. Liberals in the region focused on a three-pronged approach for transforming the planned economy into a market: price liberalization, macroeconomic stabilization, and privatization and restructuring. Although liberal economists differed on the pace or sequence of these reforms, they agreed on the basic principles. Liberalization entailed the freeing of prices and relaxing of control over the exchange rate. Macroeconomic stabilization was designed to get the ensuing inflation under control through tight monetary and fiscal policies, and thus establish the conditions that would encourage foreign direct investment. Privatization and restructuring would eliminate state-owned property and destroy the system of monopolistic complexes favored by integralists. According to market liberals, the old industries needed to be restructured

---

[52] Or rather, successful entrepreneurship is simply assumed.

or destroyed, their inefficient machines cut apart with "acetate and a blow-torch,"[53] and a new economic order was expected to emerge spontaneously in their stead.[54]

Thus, translated into a concrete policy agenda, liberal economic thought leads to the pursuit of the following:

1. *Free prices.*
2. *Macroeconomic stabilization, i.e. a stable national currency and low inflation.* Budget deficits should be eliminated. Tight control over the money supply should be maintained to prevent inflation and exchange rate fluctuations. This allows foreign investors the security of knowing that the returns on their investments will not be devalued by currency fluctuations.
3. *Privatization and the establishment of inviolable private property rights.* Improvement of physical plant will not take place unless actors feel they will reap the benefits of their investment of time and money. This requires the establishment of a clear and inviolable public–private boundary through the establishment of secure private property rights and a limited state.
4. *Hard budget constraints for enterprises.* All subsidies to industry should be eliminated. All domestic prices should be brought into line with world prices. This forces the enterprises to innovate and become competitive and not take resources away from more productive ends.
5. *Destruction of the monopolistic complexes of the Soviet system and its replacement with competing enterprises.* The existing complexes are seen as engaging in *negative value-added* production. In short, the production process subtracts from the value of initial inputs.[55] Many

---

[53] Interview, G19.

[54] As Russian President Boris Yeltsin stated in his autobiography, "[Russian Prime Minister Yegor] Gaidar's reform had led to macroeconomic improvement or, to be more precise, to the destruction of the old economy. It was achieved with terrible pain . . . but achieved nonetheless. There was probably no other way to do it. Except for Stalinist industry, adapted to contemporary conditions and a Stalinist economy, virtually no other industry existed here. Just as it had been created, so must it be destroyed." Boris N. Yeltsin, *The Struggle for Russia*, trans. Catherine A. Fitzpatrick (New York: Times Books, 1994), p. 146. Cited in Aslund, *How Russia*, 64). I have replaced the translation of *sovremennyi* as "modern" with "contemporary." This is more appropriate to the context.

[55] For those not familiar with the concept of negative value-added production, a useful analogy is a bad cook. A bad cook, like an inefficient factory, takes perfectly good inputs (raw foods) and makes something that no one wants to eat. The raw foods had more value than the awful dish created by the cook. Hence, the value added by the chef is *negative*.

factories must simply be destroyed and sold for scrap. They must be prevented from further diverting resources away from other ends.

6. *Low tariffs/trade restrictions.* To facilitate technology transfer, lower costs to consumers, and force competition. But with budget conditions primary, tariffs are accepted as a temporary fiscal measure. WTO entry is of first priority.

MERCANTILISM

In its essence, the "mercantilist" position taken by some elites in the region is quite simple, although it is more a theory of international trade than a general theory of economics.[56] The central tenet of mercantilism is that economic relations are zero-sum. As noted by Viner, "What was apparently a phase of scholastic economics, that what is one man's gain is necessarily another man's loss, was taken over by the mercantilists and applied to countries as a whole."[57] As a result, the path to growth is the largely political task of securing or protecting one's share of a fixed pie. The key to maximizing national wealth is having as high a balance of payments as possible. Exports should exceed imports by as large a margin as possible, for in the mercantilist calculation, expanding incomes relative to financial outflows is the key to expanding wealth. The method for achieving this goal is to achieve self-sufficiency, i.e. to develop the capacity for the full cycle of production in as many goods as possible, thus reducing the need for imports and allowing any production exceeding domestic demand to be sold on world markets for a profit. In this way, the post-Soviet mercantilists reject both the liberal ideas about the benefits of producing only those goods in which one has comparative advantage and the integralist notion that the economic totality can be made more efficient through a specialized division of labor. Rather, the mercantilists seek to reduce their international specialization and generally reject regional institutions.

Mercantilism as we encounter it in the post-Soviet context also finds its roots in the Soviet economic tradition. Whereas the integralist views the economic relations of the post-Soviet states in terms of the Marxist view of economic relations under Socialism, the mercantilist views those same

---

[56] Here, I am speaking only of what I am calling the "mercantilist" approach as I see it in the region. I am not trying to categorize the modes of reasoning prominent in Europe prior to the nineteenth century, although it is certainly because of the similarity with those modes of reasoning that I refer to the post-Soviet logics as mercantilist.

[57] Jacob Viner, "Power versus Plenty as Objectives of Foreign Policy in the Seventeenth and Eighteenth Centuries," *World Politics* 1 (1948): 9.

relations under the Soviet rubric of economic relations under capitalism. If Socialism was marked by monopolistic cooperation, capitalism was characterized by exploitation – the unequal distribution of surplus capital and the exploitation of the colonies by imperialist powers. Because the application of a theory of exploitative relations among capitalist states to the relations among Soviet republics would have been heretical (and extremely dangerous) in Soviet times, the mercantilist account could not be openly formulated and expressed. As a result, mercantilist ideas had no direct scientific base of development and even in the post-Soviet period more often took the form of a folk doctrine. The incoherence that results from surviving as a doctrine privately maintained through kitchen conversations and samizdat tracts during a period of Soviet rule in which the reigning public orthodoxy was integralism is still very much in evidence. For this reason, perhaps, the mercantilist mode of reasoning is rarely expressed abstractly as a set of causal relationships. Instead, the causal notions are embedded in narratives about specific instances or relations in the past and present.

The primary narrative of mercantilist reasoning among elites in the post-Soviet space is what we might call "the myth of imperialism." The essence of this argument is that the nation is being exploited by a foreign or domestic power and economic hardship is explained as the result of the nation's resources being siphoned away by this exploitative force. In short, the failure of one group is explained by its "exploitation" by an imperial other. However, the nature of this exploitation is not always clear and the category of "the exploiter" can be filled by anything from an "imperialist" power (usually Russia in this case) to a Zionist conspiracy. The occupants of the "exploiter" category often seem to be combined almost indiscriminately, as in the "Jew-Bolshevik-Muscovite" oppressor imagined by some Ukrainian nationalists. The more sophisticated accounts generated by nationalist exiles during the Cold War focused on the distortions of Soviet pricing, which they believed were designed to undervalue the commodities of their subject nations in favor of Russia and the other Soviet republics.[58] These accounts, of course, were not "objective" in that they deeply underestimated the mutual subsidization that took place among republics. Nonetheless, this mode of thinking is still powerful in some states and has been almost impervious to counterevidence. Many continue to see price increases – particularly for Russian oil and gas – as part of a deliberate attempt to siphon away national resources and undermine national autonomy. It is worth repeating that in most of the forms that it is expressed, the mercantilist reasoning is

---

[58] The Ukrainian émigré literature was the most extensive. See Wilson *Ukrainian Nationalism*.

not based on any concept of a larger economic system or its functioning. There are no systemic or structural causes here. Behind all economic failures lies someone's intentional design.

In the mercantilist mode of reasoning, the key to economic success is to break the harmful relationship by freeing oneself from the exploiter and unleashing the talents and will of the nation to serve its own ends. The past Soviet interdependency is viewed and experienced primarily as a combination of *dependency* and *exploitation*, and it is precisely the ties that the integralist seeks to preserve that the mercantilist hopes to destroy. It is often the case that nation-building is seen as the most immediate step to economic growth. Nationalism – both as linguistic–cultural revival and as antagonism toward a neighboring "other" – is a formula for growth to the extent that it further increases the autonomy and self-interested identity of the country, thereby preventing the reestablishment of the past exploitative relationship. To some extent, this model accepts that an important part of growth will result from the exploitation of aid from others – which can lead in some cases to an ethic of deception and entitlement before international donors as well as trade partners. In extreme versions of this way of thinking, relations between cause and effect are not tied down by physical laws or technical constraints. All can be achieved with the revitalization of national spirit, the focusing of national will, and bountiful foreign aid.

This mode of reasoning needs to be distinguished from simple self-interested action on the part of individuals – which is an important element of all cases. Self-interested action can lead to cooperation on selfish grounds. Both the integralist and liberal conceptions lead actors to believe that to some extent individual or national gain can best be attained through cooperative outcomes. The mercantilist model, however, rejects the possibility or utility of cooperation in principle, at least with some states. The proper path to growth is through greater and greater national autonomy, if not autarky. In extreme cases, these elites will prefer to continue state ownership to avoid the sale of national assets to foreign powers.

Mercantilist reasoning leads to the following programmatic agenda:

1. *Exports should exceed imports by as large a margin as possible.* Increasing the balance of payments is the key to increasing wealth.
2. *Strive for closed-cycle domestic production.* Goods should be produced domestically and the domestic market should be protected from outside competition if necessary. At the very least, all high-value-added production should be done domestically. A rapid decoupling from the specialized Soviet production complex is desirable.

3. *Those products that cannot be produced domestically should be secured through multiple sources of supply,* so as to reduce vulnerability and maximize autonomy, particularly in food and energy.
4. *Membership in international organizations should be pursued solely to achieve national recognition and to secure resources.*

INDICATORS, CODING, AND MEASUREMENT

To code each of the post-Soviet governments according to the dominant economic ideas among the elite, I use two sets of indicators based on complementary methodologies. The first set of indicators uses content analysis to code the different ways that actors express their ideas. The second set of indicators codes the different ways that government actors understand economic reality by observing their economic policies and determining whether they are consistent with expectations we have about how actors holding different sets of economic beliefs would be expected to govern the economy.

Interviews and Content Analysis

The first method, content analysis, is based on the assumption that in responses to interview questions and in public statements, actors generally reveal some of their main assumptions about how the economy works. And whereas the coding of actors' basic causal assumptions, as opposed to their values or opinions, is not widely done, it is a good method for getting directly at the ideas that lie behind human behavior and state policy.[59]

This mode of inquiry is not flawless, as behaviorists rightly point out. Actors certainly do not always say what they think, and the task of coding the different ways that actors think on the basis of the content of what they say is not simple. The problem is lessened somewhat in areas where actors have no clear material or emotional motivation to lie or disguise their genuine thoughts, or when they are unaware of what is of interest to the researcher. In any case, all researchers inevitably incorporate actors' statements into their analysis, if only by reading newspaper accounts about the events they study, and do so in ways of which they are not immediately conscious. Our goal here is simply to try to do so systematically.

The coding scheme for the content analysis was initially developed and refined with interviews conducted in 1996 and 1997 in Armenia, Georgia,

---

[59] The policy coding is more "direct" in the sense that it does not require the additional assumption that action is based on subjective mental states. It provides a method for assessing subjective mental states that does not rely on the observation of action.

Russia, Belarus, Ukraine, Kazakhstan, Kyrgyzstan, and Uzbekistan, with a new round of interviews in Russia in fall 2000. These interviews were designed to draw out the officials' ideas about how economies function, assess their understanding of and degree of interaction with regional economic institutions, and get factual information about the formulation of the state's economic policy. Toward this end, I conducted more than 200 interviews with decision makers in the presidential administration; the Ministries of Finance, Economy, Trade, Industry, Foreign Affairs, Foreign Economic Relations, Fuel and Energy, Electricity, and CIS Affairs; and the Customs Commission between May 1996 and December 1997.[60] In this chapter, our concern is solely with the way the interviews were used to draw out officials' ideas about the functioning of the economy. The primary means for identifying officials' economic ideas was to ask them to explain the causes of the economic crisis facing their country. Their responses could then be coded according to the causal ideas that the officials employed in their explanations. At the outset of each interview, officials were asked, "What are the causes of the economic crisis facing your country?" This was an unambiguous question at the time the interviews were conducted. Each country faced a severe economic crisis and it was a central topic of discussion in all quarters of society. Not once did a respondent ask me to clarify to which "crisis" the question was referring. The question was also very open. It was general enough not to beg any particular response and did not limit the range of causes that could be cited. The responses were then classified according to the type of cause-and-effect relationships that were employed in explanations of the economic crisis. The purpose was not to interpret some set of hidden meanings or intentions.[61] The goal was simply to identify their causal statements and to get a sense of the salient economic ideas.

The question about the causes of the economic crisis proved quite useful for dividing up respondents into different conceptual camps. Officials generally answered the question in one of three ways.

Some officials would begin to explain how the breakup of the Soviet Union had caused the economic collapse. They would generally explain that the Soviet economy was constructed as a single organism or mechanism and that the severing of the interrepublican economic ties had caused a collapse

---

[60] Not all ministries were available for interview in all nine states. Interviews also included the president or vice president of the National Association of Industrialists and Entrepreneurs, and the IMF and World Bank mission representatives.

[61] The respondents were not aware that the main purpose of the question was to code their ideas about the economy. I presented myself as a graduate student studying economic relations in the CIS.

in production. More often than not, they would go on to clarify this general picture by providing me with the example of a particular enterprise: "X factory in (city) used to receive its (raw material) from (city in another republic) and make parts to be assembled at a factory in (city in a third republic). The construction of national borders and the collapse of the economic complex have left this factory working at 10% of capacity." Such responses were coded as integralist.

Other respondents would launch into a list of the ways that their national economy had been stripped and exploited under the USSR and raise several current practices that Russia or some other republic was engaging in that were punishing their economy. Here, the standard answer usually identified a natural resource (grain, gold, cotton, etc.) that had been taken out of the country, or some system of exchange perceived to be unequal ("they gave us coal; we gave them refrigerators"). These responses, which were generally indicative of themes that would return repeatedly throughout the interview, were coded as mercantilist.

A third set of respondents identified the inefficient nature of the Soviet system as the reason for the economic collapse. On these accounts, the legacy of the USSR was its uncompetitive enterprises, corrupt management, and poorly structured incentives due to the lack of market competition. As the first group of respondents, these, too, often cited examples of Soviet production chains – but with the opposite intent. They generally identified a factory that was emblematic of poor central planning, e.g. a sugar factory deep in Central Asia that was designed to process raw sugar cane imported from Cuba, rather than locally grown sugar beets. Often these respondents saw the economic crisis as a necessary and/or inevitable destruction of the old system and expected economic decline to be a temporary phenomenon so long as market reforms took hold. Respondents drawing on these causal ideas were coded as liberal.

Respondents could also be coded according to their proposed solutions to the crisis: the reintegration of the economic complexes, the establishment of economic independence/statehood, or rapid market reforms.

The coding scheme, with examples, is shown in Table 4.2.

The coding scheme derived from the interviews proved useful for the analysis of public statements by economic officials – the primary basis upon which countries were coded for the years 1991 to 2000. Because public statements and newspaper interviews did not always address the question of the economic crisis directly, the method was modified to code all of the causal statements within the text, but the basic rules remained the same. If officials referred to the importance of competition, individual incentives,

TABLE 4.2. *Content Coding Scheme for Interviews, Speeches, and Textual Sources*

	Cause of the Crisis	Solution to the Crisis
Integralist	Breaking the productive ties of the Soviet economy *"The catastrophic crash of the economy has been caused primarily by destroying the single economic complex that had been formed in the Soviet Union, by dismantling mutually advantageous economic ties between enterprises and organizations."*[a]	Reintegration of production complexes *"To achieve something real, we need to unify into one mechanism that economic organism which we broke up some time ago."*[b]
Mercantilist	Historical oppression/exploitation *"They took 5 million metric tons of cotton out of our republic at the same time that they counted us in the ranks of subsidy recipients."*[c]	Economic independence *"We must end the disproportions allowed in the development and distribution of productive forces as a result of so-called Union specialization and break off of the chains of neo-colonial economic dependency."*[d]
Liberal	Inefficient Soviet economic structures *"The economy developed as a system of rigid central planning.... As a result, the economy was in a state of serious crisis, manifesting in the fall of production, the acceleration of inflation, the obsolescence of fixed capital investments, crude distortions of price relationships and serious structural disproportions."*[e]	Rapid market reforms, competition *"The elimination of the root causes of the crisis requires the transition to a market economy and the achievement of macroeconomic stabilization."*[f] *"If there is price competition, decontrolled prices stabilize, and the quality of goods improves. If there is competition between goods – production gets modernized, and the resources of enterprises that go bankrupt shift into the hands of more effective ones. When competition is present in the banking sector, the currency is not devalued and investment resources 'work' for expanded reproduction and modernization. When political competition is present, the authority works for the society."*[g]

[a] Vitaliy Masol, "What Has the 'New Policy' Brought Us? My View of the Socioeconomic and Political Processes in Ukraine," (FBIS Translation), *Silski Visti* 3, 7, 9, 10, 14 June 1994.

[b] Belinform interview with Belarusian prime minister Mikhail Chygyr published in *Zvyazda* (Minsk) in Belarusian 13 September 1994, p 1.

[c] Islam Karimov, president of Uzbekistan, quoted in Elmira Akhundova, "Aliyev and Karimov Do Not Long for the USSR and They Are Not Inspired by the 'Pact of the Four," *Literaturnaia Gazeta* in Russian (FBIS Translation), 5 June 1996, no. 23, p 2.

[d] Islam Karimov, *Building the Future: Uzbekistan – Its Own Model for Transition to a Market Economy* (Tashkent: Uzbekiston, 1993), pp. 4–6.

[e] Memorandum on the Economic Policy of the Russian Federation, passed by the government on 27 February 1992. Reprinted as "Memorandum of Russia's Government," *Nezavisimaia Gazeta*, 3 March 1992.

[f] Ibid.

[g] *Kazakhstansaia Pravda* (Almaty) 24 August 1994, pp. 1–2. Interview with P. Svoik, chairman of the State Committee for Price and Antitrust Policy, by unidentified *Kazakhstanskaia Pravda* correspondent; place and date not given: "We Cannot Stop the Prices Until We Stop Monopolism."

private property, or the inefficiency of the Soviet economy, they were categorized as liberal. If officials stressed the importance of specialization; the regional division of labor; the preservation of the economic organism, mechanism; or unified national-economic complex, and emphasized the need for preserving the economic complexes' and the role of the state, they were coded as integralist. Officials drawing on themes of economic exploitation and stressing the importance of exports exceeding imports were coded as mercantilist. For additional details on the coding process, see Chapter 9 and Appendix A.

Additional Empirical Implications: Domestic Economic Policy Indicators

Any coding scheme involves measurement error, and perhaps content analysis even more so than others. For this reason, I also supplement the content analysis by looking for additional observable implications of officials economic ideas, using an alternative set of indicators based on what one would expect in a state's energy policy, privatization policy, and macroeconomic and industrial policy if elites were employing these different economic ideas in their decisions. These policy areas are not included in the international economic institutions or trade policies that we are seeking to explain (our dependent variable), and thus provide an additional measure of confidence in both the theory and the measurement if we find that actions taken in these areas reflect our expectations given the ideas we identified as prevalent in the government.

The use of policies as an indicator for governing ideas is based on the assumption that if government decision makers have adopted a particular way of thinking about how the economy functions, they will then employ this conceptual framework in decisions taken in key areas of economic decision making. Although clearly we would expect other influences on economic policy in addition to the ideas of the governing elite, the domestic economic policies pursued by a government can thus be expected to provide some indication of the ideas of the governing elite. Our general expectations of the policies to be pursued by integralists, liberals, and mercantilists in each the three policy fields are as follows.

Energy Policy. In approaching the problem of how to manage the country's energy needs, integralists would be expected to act in a way that gave priority to the maintenance of the complex of economic ties that bound the former republics together under the former Soviet system. Because the maintenance of Soviet-era industries and interindustry trade relied on lower-priced energy inputs, one would expect integralists to favor energy subsidies as well. In countries that are net importers of energy, one would expect continued reliance on traditional Soviet-era partners for imports and would assume that integralist governments would be receptive to proposals to create multinational joint-stock companies or financial-industrial groups that link national energy monopolies. In countries that are net exporters of energy, one would expect a willingness to supply energy to prior partners at subsidized prices, and a tendency to favor, where feasible, new export routes allowing post-Soviet partners to receive transit payments. In sum, policies that maintain and reinforce existing ties with Soviet-era partners, rather than seek alternative sources of supply or alternative export routes for oil and gas, are indicative of integralist ideas among the leadership.

Mercantilists, in contrast, would place the highest premium on energy autonomy. Mercantilist states would seek to attain self-sufficiency in the production of energy even if at additional cost. Mercantilists view prior Soviet-era interdependence as the harmful legacy of imperialism and consider dependence on other post-Soviet states in the supply of energy or as an export route a point of weakness that can be used to undermine the country's autonomy. Mercantilist states that are not naturally endowed with energy resources will seek to establish multiple sources of supply to reduce their dependence on any one partner. They may also maintain control of national energy monopolies and use them to subsidize national industrialization programs. Costly programs to achieve energy independence or active pursuit of alternative supply routes are taken as evidence of mercantilist leadership.

Liberals, who view competition as the key to productivity and growth, would pursue this course as far as possible in the energy sector and seek to remove the state from the business of supplying energy entirely. Liberals should therefore seek to establish private ownership and restructure the national energy monopolies so as to create a competitive market, generally along the lines of programs developed by the World Bank. Liberal states may also seek to diversify energy supply, as part of a general goal of increasing competition so as not to pay monopoly prices.

Privatization. In looking at privatization policy, our attention focuses on the large-scale enterprises that were most tightly linked into the union-wide production complexes. It is the variation in the way these assets are viewed that critically distinguishes the different modes of economic thought. We would expect integralists to maintain these enterprises as the republic's crowning achievement and to work to create state-controlled joint-stock companies linked to enterprises in other post-Soviet states as a way of preserving the Soviet production complexes. This concern could manifest either as an outright resistance to large-scale privatization; as an effort to transfer state-owned shares to the enterprises of other post-Soviet partners, government or private; or as assignment of a privileged role in the privatization process to other post-Soviet states. In the latter case, this is generally done by first offering enterprises for sale to the post-Soviet enterprises to which they were once linked, in a single production complex, prior to the official privatization tender. It is also very often the case that a voucher privatization that effectively allows the firm to be privatized to its existing management, which is generally committed to maintaining the links with the prior Soviet production complex, will achieve the same effect.

Mercantilist governments would be wary of allowing national assets to be under foreign control and would seek to preserve the state's authority to deal with the nation's "strategic assets." Mercantilist governments would be expected to resist privatization and to keep industries under national control. For this reason, an examination of privatization policy alone may not allow one to distinguish between mercantilist and integralist regimes. Unlike integralists, however, mercantilist governments would be expected to resist the foreign involvement of other post-Soviet states in their economies and use state control to direct key enterprises away from prior links with Soviet-era partners.

Liberal governments should place great weight on the virtues of private ownership and management with market experience. This would lead liberal states to pursue an active policy of privatization and demonopolization and to open tenders to both national and international buyers.

Macroeconomic and Industrial Policy. The direct implications of economic ideas in macroeconomic and/or industrial policy are potentially manifest in a wider range of practices, making them somewhat more difficult to identify.[62] The easiest to classify are the liberal states. Liberals should eliminate price controls, subsidies, and state orders for goods; maintain balanced budgets and stable currencies; and eschew industrial policy: i.e. true liberals would make no efforts to support specific industries and would force loss-making enterprises into bankruptcy.

---

[62] Macroeconomic policy is the policy area that is most subject to international pressure. In most cases, IMF policies have had some influence on policies at least for a short period. In areas such as price liberalization, states were also heavily influenced by the actions taken by neighboring states.

Distinguishing the expected policies of mercantilists and integralists requires greater scrutiny. Both integralists and mercantilists may pursue price controls, industrial subsidies, persistent state orders for goods, budget deficits, inflationary policies, and state-controlled investment. The key in distinguishing the two policies is to identify, if possible, the enterprises or sectors toward which the policies are directed. Integralist states will seek to maintain existing union-linked enterprises through subsidies and will not seek to develop new industries to replace traditional imports from their prior post-Soviet partners. In short, their policies are interventionist, but conducted in a way so as to maintain the division of labor as it was crafted under the USSR with investment directed at areas of traditional strength, although generally not areas that facilitate entry to world markets.[63]

Mercantilists, in contrast, will direct their intervention in the economy toward the goal of developing new industries to replace imports from their traditional Soviet partners and to redirect their own resources toward home use. In contrast to the integralists, who run inflationary policies to support firms that maintain the Soviet division of labor, mercantilists intervene to support the development of new industries to enhance national autonomy and self-sufficiency and extract their economies from the Soviet division of labor. In both cases, however, real interest rates will often fall below the rate of inflation, so that a direct subsidy is given to the sectors chosen to receive state support.

The various policies we would expect from officials of each ideational type are shown in Table 4.3.

The use of these policy indicators outside the post-Soviet space would clearly carry certain risks and limitations. Other factors may influence the selection of domestic economic policies in addition to the economic ideas of officials. Governments face different constraints that affect their policy choices in ways not directly tied to their understanding of the economy.[64] For this reason, policy choice may be an imperfect indicator of elite intentions in many states. But it is useful, particularly with such difficult-to-measure qualities as ideas, to have an additional set of implications to observe. For even if our coding methods used in isolation present certain problems or uncertainties, the fact that diverse methods, drawing on three independent

---

[63] In certain cases, integralist states may maintain stable currencies but continue to subsidize enterprises by allowing them to run up large debts to state-owned energy producers or by allowing them to pay in barter arrangements.

[64] The implicit claim here that governments were effectively free to choose from a wide range of policies/strategies appears to hold true for all cases except Armenia, where the war with Azerbaijan placed severe limits on the type of economic policy the country could pursue.

TABLE 4.3. *Additional Observable Implications of Economic Ideas in Domestic Economic Policy Areas*

	Energy Policy	Privatization (Large-Scale Enterprises)	Macroeconomic/ Industrial Policy
Integralism	Maintain or increase energy dependence on prior suppliers or delivery routes; transfer shares to FSU partners	Encourage purchase by regional buyers; create joint state-controlled regional FIGs	Union-linked enterprises maintained through subsidies; inflationary
Mercantilism	More costly state exploitation of national resources; diversify sources of supply, delivery routes	Resist privatization and keep industries under national control	Import-substituting industrial policy; inflationary
Liberalism	Privatize and break up energy monopolies	Full privatization; auctions open to national and international bids	Prioritize stable currencies, balanced budgets; no direct intervention in production

bodies of data, suggest a similar pattern allows for some confidence that the economic ideas of the region's elites are being identified accurately.

CONCLUSION: OUTLINES OF A METHOD FOR STUDYING THE EFFECTS OF IDEAS

In sum, this chapter provides a history and typology of the economic ideas salient to actors in the region and sets out a three-stage process for constructing ideational variables. The first step is interpretation – or the use of inductive methods to identify the beliefs that are salient among the key actors in the region. For this first stage of research, I conducted more than 200 interviews designed to elicit an individual's understanding of how the economy worked using traditional interpretive and ethnographic methods and extensive work with a variety of textual sources. Taken in aggregate, the interviews provided a good sense of the ideas relevant to the actors in this particular time and place.

The second step is conceptualization – or the development of a general typology of the different economic ideas in the region based on the specific causal statements collected in interviews. As noted later, the causal stories told to me by the interview respondents fell rather easily into the three main categories of integralism, liberalism, and mercantilism. I then reconstructed the history of these ideas and traced, where possible, how those ideas have come to be part of the cultural repertoire of officials in the region. I also identified the domestic and international economic policy preferences that their adherents of each economic ideology would pursue and stipulated the institutional outcomes that they would prefer to see in the region on the basis of their economic ideas.

The final step is measurement. Toward this end, this chapter laid out a system for coding the content of officials' public statements to determine which economic ideas prevailed in a government in each six-month period between 1991 and the end of 2000. The quantitative version of this process is described in Appendix A and put to use in the cross-sectional analysis of Chapter 9. But in the next section, we use the same set of criteria to chart the shifts in ideas within each of the countries over the decade using more conventional qualitative discussion. That is the task to which we now turn.

PART TWO

CONTINGENT SELECTION AND SYSTEMATIC EFFECTS

Country-Level Analyses of Elite Selection, Ideational Change, and Institutional Choice, 1991–2000

The next four chapters chart the changes in economic ideas in each of the 15 post-Soviet states over the first 10 years of their independence, and their purpose is to demonstrate contingency in the selection of ideas and the systematic effects of officials' ideas on policy and institutional choice. To do this, the chapters trace the leadership changes in each country during the 1990s, identify the economic ideas prevalent in each of the governments, and show how these ideas manifest in each country's choice of international trade institutions, as well as macroeconomic, privatization, and energy policies. To make the case for contingency, the chapters highlight the idiosyncratic, nonsystematic factors determining the selection of economic ideas – and hence the exogeneity of those ideas. Second, they show the systematic effect of economic ideas on political preferences and institutional choice. Before moving to the empirical studies, let us briefly examine the logic of the argument and the methods used for making this case in the post-Soviet context.

THE CASE FOR CONTINGENCY OF SELECTION

As noted in Chapter 1, contingency is inherently a part of ideational selection. In the post-Soviet states in particular, the contingency of idea selection was heightened by a combination of political institutions that gave individual leaders a great deal of authority, as well as idiosyncratic features of the process by which the region's leaders came to power and by which they came to hold their ideas.

Because political authority in these countries was highly centralized, the ideas of top leaders played a much greater role than popular opinion or interest group pressures in determining institutional choice. Although there is certainly variation across the post-Soviet states, if we use the criteria identified in Chapter 2 for distinguishing whose ideas matter, we generally find that post-Soviet countries have low accessibility, low accountability, and a high level of control over ideas and information.[1] This is no accident. The political and economic institutions of the Soviet Union had been designed for the purpose of implementing centralized directives, not representing a diversity of interests and perspectives, and each of the post-Soviet states inherited a wide range of institutional tools for executives to suppress dissent and secure compliance with their directives.[2] As a result, the selection of ideas, policies, and personnel remained generally the prerogative of executives and was subject to their idiosyncratic viewpoint and criteria of selection.

Second, the process by which leaders were themselves selected was generally not systematic or predictable, and to the extent that we can discern the systematic factors determining the selection of leaders, they generally had little to do with the economic beliefs leaders held. Top leaders were not, for the most part, chosen because of their economic ideology. In the Caucasus and Tajikistan, for example, changes in the executive occurred through wars, revolutions, and coups d'etat rather than elections. The discernable criteria of elite selection were battlefield prowess and/or the strength of a leader's Soviet-era patronage ties. In both Azerbaijan and Georgia, for example, the men who controlled the republics during the Brezhnev years returned to rule their republics as independent states. The two men, Haidar Aliev and Eduard Shevardnadze, respectively, happened to hold different economic views, but it was their powerful patronage networks rather than their personal views about the economy that led to their choice as the leaders of their war-torn countries. Similarly, in Kazakhstan, Uzbekistan, and Turkmenistan, the first secretaries of the Communist Party simply retained

---

[1] The differences in regime are discussed in the individual cases that follow.

[2] William Odom's description of the making of Soviet military policy, although stark, nonetheless captures the fundamental nature of the system: "No Western political leader could bring a mere dozen of his close associates into a closed room, deliberate with them based only on materials prepared by the staff of his military department and reviewed only by his own political staff, and then push through his preferred policy (occasionally over the objections of a disgruntled fellow official), a policy sometimes involving scores of billions of dollars at a cost not even known by himself in terms of the market value of the resources involved. Yet this is precisely how the general secretary of the party made military policy in the Politburo." William E. Odom, *The Collapse of the Soviet Military* (New Haven, Conn.: Yale University Press, 1998), p. 37. The precise extent to which post-Soviet executives determined policy free of pressure from organized interests or political factions certainly varied among countries, but it is important not to ignore how high it was overall, even in the formally democratic countries.

their posts – for reasons that had more to do with the continuity or reorganization of authoritarian rule in those countries than with the economic views of the leaders themselves.[3]

Even in countries where leaders were genuinely selected through popular vote, the link between economic ideas and leadership selection was tenuous at best. More often than not, incumbents were tossed out of office as a result of scandals, corruption, or poor economic performance, and there is little to suggest that their successors were elected because they shared the economic ideas of the majority. In part this was because candidates easily deceived voters. Ukraine's president, Leonid Kuchma, for example, expressed one set of economic views during the election campaign for the purpose of winning the presidency in 1994 but drew on an entirely different set of beliefs once firmly ensconced in office. Even where candidates honestly expressed their economic views, it is clear that voters chose their candidates according to many different criteria, not simply the candidate's economic views.

The fact that leaders were not selected primarily for their economic views, and their economic views tended to be "sticky" – i.e. they did not change easily and were generally formed before they took office – means that even where the selection of leaders was systematic and predictable, the selection of a set of economic ideas was not.[4]

In some cases, there also appeared to be a random or unsystematic character to the process by which leaders chose their economic ideas. What Hirschman wrote of the Latin American leaders in the 1950s could also be applied to a few leaders in the post-Soviet period: "Rapid political and social changes... lead to the sudden appearance of new leaders. Without much experience in the handling of public affairs and with a strong desire to quickly solve their country's problems, they are apt to reach out for the ready-made policy prescriptions of various ideologies."[5] Leaders often lacked strong initial motivations or drives in their choice of economic ideas; ideas were selected on a provisional basis and discarded when they seemed

---

[3] Jones Luong, *Institutional Change*.

[4] Because the criteria of selection are not the variables of interest to us, and the variables of interest bear no necessary relation to the criteria of selection (i.e. they are independent), we can treat their choice as contingent and exogenous rather than endogenous. Where there are exceptions to this, i.e. where the economic ideas of leaders did have an influence on their political success, I carefully note it in the discussion that follows.

[5] Albert O. Hirschman, "Ideologies of Economic Development in Latin America," in *Latin American Issues – Essays and Comments*, ed. A. O. Hirschman (New York: Twentieth Century Fund, 1961).

to fail. But in the cases discussed later, far and away the most prevalent cause of changes in the ideas of the government was a change in personnel: cadres changed more frequently than minds, and the causes of cadre change could be highly contingent.

To say that the selection of economic ideas was contingent is not to suggest that leaders were subject to no constraints or that the choice of institutional membership or economic policy had no impact on how they stayed in power. The region's leaders clearly wished to stay in power, and their economic strategies had to remain consistent with this end.[6] But this did not eliminate any of the three sets of economic ideas presented here, as each of the economic strategies presented earlier could, and did, serve as an effective means to sustain the existing leadership in the state in which it was adopted. The adoption of a liberal program allowed for a significant reallocation of wealth and power. Privatization allowed governments to take away profit-making enterprises from political enemies and place them in the hands of political loyalists, or to buy political support by transferring state assets to new management, who would be deprived of those assets if the liberal order were toppled.[7] Moreover, the reduced influence of the state on the economy and the elimination of subsidy programs allowed leaders to undercut the influence of rivals within the state apparatus. Alternatively, leaders who adopted mercantilism and integralism could sustain support by retaining administrative controls over enterprises and trade, which provided considerable political muscle and allowed leaders selectively to dole out favors to loyalists.[8] In short, because viable political strategies existed for each of the economic frameworks, the exigencies of political survival did not determine the selection of ideas; leaders were ultimately not forced to choose one economic pathway over another in order to stay in power.

As a result of this combination of state centralism, the critical role of individual leaders, and the fact that leaders were selected on criteria other than their economic views, the role of chance or idiosyncratic factors in leading a set of economic ideas to be employed in government policymaking was heightened. One purpose of the next three chapters is to demonstrate this contingency and simply detail the history of ideational change within the region over the first decade of independence.

---

[6] Following Hall, *Political Power,* p. 374, it was necessary that the ideas be "politically viable."

[7] This was the acknowledged strategy of the liberal architect of Russia's privatization program, Anatoly Chubais.

[8] Keith A. Darden, "The Dark Side of the State: Formal and Informal Mechanisms of State Supremacy," paper presented at State-Building in Post-Communist States: Toward Comparative Analysis, Yale University, 27–28 April 2001.

DEMONSTRATING SYSTEMATIC EFFECTS

A second purpose of the next three chapters is to demonstrate that despite the idiosyncratic and undetermined process of idea selection, once a set of ideas was chosen by the leadership – or, more commonly, once new leaders with different ideas came to power – the effect of those ideas on the choice of international institutions was systematic. The chapters demonstrate the systematic relationship between economic ideas and institutional choice in two ways. The first approach examines changes within each country over time. By exploring each country individually, country-specific factors are held constant and we can demonstrate with the sequence of events how new leaders, bringing to power a new set of economic ideas, subsequently produced significant changes in international institutional choice and economic policy. Moreover, we can more easily identify the specific historical events – the civil wars, economic crises, and political violence – that led to sometimes long and variable lags between the adoption of a set of ideas and its manifestation as policy. In this respect, the qualitative analysis, by linking the intentions and motives of actors to outcomes through historical narrative, proves to be an effective tool for showing causation. Moreover, by showing precisely how events were linked, we are able to exclude some rival explanations that statistical analysis cannot.

Second, the following chapters make use of comparisons across cases to show a link between the economic ideas of the government and a country's choice of institutions. This method works, in general, across the 15 states because they share so many features, but it is particularly important for comparing specific groups of countries where the similarities are most marked. Because in many respects the most similar states are those that neighbor one another, the countries have been grouped by region to facilitate comparison.

To a certain extent, regionally organized chapters also allow for specific treatment of alternative explanations, although this is primarily taken up in Chapter 9. Chapter 5, on the three Baltic states and Moldova, examines more closely the relationship between nationalism and institutional choice, as all four states had strong nationalist movements in the late 1980s and it is the interpretation of these states' choice of liberal international institutions that drives the nationalist arguments. Chapter 6, on Russia, Belarus, and Ukraine, provides an ideal laboratory for evaluating theories that privilege economic structural conditions, as the economies of Ukraine and Belarus were the most similar of any two post-Soviet states. Chapters 7 and 8, on Central Asia and the Caucasus, allow for closer examination of the hypothesis that energy or security interests drive the choice of institutions in the region, as neighbors often faced a similar environment but acted quite differently. The fact that similar countries make such different institutional choices at times during the decade allows us to isolate the economic ideas of the elite as a critical explanatory variable.

In sum, the chapters serve multiple purposes. Those able to follow the differences across the 15 cases will have a strong sense of the causal role of economic ideas in explaining differences between these similar countries, and a deeper understanding of the politics of the decade. Those with less interest in the politics of the region or more historical demonstration of causation should turn to the cross-sectional time-series analysis of Chapter 9, where a wide range of variables are controlled for and the results are more easily summarized.

5

The Baltic States and Moldova

At first blush, Estonia, Latvia, Lithuania, and Moldova would appear to be ideal cases for the argument that countries with stronger national identities redirect their trade and institutional ties away from Russia and toward global multilateral or Western institutions. The four countries had a shorter spell as part of the USSR; they were incorporated only after World War II.[1] Each country had a strong nationalist movement that came to power in the Supreme Soviet elections of 1990, and each subsequently boycotted the March 1991 referendum on the preservation of the USSR on the grounds that their countries were forcibly annexed and never recognized the legitimacy of the Soviet rule. And if we look at institutional membership at the end of 2001, these countries all also look fairly similar in their institutional choices; all four countries had secured membership in the WTO.

But to draw conclusions simply on the basis of the conjuncture of evidently strong nationalist sentiments in 1990 and institutional membership as it stood in 2001 would be an error for two reasons. First and foremost, the fact that these countries had strong nationalist movements and also, ultimately, all joined liberal international trade institutions begs the empirical question of whether and how nationalism was linked to institutional choice. Second, a look only at the end of the period elides important variation within these countries over the decade. At critical points in the decade, Lithuania, Latvia, and Moldova pursued alternatives to liberal trade institutions with considerable vigor and these choices need to be explained.

This chapter addresses these problems directly. It shows that although nationalism certainly influenced the policies of each of the four states, the

---

[1] The Baltic states also experienced Soviet occupation from 1939 to 1941 and the Transdniester region of Moldova was part of the USSR during the interwar period.

critical differences over time in institutional choice stemmed from differences in the economic ideas of the elite in power. To capture this relationship, I first examine each country individually and then briefly turn to a more general critique of the nationalist argument, as a closer examination of the *process* by which the Baltic countries came to define their trade relations with their post-Soviet partners runs counter to the central tenets of the identity-based approaches, even if the final outcome is precisely as hypothesized.

ESTONIA

Estonia is a particularly interesting individual case, as it is the only one of the 15 countries that was consistently and unambiguously liberal from 1990 to 2000. The Estonian case also nicely exemplifies the core argument of this book, as the roots of liberal dominance in Estonia are, in many respects, an outcome of a peculiar and largely contingent aspect of its history as a Soviet republic, yet the effect of those ideas was remarkably consistent across the decade.

Economic Ideas: The Contingent Historical Sources of Liberalism

Although it is not widely noted in academic writing on the country, the Estonian Soviet Socialist Republic (ESSR) was the site of several liberal economic experiments conducted by the Soviet government in the 1970s and 1980s.[2] Selected because it was the union republic of the smallest size and thus least likely to wreak havoc in the system as a whole should the experiments fail, the ESSR was a laboratory for Gosplan, the state economic planning agency of the USSR. The experiments began in the agricultural sector, and after a series of organizational experiments starting in 1975, a unified Ministry of Agriculture was created in 1982 that became a breeding ground for liberal economic ideas and experimentation in the republic. This ministry pioneered "self-financing in agriculture which made profit the most

---

[2] From the existing record it is not clear whether these experiments were part of the so-called large-scale experiment conducted by Gosplan of the USSR beginning in 1984, in which plan targets were supposed to be simplified and enterprise managers given more autonomy in select industries and republics. According to Oleg Yun', one of the experiment's organizers, the original scope of the "large-scale experiment" included enterprises subordinate to the Ministry of Heavy Engineering, the Ministry of Electrical Engineering, the Ministry of Food-Processing Industry of Ukraine, the Ministry of Light Industry of Belarus, and the Ministry of Local Industry of Lithuania. For a discussion of the experiment see Michael Ellman and Vladimir Kontorovich, eds., *The Destruction of the Soviet Economic System: An Insiders' History* (New York: M. E. Sharpe, 1998), pp. 108–117.

important of a reduced number of plan indicators and gave farms the right
to sell above plan production at a 50% premium above state procurement
prices."[3] While a free market was not created in the republic in Soviet times,
the focus on profit as a driving motive was clearly inspired by liberal ideas
that were forbidden elsewhere in the USSR of the early 1980s.

Similar reforms in the service sectors that replaced vertical directives
and plans with contracts between enterprises were later introduced in the
USSR as a whole under Gorbachev.[4] Estonia reorganized its light industry
starting in early 1985, giving the enterprises more autonomy, shifting plan
targets toward a focus on profits, and allowing enterprises to retail their
own products. To encourage competition, in 1987 the government had
a policy that gave incentives to small-scale state enterprises producing for
local markets – a program ultimately extended to other branches of industry.
Similar radical experiments in the decentralization of wage setting and tying
wages to productivity were initiated in the ESSR in the mid- to late 1980s.
At the same time, the receptiveness of the population to such measures, to
the extent that this was relevant under a Soviet dictatorship, was enhanced
by the fact that the Estonian population had been able to watch Finnish TV
from 1956 onward – an accident of geography and language that gave them
greater exposure to Western ideas than any other republic of the USSR.[5]

The cultivation of liberal ideas in the republic ultimately manifest in a
liberal reform proposal for a "Self-Managed Estonia" (IME) – advocating
a shift to a market economy in the ESSR – in September 1987. Produced
by four Estonian economists, the published proposal aroused significant
popular support, was generally accepted by the Estonian Communist Party,
and was worked into a more concrete "Concept on Self-Accounting for
the Estonian SSR" adopted in May 1989 by the Estonian Supreme Soviet.[6]
Both the IME and the concept were partly authored by the liberal economist
Edgar Savisaar, who was made the chairman of Estonian Gosplan in fall
1989 and later served for two critical years as the prime minister of Estonia
(1990–1992). The IME proposal was coauthored by Siim Kallas, who went
on to serve as Estonia's first Central Bank chairman, as finance minister,

---

[3] Brian Van Arkadie and Mats Karlsson, *Economic Survey of the Baltic States: The Reform Process in Estonia, Latvia and Lithuania* (London: Pinter, 1992), p. 103.

[4] Indeed, as noted by Van Arkadie and Karlsson, the Soviet Union's laws on individual enterprise (*Economic Survey*) and cooperatives (1988) were largely based on Estonian experiences, pp. 103–104.

[5] Raphael Shen, *Restructuring the Baltic Economies: Disengaging Fifty Years of Integration with the USSR* (Westport, Conn.: Praeger, 1994), p. 216.

[6] Van Arkadie and Karlsson, *Economic Survey*, p. 105.

as chairman of the liberal Reform Party, and ultimately as prime minister in 2002. As a result, unlike any Soviet republic other than Russia, Estonia appears to have developed an indigenous cadre of liberal economists during the Soviet period that grew increasingly influential in the years prior to the Soviet collapse and played a significant part in running the country after independence.[7] Yet in contrast even with Russia, where liberal economic ideas were still held only by a small minority of economists in Moscow, liberal economics in Estonia had achieved near hegemony. And hence we see a clear link between an odd, idiosyncratic aspect of Soviet planning, the cultivation of liberal ideas among economists in the republic under the USSR, and the political influence of those same liberal economists when Estonia achieved independence. When it came to liberal economics, the Estonian elite had a particularly "usable past."[8]

Presumably as a result of this difference in Estonia's Soviet experience, leaders with liberal economic ideas have governed Estonia since the Supreme Soviet elections of March 1990 yielded overwhelming victory to the Estonian Popular Front and the Estonian National Independence Party. Following the elections, Arnold Ruutel was named head of state (chairman of the Supreme Soviet) and Savisaar as prime minister (head of the Council of Ministers). Ruutel, too, had strong liberal credentials extending back to his experiences in Soviet Estonia – he had previously served as an ESSR deputy minister responsible for the earlier agricultural experiments of the 1970s and 1980s. New elections in September 1992 introduced an even more orthodox neoliberal government under 32-year-old Mart Laar of the Fatherland Party (Isamaa). Elections in 1995 brought in another liberal coalition government under Tiit Vahi with Savisaar's Centrist Party, Ruutel's Rural Union, and Kallas's Reform Party serving as part of the coalition in various configurations until March 1999, when Laar returned to the prime minister's position to lead a coalition of his Pro-Patria Party and Kallas's Reform Party.[9] In short, while there were many changes in the composition of parties and leadership of Estonia's government from 1990 to 2000, this was simply a

---

[7] Indeed, in an early meeting in which six Western economists traveled to the USSR to advise the Soviet government on economic reform, the only person involved in the discussions who was not a Moscow official was Kalle Tenno, a young economic adviser to the ESSR Council of Ministers. See Ellman and Kontorovich, *The Destruction*, p. 247.

[8] On the concept of "usable pasts" and the role of the practical skills and understandings of elites gained under Communism, see Anna M. Grzymala-Busse, *Redeeming the Communist Past: The Regeneration of Communist Parties in East Central Europe* (Cambridge: Cambridge University Press, 2002).

[9] Note that Mart Siimann took over as prime minister after corruption allegations forced the resignation of Vahi, but the liberal coalition remained intact.

constant reshuffling of the same cast of liberal political–economic figures, many of whom had learned their liberal ideas from their unique experience in Soviet Estonia. As a result, the liberal economic ideas that informed the government remained highly constant.

Institutional Choice

These liberal ideas were manifest in a wide range of policies. With regard to trade and foreign economic policy, the Estonian government has been the most liberal of all post-Soviet states. In 1992, Estonia abolished all import tariffs. Progress toward WTO entry was exceptionally rapid and active, as its Working Party had held its fifth meeting already in 1995, before many post-Soviet states had even held their first. Estonia, with Kyrgyzstan in 1998, was in the first pair of FSU countries to be approved by the WTO for membership. Indeed, the only reason that Estonia's membership was delayed until 1998 was that the government had to make arrangements for the country's entry into the EU, which required a substantial increase in the country's external tariff. The country was never a CIS member and rejected any illiberal institutions (and was even close to rejecting membership in the EU on the grounds that the organization was not liberal enough), but nonetheless made every effort to pursue free trade with its former Soviet partners – including overtures to Russia as early as 1992 to establish a free trade area between the two countries.

In its domestic economic policies, Estonia was the model of the Washington Consensus. Other than the energy production sector, where the Estonian government converted facilities that relied on fuel imported from Russia to reliance on wood chips and shale, and where privatization has not been fully completed, the Estonian policies have been a textbook case of liberalism. The privatization of large-scale enterprises began in June 1991, with the creation of a state privatization agency, Eesti Erasmus, modeled on the German Treuhand. This was considerably earlier than in other post-Soviet republics and began prior to the end of the USSR. Moreover, aside from the energy sector, the privatization was total and included a complete sell-off of all state-owned companies[10] and a full-scale privatization of land. Likewise, in macroeconomic policy, the Estonian government pursued the early introduction of its own currency and an early price liberalization (1991–1992) and established a currency board legally fixing the Estonian kroon to the German mark at a rate of 8:1 with its introduction in 1993. A mandatory

---

[10] This was initially done through vouchers, followed by a cash auction.

balanced budget is also enshrined in Estonian law and in 1992 the government stopped all subsidies and other forms of support for enterprises. This, along with the strong kroon, has meant that domestic industry, which was primarily linked to Soviet production chains, has been almost completely eliminated. In sum, Estonian governments have consistently favored private property and a stable currency through policies that have destroyed industries linked to the former Soviet Union.

Hence, as a result of a quirk of Soviet planning, there was a group of economists working in Estonia who had privileged access to and considerable experience with liberal economic ideas that were otherwise limited to select, often underground, economic circles in Moscow and Leningrad. As a result, liberal economic ideas were well entrenched in Estonia by the time it achieved independence. Several liberal economists went on to take very high positions in an independent Estonia, two of whom later served as prime ministers, and consistently implemented their ideas in Estonia's economic policy and international institutional choices.

LITHUANIA

In contrast to Estonia, there was neither as sizable nor as influential a group of liberal economists at work in Soviet Lithuania or Latvia, a difference that was particularly noticeable in the first governments of these two countries. In both countries, political parties with mercantilist ideas were important political forces. In Lithuania, nationalist parties with mercantilist economic views (first Sajudis and later the Homelands Union) contested with liberal parties (the Democratic Labor Party and the independent leader, Valdus Adamkus) for control of the government throughout the 1990s, with each transfer of power producing significant changes in foreign economic policy.

Economic Ideas

The alternation of power began when the nationalist Sajudis movement took control of the republic in the March 1990 Soviet elections. Sajudis's leader, Vytautas Landsbergis, was a professor of musicology notable for his lack of any economic training or clear economic ideology. Most commentators have identified Landsbergis as having primarily a political strategy of confrontation with Moscow and a commitment to securing Lithuanian independence. And indeed, arguments that nationalist goals determined foreign economic policy appear to be most appropriate in the case of Landsbergis – economic ideas or motivations were a secondary or tertiary concern at best and the breaking of economic ties with Moscow appeared to be seen as desirable.[11] Regardless of its determinants, there is little to suggest that for-eign economic policy was much of a priority for a government concerned first with eliminating Soviet authority and then with removing Soviet troops from Lithuanian territory.

To the extent that Lithuanian policy was informed by a set of economic ideas or an economic agenda in the Sajudis government of 1990–1992, it appears to have been set by the prime ministers. Lithuania's first three prime ministers were generally liberal in orientation but consistently encountered opposition by illiberal mercantilist forces in the parliament who viewed "self-sufficiency" as an economic program appropriate to an independent nation. Lithuania's first prime minister, Kazimiera Prunskiene, put forward a draft program for economic reform in November 1990 stating vaguely that "the essence of the economic reform being conducted in Lithuania consists of transforming the Soviet model of the economy into a moderately state-regulated socially-oriented market economy."[12] Yet even this moderately liberal plan was rejected by parliament and further efforts to introduce price reforms in January 1991 also failed. After the appointment of Gediminas Vagnorius, an economist, to the position of prime minister the government can be said to have been informed in part by liberal ideas, but the decollec-tivization reform put forward by Vagnorius was justified more by the logic of undoing Soviet history than by efficiency concerns. Laws were passed for the privatization of land, but the purchase of land was limited to Lithuanian citizens and citizens of states that were members of OECD countries prior to 1989, thus preventing Poles and Russians from buying land – a constant concern of the right-wing nationalist parties. Moreover, agricultural land was excluded from privatization and was kept under state control for the duration of the decade.

In general, most commentators agree that the defining feature of the Sajudis government's economic principles was confusion.[13] As Aleksandras

---

[11] Alfred Erich Senn, "Post-Soviet Political Leadership in Lithuania," in *Patterns of Post-Soviet Leadership*, ed. Timothy J. Colton and Robert C. Tucker (Boulder, Colo.: Westview Press), pp. 123–140. See also Shen, *Restructuring the Baltic*, pp. 217–218, and Rawi Abdelal, *National Purpose in the World Economy: Post-Soviet States in Comparative Perspective* (Ithaca, N.Y.: Cornell University Press, 2001).

[12] Van Arkadie and Karlsson, *Economic Survey*, p. 51.

[13] Shen, *Restructuring the Baltic*, p. 218; Van Arkadie and Karlsson noted after conducting interviews in Lithuania in 1990 and 1991 that "in early 1991, the economic situation in Lithuania could only be characterized as one of confusion.... Because of the stalemate at the political level, discussions of economic matters had not proceeded far." *Economic Survey*, p. 51.

Abisala, prime minister from July to December 1992, noted in 1992, "Our preparation for reform was done under very difficult conditions. After March 11, 1990 [Lithuania's declaration of independence], we did not have a finalized reform model. We do not have the full spectrum of everything we must do.... I would like to have such a plan. But we do not."[14] The fact that Lithuania's economic ties with its Soviet-era partners disintegrated during this time appears to have been more a function of neglect than principled design.

The majority of observers also agree, however, that much of this confusion came to an end with the election of the Democratic Labor Party (LDLP), the renamed Lithuanian Communist Party, and its chairman Algirdas Brazauskas, in October 1992 on a program of improving ties with Russia and imposing superior economic management.[15] The election of the former Communists was generally seen as a referendum on the failure of nationalist economic policies and the emergence of hostile relations with Russia and Poland, radical economic decline, and also a more idiosyncratic negative reaction to the demagogic personality of Landsbergis, who almost indiscriminately charged his political opponents with treason. And while not the radical free-marketeers that governed Estonia, the party had undergone a transformation similar to that of the former Communist Parties of Poland and Hungary, and the liberal nature of the Brazauskas government was immediately made clear.[16] Brazauskas drew several economic liberals into the government, including Bronius Lubys of the Liberal Union as prime minister, and all statements made by the new government on economic policy matters stressed the need to create the conditions for free market competition. In February 1993, Brazauskas was elected to a newly empowered presidency.

It was at this point, notably with liberal (and, indeed, pro-Russian) leadership and with the nationalist movement politically neutralized, that the

[14] Interview with Abisala in 1992, quoted in Shen, *Restructuring the Baltic*, p. 218.
[15] Senn in "Post Soviet Political," p. 134, notes that "relations with Russia and the Commonwealth of Independent States constituted a major issue in the elections" and that Brazauskas "symbolized the hope of better economic relations with Moscow." Indeed, on election night, Brazauskas declared, "I have thirty years experience with the Moscow bureaucracy. I know how things work there. I won't get lost in those Moscow corridors." Quoted in Anatol Lieven, *The Baltic Revolution: Estonia, Latvia, Lithuania and the Path to Independence* (New Haven, Conn.: Yale University Press, 1993), p. 268. The extent to which Brazauskas symbolized closer ties to Russia is also stressed in election reports produced at the time (EIU December 1992, 34).
[16] On the regeneration of Communist Parties in East Central Europe see Grzymala-Busse, *Redeeming*.

Lithuanian government began to be consistent in its support for and enactment of the ideas of economic liberalism. The government embarked on a privatization program that had been resisted by the nationalist government. Prices were liberalized in 1993. The national currency, the litas, was introduced and macroeconomic stability and tight fiscal and monetary policy achieved. Subsidies to enterprises were cut and a currency board was formed in 1995. A privatization law drafted in 1995 allowed for cash privatization of the remaining large-scale enterprises and a State Property Fund was created for the purpose of selling off remaining assets, but many "strategic" assets were excluded from privatization, including state monopolies, state-owned banks, the transport and shipping infrastructure, and large stakes in many industrial enterprises. Trade was liberalized shortly after Brazauskas and the LDLP took power and MFN status was awarded to Lithuania's main trading partners – including Russia, Belarus, and Armenia – giving Lithuania lower tariffs with these post-Soviet partners than with the EU.[17] In January 1994, Lithuania applied for WTO membership and the period of greatest activity toward accession took place between 1994 and 1996.

It was only in November 1996, with the election of the Homeland Union, a nationalist party formed on the ruins of Sajudis, to a majority in parliament and the reinstatement of Gediminas Vagnorius as prime minister that mercantilist ideas crept back into the sphere of economic policymaking. But given the strength of the Lithuanian presidency, the new government served mainly to block further liberalization rather than implement its own agenda. The presence of the nationalists, who idealize the Lithuanian peasantry as an essential part of the national mythology, did, however, have a notable effect on the state's role in agriculture and in some aspects of privatization. In 1998 the government established the Agricultural and Food Products Market Regulation Agency to set prices and buy up surplus production. The government also provided a subsidy to farmers by raising the minimal price for grain and by paying in advance of the harvest. As a result of these policies, and the use of various tariff and nontariff measures to protect agriculture, Lithuania's progress toward WTO membership stalled. There were no meetings of the WTO Working Party in 1998 or 1999 while Homeland Union held a parliamentary majority.

---

[17] Ironically, a slightly higher tariff schedule was applied to goods imported from about 20 countries with which Lithuania had a free-trade agreement, such as Estonia, Latvia, and the members of the EU. These tariffs were reduced during the six years following 1995 as part of the agreement.

Tensions between liberals and nationalist parliamentarians with more mercantilist leanings came to a head on the issue of privatization, particularly with the election of the liberal Valdas Adamkus as president in February 1998. Adamkus, an American citizen and former bureaucrat at the U.S. Environmental Protection Agency, moved quickly to advance the privatization of large-scale enterprises. A 60% share of the telecoms sector was sold off at an auction in 1998, but the most contentious issue was the privatization of the Mazeikiu oil refinery – which counted for a significant portion of Lithuania's export earnings. In 1998 the government implemented the first stage in a plan to privatize the oil sector by selling 33% stakes in the country's oil refinery. Even though the sale was set up to prevent purchase by Russia's Lukoil, and the tender was awarded to a U.S. oil company (Williams Oil), the sale of what nationalists considered a strategic asset to a foreign company brought about the resignation of Prime Minister Rolandas Paksas of Homeland Union.[18]

In other aspects of energy policy, the Lithuanian government has generally continued to rely on its own means of supply. The country has gained most of its electricity from its own Ignalina nuclear power plant, a Chernobyl-style plant that Lithuania's neighbors and the European Union have been encouraging the government to close. The decision, in the face of external pressure, not to close down the nuclear power plant is not necessarily illiberal. From the beginning of independence, however, Lithuania has been resistant to move away from reliance on its own supplies. The country has continued to import oil and gas from Russia, its traditional supplier in the Soviet era, but since 1997 has moved forward on privatization of the sector.

Institutional Choice

In its foreign economic policy and institutional membership, Lithuania tracks closely the shifts in the economic ideas of the government. With the mercantilist Sajudis government in power, the country had significant export restrictions on all partners – primarily licenses, quotas, or outright bans.[19] There were no tariffs on imports, but the undervalued currency essentially made most imported goods unaffordable.[20] In October 1992, immediately

---

[18] But signaling the extent to which liberals have come to take the upper hand in the Lithuanian government, the Williams stake was sold to the Russian company Yukos in August 2002.

[19] Piritta Sorsa, "Lithuania: Trade Issues in Transition," in *Trade in the New Independent States*, ed. Constantine Michalopolous and David G. Tarr, Studies of Economies in Transformation No. 13 (Washington, D.C.: World Bank, 1994), pp. 157–170.

[20] Ibid., p. 163.

following the parliamentary elections and the shift to a liberal government, most license requirements were lifted and most export bans removed and in June 1993, after Brazauskas took over as president, export taxes were reduced considerably.[21] And in February and May 1994, export restrictions were further reduced. Lithuania added an import tariff regime under LDLP control. This was done primarily to gain the necessary revenue to balance the budget, but the government also added several quota restrictions, particularly on agricultural goods.

Lithuania's participation in international institutions reflects a similar pattern. Lithuania never joined the CIS, but after the liberal LDLP came to power in 1993, it did establish several close bilateral relationships with post-Soviet states and was the fifth of the post-Soviet states to secure membership in the WTO. Lithuania was slower to enter the WTO than its two Baltic neighbors, largely because of the government's resistance to giving up tariffs on agricultural goods while mercantilist (and more nationalist) parties were in power. Lithuania first submitted its application in January 1994, shortly after Sajudis was removed from power and the liberal Brazauskas government took over. The government followed with its Memorandum on Foreign Trade only a month later. Between 1994 and 1996, the government met actively with WTO representatives and made considerable progress toward WTO membership, but efforts were put on hold with the election of Gediminas Vagnorius, of the Homeland Union, to the post of prime minister. It was only after the liberal President Adamkus pressed the issue that Lithuania secured membership in the WTO in December 2000.

LATVIA

Latvia, like Lithuania, was split between nationalist parties with mercantilist economic ideas, such as the Farmers' Union and For Fatherland and Freedom, and two more liberal parties, Latvia's Way and, especially, the People's Party. The country's international trade policies reflected which of these two groups was in the majority, and when both parties were in the coalition the result was a strange and inconsistent amalgam of the two positions.

Shifts in Economic Ideas

The principles behind Latvian economic policies began with a considerable degree of incoherence, but with a heavy dose of mercantilist ideas. According

---

[21] Ibid., p. 162.

to Lieven, economic policymaking in Latvia was initially "in a state of the deepest confusion" and he noted that "during 1991, I noticed a strange tendency in Latvian officials to cackle like chickens when asked about state economic policy – the implication being that anyone who tried to understand it would infallibly go insane."[22]

As in the other two Baltic republics, the Latvian Popular Front took control of the government after the 1990 Supreme Soviet elections, placing Ivars Godmanis, a physicist by training, as the effective head of state in May 1990. As in Lithuania, economic policymaking was not a priority for this first government and economic ideas were secondary to nationalist concerns about independence until the end of 1991. Godmanis himself, according to some sources, was committed to broadly liberal ideas in both politics and economics but faced an increasingly radical nationalist parliament with strongly mercantilist ideas. The nationalists viewed non-Latvians (in particular Russians and Jews) or their Latvian "collaborators" as enemies of the nation seeking to "plunder Latvian resources."[23] This zero-sum economic relationship with "national enemies" was seen as both a domestic threat, represented by the country's large Slavic minority, and an international threat manifest in foreign trade.

In that first freely elected government, the ideas behind Latvian economic policy were an odd cocktail of liberal and mercantilist ideas reflecting the composition of the coalition. The contradictory nature of this mixed set of ideas is clear in the first Latvian economic reform program in 1991. Writing on the program, Van Arkadie and Karlsson note that "the 'overriding goal' is said to be a smooth transition to a market economy while 'at the same time recreating the integrity of the Latvian economy as a separate unit.'"[24] The contradictory mix of liberal and mercantilist principles was evident in the seven goals of the program. While the fourth goal sets out "to protect the domestic market through trade quotas, our own currency and customs," the fifth seeks "to develop a unified Baltic market and close ties to the Scandinavian and other West European nations."[25]

It was only in mid-1992 that Godmanis and the liberals were able to gain ground, primarily with the support of the International Monetary Fund. Lieven notes that both the prestige and the monetary resources of the IMF were critical in swinging the government, as Godmanis "was able to

---

[22] Lieven, *Baltic Revolution*, p. 295.
[23] A "moderate" Popular Front deputy quoted in Lieven, *Baltic Revolution*, p. 299.
[24] Van Arkadie and Karlsson, *Economic Survey*, p. 77.
[25] Quoted in Van Arkadie and Karlsson, *Economic Survey*, p. 78.

blackmail his opponents by threatening that if they did not fall into line, the IMF would cut off its loans."[26] As the severe economic crisis facing the country deepened, particularly a fuel crisis that left the country without heat or hot water, the fact that liberals were able to draw in desperately needed resources gave them a modicum of influence.

But it was only with the elections of August 1993 and the victory of the newly formed liberal Latvia's Way party that the liberals truly began to secure control of the government. Latvia's Way initially formed a coalition with the more radical nationalist Farmer's Union and in August, Valdis Birkavs, a moderate liberal lawyer and onetime founding member of the Popular Front, was elected as prime minister. Birkavs, who held important posts in all Latvian governments in the 1990s, certainly had strong nationalist credentials, and, true to the arguments put forward by Tsygankov and Abdelal, he was oriented toward bringing Latvia into the European Union.[27] But as in Estonia, the liberal government saw Russia as a critical partner with which economic ties should be cultivated rather than severed. Birkavs was famously quoted as advocating "one step towards Russia, and two or three towards the EU and NATO."

Birkavs's stint as prime minister lasted only until July 1994, when the Farmer's Union pulled out of the governing coalition to protest the failure to meet their demands for high agricultural tariffs. The withdrawal of the more mercantilist Farmer's Union only meant the further consolidation of the liberal hold on decision making within the country. The new Latvia's Way government selected a reformer, Maris Gailis, as prime Minister until the new round of parliamentary elections in 1995. The 1995 elections produced a relatively even balance among four parties, but Andris Skele, a liberal businessman, was put forward as prime minister by President Guntis Ullmanis. In mid-1997, the rightist parties withdrew their support from Skele and Guntars Krasts, from the rightist For Fatherland and Freedom Party, took the post of prime minister in 1997. Skele's liberal cabinet, however, remained intact. Following the elections in 1998, Latvia's Way once again took a position of strength – which ensured that Latvia had liberal prime ministers from 1998 onward, first with Vilis Kristopans of Latvia's Way, and then again Andris Skele, who had now established the People's Party as a more coherent base of support of liberal reforms, from July 1999 to May 2000.

[26] Lieven, *Baltic Revolution,* p. 295.
[27] A. P. Tsygankov, "Defining State Interests after Empire: National Identity, Domestic Structures, and Foreign Trade Policies of Latvia and Belarus," *Review of International Political Economy* 7 (2000): 101–137; Abdelal, *National Purpose.*

Institutional and Policy Choices

As predicted if Latvia's economic policies reflect shifts in the ideational composition of the government, the Latvian government has pursued liberal trade institutions since 1994. Efforts to relax the initially autarkic trade regime started only in late 1992 and true opening began only after the liberals had consolidated their position in 1994. The revised tariff schedule introduced by the Latvian government in October 1992 was still highly protectionist. The country had a high standard import tariff of 20% and a formidable array of special export tariffs, quotas, and other restrictions.[28] According to Tsygankov, who provides a careful account of the policy shifts, the Latvian government sought to limit these restrictions on trade with several former Soviet republics in 1992 by signing MFN agreements, including one with Russia in October 1992.[29] In the MFN agreement with Russia, the partners agreed to extend MFN status to one another and eventually to establish a free trade agreement. The agreement would have gone forward were it not for resistance in the Russian parliament, which refused to ratify the agreement as punishment for Latvia's nationalization of the trunk oil pipeline and a critical oil terminal at Ventspils and its disenfranchisement of the Russian minority in Latvia.[30] Indeed, Russia instead applied a double import tariff on goods from Latvian goods, charged world prices for oil and gas, and forced the country to pay for all of its imports in hard currency.[31] To the extent that Latvia's trade ties were diverted away from Russia and the other post-Soviet states, it was on Russia's initiative and was in opposition to the active efforts of the Latvian government.

The Latvian government's choices on domestic economic policy also follow directly on the shift in ideas. In energy, the government pursued a combined policy of diversification of supply and privatization.[32] The government pursued the diversification of supply by endeavoring to link the country's gas network to the Nordic gas system by means of a pipeline through Finland and Estonia.[33] The government has also sought to privatize the formerly state-controlled monopolies, Latvian Gas and Latenergo:

---

[28] Riga, Radio Riga International, "Government Introduces New Import, Export Tariffs," in FBIS-SOV-92-206, 23 October 1992, pp. 73–74.

[29] Tsygankov, "Defining State Interests," p. 63.

[30] EIU Country Report No. 1, 1993, p. 26.

[31] The double import tariff was charged on goods from the three Baltic states and Georgia beginning in January 1993.

[32] Latvia imports 93% of its energy.

[33] In 1998, the proposed cost of the pipeline was $1 billion, and the project was expected to take 10 years, so it remains to be seen whether the plan will be implemented.

Latvian Gas was privatized in 1997. Latenergo was restructured in 1998 to prepare for a future privatization but despite an active campaign by the governing Latvia's Way and Skele's People's Party, the company was taken off the privatization list after a public referendum rejected privatization.[34]

In its general privatization policy, the Latvian government moved quickly after 1994 to privatize state-owned assets through large-scale privatizations open to international tender. A privatization bureau based on the Estonian model was established in 1994, and privatization of large-scale enterprises was begun in earnest in January 1995. The mid-1998 deadline for the completion of privatization was largely met. Most enterprises were sold but some political battles over large-scale enterprises and energy remained.

In macroeconomic policy, the government's policies reflect a turn toward liberalism in late 1992 with the introduction of the IMF program and have been consistently liberal since 1995. Most prices were liberalized in 1992. Unlike its two Baltic neighbors, Latvia did not create a currency board, but an independent Central Bank established in May 1992 has kept interest rates high to maintain the lat, the national currency.[35] The result, as in the other liberal cases, has been a macroeconomic policy that punished the Soviet-era industries such as machine-building, steel, light industry, and food that were once the country's key sectors. The country saw declines of 32% and 38% in industrial production in 1992 and 1993, respectively, and a major shift in employment to services.

MOLDOVA

Moldova, in contrast to the three Baltic states, saw each of the three economic ideologies (mercantilism, integralism, and liberalism) become politically relevant at different times during the 1990s. The first half of the decade was marked by a struggle between the nationalist Popular Front, which drew generally on mercantilist ideas, and the Agrarian Democratic Party, whose leaders were integralist in their economic views. By the latter half of the decade nationalist parties had largely fallen out of favor and the primary political contest was between a revived Communist Party with integralist views and a liberal Alliance for Democracy and Reforms.

Moldova, like Estonia and Latvia, is notable among post-Soviet states in that the parliament played a critical role in economic policymaking in the 1990s. There was a genuine distribution of powers between the legislative

---

[34] East European Constitutional Review, "Country Watch Latvia," 9, no. 4 (2000).
[35] The Bank of Latvia had been established earlier but gained independence only with the law "On the Bank of Latvia" signed 17 May 1992.

and executive branches that favored the legislative branch even before the creation of a full parliamentary system in 2001. In the 1990s, the parliament formed the government in Moldova and the president did not have the authority to rule by decree. For this reason, an examination of the changes in the elite thus appropriately turns to party ideologies, shifting parliamentary coalitions, and critical elections. In Moldova, there were major shifts in the economic ideology of the government in both the 1994 and 1997 elections.

Shifts in Economic Ideas

As in the Baltics, Moldova began its independence with a Popular Front government that came to power in the March 1990 Supreme Soviet elections. At the time, approximately one-third of deputies elected were supported by the Popular Front. This minority position in the parliament was not, in itself, enough to control the national political and economic agenda. However, support given to the Popular Front by what Crowther refers to as "centrist deputies" allowed it to command a majority of the votes in the new legislature.[36] By some accounts approximately 80% of the deputies supported the Popular Front.[37] As a result, Popular Front figures took up positions of power in the legislature, and a pro–Popular Front economist, Mircea Druc, was appointed to the post of prime minister. The front also backed Mircea Snegur as chairman of the Supreme Soviet, despite his prominent position in the Moldovan Communist Party.[38]

Although the Popular Front was a broad movement including some liberals, the driving economic ideas of the party were mercantilist and tied to the larger political agenda of gaining independence from the Soviet Union to unify with Romania. Economic concerns do not appear to have been terribly central to the Popular Front platform, but as other popular front organizations, they extolled the virtues of their national production and delivered hostile attacks against what they viewed as imperial exploitation at the hands of Moscow. The leadership advocated severing the economic ties that bound the country to the Soviet Union and "joining the West" through integration with Romania. Typical of the Popular Front position at the time, in a televised speech on the anniversary of Moldovan independence Snegur noted:

[36] William Crowther, "Moldova: Caught between Nation and Empire," In *New States, New Politics: Building the Post-Soviet Nations*, ed. Ian Bremmer and Ray Taras (Cambridge: Cambridge University Press, 1997), p. 319.
[37] Economist Intelligence Unit, Moldova Profile, 1996.
[38] Crowther, "Moldova," 320.

We are all feeling the burden of this inheritance [of the communist system].... Thus, the policy of excessive specialization, which was supposed to create the flourishing garden of the union, led to the artificial division of our potential into the overagricultural right bank of the Dniester River and the overindustrialized left bank and to an overintegration in the economic space of the former USSR.... Megalomaniacal and totally unjustified projects led to the barbarian exploitation of our resources and hardworking people.... With the independence proclamation, the means were created to solve these problems.[39]

From 1990 until 1992–1993, mercantilist ideas such as these were central to the thinking of the Moldovan decision makers.[40]

The combination of the unpopular and unsuccessful civil war against the separatist Transdniestr Republic that began in January 1992 and economic collapse rapidly undercut popular support for the Popular Front government and its mercantilist ideas. The violent actions of the government received little popular support even in western Moldova. Moreover, the state of the economy had considerably worsened under the Popular Front government – in 1992 alone, per capita GDP fell by 29%. In Moldova, the crisis appears to have led many to reject the Popular Front and virtually all of the ideas associated with them.

The shift in popular and elite opinion began to yield changes in the country's leadership by the second half of 1992. Andrei Sangheli, of the integralist Agrarian Democratic Party, replaced the Popular Front Muravischi as prime minister in July 1992. By January 1993, the Popular Front chairman of parliament resigned and was replaced by Petru Lucinschi, the former first secretary of the Moldovan Communist Party (CPM), who became chairman of the Agrarians when the CPM was banned. Of the three top leaders – President Snegur, Prime Minister Sangheli, and Parliamentary Chairman Lucinschi – only Sangheli could be described as a consistent integralist on the basis of his interviews and public speeches. Snegur appears to have been something of a political opportunist who conveniently switched his economic rhetoric and political affiliation in order to maintain his hold on the presidency. Lucinschi advocated closer ties with Moscow, but there is nothing from his speeches or interviews to indicate that this was grounded in an underlying set of integralist ideas. All three men were former members of

---

[39] Speech by Mircea Snegur, president of the Republic of Moldova, at a parliament session on 27 August 1992. FBIS translation. FBIS-SOV-92-168, p. 41.

[40] In December 1991, after the parliament refused to ratify the Almaty Declaration that created the CIS, the main integralist parties – Unity, the Socialist Party, and the Agrarian Democrats – abandoned the legislature. This left control entirely in the hands of the Popular Front.

the Moldovan Politburo and the elections appeared to be decided predominantly by the ability of these figures to mobilize their prior Soviet patronage networks in the new political environment.

In 1993, the actual representatives serving in parliament had not changed since 1990. Even though many of the representatives had changed their political affiliations, the Popular Front remained a coherent enough force in parliament to block any initiative that was not to its liking. It was only through the elections to the legislature in February 1994 that deputies with integralist ideas made up a secure majority of the parliament. Parties contending that the only way out of the economic crisis was through some form of economic union with the former Soviet republics took 65.2% of the vote, giving them 84 of the 104 seats in the legislature.[41] The overwhelming result is particularly striking given that the Dniester region did not take part in the elections, although observers noted that thousands crossed the river to vote. The Agrarian Democrats alone secured 56 of the 104 seats, allowing them to rule without coalition partners.

The new head of the Agrarian Democratic Party, and deputy chairman of the Supreme Soviet, gave a very clear statement of the new government position:

> Our attitude toward the CIS, in particular mine as chairman of the Agrarian-Democratic party, is positive, of course.... In order to mend the holes that have appeared with the breakup of the Union, we badly need constant, businesslike meetings at the level not only of state and government heads, but also of parliaments.[42]

Over time, however, as the economy continued to deteriorate and Snegur and Lucinschi began to build their own political parties, defections from the Agrarians led to a weakening of their position in parliament. In mid-1995, the Agrarians dropped from 56 to 43 seats. This merely led to coalitions with the Socialist Party, however, and did not change the overall orientation of the government.[43]

---

[41] For an analysis of the election see Crowther, "Moldova," p. 325.

[42] Interview with Dmitri Mostkan, Moscow *Rabochaia Gazeta*, in Russian, 18 November 1994, p. 3 (FBIS-SOV-94-225, 22 November 1994, p. 1) (article on the meeting of the Interparliamentary Assembly).

[43] Although left with a minority of seats in parliament, the Popular Front remained in the opposition and rejected the government's economic program as being politically motivated and began to remake itself as a liberal party, adopting a resolution at its 1996 party congress stating that "the economic collapse has been triggered by misorientation to cooperation with Former Soviet Union republics only, primarily with Russia, by preservation of the administrative-command system, and by undermining of reforms.... The all-out revision of the privatization concept by the government and ruling party has led to a profanation of the

By January 1997, however, liberal ideas began to find an audience in the government. Petru Lucinschi defeated Snegur in the presidential elections of December 1996 and the former first secretary remade himself as a moderate liberal. After his electoral victory, Lucinschi engineered the removal of Andrei Sangheli, who had run against him in the election, and supported Ion Ciubic, a liberal economist and former collective farm director, for the prime minister's post. Although Ciubic left most of Sangheli's government intact, his relatively weak position led him to strengthen ties with liberal international institutions. By June 1997, support for the Agrarian Democrats had dropped to a mere 32 seats.

The critical shift towards liberalism occurred with the 1998 parliamentary elections. Although the Communist Party won the largest number of seats of any party in the elections, they did not manage to secure an outright majority. As a result, Ciubic managed to cobble together an Alliance for Democracy and Reforms to underpin a new more liberal government. Although Ciubic himself remained prime minister only until the economic fallout from the Russian financial collapse caused his resignation in February 1999, liberal ideas remained dominant in the government. Ciubic was replaced by his first deputy, Ion Sturza, also a liberal economist from the same coalition, who was, according to most sources, a more ardent economic liberal than Ciubic.[44] After coalition infighting led to Sturza's resignation, he, too, was replaced by another liberal, Dmitry Braghis. This gave the liberals control of the government consistently from 1998 through the end of the decade. It was only in Febuary 2001, when new elections gave the Communist Party more than 70% of the seats in parliament, that integralists returned to power.

Institutional and Policy Choice

In Moldova, the policy changes shadow precisely the shifts in the ideas of the government. Prior to 1992, when the mercantilist Popular Front was at its peak, Moldova eschewed membership in the CIS, abandoned the Soviet system of state contracts, and simultaneously sought to reorient trade toward Romania while the economy was still under state control. Even as integralist ideas began to revive within the government in 1993 and the Popular Front disintegrated as a coherent political force, the composition of parliament still prevented Moldova from joining the CIS or taking other "unionist" actions.

state property privatization, and to enrichment of the old communist nomenclatura at the expense of the national property." Chisinau *Infotag* in English, 1930 GMT 10 June 1996.
[44] EIU Country Profile 1999/2000.

In 1991, Snegur signed the Almaty declaration that formally created the CIS, but the Popular Front–dominated legislature refused to ratify it.

After the February 1994 elections brought the Agrarian Democrats to power, changes in foreign economic policy and institutional membership followed swiftly on the heels of the ideational shifts in the elite. In a radical departure from the policies advanced by the previous governing coalition of the Popular Front, Moldova joined the CIS on 8 April 1994 and shortly thereafter became a party to the Treaty on the Economic Union[45] and to the Interparliamentary Assembly. Notably, Moldova did not enter any of the military–political agreements – its motivations were purely economic. Months later, Moldova became a strong advocate for the transfer of supranational authority over economic matters to the Inter-State Economic Commission of the CIS.[46]

Moreover, in the Moldovan case we see a rapid change in the orientation of Moldova's economic exchange from West to East after the 1994 elections. The timing of these radical changes in trade flows suggests that trade patterns are, in this case, at least partially an effect of government policy. Trade with Romania, which had grown steadily since 1991, fell off precipitously after the 1994 election. In 1993, 21.5% of Moldova's exports were to Romania and 10.7% of its imports were from Romania. By 1995, Romania constituted merely 13.9% of Moldova's exports and 6.8% of imports,[47] approximately a 35% drop in Romania's share of Moldova's trade. Likewise, trade with CIS states, which had fallen considerably since 1991, began to rise in 1994. Russia, in particular, became an increasingly important trade partner. The percentage of exports to Russia, after falling from 58% in 1991 to 35.6% in 1993, rose dramatically to 48.3% in 1995.[48]

---

[45] Encompassing a customs union, payments union, scientific-technical union, and eventual common currency.

[46] Chisinau *Basapress* in English 2115 GMT 25 October 1994 (FBIS-SOV-94-209, 28 October 1994, p. 28):

> The results of the recent meeting of the CIS heads of state can be regarded as sufficiently positive for Moldova and the CIS as a whole, stated to BASA Iacob Mogoreanu, Moldovan representative to the CIS statutory organs. "We are now on the path of natural evolution of events; decisions are made by consensus and not by posing pressure on other states," Mogoreanu said. According to him, the signing of the agreement on creating the [CIS] Interstate Economic Committee is of great importance. "The CIS lays the foundation for an economic union, that is, a secure economic space for Moldova and other CIS states, and a result of its activity should be the overcoming of the economic crisis and the joining of the international economic community," Mogoreanu said.

[47] EIU Moldova Country Profile 1996–1997.

[48] World Bank 1995.

Moldova's progress toward WTO membership closely tracks the influence of liberal ideas in the government. Moldova applied for membership to the WTO in November 1993, just before the integralists took control of the parliament in 1994. Immediately after the application, however, no moves were made toward WTO membership until the Memorandum on Foreign Trade was finally sent in September 1996. It was in the period between 1997 and 2000, the years when liberal ideas were most influential in the government, that the Moldovan government moved actively toward WTO membership, with the government being approved for membership in May 2001.

The same shifts can be seen in energy, privatization, and macroeconomic policy. Beginning in 1994, cooperation with Russia in the provision and transit of energy resources was suddenly initiated. In 1995, the Russian company Gazprom was given a 51% stake in a new pipeline venture with the state-owned company Moldovagas in exchange for a debt write-off of $220 million of Moldova's gas debts.[49] By March 1998 gas debts were again at $650 million, and the government, rather than seeking rescheduling and external loans, transferred equity in the national gas complex in exchange for a debt write-off. The state-owned gas company Moldovagaz was merged with Gasnabtransit to form Moldovagas and Russia's Gazprom was given a 50% stake.[50] After the liberals took control of the government, there were plans made in 1998 to privatize the few bits of infrastructure that exist on Moldovan territory, which include only three generators and five distributors, but as of 2000 this privatization had not been carried out.[51] The largest privatization to date has been the sale of half the country's electricity network to Union Fenosa (Spain) in 1998.

Moldova's record of large-enterprise privatization is hard to decipher, with significant differences in the available secondary sources – all of which question the government's statistics. The Privatization Act of 1991 laid the basis for the privatization of all except land, but the country's largest enterprises were not privatized. Some reports indicate the privatization of the majority of large enterprises by 1995, but others suggest that there was little effective privatization of large enterprises until a second privatization program was introduced by the liberal government between 1997 and 2001. Even so, in the few areas – cement and tobacco – where tenders for large enterprises were held, parliament subsequently annulled the sales.

---

[49] EIU Country Profile 1996.
[50] Transdniestr owns 14% and Moldova 36%.
[51] Moldova's primary electricity producers lie in Transdniestr and are firmly under the control of the separatist government.

As Moldova's primary enterprises are agricultural, land privatization is probably a better measure in this case. Privatization of agricultural enterprises began in 1997 through liquidation of state farms and distribution of ownership titles to private farmers, and in late 1997, the government passed a law allowing land to be traded on a restricted basis. In 1998 this pilot project of 73 farms was expanded nationwide with a goal to complete titles transfer to more than 1 million farmers in 2000. All of this occurred during the window of time that liberals were in control of the government.

In macroeconomic policy the government continued to give soft credits to industry and agriculture, running large deficits financed by loans from the National Bank of Moldova.[52] The government has nonetheless received significant financial support from international lenders, which has helped maintain a relatively stable currency.

Moldova also affords something of an experiment within an experiment, because the country was divided in two after the civil war in 1992. It is noteworthy that mercantilist and liberal ideas were only employed in Moldova proper. In the Transdniestr region of Moldova, which has carried out its own economic policies since 1992, integralist ideas prevailed. Consistently with these ideas, the energy monopolies were kept under state control and continued to be supplied with oil and natural gas from Russia. No privatization took place, and the government retained the Soviet ruble as the currency and pursued hyperinflationary subsidization of Soviet-linked industries. The government also worked to establish direct economic ties and to organize barter arrangements with enterprises in Russia and Belarus.

A CASE FOR NATIONALISM?

In sum, although Estonia, Latvia, Lithuania, and Moldova all ultimately joined the WTO, there was considerable variation in the economic choices and institutional participation of these countries across the decade as groups with different economic ideas moved in and out of power. Of the four countries, only Estonia consistently steered a liberal institutional course, a course tied to the historically contingent fact that it was a liberal economic laboratory within the USSR and thus a home of liberal views even prior to its independence. Latvia and Lithuania, in contrast, found their policies buffeted between newly created liberal parties and mercantilists associated

---

[52] The budget deficits were 5.9% of GDP in 1995, 10% of GDP in 1996, and 7.7% of GDP in 1997 (EIU 1999). The Central Bank was made independent in November 1993, just before the Popular Front was forced out of the government by the February 1994 elections.

with the more nationalist parties who drew on the model of the country's interwar independence. As virtually each election saw the incumbents tossed from power, these countries exhibit almost a random cycling between these two economic ideologies. A similar pattern of electoral cycling between different parties with different economic ideologies is evident in Moldova, but in the Moldovan case integralist ideas also played a significant role. Hence, Moldova was the only one of the four countries to join the CIS and did so immediately after the integralist Agrarian Democratic Party was given its turn at the reins in 1994.

Latvia and Lithuania have served as critical cases for the nationalist argument, but to what extent do these four cases, upon closer scrutiny, bear out those claims? Consistently with the work of Abdelal, Tsygankov, and others, widespread nationalist sentiment did serve to censor integralist ideas, which were correctly associated with the policies and institutions of the USSR. In the three Baltic states, integralist ideas were unacceptable in public discourse or as a guide for policy, no relevant political parties or factions adopted them, and none of their governments ever seriously considered membership in the CIS. Only Moldova is distinct in this regard, as the Agrarian Democrats and the Communist Party both drew on integralist ideas during the 1990s, and Moldova joined the CIS and signed on to most of the regional economic agreements in 1994 despite the opposition of the nationalist parties. The nationalist hypothesis correctly anticipated that states with stronger nationalist movements would move more rapidly into liberal international institutions and reorient their trade away from Russia.

But this chapter also shows how reliance on Humean "constant conjuncture" to identify causation can be misleading, as the *path* by which each of the states moved to WTO membership shows some important inconsistencies with the nationalist argument; indeed the outcome happened in a way that was inconsistent with the logic of the theory. The most problematic datum is that once Russia had recognized the independence of the Baltic countries, *the Baltic countries made efforts to cultivate rather than curtail their economic ties with Russia and other former Soviet republics.* In the early 1990s, each of the three Baltic countries sought to sign a free trade agreement with Russia (and Moldova succeeded in doing so). As stated by the Estonian prime minister Tiit Vahi in an interview in 1992:

I believe that all operating relations with the eastern regions must be preserved. This is why the Baltic countries have agreed to start unrestricted commodity exchange and non-visa border crossing as of May 1 [1992]. We have also proposed to Russia that we change over to trade free of customs limitations. . . . Parallel to this, we are stepping up economic contacts with our Western partners. Why do I say this? In order to confirm the principle position of our cabinet: The strengthening of Estonian sovereignty must in no case grow into self-isolation. On the contrary, Estonia may really become a unique bridge between the East and West, as well as between the North and the South.[53]

Indeed, the only reason that there was no free trade area between Russia and the Baltics in the early 1990s was that the Russian side refused these overtures – both because of its concerns about reexport of its oil, minerals, and metals, and as a way of punishing these countries for their treatment of Russian minorities.

In fact, far from drawing their countries into Western economic institutions, it was the more nationalist parties in these countries that provided the strongest political *impediment* to greater trade openness and membership in Western multilateral liberal trade institutions. The Lithuanian and Latvian national myths, forged in the romantic tradition of the nineteenth century, idealized a nation of independent farmers organically tied to the land. Efforts to re-create or preserve this national vision left the nationalist parties ideologically committed to the high agricultural tariffs and subsidies that delayed their entry into the WTO. Indeed it was the presence of economic liberals who, like Vahi, viewed Russia as a valued trading partner that best explains the ultimate choice of these states to enter the WTO and the timing of their liberalization. Such liberal ideas ultimately led all four countries actively to court free trade, WTO membership, *and* closer market ties with Russia and other post-Soviet states, rather than to reject economic ties with the historical "other" as the nationalist argument suggests.

But the nationalist arguments do certainly point to a shift in the composition of trade of the Baltic states away from the former Soviet countries and toward Western Europe. Why might this be the case if a reorientation of trade away from Russia was not something that these countries actively pursued? There are several reasons, but the most obvious is that it is very dangerous to treat aggregate trade flows as a measure of government intentions. Political factors, let alone specific trade policies or government intentions, are only one subset of many factors that impact trade flows. For this reason, aggregate data on trade flows are problematic as a measure.

This problem is compounded by existing analyses, which do not control for other factors. Without such controls, one would have no way of knowing whether Estonia, for example, has had a highest percentage of trade with the European Union of all of the post-Soviet countries because it has a strong

---

[53] Tiit Vahi, "The 'Curtain' is Being Lifted, or the View of Today's Estonia by Prime Minister Tiit Vahi," *Delovoi Mir*, 25 April 1992, p. 3. FBIS-USR-92-057 (13 May 1992).

European national identity or because its capital and largest city, Tallinn, is only 82 kilometers from the nearest EU capital (Helsinki). Indeed, if one were to run a simple gravity model of the type that economists generally use to predict trade flows on the basis of nonpolitical factors such as geographical proximity and GDP, one would find that the share of *each post-Soviet country's trade with their former Soviet partners was significantly greater than predicted (the Baltic states included).*[54] For this reason, one should view the relative decline in intrarepublican trade as a deliberate policy choice only with some significant qualifications. It is telling, perhaps, that the country with the most radical and precipitous drop in trade with former Soviet countries as a percentage of its total trade was Tajikistan, falling from 86.2% in 1988 to 33.1% in 1993; few would attribute this decline to the intentions of the Tajik government.[55] Likewise, the radical decline in Lithuanian exports to Russia from 46.4% in 1997 to 18.2% in 1999 took place when there was no discernable change in the politics or economic strategy of the Lithuanian government. What changed was that the collapse of the Russian ruble in 1998 meant that Russians could no longer afford to purchase Lithuanian products.

In sum, because it is not clear precisely what mixture of political, economic, or geographical features determines trade patterns, trade flows are not very useful as an indicator of political choice. Tracing policies is absolutely critical, especially in the cases discussed in this chapter. By examining the institutional and policy choices of the Baltic countries and Moldova across the decade, we get a much clearer picture of the government's motivations, and the extent to which those intentions were informed by economic ideas.

[54] Bert Van Selm, Bert, *The Economics of Soviet Break-Up* (New York: Routledge, 1997), pp. 64–65.
[55] Ibid., p. 65.

6

Russia, Belarus, and Ukraine

The three Slavic states, both individually and in comparison, also provide excellent material for testing the argument that economic ideas drive international institutional choice. We should not overstate the prospects for controlled comparison of the group despite the fact that the three states were carved out of a single country and had been unified for more than 300 years. Russia's distinctiveness – its large size, its nuclear forces, its oil and gas reserves, its international presence, its absorption of the Soviet bureaucracy, elite, and economic institutions after 1991 – obviously limits its utility for isolating causal factors through paired comparisons with its Slavic neighbors. But given the undeniably idiosyncratic and practically stochastic nature of President Boris Yeltsin's personnel changes,[1] and the high level of variation over time in the economic ideas holding sway in the government, Russia on its own provides the means for a formidable test and demonstration of the argument in action. Indeed, Russia's nearly constant turnover in officials and the resultant shifts among economic ideologies over time make the country a laboratory unto itself if we take a longitudinal approach.

And whatever difficulties Russia may present in terms of its comparability with other cases are happily compensated for by Ukraine and Belarus, which provide extraordinary leverage in comparison. The similarities between the two countries are remarkable; it is as if the republics were designed specifically for the purpose of controlled experimentation for the effects of differences in economic ideas of the leadership.

---

[1] On Yeltsin's idiosyncrasies and the role of unpredictability and spontaneity in Yeltsin's leadership style, see George W. Breslauer, *Gorbachev and Yeltsin as Leaders* (Cambridge: Cambridge University Press, 2002).

TABLE 6.1. *Similarity of Belarus and Ukraine on Key Variables*

	Belarus	Ukraine
Production controlled by Union-level (Soviet-specific assets):[a]		
As % of total production volume	54	58
As % of industrial personnel	54	63
As % of fixed assets for industrial production	74	73
Heavy industry as % of total[b]	65	68
Percentage employed in industry	30	30
Military-industrial employment as % of total	17	19
Percentage of imports from Russia[c]	54	57
Percentage of exports to Russia	47	53
Percentage fluent in national language[d]	78	78
Percentage fluent in Russian	83	78
Percentage of population of titular nationality	78	73

[a] Narodnoe Khoziastvo SSSR 1989, p. 331

[b] World Bank 1995, Table 7-1, 53 (data for 1990).

[c] Narodnoe Khoziastvo SSSR, 1989, 634.

[d] Language and nationality data are from *Natsional'nyi Sostav Naseleniia SSSR, po dannym vsesoiuznoi perepisi naseleniia 1989* (Moscow: Finansy i Statistika, 1991).

As shown in Table 6.1, the two neighboring countries were virtually identical in terms of their basic economic structure. Both were integrated to a great extent in Soviet production structures, heavily industrialized, and a large segment of their workforce in military production. Both countries relied on Russia for their primary energy supply and the bulk of their trade. Both countries had the same percentage of the population fluent in the titular language and had minority Russian and Polish populations of similar size. The languages in both countries were in the East Slavic family, and hence very close both to one another and to Russian. Neither country had a prior history of independent statehood.[2]

---

[2] When Russia withdrew from World War I, Austro-German forces occupied much of the European territory of the empire that is now part of Belarus and Ukraine. Under Austro-German occupation, both Ukraine and Belarus were declared independent from Russia and established as sovereign states. Nationalist historians in both states have presented this as a prior tradition of independent statehood. In actuality, however, both the Belorusian and Ukrainian National Republics enjoyed no more than a brief symbolic independence and depended entirely on the goodwill of the Austro-German occupation army authorities. The Belorussian National Republic (BNR) lasted only 10 months. The Ukrainian National Republic (UNR) lasted only slightly longer by virtue of the fact that Russian general Denikin's White Army tried to keep the territory outside Bolshevik control. This does not amount to a significant history of prior statehood.

Despite these commonalities, Belarus and Ukraine differed significantly in the economic ideas of their governments in the 1990s – which were ultimately rooted, I argue later, in contingent choices made by Communist Party elites in each country as the USSR was collapsing. In Ukraine, during the first half of the decade, mercantilist ideas were dominant and their advocates sparred with integralists within both the government and the parliament, but toward the end of the decade this dynamic gave way to an increased political role of liberal economists. In Belarus, integralist ideas held sway within the government throughout the period and the few economic liberals who received minor portfolios in the government in the mid-1990s disappeared (in some cases physically) as the decade wore on.

As a result, these two countries followed very different institutional trajectories in the 1990s. Belarus was the strongest advocate of the regional trade institutions, whereas Ukraine participated in the CIS in only a very limited way and continually rejected membership in the Customs Union. The remarkable similarities of the two states allow us to isolate the causal role of economic ideas. But let us begin with the Russian case.

RUSSIA

Throughout the 1990s the economic ideas informing Russian policy fluctuated between integralism and liberalism as President Boris Yeltsin shifted his support back and forth between the two groups. Indeed, Boris Yeltsin's leadership style, as detailed carefully by Breslauer,[3] relied on unpredictability, spontaneity, and impulse, and he preserved his post by ensuring the constant insecurity of official cadres and rapidly eliminating potential rivals. As a result, Yeltsin admirably plays the role of "randomizer" in the selection of ideas. His reckless alcoholism and idiosyncratic reasons for replacing officials – and his lack of personal attention to any details of economic policy – provide us with an important source of contingency (and thus exogeneity) in the selection of the elites and economic ideas that guided Russian policy.

Because Yeltsin had little personal involvement in economic policy and primarily devolved such decisions to his subordinates, an understanding of the Russian case necessitates a greater attention to shifts in government personnel. Fortunately, Russia is the easiest of the 15 countries when it comes to identifying the ideas of government officials. Throughout the 1990s, Russia had free and vibrant media, many government officials have published

[3] George W. Breslauer, *Gorbachev and Yeltsin as Leaders* (Cambridge: Cambridge University Press, 2002), pp. 34–39.

memoirs, and there are some excellent secondary accounts by American scholars;[4] in short, there is no shortage of information on Russian officials. Moreover, the task itself in Russia is made easier because the ideological camps were so starkly defined.

Economic Ideas

In Russia, the first period in which liberal ideas clearly dominated policymaking was the time that economic management was under the direct control of Yegor Gaidar, which lasted from November 1991 until December 1992. Gaidar, a 35-year-old economist, was the de facto leader of a group of liberal economists in Moscow and Leningrad and drew many of his colleagues into the government.[5] In November 1991, Gaidar was made the deputy chairman of the Supreme Soviet of the RSFSR under Yeltsin's chairmanship, as well as the minister of economy and minister of finance – hence he controlled the direction of economic policy in the country. His administration included several liberal academics: Anatoly Chubais was appointed the chair of the State Property Committee. Aleksander Shokhin, who had been minister of labor since August 1991, was appointed deputy prime minister. Pyotr Aven was made minister of foreign economic relations. Vladimir Mashitz, of Gaidar's Institute for Economic Policy, was made chairman of the Committee on Cooperation with the CIS. Victor Khlystun was appointed minister of agriculture. And Andrei Nechaev, also of Gaidar's institute, was made the first deputy minister of economics and finance under Gaidar. Several other liberal economists, including Sergei Vasiliev, whom Gaidar describes in his memoirs as "a confirmed liberal, ideologically even stricter than I," took on an active advising role and later held positions in the government. In sum, the government was stocked with a cohesive team of liberal economists, many of whom, especially Chubais, Shokhin, and Vasiliev, were old student friends of Gaidar's or were involved in his liberal economic policy institute.[6]

[4] Particularly nuanced and detailed accounts of the early 1990s may be found in Michael Urban with Vyacheslav Igrunov and Sergei Mitrokhin, *The Rebirth of Politics in Russia* (Cambridge: Cambridge University Press, 1997), 257–290 and for the decade as a whole in Michael McFaul, "The Fourth Wave of Democracy and Dictatorship: Noncooperative Transitions in the Post-Communist World," *World Politics* 54, no. 2 (January 2002): 212–244.

[5] Yegor Gaidar and Jane Ann Miller, trans., *Days of Defeat and Victory* (Seattle: University of Washington Press, 1999), pp. 91–103.

[6] Ibid., p. 109.

Although Gaidar was demoted in December 1992 and replaced by Victor Chernomyrdin as prime minister, an integralist who had previously managed the Soviet natural gas complex, many of the liberals remained in the government. Gaidar moved only one rung down the hierarchy to first deputy prime minister, and another liberal economist, Boris Fedorov, was named a deputy prime minister and served until January 1994. From March 1993 until January 1994 Fedorov also served as minister of finance. Shokhin retained his post as deputy prime minister and was responsible for supervising the Ministry of Foreign Economic Relations and acted as chair of the Monetary and Economic Commission. Indeed, aside from the brief period between January 1996 and March 1997, the government prior to 1998 was split between integralists under the tutelage of Prime Minister Chernomyrdin, and liberals, generally in control of the Ministries of Finance and Economics. The liberal group was led and organized from the first deputy prime minister's position, which was held by Gaidar between September 1993 and January 1994, and by Anatoly Chubais from November 1994 until January 1996. As a result, during this period, different branches of the government were often acting independently of or in pitched battle with one another.

Beginning in March 1997, the government began to take a decidedly more liberal tilt. Chubais and Boris Nemtsov were named first deputy prime ministers in March 1997. Oleg Davydov, an integralist, was ousted as minister of foreign economic relations in April 1997 and replaced by Mikhail Fradkov, a liberal who had been Russia's representative to the GATT/WTO. Prominent liberals, Yakov Urinson and Mikhail Zadornov, headed the Ministries of Economy and Finance (respectively), and two leading liberal economists, Sergei Ignatiev and Alexei Kudrin, secured deputy slots in the Ministry of Finance. Alfred Kokh and the liberal economist Maksim Boiko controlled the Privatization Ministry. The shift toward liberalism was strengthened by the removal of Victor Chernomyrdin from the post of prime minister in March 1998 and the appointment of Sergei Kirienko.

The economic crisis of August 1998, however, again put integralists in power. In September 1998, the integralist foreign minister and Soviet-trained economist Yevgenii Primakov was installed as prime minister. Yuri Masliukov, the former head of the Soviet State Planning agency (Gosplan), was named first deputy prime minister. Moreover, Fradkov was ousted and Gyorgy Gabunia, an integralist in the ministry who was responsible for trade policies with the CIS countries, was made minister of foreign economic relations. Particularly with regard to foreign economic policy, the integralists were firmly in control.

In May 1999, however, Yeltsin unexpectedly sacked Primakov and temporarily put in Sergei Stepashin as an interim prime minister until the appointment of Vladimir Putin in August 1999. The appointment of Putin secured the position of the liberals. While Putin himself had no effective economic training, he had served in the liberal St. Petersburg government of Mayor Anatoly Sobchak and had close ties to liberal economists. Putin immediately reinstated Fradkov as the minister of foreign economic relations and installed other St. Petersburg economic liberals in the government. Following his assumption of the presidency in January 2000, Putin handed the entire economic portfolio over to liberal economists, many of whom were drawn to government directly from Gaidar's economic institute. In May 2000, a new Ministry of Economic Development and Trade was established, with German Gref (of Gaidar's institute, now renamed the Institute for the Study of the Economy in Transition) placed at the head, with his key deputy ministers also bearing strong liberal intellectual credentials. Another St. Petersburg liberal, Alexei Kudrin, was made a deputy prime minister and minister of finance. Andrei Illarionov, an economist known for his radical free-market views, became Putin's chief economic adviser. In general, liberals secured control of Russian economic policy and remained in control for the first years of Putin's administration.

Remarkably, throughout the 1990s the liberals generally managed to retain control of the Ministry of Finance. Indeed, a survey of all of the articles written by government officials in the publication of the academic institute associated with the Russian Ministry of Finance revealed that only 4 of 26 articles had integralist reasoning. The remaining 22 were liberal in nature.[7] It is noteworthy that the single integralist article by a top official was written in 1995, by Viktor Panskov, then minister of finance. This was during the brief window of time when the liberals were completely out of the government.

INSTITUTIONAL AND POLICY CHOICE

The relationship between the ideas of the government and economic policy maps very closely in the case of Russia, although the rapid personnel changes typical of Yeltsin's leadership make it somewhat difficult to follow. It was during the period of liberal control between 1991 and the beginning of 1993 that the Russian government pursued its most radical liberal economic reforms and most actively destroyed the regional economic

[7] Darden, Statistical Dataset.

institutions. Shortly after Gaidar's team took control, on 2 January 1992, prices were liberalized and within 18 months the ruble zone had been scuttled (see Chapter 10). The liberal government also raised prices for gas and electricity deliveries to enterprises by 500% in 1992 to shift them closer to world price levels.

With the diminished influence of the liberals and return of integralists under the Chernomyrdin government, policies shifted accordingly. Some price restrictions were reimposed and the Chernomyrdin government increased credits to Soviet-era industries. The Central Bank, governed by Viktor Gerashchenko, opposed the monetarist ideas behind Gaidar's reforms and kept a steady flow of credits to industry. It was only after Gerashchenko was ousted from the chairmanship of the Central Bank in October 1994 that the Central Bank restricted the monetary supply and stabilized the currency. In 1995, an exchange rate corridor was established for the ruble. Notably, the ruble was kept relatively stable under liberal governments until the world economic crisis began in spring 1998.

One area where the liberals retained significant influence was privatization policy.[8] From 1992 to 1994, a massive voucher privatization scheme was implemented under the leadership of Anatoly Chubais that put 70% of Russian enterprises under private control. In the majority of cases this led to enterprises' winding up in the hands of so-called enterprise insiders. In a few cases, however, vouchers were purchased by voucher funds, which then took over key enterprises at voucher-based auctions.[9] Several of the most lucrative large-scale enterprises were not included in this privatization, however, and these enterprises were privatized through an arrangement orchestrated by Chubais in advance of the 1996 presidential elections that effectively amounted to a transfer of these enterprises to individuals who were expected to be loyal to Yeltsin and assist in securing his reelection. In both privatization schemes, political motives and economic ideas were closely entwined. Liberals like Chubais and Gaidar wanted to secure private property in principle, but they also sought to create a class of new owners who would have a vested interest in maintaining the current regime.[10]

Privatization of the state gas monopoly (RAO Gazprom) and the electricity system (RAO UES) was undertaken in the early 1990s, but there were

---

[8] Hilary Appel, "The Ideological Determinants of Liberal Economic Reform: The Case of Privatization," *World Politics* 52, (July 2000): 520–549.

[9] See Anders Aslund, *How Russia Became a Market Economy* (Washington, D.C.: Brookings Institution, 1995), pp. 252–257.

[10] Lynnley E. Browning, "Rebel Chechen Currency New Salvo to Moscow." *Reuters*, 24 April 1997.

no auctions and the state retained a controlling packet of shares in the two firms. Effectively these privatizations amounted to the transfer of the intact Soviet complexes into semiprivate holdings and were more a manifestation of integralism than of liberalism.[11] With market liberals in the top positions of authority in the government after March 1997, an attempt was made to break up and privatize the state gas monopoly, but this failed. This proposal was first rebuffed by Prime Minister Victor Chernomyrdin, and after Chernomyrdin was fired, Prime Minister Sergei Kirienko's government was too weak to impose any changes on the gas monopoly – which remained an integralist stronghold under the control of Rem Viakhirev until Putin secured his ouster.[12]

The volatile "dual power" arrangement between liberals and integralists was also manifest in the trajectory of Russia's foreign economic policy and institutional membership. In June 1993, when most of Gaidar's people were still in office, Russia applied for membership in the WTO. It was the first of the former Soviet republics to do so, but the application soon languished and Russia's import tariffs increased dramatically after a March 1994 decree – i.e. precisely during a window in which the liberals were out of power.[13] Regarding Russia's participation in CIS matters, the situation changed dramatically toward the end of 1993 and, especially, during 1994, again during the period that the liberals were out of power. In late 1993 and early 1994, Chernomyrdin worked actively to promote the unification of the Russian and Belarusian monetary systems against Gaidar's wishes, a fact noted in Gaidar's January 1994 letter of resignation to Boris Yeltsin:

> To my regret, more and more resolutions which I have neither helped prepare nor with which I can in any way agree are being adopted. Let me give you just two recent examples. An interbank agreement on the unification of Russian and Belarusian monetary systems has just been signed. . . . I repeatedly objected to this decision, but my protests went unheard.[14]

Following the resignation of Gaidar and other prominent liberals in January 1994, Russia stepped up its activity with respect to regional institutions. After having signed the Treaty on Economic Union in November 1993, Russia was one of the strongest supporters behind the creation of the IEC at the

[11] The "privatization" of Gazprom was conducted by Chernomyrdin.
[12] Personal communication, Boris Nemtsov, Washington, D.C., November 1998. See Chapter 4 on post-Soviet integralism and a discussion of Gazprom.
[13] Vladimir Konovalov, "Russian Trade Policy," in *Trade in the New Independent States*, ed. Constantine Michalopolous and David G. Tarr, Studies of Economies in Transformation No. 13 (Washington, D.C.: World Bank, 1994), pp. 29–51.
[14] Gaidar, *Days of Defeat*, p. 269.

CIS meetings in fall 1994. The Agreement on the Customs Union, prepared during 1994, was signed in January 1995. Even after key liberals Anatoly Chubais and Yevgenii Yasin returned to the government in November 1994, in the political aftermath of Black Tuesday,[15] Chernomyrdin's position as prime minister was strong enough to secure the implementation of the signed agreements. It is noteworthy that it was precisely during the period when the liberals were again out of power between January 1996 and March 1997 that an additional set of key CIS agreements was signed. In March 1996 the Russian government pushed for the creation of the closer "Treaty on Deepening Integration" and in April the Belarusian-Russian Union Treaty was signed.

Similarly, despite consistent biannual meetings of the Working Group, Russia actively pursued entry into the WTO only after Putin took power and Gref, the liberal from Gaidar's institute, became minister of economic development and trade. Interviews conducted in November 2000 with Maksim Medvedkov, the deputy minister of economic development and trade who was the architect of Russia's WTO strategy, demonstrated that this policy flowed directly from the liberal ideas of the new government. Medvedkov, a liberal economist, had worked at Gaidar's institute before his appointment as deputy minister. The decision to pursue WTO entry was essentially taken by fiat by Putin on the advice of his liberal economic advisers.[16] As of late 2000 when the decision was taken to pursue entry decisively, no pro- or anti-WTO lobby had formed and no interest groups were involved in the decision.

CONTINGENT ORIGINS OF THE IDEATIONAL DIFFERENCES
BETWEEN BELARUSIAN AND UKRAINIAN ELITES

Turning to the cases of Belarus and Ukraine, it is worth recalling their similarities. As late as 1990 there was little prospect of any alternative to integralist ideas in either country. Ukraine had been ruled by the Soviet hardliner Vladimir Shcherbitsky from 1972 until September 1989 and was one of the least open and reformed of the Soviet republics. Belarus, despite greater turnover in first secretaries (there were five between January 1980 and December 1990), had similarly conservative Soviet leadership. And although Ukraine had strong anti-Soviet popular sentiments in 5 of the

[15] On 11 October 1994 the ruble lost 25% of its value.
[16] Author's interview with Maxim Medvedkov, deputy minister of economic development and trade, November 2000.

country's 26 regions, this was only a small minority of the population.[17] In both Ukraine and Belarus, the 1990 Supreme Soviet elections brought nationalist groups into politics, but in both countries the groups secured only a minority of seats and both countries voted overwhelmingly to preserve the USSR in the March 1991 Soviet referendum. Indeed, intelligent observers in Ukraine as late as spring 1991 were writing of the cohesion of the Ukrainian Communist Party and its failure to "nationalize" along the lines of the Communist Party of Lithuania.[18]

Why did these countries have different sets of elite ideas given their similar histories and structural condition? To answer this question, we must look at differences in the strategic choices made by the leadership of the Communist Parties of the two countries in 1990 and 1991. The critical point occurred with choices leaders made during the August 1991 coup attempt. In Ukraine, the chairman of the Supreme Soviet, Leonid Kravchuk, chose to oppose the coup. The Communist Party leadership in Belarus chose to support it. The failure of the coup had significant implications for the composition of the elite in both countries. In Ukraine, the former Communist Party leadership, sensing the imminent demise of the party's authority following the failed coup, chose to ally themselves with the small but politically active national movement against the central government in Moscow. Former Communist ideologists like Leonid Kravchuk shed Communist Party ideology and loyalty to the USSR so that they could effectively preserve power and privilege of the Ukrainian nomenklatura. The result was that the Ukrainian party leadership recast itself, opened the door to mercantilist ideas (a mix of nationalism and Socialism), and, upon independence, gave nationalists from Galician Ukraine effective control over the armed forces and the newly created foreign ministry – leaving them with an important and enduring institutional stronghold within the state.

In Belarus, in contrast, the top leadership resigned, the Communist Party was disbanded, and the Supreme Soviet named Stanislav Shushkevich, a physicist associated with the Belarusian Popular Front, as chairman. Shushkevich was ousted as the economic crisis wore on and the memory of the August 1991 coup began to fade. As a result, the nationalists, who were mercantilist or liberal in their economic views, were subsequently marginalized within Belarusian politics.

---

[17] Wilson, *Ukrainian Nationalism;* Darden, "The Scholastic Revolution," unpublished Mimeo, 2003.

[18] Chrystia Freeland, "Rukh: The New Ukrainian Nationalism" (A.B. honors thesis in History and Literature, Harvard University, 1991).

In sum, the Communist elites in both Belarus in Ukraine were trying to preserve their position of power in the confusing transitional environment of the USSR in 1991, but they placed their bets differently. Strategic choices made by elites in Ukraine led both to the preservation of Ukraine's Soviet-era nomenklatura and to a broadening of the economic views represented among the elite. In Belarus, where the elite cast its fate with the coup plotters of August 1991, thinking that the coup would be successful, a temporary loss of power of the integralist nomenklatura occurred; the ultimate outcome, however, was complete marginality of nonintegralist views among the Belarusian elite. Reading history backward, we have a tendency to see the different trajectories of these two countries as historically determined, but it is telling that *one cannot find a single observer* who anticipated the differences in Ukrainian and Belarusian policies even as late as spring 1991. As a result of the different and, I would argue, largely contingent choices that leaders made at the time of the coup, the ideational terrains of the two countries were quite different. To get a sense of these differences and their effects on institutional choice, let us examine the two countries individually.

BELARUS

Throughout the 1990s, there was little in the way of "separation of powers" in Belarus, and authority was centralized in the office of the president. At the outset of Belarusian independence, the Supreme Soviet played an important role in selecting the government and carried the right to impeach the head of state, but in 1994 a new presidency was created that centralized most powers of relevance. In 1996, any further challenge to presidential authority was removed when the legislature was disbanded, and a new constitution that essentially put all power in the hands of the president was adopted by referendum.[19] Since 1996, the Belarusian legislature has been no more than a rubber stamp, and the remaining political opposition has been forced outside institutionalized political life and into sporadic street demonstrations. In examining the ideas that matter in Belarus, one's gaze naturally turns to the office of the head of state and his surrounding advisers.

Unlike the authoritarian regimes of Central Asia, however, Belarus has had considerable political turnover with three leaders since achieving independence. All three leaders have been integralist thinkers and integralism has

---

[19] The Belarusian parliament, the Supreme Soviet, still exists, but the president has the right to appoint a significant number of its representatives and the elections for the remaining deputies appear to be rigged.

been particularly pervasive among the Belarusian elite. Consequently, there are no significant political groups in Belarus that oppose economic union. The Belarusian National Front, which advocates Belarus's withdrawal from the CIS, has never garnered more than 15% of the vote, even in the relatively free and fair elections prior to 1996. Aside from a brief period following the 1994 elections, in which a mix of different economic ideas were expressed in public statements by top officials, the Belarusian elite consistently expressed integralist ideas when speaking about economic matters.

Economic Ideas

The leader of the first postindependence government, Stanislav Shushkevich, who had been party to the agreement that replaced the Soviet Union with the CIS, justified the need for economic union in integralist terms, although he opposed any form of CIS military alliance or political union. Indeed, since leaving office Shushkevich has continued to express integralist ideas.[20] On 27 January 1994, he was ousted by the Belarusian Supreme Soviet on corruption charges and replaced by Vyacheslav Kebich.

Kebich, a Soviet-trained economist who was later considered for the post of CIS executive secretary, was a particularly devout integralist. In a 1994 New Year's speech, a month before he deposed Shushkevich, Kebich explained the economic situation in the following way:

The socioeconomic development of Belarus has recently been accompanied by further exacerbation of critical phenomena, the shrinking of production and investments, inflation and deregulation of the consumer market. This has led to a deterioration in living standards. The main cause of the crisis is the destruction of the single economic space of the former USSR.... Serious problems emerge on our way. The "invisible" hand of the market brings changes undesirable for society. This is demonstrated by the experience of many countries living through a transitional period. When prices are set free, the application of Western-type monetary methods is often inefficient and may bring opposite results.... The government has a concept of how to solve these problems. This concept is based on the sober evaluation of our potential and understanding of an active involvement of the state in realigning the economy. Joint action with Russia is the cornerstone of this concept.... We are absolutely positive that we took a correct line in stipulating an economic union within the CIS framework, a single ruble zone with Russia, and a coordinated customs legislation. This will give our people the possibility to live and work in a civilized manner.[21]

[20] Shushkevich was, and still is, a true believer in the need for CIS economic union. He reasserted this position in a talk at Harvard University in May 2000.

[21] Minsk *Respublika* 31 December 1993, p. 2. Speech by Prime Minister Kebich to the diplomatic corps (FBIS translation).

Kebich was particularly keen on integration with Russia, arguing later that union was "the only way to save the Belarusian economy" and that the two states were so closely integrated that they "cannot exist without one another."[22] Kebich noted that if monetary union were not to take place, "our enterprises will simply collapse."[23]

Although Kebich was defeated in the July 1994 elections, and most of his government was replaced by the new president, Aleksandr Lukashenko, the new government was also integralist. Indeed, aside from the Belarusian Popular Front candidate, all of the candidates in the 1994 elections favored some form of economic integration with Russia and justified their positions in integralist terms. Moreover, the Popular Front candidate, Zyanon Paznyak, received only 12.9% of the votes in the first round and did not advance to the second. Lukashenko received the largest percentage of the vote in the first round (44.8%) and handily defeated Kebich in the second, earning 80.1% of the votes. Integration was also a strong plank of Lukashenko's campaign, and his credibility was reinforced by the fact that he had been the sole member of the Belarusian Supreme Soviet to vote against the ratification of the Viskuli accord that dissolved the Soviet Union and created the CIS. What apparently distinguished the two candidates were that Lukashenko successfully presented himself as a corruption fighter and Kebich prevented all other major political figures from running.

Only two months after the election, Lukashenko's prime minister, Mikhail Chygyr, gave an interview upon his return from the CIS summit at which the Interstate Economic Commission was formed, and at which the Belarusian delegation was a strong advocate for greater union:

I have an impression that everyone has begun to understand: We must overcome the current situation together. Attempts to overcome the economic crisis separately have collapsed, and, as of today, none of the former USSR republics can claim positive economic results.... I think that there is no other way. To achieve something real, we need to unify into one mechanism that economic organism which we broke up some time ago.[24]

Deputy Prime Minister Mikhail Miasnikovich, who went on to become the Belarusian prime minister in 1996, made similar comments and voiced the sentiment that the IMF was trying to prevent the union with Russia.[25]

---

[22] Radio Minsk Network in Belarusian 1700 GMT 12 January 1994.
[23] Radio Minsk Network in Belarusian 1700 GMT 12 January 1994.
[24] Belinform interview with Prime Minister Chygyr published in Minsk *Zvyazda* in Belarusian 13 September 1994, p. 1.
[25] Interview with Mikhail Miasnikovich, Moscow *Rossiyskaia Gazeta* in Russian 17 September 1994 first edition p. 6.

The new minister of foreign economic relations voiced no such views, however, and explicitly argued that Belarus would give equal treatment to all partners and would accord no special status to relations with post-Soviet states.[26]

The government arrived at a consistent integralist "party line" by the beginning of 1995, however. From this point onward, Lukashenko was consistent in his arguments that the salvation of the Belarusian economy required closer ties with the former Soviet republics.

Lukashenko, unlike Kebich, could not embellish the underlying set of organic principles with the skill of a Soviet economist, but his practical understanding of the economy clearly arose from the integralist framework. When asked by an interviewer about the relationship between the "economic lives of people" and integration, Lukashenko responded:

Let me cite an example. Do we need clothes? We do. Are there weavers in Ivanovo [a Russian city that was center of Soviet textiles]? There are. They have not moved anywhere. There is also the cotton combine in Baranavichi which produces cotton yarn for Ivanovo weavers, textile factories in Belarus, and the like. Can Russia and Belarus reach agreement with Uzbekistan [a major Soviet cotton grower], in line with which the Baranavichi cotton combine would produce yarn for Ivanovo weavers who would produce fabric for us? Why did we destroy the links that were typical of our economy? This is an example of living integration at the economic level. Why do we not do that? At this point Russian agriculture does not have tractors – the principal agricultural machines. Why? Can we not engage the Minsk Tractor Plant to produce tractors for farmers in Voronezh Oblast or in the Don area, where they are badly needed? Why is it that the Americans buy batches of Minsk tractors? I repeat: batches. Do Russia and Belarus not need them? They do. This is concrete integration.[27]

The example of the Ivanovo textile region was commonly employed by integralists as a paradigm of the type of productive interdependence that they believe was destroyed with the collapse of the USSR.[28] In the preceding typical statement, Lukashenko looked to the revival of "the links that were typical of our economy" as a means to escape the crisis. "Living integration at the economic level" was his recipe for ending the lifelessness of the economic collapse. These are the hallmarks of integralist thinking in the "vernacular" form that was commonly expressed.

[26] Interview with Foreign Economic Relations Minister Mikhail Marynich by Uladzimir Hoytan; place and date not given: "Mikhail Marynich: 'Terms Like Far versus Near Abroad Are Obsolete. There Is Only Abroad'" Minsk *Zvyazda* in Belarusian 27 September 1994, pp. 1–2.

[27] Minsk BTK Television Network in Belarusian, 11 December 1996.

[28] This same example was noted in several interviews with officials in the Interstate Economic Commission of the CIS. Author's interviews R17, R18, R20.

Clearly, other members of Lukashenko's cabinet shared this vision of the economy. Note the excerpt from an interview with the minister for CIS affairs:

[Minister] . . . I would like to recall those good things existing in the past: division of labor, cooperation and specialization within the framework of a single national economy. I think it is necessary now to restore that division of labor – providing it brings practical advantages to Belarus and Russia. Therefore, the treaty [the Community Treaty between Russia and Belarus of 1996] provides for the creation of single economic complexes.

The point is in combining the interests of both parties, as well as improving and modernizing their scientific, technical, and production potential. There is no need to organize production capacities that will duplicate one another [cf. irrational parallelism]; it is necessary to rationally use the existing capacities. Such an approach undoubtedly serves Belarus' interests.

[Interviewer] Does this refer to bilateral relations or those within the CIS?

[Minister] This also refers to the CIS as a whole. Look: Russia has not been able to revitalize the Lipetsk Tractor Plant; Uzbekistan has not been able to make its cotton-picking equipment competitive (tractors made according to a technology from the Minsk Tractor Plant with the Minsk D-240 engine and assembled in Uzbekistan are lower in quality than those produced in Minsk). Is it not simpler to return to cooperation with the Minsk Tractor Plant which today has a program for producing new tractors? I think that such problems will be seriously considered at the meeting of CIS heads of governments on 12 April – when it is planned to adopt a unified program of agricultural machine building in the Commonwealth [of Independent States].[29]

Lukashenko went through three prime ministers between 1994 and 2000, but each was an integralist. Thus, in Belarus, leaders changed between 1991 and 2000, but all shared a common integralist understanding of the economy, and Belarus remained one of the strongest supporters of CIS economic institutions during this period.

Institutional and Policy Choice

Belarusian economic policies and choices of institutional membership conform tightly to expectations from the integralist ideal-type. The Belarusian government has been the most ardent advocate of regional institutions among the post-Soviet states. The country has the best record of all of the

[29] Minsk *Respublika* in Russian, 10 April 1996, p. 2. Interview with Ivan Bambiza, Belarusian minister for CIS affairs, by Andrey Patrebin; place and date not given: "The Point Is in Rationally Combining Interests."

post-Soviet states in signing and implementing CIS economic agreements and has been a party to every major regional institution. Belarus was one of the last countries to leave the ruble zone and, under the Kebich government, tried to establish a bilateral currency union with Russia immediately after the zone collapsed. In 1993, Belarus was an active supporter of the Economic Union Treaty and subsequently became a strong supporter behind IEC, backing each effort to give the institution greater authority and scope of activity. The country was a founding member of the Customs Union with Russia and Kazakhstan in January 1995 and a founding member of the union that resulted from the Treaty on Deepening Integration in 1996. In May 1995, Lukashenko put forward a referendum seeking further backing for union with Russia, which passed by a large margin, and in 1996, Belarus signed a Union Treaty with Russia that has progressed whenever the Russian side has shown a willingness to pursue greater integration. In 1999, Belarus formed the Eurasian Union with Kazakhstan, Russia, Kyrgyzstan, and Tajikistan.

In terms of WTO accession, Belarus has made only halting progress. Belarus applied for membership in September 1993, shortly after Russia submitted its application, but did not follow through with its Memorandum on Foreign Trade until three years later. After a few meetings of the Working Group in 1996, 1997, and 1998, there were no further meetings until March 2001.

In energy policy, the Belarusian government has not made any attempts to diversify the country's sources of supply, which are almost entirely imported from Russia. Nor has there been any effort to cut down on energy use as a means of limiting dependence. The Belarusian government has also blocked proposals by neighboring states to create a Baltic–to–Black Sea energy corridor that would bypass Russia and give the country alternative sources of supply.[30] Rather, the Belarusian government has increased its ties to Russia by transferring ownership of the country's major gas storage facilities and pipeline network to Russia's Gazprom in exchange for a write-off of its debts. The government has also provided for the construction of a new gas export pipeline to the West across its territory. Moreover, Belarus pays for its debt in complex international barter arrangements that allow Soviet-era industries to continue their production in exchange for energy supplies. All of this has served to preserve Soviet-era industrial ties. The privatization of large-scale enterprises has yet to take place in Belarus, but

---

[30] The active participation of Belarus in this alternative energy supply network was part of the Belarusian National Front Party platform. Author's interview B7.

as with its gas network, the Belarusian government has been eager to form joint stock companies and financial–industrial groups in which shares are held by post-Soviet governments or enterprises, in particular those in Russia and Kazakhstan.

In macroeconomic policy, the Belarusian government pursued a policy in which credits are directed toward Soviet-era enterprises through banks that charge interest rates significantly lower than the rate of inflation, effectively a subsidy. This led to budget deficits throughout the 1990s that were financed by printing currency to meet obligations, a declining ruble, and repeated efforts to slow inflation using state pressure to limit price increases and legally mandated price controls. For a brief period in 1994 there was some financial tightening, but shortly thereafter presidential control over the Central Bank was established, and the head of the bank imprisoned, and all efforts to limit support for the country's Soviet-era industrial complex were abandoned. As a result, Belarus has retained its Soviet-era industrial foci, and industrial production has even grown in the country since 1996.

UKRAINE

In Ukraine, more so than in Russia and Belarus, power remained divided between the president and the parliament throughout the 1990s. The division favored the presidency, but the Ukrainian parliament managed to retain some of its authority after independence. Parliamentary support was required for the appointment of a new prime minister, the adoption of tariffs, and the drafting and approval of the budget. For this reason, the ideas of the parliamentary majority – when it existed – must be examined. At the same time, parliament's role was significantly limited by the fact that the body needed a two-thirds majority to overrule any presidential decree. So long as the president held sway over a significant minority in parliament, he was effectively able to rule by decree.[31] For this reason, the ideas of the president and the government must be given precedence.

Economic Ideas

Ukraine had two presidents prior to 2000. From 1991 to 1994, under Leonid Kravchuk, the primary economic logic behind the government's policy was mercantilist.[32] As stated in an economic policy paper

---

[31] Interview with parliamentary representative, U2.
[32] According to Dawisha and Parrott, the ideas behind Ukrainian government policies were that "political independence and economic reform can be safeguarded only if Ukraine uncouples

drawn on by Kravchuk entitled "The Catastrophic Consequences of Temporizing Economic Policy," the purpose of government policy was to "guarantee the impossibility of drawing Ukraine into...the restoration of a 'single national-economic complex.'"[33] The operative mercantilist logic – economic interdependence is a threat to the nation – was reflected in a statement by Ivan Plyushch, the chairman of the Supreme Soviet, in 1992:

At present our economy is not a national one. And that is the chief cause for all of our misfortunes. So long as it is not a national one, we will not have normal relations with a single republic. Incidentally, we never had relations, but rather direct dependence and "'diktat." Relations have not existed between Ukraine and Russia since 1654.[34] What kind of relations can there be if I am dependent, if I am a part of the other, and if a great number of structures have been created over me to make me dependent?[35]

The nationalist government blamed "imperial exploitation" for all of Ukraine's contemporary economic troubles and claimed that self-sufficiency was the key to economic revival. In these years, the government claimed that Ukraine could be self-sufficient in energy and that Soviet-era imports were designed to make Ukraine dependent on Russia.[36]

During these crisis years there was tremendous turnover among government officials responsible for the economy. The Ukrainian prime minister was replaced three times between 1992 and mid-1994, and the government was reshuffled even more frequently. Beginning with the appointment of Leonid Kuchma in October 1993, the Ukrainian prime ministers serving under Kravchuk were integralists from the eastern strongholds of Soviet power, Donetsk and Dniepropetrovsk. Thus, the Ukrainian government is best coded as consistently mercantilist only until October 1993, after which the integralists sustained a strong minority within the government. Unlike in Russia or the Baltic states, liberals in Ukraine had almost no role in government decision making in the early independence period.

itself economically from Russia." Karen Dawisha and Bruce Parrott, eds., *The End of Empire? The Transformation of the USSR in Comparative Perspective* (New York: M. E. Sharpe, 1997), p. 177.

33 Cited in Mikhail Leontyev, "Couponization at a Faster Rate: The First Concept of Ukrainian Economic Reform," *Nezavisimaia Gazeta*, Moscow, 1 April 1992, p. 1. FBIS-USR-92-045.

34 In the year 1654 the Pereislav treaty subordinated the Zaporozhian Host (on the territory of what is today Ukraine) to Muscovy.

35 Interview with Ivan Plyushch, *Golos Ukrainy*, 18 March 1992 (FBIS translation). FBIS-USR-92-040-072.

36 Olexiy Kirichenko "Moving Forward into the Past," *The Ukrainian Panorama* 1 (1997): 2.

A major shift in the governing elite took place with the parliamentary and presidential elections held in spring and summer 1994.[37] In the parliamentary elections, integralist themes featured prominently in the campaigns of those parties that performed well. Integralist parties advocating regional integration gained 60.5% of the seats.[38]

In Ukraine, however, as in most other post-Soviet states, the president plays the most important role in selecting the government; thus the presidential elections were far more significant to the future of government policy. During the campaign, Leonid Kuchma presented a popularized version of basic integralist tenets. Regional integration was put forward as a cure-all for the woes of the economy. Responding, for example, on a national broadcast three days before the run-off election to the question of how he would fight unemployment, Kuchma responded that "most important, we need economic integration with all the republics of the former Soviet Union and Eastern Europe. We need to dismantle all customs barriers."[39]

In speaking of his support for economic union with Russia during the campaign, Kuchma stated:

I understand the economic union with Russia as economic cooperation – equal and good-neighborly cooperation. This is the main thing, because throughout the entire history of Soviet power we have been developing together. Our plants, our enterprises, depend on one another in many areas. We were receiving raw materials from there, and components were being shipped from here. These flows – these *arteries*, as they say – have existed for more than 70 years. So, even from this point of view – to say nothing about our 1,000-year-long history – we must cooperate with our great neighbor.... As far as economic cooperation is concerned, I would like to say that today any country's national economy is unable to survive on its own. The future of any country, including Ukraine, is in macroeconomic transnational associations. We must work tirelessly for the creation of financial-industrial groups

---

[37] Economic ideas were very salient in these elections. The central political cleavage in both elections, the first elections following the collapse of the USSR, was over the issue of whether full national independence or some form of more integrated economic union with the former Soviet republics was the more desirable future course.

[38] This is the combined figure for the Communists, Socialists, Agrarians, Edinstvo (Unity), and Interregional Bloc. A direct tally of support is difficult to determine because the electoral laws were not conducive to party affiliation, and more than 60% of the candidates elected in the first round were officially unaffiliated. However, on the basis of a study of candidate programs and press reports, Wilson concludes that nationalists, who in terms of their economic views were a mix of liberals and mercantilists, garnered approximately 24% of the seats, as opposed to 43.5% (147 seats) for the Communists, Socialists, and Agrarians.

[39] Kiev Radio Ukraine World Service in Ukrainian 1830 GMT 7 July 1994. Studio phone-in program with President Leonid Kravchuk and former prime minister Leonid Kuchma, candidates in the 10 July run-off presidential election, moderated by Zynoviy Kulyk; from the *Hot Line* program – live (FBIS translation).

with the countries of the East and the West, with all those who wish to cooperate with us in a normal manner. I again underline that this is the future, because self-isolation leads to unpredictable consequences and, in principle, to self-destruction of one's own economy.[40]

Here, as elsewhere, Kuchma draws on integralist reasoning, stressing the historical economic and cultural "arteries" that connect Ukraine and Russia and criticizing the previous government's policy of mercantilist autarky as leading to "self-isolation" and "self-destruction." Kuchma won the election handily, with 52% to Kravchuk's 45%.[41]

Given the content of Kuchma's campaign and the popular mandate of the election victory there was every reason to think that Ukraine would have an integralist-minded governing elite not significantly different from the one in neighboring Belarus.[42] And following the elections, it indeed appeared that a shift to an integralist elite was about to take place. Kuchma retained as prime minister Yevgenii Masol, a former high-level Soviet official.[43] Masol clearly thought about the economic situation faced by Ukraine in integralist terms:

Who today will dare to deny that the catastrophic crash of the economy has been caused primarily by destroying — to satisfy the political ambitions of nearby leaders — the single economic complex that had been formed in the Soviet Union, by the collapse of the single currency, financial, transport, and energy space, by dismantling mutually advantageous economic, scientific, and other ties between enterprises and

---

[40] Ibid. (emphasis added).

[41] The Kuchma victory is all the more significant given the announcement on the day before the run-off election that the G-7 had approved a $5 billion aid package to Ukraine. The national television coverage linked the money to Kravchuk's presidency and conspicuously failed to note that the $4 billion package was a complex of loans rather than grants to be released over a long period. Kiev UT-1 Television Network in Ukrainian 1600 GMT 9 July 1994 (FBIS translation). As Wilson puts it, "The choice facing voters was characterized in the starkest terms and Kravchuk lost." Wilson, *Ukrainian Nationalism*, p. 145.

[42] On the basis of Kuchma's personal background, voters would be expected to believe that these campaign statements were made in earnest. Kuchma in many respects fit the profile of a candidate who would have the strongest commitment to CIS economic integration. He was from the Soviet-nationalized East (Kravchuk was from the former Polish province of Volhynia). He was the general director of one of the leading Soviet rocket production facilities, hence a creature of the military-industrial complex. Kuchma was also the president of the Ukrainian Union of Industrialists and Entrepreneurs, an organization (linked to others like it throughout the former Soviet Union) for which the reintegration of the Soviet economic complexes was a central goal. All of these biographical elements, as well as Kuchma's pro-CIS actions during his stint as prime minister, signaled to the voter that a Kuchma presidency would produce economic integration with Russia and the other post-Soviet states.

[43] Masol was chairman of the Council of Ministers of the Ukrainian SSR before being forced to resign by the nationalist student protests in 1990.

organizations, which after the destruction of the single Soviet state ended up in different countries, henceforth divided by borders, which were initially proclaimed "invisible," but in reality are becoming increasingly tighter and more impenetrable. According to various estimates, close to 60 percent of the production decline in the CIS countries is directly attributable to this cause. There is nothing odd about this if we take into consideration that in Ukraine, for example, only 20 percent of all industrial enterprises had a closed production cycle. No matter what lofty considerations are cited to justify the policy of self-isolation and the separation of former republics of the USSR from one another, the price that our peoples are forced to pay for this shortsighted policy is much too high to allow us to regard this unfolding of events as normal.

. . . Where else in the world do you find countries that deliberately destroy cooperation and integration that had taken many decades to establish? One might well ask: why utterly destroy something that has already been built, that worked successfully, that – despite all its flaws – justified its existence, multiplied our forces, made it possible to create on a vast territory a mighty industrial, scientific, and defense complex, which served the interests of all the republics and their peoples and reliably defended a large country? Was it not possible to overhaul gradually and in a civilized manner the ties and relations that already existed, without upheavals and destruction, making them more effective and more mutually advantageous? Would this have hindered the consolidation of their sovereignty by the new states?[44]

The key elements of integralist thinking are all present here. However, in a very short period the position of the government changed. Kuchma, after disappearing from the public eye shortly after the elections, returned to deliver a speech in Ukrainian rather than his usual Russian, much to the dismay of his supporters in the Russian-speaking regions. The key foreign economic policymaking portfolios were handed to officials of a distinct anti-integralist stripe. The incoming foreign minister, Gennady Udovenko,[45] employing "anti-imperialist" mercantilist language, asserted that Russia would no longer be the "big brother" to Ukraine.[46] The new deputy minister of foreign economic relations, Sergei Osyka, stated in interviews that early entry into the WTO was in Ukraine's best interests, noting that this was one of the main conditions for receiving Western financial aid (not, however, that freer trade was directly good for the economy).[47] While the portfolio of the Ministries of Economy and Industry were placed in the hands of

[44] Masol, "New Policy."

[45] Udovenko is from the western part of Ukraine that was once part of Austria.

[46] Moscow *Interfax* in English 1559 GMT 26 August 1994; Moscow ITAR-TASS in English 1218 GMT 7 September 1994.

[47] Interview with Serhiy Osyka, deputy minister of foreign economic relations of Ukraine, special representative of Ukraine for issues of joining GATT, Kiev *Holos Ukraiyny* in Ukrainian 2 August 1994, p. 3.

integralist economic managers, these ministries came to have decreasing influence over foreign economic policy.[48]

The intragovernmental division between integralists and mercantilists came to a head in September 1994 as negotiations were under way concerning the creation of the CIS Economic Union and the transfer of decision-making authority to the CIS Interstate Economic Commission (IEC). In discussions on the formation of the IEC, Prime Minister Masol argued that participation in the IEC and economic union were necessary for entering the Russian market.[49] Similarly, the deputy minister of economy explained that there should be no apprehensions that the IEC would become a "supranational" body akin to the former Soviet State Planning Commission, because "everything depends on the powers to be vested in the Commission by each of the countries, and it will act within the framework of these powers."[50] When it came time for the heads of state to sign the agreement, however, Ukraine signed only with appended "reservations" that effectively voided the agreement.[51] In interviews conducted in 1997, respondents noted that the impetus behind the decision to reject any transfer of decision-making authority away from the national level had been made by the presidential administration and the Foreign Ministry, not the prime minister.[52]

This ideational split within the government can be seen in interviews published at the time, in which Prime Minister Masol continued to focus on broken economic ties and the harm that the collapse of the Soviet Union had done to the Ukrainian economy, while Foreign Minister Udovenko took every opportunity to undercut this position. For example, upon returning from an official visit to Kazakhstan, Masol noted, in typical integralist fashion, that the Ukrainian electrical industry relied on supply links established with Kazakhstan under the Soviet system and that the Kazakhs needed diesel locomotives from an idle Ukrainian plant in Luhansk.[53] Less than a week later, however, Foreign Minister Udovenko, speaking of the same plant, noted that "the old ties must not be mechanically restored. In Luhansk, for instance, there is a diesel locomotive construction plant which had suppliers in 800 cities in the former Union. Needless to say it is unprofitable to

---

[48] Personal communication, Lucan Way, World Bank consultant, Ukraine, August 1997; interview U15.

[49] Kiev Radio Ukraine World Service in Ukrainian 1500 GMT 10 September 1994.

[50] Kiev Radio Ukraine World Service in Ukrainian 1500 GMT 10 September 1994.

[51] Kiev Radio Ukraine World Service in Ukrainian 1500 GMT 10 September 1994.

[52] Interview U2.

[53] Kiev UT-1 Television Network in Ukrainian 1600 GMT 18 September 1994.

import screws for it from the Far East [Russia and Kazakhstan]."[54] This is characteristic of the divisions in the government between mercantilist elites with foreign-policy portfolios, including the Ministry of Foreign Economic Relations, and the integralist industrial ministries.

The Foreign Ministry began to have increasing influence over foreign economic policy toward the end of 1994. Foreign Ministry officials repeatedly stated that the CIS countries were important as export markets, given that Western markets "had already been divided up."[55] Production ties, however, were to be national in scope rather than rely on old Soviet ties. New production facilities were to be financed by Western aid that the officials in the Foreign Ministry thought would be forthcoming because Ukraine was a "great power" and a valued European partner of the West, in particular the United States.[56]

By March 1995, the ideational shift toward mercantilism was formalized when Prime Minister Masol was replaced by Yevhen Marchuk. Marchuk was a career KGB officer with no training in economics, but his speeches reflect mercantilist views.[57] Pockets of integralist-minded elites remained in the Ministries of Economy and Industry, but these organs had little influence over key policymaking matters.[58]

Several months after taking office, Marchuk presented the government's new economic policy, worked out by the Council of Ministers, with the assistance of Ukrainian academics. The document laid out an agenda entailing autarkic national control of industry with no privatization to foreigners, import substitution, the restriction of raw-material exports, closed-cycle national production in the form of state-sponsored monopolies, and greater state control over foreign exchange. The plan, delivered as a speech by Marchuk, both was indicative of the mercantilist thinking among the top Ukrainian policymaking elite during the 1990s and was itself an important statement of the country's economic policy doctrine under Kuchma.[59]

A central theme of the new economic policy was that Ukraine was unique, that general economic theories did not apply to the country, and that the

---

[54] Hennady Udovenko, Moscow *Rossiyskaia Gazeta* in Russian 24 September 1994, p. 6.
[55] Hennady Udovenko, Moscow *Rossiyskaia Gazeta* in Russian 24 September 1994, p. 6.
[56] Interview with Foreign Minister Gennady Udovenko in *Uryadovnyy Kuryer* (Kiev) in Ukrainian, 10 August 1996, p. 6.
[57] There was some suggestion that Masol's replacement was linked to an effort to gain IMF aid. Just over a week after the change in prime Minister, IMF Managing Director Michel Camdessus announced that a $1.492 billion credit would be appropriated to Ukraine.
[58] Interview U15.
[59] The source for Marchuk's speech is Radio Ukraine World Service, Kiev, in Ukrainian, 16 September 1995 (FBIS translation). Hereafter, Marchuk, 1995.

country had to develop its own self-sufficient economy with limited external involvement.[60]

State controls were a central feature of the Marchuk economic program, and while critical of both integralist and market liberal tenets, the prime minister reserved particular invective for the latter for calling for the retreat of the state from the economic life of the nation. Marchuk criticized the "market blitzkrieg, intended to generate and accelerate self-regulating economic processes by using and demonstrating the laws of a classic market economy" as "premature" and described monetarist policies as "pseudo-market dogma."

> I would like to say that, unfortunately, in the recent past there was a phenomenon that could be described as restriction of the state's influence on the economy. It was believed at the time that a self-regulating free market would fix all problems at once in the best possible way.... That is, the state should not either help or interfere with the so-called invisible hand of the market. The other extreme was the overt or covert desire to restore the command system. Both brought nothing but chaos and destruction to the economy.[61]

In contrast to integralism, which also reserves an important role for the state, the Marchuk program focused on using the state to foster economic self-sufficiency and to remove the country from the Soviet division of labor. Marchuk's team argued that in all cases of successful economic reform, "the intention primarily was to feed and clothe their country on their own as a precondition for other nationwide in-depth reforms to take place" with "precedence given to support for goods manufacture and the stimulation of agriculture."[62] The plan argued that import substitution and state aid to key industries would provide "a boost to a whole productive complex and stimulate closed cycles of cooperation."[63]

In the field of foreign economic relations, the government saw inherent conflict with other states. As opposed to the mutually beneficial trade relations seen by liberals or the efficient monopolistic regional specialization envisioned by integralists, Ukraine's national–mercantilist government

---

[60] The Marchuk plan, ironically, mimicked the mercantilist Uzbek policy program drafted two years prior. Marchuk's speech stressed the need to seek out "our own, Ukrainian, model of market reforms," modeled on a favorite expression of Uzbek president Islam Karimov. Note the title of one of Karimov's books: *Building the Future: Uzbekistan – Its Own Model for the Transition to a Market Economy*.

[61] Marchuk, 1995.

[62] Ibid.

[63] Ibid.

assumed that the "objective" reality of economics is that relations are zero-sum and inherently conflictual. According to Marchuk:

[It is a] well-known fact that no foreign economic environment is favorable towards any new partners, which is an objective economic law. There is severe competition and the customary protectionism and lobbyism there.... It would be logical to expect that [the foreign economic environment] will attempt to suppress and convert to its own use the economy of Ukraine, which, [is] an objective characteristic of economics.[64]

Consistently with mercantilist ideas, the government's economic program advocated protectionist customs tariffs on the import of "goods which can be produced in sufficient quantities at home," as well as restrictive tariffs on the export of "raw materials badly needed by domestic industry."[65] Moreover, state controls were to be implemented to stop "the spread of the black market to the export of domestic capital," which was "drawing blood from the national currency market and monetary system."

In discussing the government's "antimonopoly policy" Marchuk makes the goal of creating/preserving monopolistic national complexes explicit:

The enterprises most capable of breaking through to Western markets are highly-concentrated large enterprises and associations, which, due to their scale and technological support, are almost always... monopolists. It is economically inexpedient, and even dangerous, to tear apart or disperse these complexes into mini-enterprises, and to disintegrate their potential, personifying the state's highest priority scientific, technical and other possibilities. It is extremely important to preserve these production structures as a national achievement, and they should be under the government's care. Precisely in this context of combating monopolism, the government is ready to and will actively cooperate with the Anti-Monopoly Committee, striving for maximum support for goods production by joint efforts.[66]

Thus, the national "anti-monopoly" policy is designed to promote the maintenance of the national monopolies.

In sum, the Marchuk economic plan was a clear expression of mercantilist thinking. Despite the fact that Kuchma replaced Prime Minister Marchuk in May 1996, the main orientation of the government remained primarily mercantilist. Marchuk's successor, Pavlo Lazarenko, was, like Kuchma, a corrupt official from the Brezhnev-era stronghold of Dniepropetrovsk, but he consistently expressed mercantilist views, both during his tenure as prime

[64] Ibid.
[65] All quotations in this paragraph are from Marchuk, 1995.
[66] Ibid.

minister and as head of the Hromada bloc in parliament after his dismissal from his government post.

Interviews conducted in Ukraine in summer 1997 also reflected the strength of mercantilists in the government, although there were small but generally weak groups of integralists and a few liberals notable in interviews in less influential ministries and in the Verkhovna Rada, the Ukrainian parliament. Western economic officials dealing with the government on a regular basis made note of these divisions in informal interviews and often remarked that the government had difficulty pursuing coherent policies.[67] It was often the case that different parts of the government worked at cross-purposes.[68]

Interviews suggested that the presidential administration and the Foreign Ministry were strongholds of mercantilist views, and these two institutions played the critical role in the formulation of economic policy.[69] A close economic adviser to President Leonid Kuchma from the presidential administration cited "Russian imperial tendencies" as a cause for Ukraine's economic troubles.[70] The representative in the Foreign Ministry responsible for economic affairs, a native of the western Ukrainian city of Lvov, spoke similarly and cited Russia's sugar tariffs and increased natural gas prices as examples of Russian efforts to punish Ukraine for its independence.[71] Even the accountants in the Finance Ministry explained that economic ties with Russia were complicated by Russia's "imperial tendencies" and blamed Russia's sugar tariffs and value-added taxes for many of Ukraine's economic problems.[72] These officials also noted that all decisions on financing regional institutions were made by the Ministry of Foreign Affairs – hence the ideas of the Ministry of Foreign Affairs were very significant in the Ukrainian case.[73]

The notion that mercantilist ideas held sway in the Ukrainian government was reinforced by other Ukrainian officials, who did not share the mercantilist viewpoint and considered themselves isolated from the country's

---

[67] Interviews U11, U14, U15, U20.

[68] This was particularly noted by an IMF resident representative.

[69] Interviews U1, U3, U19.

[70] Interview U1. But when asked to provide details or examples, none came to mind.

[71] Prices charged to Ukraine for gas are lower than world market prices and than prices Russia charges for shipments to Western Europe. Ukraine is generally incapable of payment.

[72] Interviews U17, U4, U5.

[73] Finance Ministry officials also stated that some CIS organs are financed directly out of the ministerial budgets, over which the Ministry of Finance (and Ministry of Foreign Affairs) have no control. The officials said that the Coal Ministry and the Electrical Energy Ministries both financed the CIS organs relevant to them out of their own budgets. Interviews U5, U17.

decision-making process. A prominent Ukrainian economic figure noted that among Ukrainian industrialists, a belief that closer ties with the post-Soviet states were needed to pull the country out of economic crisis was widespread, but that the presidency, the Ministry of Foreign Affairs, and the military prevented such ties from re-forming.[74] The respondent expressed the idea that economic policy flowed directly out of the "political" ministries and that these cadres had an interest in Ukraine's remaining independent of the CIS. The result, he said, was a CIS economy where "you previously had one system, where one part of that system produced for all the others, now you have the beginnings of 'double production' in Ukraine, where the country is trying to provide all things for itself."[75] Integralist members of parliament also expressed concern over the course of Ukrainian economic policy but substantiated the claim that the policy was governed by mercantilist ideas.[76]

After July 1997, with the appointment of Valery Pustovoitenko, there was some indication that integralist ideas appeared to have gained ground within the government. Pustovoitenko's public statements were consistently integralist, although given that polls indicate that integralist ideas were quite popular in the country it is difficult to determine whether this was simply an effort to curry favor for an unpopular government in the lead-up to critical elections in 1998 and 1999. Nonetheless, islands of integralist thinking had clearly persisted within the government, primarily at the subministerial level within the economic and industrial ministries.[77] Such groups participated regularly in the institutions of the CIS Economic Union although Ukraine is not formally a member, and often used money from their budgets to support CIS projects and institutions.

The parliament also became divided at this time, but integralists remained the most strongly represented. In the 1998 parliamentary elections, parties espousing integralist views again performed well. The Communists secured

---

[74] This respondent cited a survey done by a market research company in 1993 asking people whether they thought Russia was a potential enemy or a friendly relation. Among the general population, 20% saw Russia as a potential enemy, 80% thought a friend. Among government officials, however, 66% thought Russia was a potential enemy and 34% thought a potential friend. (There was no way to verify the survey results cited by the respondent.) Interview U19.

[75] Interview U19.

[76] Interview U2.

[77] For example, the deputy minister in charge of military production noted in an interview that multinational FIGs with post-Soviet partners were necessary to providing the investment and production links needed to save the industry. Such sentiments were common at the lower levels of government even in 1997 when I conducted my interviews in Kiev. Kiev *Vechirniy Kyyiv* in Ukrainian, 30 May 1995, p 2.

the largest share of the vote in voting for party lists (which determined half of the seats in the 450-seat Rada). Combined with the single-mandate districts, the Communists had a total of 123 members elected and the Socialist-Peasant Party bloc, 34 members. This was despite considerable efforts by the presidential administration to undermine these two parties.[78] The result, however, was a parliament so ideologically divided that on most critical issues it was paralyzed. Indeed, it took eight weeks of debate and 20 rounds of voting, during which some 90 candidates were presented, before the Rada finally elected (integralist) Oleksander Tkachenko of the Peasant Party as its chairman.

Kuchma's own views during this time are difficult to discern, as his comments varied according to the audience he addressed. On Russian television he stressed that he was committed to integration, but that the Russian side had frustrated his efforts. Before Western audiences he stressed his commitment to the European Union, noting on one occasion that Ukraine was the last to "free itself from a colonial regime and join other European nations who ditched Communism," and stating that Ukraine's "strategic goal is to become a full-fledged member of the European Union."[79]

As the 1990s wore on, liberal ideas began to make some inroads into the government. Ukraine was the beneficiary of numerous training programs for midcareer officials, an active Western diaspora, and copious amounts of Western aid designed to promote liberal ideas and policies within the administration. As a result, pockets of liberal-minded elites existed in the Ministry of Finance and the National Bank.[80] At sporadic moments these groups were able to influence certain aspects of government policy. They had the support of liberal international institutions, which allowed them some influence over policy, usually in the run-up to decisions of Western creditors on the release of further loan tranches.

In 1998, the liberal Boris Tarasiuk replaced Gennady Udovenko in the powerful Ministry of Foreign Affairs, but the critical shift in favor of the liberals occurred with the appointment of Victor Yushchenko as prime minister

---

[78] See Organization for Security and Cooperation in Europe (OSCE), Office for Democratic Institutions and Human Rights (ODIHR) report for the 1998 Ukrainian Parliamentary Elections.

[79] Moscow *Interfax* in English, 1552 GMT 23 April 1996.

[80] Note, for example, that the finance minister's solution to the economic crisis closely follows the market-liberal maxims propagated by the Western institutions: economic stabilization begins with financial stabilization. Without financial stabilization it is impossible to end the decline in production, increase the level of the population's income, and revive investment activities. Kiev *Intelnews* in English, 0806 GMT 11 December 1995, interview with Finance Minister Petro Hermanchuk.

in December 1999. Yushchenko had previously headed the National Bank, a liberal stronghold that had been heavily influenced by daily contact with the IMF representative. Yushchenko himself was a trained economist, served as the country's representative to liberal institutions such as the IMF and the EBRD, and had considerable contact with the West; his wife was an American citizen. Yushchenko was brought in immediately after Kuchma had secured the presidency through a rigged election in November 1999, was given broad scope to set Ukrainian economic policy, and collected a liberal team to run the government. Thus, liberal ideas were predominant in the government until Yushchenko was forced to resign in May 2001.

Institutional and Policy Choice

With mercantilist forces primarily in control of the government and integralists prevailing in parliament, Ukrainian institutional choices and economic policies reflect the enduring role of illiberal economic ideas in the country throughout much of the decade. For much of the 1990s, Ukrainian policy was primarily autarkic, as reflected in high tariffs, soft credits to industry, and resistance to privatization of the large enterprises. As the economy was the most industrialized and diversified in the former Soviet Union after Russia's, there was no need to create additional industrial capacity. The mercantilist strategy can thus be seen in the efforts to maintain the existing industrial capacity but to make it autonomous from prior Soviet partners.

In terms of foreign economic relations and institutional membership, Ukraine has had a somewhat unambiguous trajectory. In the early 1990s, Ukraine was one of the most closed economies in the region, but it has undergone a limited process of opening. In the initial independence period, under President Leonid Kravchuk and Prime Minister Vitold Fokin, the country maintained a terrible record with interstate economic contracts, not delivering goods that it had promised to other CIS states while still receiving subsidized imports in "exchange."[81] In 1992 and 1993, Ukraine had comprehensive export quotas covering virtually all products and licenses applied to all exports except manufactures. By the end of 1993, quotas were reduced to cover only 285 goods, but this still amounted to approximately 60% of the country's export value. In May 1994, quotas were limited to 104 goods – still 30% of export value – but import tariffs into the country were progressively increased throughout the decade until they gradually began to

---

[81] As these were government contracts, and the government controlled the country's enterprises, this can be seen as a matter of policy.

be reduced in 1999. Before a new law in 1999 capped the tariff levels at 25%, Ukrainian tariffs ranged from 5% to 200% and excise taxes from 10% to 300%.[82] Even as late as 2000, however, Ukraine sustained a complicated tariff structure with more than 10,000 distinct tariff lines. This allowed the government to target protective measures toward specific goods that were produced in Ukraine while overall maintaining a somewhat lower average tariff. A new law in 2001 reduced the maximal tariff further to 20%, but throughout the 1990s, Ukraine remained one of the most closed economies in the region.

Specific trade relations with Russia and other CIS countries are complicated and opaque. The majority of Ukraine's trade throughout this period was conducted with other post-Soviet states, and well into the middle of the decade, Ukraine was still conducting a significant amount of its trade through state contracts and bilateral agreements – which accounted for the majority of Ukraine's trade even as late as 1993. Significantly, after Kuchma became prime minister, a free trade agreement was signed with Russia in June 1993, but trade in key commodities was excluded and the agreement did not apply to state trading. As a result, according to some estimates, the agreement actually covered less than 10% of trade between the two countries.[83] In 1994, Ukraine signed the CIS Free Trade Agreement, but this agreement has had limited effectiveness because it allowed multiple exemptions to be added after the fact. In practice, extensive lists of goods have been added to the agreement by Ukraine, effectively nullifying the agreement.

Ukraine's support for CIS institutions, at least officially, has been weak. In 1992 and 1993, Ukraine participated in very few economic agreements and had one of the worst records in the region on implementation. In 1994, with Kuchma as president and Masol as prime minister, Ukraine's participation increased, but the government still signed less than half of the agreements. In 1995, Ukraine had a relatively active year, signing all of the agreements and implementing a majority. Nonetheless, Ukraine has resisted the most important agreements. Ukraine refused to sign the 1993 Treaty on the Economic Union and opposed the transfer of supranational authority to the IEC. Ukraine was also one of the most active opponents of the CIS Customs

---

[82] U.S. Department of State, *Country Reports on Economic Policy and Trade Practices: Ukraine*, 1997.

[83] Francoise LeGall, "Ukraine: A Trade and Exchange System Still Seeking Direction," in *Trade in the New Independent States*, ed. Constantine Michalopolous and David G. Tarr, Studies of Economies in Transformation No. 13 (Washington, D.C.: World Bank, 1994), p. 77.

Union and rejected calls for membership in the Treaty on Deepening Economic Integration and the Eurasian Union. And from 1996 on, Ukrainian participation in CIS economic agreements lessened. Since 2001, however, the Kuchma government has shown greater interest in CIS institutions and in 2003, Kuchma took over as the chairman of the Council of Heads of State.

With respect to membership in the WTO, Ukraine's progress during the 1990s was extremely limited. Ukraine applied for membership in November 1993 and sent its Foreign Trade Memorandum in July 1994, but after six years of regular meetings of the Working Party the country was not close to membership in 2000. In part, the combination of demonstrable activity with fundamental lack of progress that we find in the Ukrainian case stems from the fact that Ukraine was a recipient of enormous amounts of Western aid. As one of the top priorities of international lenders was trade liberalization and, in particular, the appearance of progress toward membership in the WTO, the formal execution of procedures suggesting an interest in WTO membership may have been the result of efforts to secure foreign aid. As a strategically important country with a well-organized and politically powerful diaspora, Ukraine was more subject to these pressures (and opportunities) than its neighbors. As a result, efforts to provide the appearance of progress toward WTO membership, despite the lack of substance, appear to have been greater in the Ukrainian case.

The effect of the government's economic ideas could be seen in domestic economic policy as well. Between 1991 and 1994, the government's mercantilist ideas were manifested in state control over all large-scale enterprises, massive government subsidies leading to perennial budget deficits and hyperinflation, and efforts to limit trade with Soviet-era partners. In the first years of independence, government subsidies flooded the economy with currency (the karbovanets), leading to a drop in the exchange rate from 0.56 karbovanet to the dollar on 1 January 1992 to 12,610 to the dollar by 1 January 1994.

During 1994, after Kuchma took office, the government initiated an IMF macroeconomic stabilization program that lowered inflation, stabilized the currency, and replaced the karbovanets with the hrivna, but the government continued to run deficits and subsidize national enterprises. Privatization of large-scale enterprises also began in 1994 but proceeded at a slow pace until 1996, at which point approximately half of the country's large and medium-size enterprises were at least partially in private hands. A second push toward privatization in the run-up to the elections in 1998 pushed the percentage of privatized firms to approximately 80%. Nonetheless, the largest and most financially powerful enterprises, such as the Mikhailovsky Aluminum Factory, remained in state hands and even those enterprises that had been privatized were subject to heavy state influence.[84] Hence, the extent to which the large enterprises were truly in private hands was nominal. Moreover, unlike those of neighboring Belarus and Moldova, the Ukrainian government refused to transfer shares in its enterprises to Russia in exchange for the country's massive energy debts. The interstate joint-stock companies favored by integralists were rejected by the Ukrainian government in the 1990s in favor of sole national control, even in such previously tightly linked areas as military technology. The government justified the delays in privatization on the grounds that it would be against national interests for a foreign power such as Russia – which is the primary prospective buyer – to own the country's industrial jewels.[85]

In energy policy, the Ukrainian strategy entailed increased reliance on domestic energy sources such as nuclear power, including restarting the Chernobyl reactor, and especially coal. In 1993, a national program, Oil and Gas in Ukraine to the Year 2010, was approved by the parliament, followed by the revised National Power Engineering Program of Ukraine till the Year 2010 in mid-1996.[86] The core of these programs was a plan to increase Ukraine's reliance on domestic coal, and to undertake elaborate measures to diversify sources of supply of oil and gas away from Russia. The program called for the retooling of Ukraine's predominantly gas-fired thermoelectric stations to be converted to coal – at considerable cost. Moreover, despite the fact that Ukraine has significant coal reserves, they are dangerous or overly costly to extract. The shift to reliance on domestic coal since Ukrainian independence led to overexcavation of reserves near the surface and a severe danger of undermining.[87] The majority of the remaining reserves are predominantly located deep below the surface and difficult to extract. According to one independent expert, it would be cheaper simply to

---

[84] PriceWaterhouseCoopers (USAID) 1998.

[85] It is for this reason, Ukrainian officials reported, that the Allumina plant and the pipeline factories have not been put up for sale or given to Russia as payment for Ukraine's enormous debts. Author's interviews U4, U20. Russia is the primary prospective buyer because of a desire to integrate companies that were once part of the Soviet production complex in which these enterprises were embedded. Russian metals firms hoped to buy the Allumina plant (the Mikhailovskiy Glinozemny Zavod), for example, because the Ukrainian factory is the supplier to the giant Russian aluminum smelter in Bratsk (and also the smelter in Tajikistan). Its sales are almost entirely within the CIS, and outside buyers have less incentive to purchase the plant because so much of its contracts are based on barter.

[86] Information about the plan is provided in Kirichenko "Moving Forward into the Past."

[87] Interview U12.

buy coal from abroad.[88] The stress on domestic coal in the country's energy program was a costly move toward energy autonomy.

Since domestic supplies of natural gas covered only about 20% of requirements in the 1990s, the mercantilist governments sought to diversify supply away from Russia, the country's primary supplier in Soviet times. In the short term, this meant purchasing gas from Turkmenistan, and an agreement was also signed whereby Uzbekistan would supply 6 billion cubic meters of gas in 1997.[89] The gas has often been purchased with the help of loans from the World Bank, which have allowed Ukraine to reduce its debt to Russia and thus at least "balance" its financial dependence on other states. In the longer term, the government proposes to transport gas from Central Asia through Iran and Turkey to a pumping station in Bulgaria that is linked to the Ukrainian city of Kremenchuk.[90]

In Soviet times, Ukraine was supplied with oil solely by Russia, but under both Kravchuk and Kuchma the government has made an effort to diversify the country's oil supply by signing deals with Iran and other states for the supply of oil. In the mid-1990s construction began on a new oil terminal at Odessa, to allow the country to import oil from tankers in the Black Sea, thus bypassing land pipeline routes that run across Russian territory.

In both its institutional choices and its domestic economic policies, the Ukrainian government reflected the enduring influence of mercantilist ideas in the government until liberal forces finally held the reins at the end of the 1990s.

CONCLUSIONS

In sum, the three cases show, in different ways, the important role played by economic ideas in selection of international trade institutions. Russia, because of its remarkable shifts in economic ideas over time, allows for testing within a single case. We find clear distinctions between the government's activities regarding international institutions depending on whether liberal or integralist elites happen to be in positions of power. And the spontaneity and aggressive cadre policies of Boris Yeltsin allow us to treat those changes in ideas as truly exogenous and unsystematic. The comparison of Belarus

---

[88] Serhiy Mylenkiy, deputy director of PHB Ukraine, the joint venture specializing in power engineering. Cited in Kirichenko, *Moving Forward*, p. 23.

[89] Estimated consumption in 1996 was 92 billion cubic meters. Kirichenko, *Moving Forward*, p. 23.

[90] Kirichenko, *Moving Forward*, p. 23; interview U12.

and Ukraine, in contrast, gives us the greatest leverage in explaining differences across cases, as there is somewhat limited change over time – indeed none in the Belarusian case. The remarkable similarities of the two countries allow us to show more clearly how countries with very similar economic structures pursue radically different institutional trajectories – a point to be taken up again in the statistical analysis of Chapter 9.

7

The Caucasus

Armenia, Azerbaijan, and Georgia make for excellent cases for looking at the contingency of idea selection but can be problematic when examining the systematic effects of those ideas. The reason is the same for both qualities: the region has been marked by war, assassinations, and instability since 1990. The prolonged state of war between Armenia and Azerbaijan over Karabakh and Georgia's multiple civil wars have both ensured a stochastic element in the selection of leaders and the adoption of economic ideas and, simultaneously, meant that states have not always had the luxury of choosing their trade institutions. Nonetheless, we find critical variation within the region both in economic ideas and in institutional choice. Let us examine each of the cases in turn.

ARMENIA

The most salient fact about Armenia is the defining role that the Karabakh problem plays in the politics of the country. This has affected its trade policies in two ways. On the one hand, it has affected Armenia's options directly, insofar as the regional conflicts have forced the country, de facto, into a situation where its economic policy had to rely on some element of self-sufficiency because the country was blockaded by two of its neighbors. Hence, unlike most of the other cases we examine, we particularly need to relax our assumption of the freedom of institutional choice in this case, as some of Armenia's trade policies were the direct consequence of its decision to support Karabakh's separatist movement. On the other hand, Karabakh was important because Armenian leaders were selected or deposed because of the way they handled the Karabakh question; i.e., we can see more clearly in this situation that they were not particularly subject to political constraints in the selection of economic ideas – their political survival depended entirely on other matters. Indeed, the Karabakh question was so salient that it can be difficult even to identify the economic views of Armenian officials.

Economic Ideas: From Liberalism to Integralism, and Back Again

On the basis of secondary accounts and content analysis of government statements, one could conclude that Armenia has had one of the most consistently liberal governments in the region. The country's first president, Levon Ter-Petrosian, was an academic polymath born outside the USSR who drew on liberal advice and personnel from the Armenian diaspora in the formation of his government and policy. Ter-Petrosian rode to power as the de facto leader of the nationalist movement during the protests over Karabakh. His government was drawn largely from outside the ranks of the Communist apparat, and as early as 1991 the government had developed a radical liberal economic reform program. In February 1993 the government became even more decidedly liberal, when the prime minister, Khosrov Arutunian, resigned because of what he considered the excessive market orientation of the reform program. He was replaced as prime minister by Hrant Bagratian, the architect of that program and a prominent economic liberal. In 1994, the liberal position was further consolidated when President Ter-Petrosian cracked down on the popular Dashnaktsutiun opposition in parliament, a 100-year-old diaspora-supported party that advocated socialist economic policies, arresting the party leadership and closing its newspapers.

Liberal economic ideas were underrepresented in the government for only a brief time. To consolidate his authority after a violent crackdown on protests following the rigged presidential elections of 1996, Ter-Petrosian temporarily appointed an integralist prime minister, Vazgen Sarkissian, who had close ties to the military, but Sarkissian's tenure lasted only four months. His replacement, Robert Kocharian, a war hero and leader of the Nagornyi Karabakh region, advocated liberal ideas and appointed a young liberal economic team. When Kocharian assumed the presidency in a bloodless coup following reports that Ter-Petrosian was prepared to sign an agreement with Azerbaijan for the return of Nagornyi Karabakh, Kocharian further consolidated the liberal hold on government by naming his young liberal finance minister as prime minister and staking out a course for further liberal economic reform. When all of Kocharian's political rivals – including the popular Communist leader Karen Demirchian (a prominent integralist) – were gunned down in a suspicious terrorist attack in the Armenian parliament in November 1999, Kocharian's authority and the primacy of liberal economic ideas in the government were further consolidated. While hardly a model of political liberalism with power being sustained through rigged elections, repression, and assassination, and transferred through coups and other forms of intrigue, Armenia appears from most printed sources to be as economically liberal as they come.

There is, however, a body of evidence to the contrary that cannot be ignored – interviews I conducted in Armenia that suggest the prevalence of integralist ideas within the government. With a few notable liberal exceptions, most officials interviewed in spring 1997 explained the economic crisis in integralist terms and had a strong understanding of, and support for, CIS policymaking and procedures. The economic crisis following the collapse of the Soviet Union was particularly severe in Armenia, and the personal trauma that even high-level official respondents experienced during the crisis was mentioned in virtually every interview. In particular, respondents noted that Armenia desperately depended on its industrial ties with the other post-Soviet states and detailed the many ways in which these ties had been severed by the instability of the region: the war with Azerbaijan had cut off the supply of oil and one of the country's two heavy rail links; civil war in neighboring Georgia had led to sabotage of the main gas line linking the country to Russia and Turkmenistan; instability in Georgia had led to theft of Armenia's gas shipments; the separation of Abkhazia from Georgia severed the only other heavy rail link between the country and the other CIS states. As Armenia was one of the most heavily industrialized of any of the post-Soviet republics and imported of all its raw materials from outside the region, the collapse of ties was described as particularly devastating.

The *Economist Intelligence Unit Report* from the first quarter of 1993 paints a grim picture:

> The scale of the economic and social crisis in Armenia this winter has exceeded most expectations.... Life in Yerevan has become practically unbearable. There is no hot water, heating or electricity for domestic purposes, and furniture and trees from the parks are being used as fuel for cooking. Cuts in the electricity supply have meant that even cold running water frequently does not work as filtration plants have closed. Sewerage pipes have cracked and there is a serious threat of epidemics of gastro-intestinal diseases, tuberculosis, viral hepatitis and measles. Medicines are in short supply and vaccines cannot be stored properly. Prices have continued to rise and most enterprises in the city have closed, leaving the population with little income.[1]

[1] EIU Armenia Country Report No. 1, 1993, pp. 24–25.

Respondents noted that the severity of the crisis had "cured" them of the notion that any country could be economically independent. They viewed "economic sovereignty" as a myth and delusion that they had harbored during the nationalist euphoria of the early 1990s and many found a new plausibility in the integralist ideas of the USSR.[2]

The interviews also revealed significant pockets of liberal ideas within the Armenian government. A respondent in the Ministry of Industry, which in most other countries was a stronghold of integralist ideas, for example, explained the crisis as being due primarily to the inefficiency and irrational placement of national industries.[3] Clear liberal sentiments were also expressed by the minister of trade, Garnik Nanagoulian, who had previously served for several years at the Armenian embassy in Washington, D.C., and who reflected an exposure to liberal ideas and a facility with Western economic concepts.[4] Nanagoulian's deputy trade ministers also expressed liberal views.[5]

Several government respondents also noted that Prime Minister Robert Kocharian's[6] personal view was that Armenia needed to conduct rapid liberal reforms to build an economy strong enough to fund the defense spending

[2] This experience was salient to respondents well into 1997 when I conducted interviews. As I recorded in my field notes from the time: "Another thing of note here was that for absolutely everyone, in every single conversation, the period from 92–94 has left an incredibly powerful impression. People were actually cold and hungry in what had been the one of the most modern republics of the Soviet Union. It went down to minus 8 outside and people were sitting in their houses in overcoats and falling asleep cold. In this apartment [I stayed with an Armenian family in the central region of the capital], for example, they would close off the kitchen and the living room and bedroom, and they and the neighbors would come into the small room that I am staying in, and use a kerosene stove to cook and have light. Then they would shut it off and go to sleep cold."

[3] Interview A9, June 1997. The respondent had not previously worked in industry, but as a professor; that may explain why his views were so atypical for an official in a post-Soviet Ministry of Industry.

[4] Interview with Garnik Nanagoulian, minister of trade of the Republic of Armenia, 1 June 1997. He was one of the few respondents in all of the CIS to employ the idea of "comparative advantage."

[5] After a long interview with one of the deputy ministers who previously worked in Gosplan but consistently expressed liberal views, I mentioned to him that many people in Moscow had told me that the USSR was created as a single economic organism and that the economic problems facing the post-Soviet states resulted from the breakup of the union. He nodded the entire time but at the end said that that was only part of the story. The other part of the story, he said, was that these economies were not competitive and now needed to figure out how to make themselves fit into the world market. Interview A20, June 1997. Liberal views were also expressed by the official in the Ministry of Economy responsible for working on WTO membership, Ara Hakobian, 6 June 1997.

[6] Kocharian was prime minister at the time the interviews were conducted in June 1997. He is currently president of Armenia.

needed to protect itself from resource-rich Azerbaijan. According to these versions of Kocharian's views, Armenia, as a state with no natural resources to sell, had no other options available to it and must find a new source of wealth before Azerbaijan became too rich and powerful. In support of this, these respondents cited the formation of a team of young liberal officials from the Finance Ministry and the National Bank who were planning to pursue rapid market-liberal reforms.[7] In interviews conducted with several members of this team, however, respondents stated clearly that the crisis in the economy was due to the collapse of the union, and that Armenia could not hope to escape from the crisis without economic integration with the other republics under the CIS. Certainly at the lower levels of the government and in most ministries, the severe economic crisis of the early 1990s had sparked a crisis of confidence in liberalism and a return to integralist economic ideas.

But regardless of the economic ideas prevalent among officials, Armenia's economic choices were heavily determined by its security choices. The government's military actions isolated the country and significantly narrowed the range of economic policies available to it. Even if the Armenian government had wished to pursue integralist policies, its capacity to do so was limited given that it was landlocked by hostile or unstable neighbors. For this reason, the "choice" of economic policy is not as revealing since many of Armenia's options were foreclosed.

In terms of their international institutional choices and foreign economic policy Armenia was highly constrained. Given that Armenia faced a trade blockade from Turkey and Azerbaijan as a result of the conflict over Karabakh, and Georgian routes were essentially closed, Armenia only had the opportunity to engage in trade through air transport or through a narrow border with Iran. Hence, there was not much scope for foreign economic policy. Nonetheless, Armenia began to participate very actively in CIS institutions beginning in 1994. At this point, Armenia became one of the strongest supporters of economic integration within the CIS. This action is consistent with the notion that the severe economic crisis of 1993 forced a change in thinking within the Armenian government. Armenia participated neither in the Customs Union, nor in the subsequent cooperative agreements, but it is difficult to determine whether this was because of the liberal orientation of the government or whether it was a realistic assessment of the limited extent to which Armenia could participate in such agreements given that it lacked not only a border with any of the Customs Union member states,

---

[7] This team was led by the 32-year-old minister of finance, Armen Darbinian.

but reliable transport routes. Indeed, the specific conditions of Armenia's isolation and the blockade were cited as the primary reasons for rejecting the union by an Armenian economic official in an interview published in January 1996.[8] Given that the country already enjoyed free trade with the CU members, and the Customs Union agreement would force Armenia to lose a vital favorable trade arrangement with Iran, the country from which it imported the majority of its food, the government decided not to join and instead pursued an open trade regime. Consistently with the notion that liberalism prevailed at the upper ranks of the Armenian government under Kocharian, Armenia's participation in new economic agreements, in sharp contrast to its active participation in all CIS security arrangements, declined after Kocharian took office in 1997. Indeed, Armenia's participation in the WTO increased at this point, but then its application languished for several years, and Armenia ultimately acceded to the WTO only in 2003.[9]

In energy policy, Armenia had no choice but to rely on its own sources of supply. The war with Azerbaijan had resulted in a blockade by both Azerbaijan and Turkey. Instability in Georgia meant that supplies of natural gas rarely reached Armenia, and the cables linking Armenia to the Soviet energy grid via Georgia were increasingly sabotaged or stolen.[10] Nor does Armenia's decision to restart the Chernobyl-style Medzamor nuclear power plant reflect a move toward autarky, as this was the only energy supply available to the country. The "choice" of policy in this case provides little information because there were so few options. The government's preferences on Karabakh clearly trumped any economic concerns and heavily impacted the range of foreign economic policy options.

Armenia was similarly constrained in its macroeconomic and industrial policy. To maintain ties between Armenian enterprises and other post-Soviet enterprises required shipments by heavy rail, but the war in the Georgian region of Abkhazia and the Azerbaijani blockade meant that Armenia had no such rail links and therefore could not maintain Soviet-era ties even if this were its intention. Ultimately, the majority of the large-scale enterprises critical to the integralists were sold off in 1996 and 1997 to managers or

---

[8] Interview with Tigran Davtyan, chairman of the Armenian Economy Ministry's Department on Foreign Trade, published by SNARK news service, in English, 1040 GMT 13 January 1996.

[9] However, it is not clear that the delay in Armenia's membership in the WTO was due primarily to its own lack of initiative. Given that Turkey was a WTO member and approval for membership requires unanimity of existing members, there may have been political reasons for the delayed membership.

[10] Interview, A3.

officials closely tied to the government, but Armenia was not in a position to reestablish its place in the Soviet production complex. There was simply no way to transport the materials even if they had hoped to do so.

Given the uncertainty in how best to code the ideas of the Armenian governments, and the very significant extent to which Armenia's policy choices were more constrained than those of any other post-Soviet country, it is less certain whether Armenia confirms the importance of economic ideas in shaping policy. To the extent that one generally codes Armenia as liberal for the decade as a whole – as one would on the basis of the public statements of officials and the composition of the top ranks of the government – Armenian policy is largely consistent with predictions based on the elite's economic ideas with the exception of 1994 and 1995, when Armenia was particularly active in economic cooperation within the CIS. To the extent that the interviews conducted in 1997 tap into a more accurate assessment of the genuine beliefs of Armenian officials, then the transformation in Armenian policy in 1994 and 1995 is much more comprehensible as a response to a temporary loss of faith in economic liberalism following the severe economic crisis of the early 1990s.

GEORGIA

Georgia, like Latvia and Lithuania, began its independence with a nationalist government with mercantilist economic views. But unlike the two Baltic states, the country soon found itself embroiled in several simultaneous civil wars and spent several years in chaos – when the economic ideas of the government were neither known nor implemented. It is only as Shevardnadze's government took root that it becomes meaningful to speak of either institutional choice, economic policy, or the role of ideas. At this time, liberal ideas – largely supplied by international actors to a receptive Shevardnadze government – played a critical role and defined Georgia's policies for the rest of the decade.

Economic Ideas

Following the October 1990 Supreme Soviet elections and the victory of the nationalist Round Table movement, the dissident nationalist Zviad Gamsakhurdia was elected chairman of the Supreme Soviet. Having assumed power while Georgia was still nominally under Soviet control, Gamsakhurdia was primarily concerned with noneconomic issues of national independence, cultural revival, ethnic purity, and, ultimately, territorial integrity.

To the extent that it can be discerned from his public statements, Gamsakhurdia's economic thinking was distinctly mercantilist. In utter seriousness, the colorful leader once referred to the Soviet practice of "building of gigantic hydro-electric power stations and enterprises" as "a manifestation of an ecological war against Georgia and in the end its aim was the genocide of its people" and decried the importation of Soviet engineers to run the factories as part of a plan for the forced assimilation of Georgia.[11] Consistently with Gamsakhurdia's unique form of nationalism – reflecting the idiosyncratic and personal nature of the movement his followers were called "Zviadists" – he continually referred to ties with Russia as imperial and dangerous to the nation and considered economic arrangements to be part of a broad Muscovite conspiracy to undermine the unity and independence of the country. His attitude toward relations with the West was not much warmer.

But Gamsakhurdia's mercantilist government was short-lived. After sweeping the 1990 elections, Gamsakhurdia kept a tenuous hold on power until he and his government were finally deposed in a violent coup in January 1992 by a loose coalition of paramilitary groups led by Jaba Ioseliani, a warlord of no evident economic convictions. In March 1992, Eduard Shevardnadze returned from Moscow to take the reins as chairman of a newly constituted (but not elected) Supreme Soviet. Shevardnadze was a complex figure whose personal economic beliefs are often difficult to discern.[12] Shevardnadze's political origins were as a Communist strongman; he ruled Soviet Georgia for 15 years under Leonid Brezhnev after making his way to the top through the Ministry of Internal Affairs and the KGB. This was hardly the standard pedigree of an economic liberal, but when Gorbachev came to power in 1985 Shevardnadze was called to Moscow to serve as foreign minister of the USSR and a member of the Politburo. In Moscow, Shevardnadze became closely associated with the more liberal wing of Gorbachev's camp.[13] Shevardnadze's primary economic adviser at the Foreign Ministry was Alexander Shokhin, a liberal academic economist who was a close friend and associate of Yegor Gaidar. Whether Shevardnadze personally held liberal views or the integralist views typical of Gorbachev and his

---

[11] "Open Letter to Eduard Shevardnadze," by Zviad Gamsakhurdia, translated from the Russian by the Zviad Gamsakhurdia Society in the Netherlands, 19 April 1992.

[12] For Shevardnadze's judgment of the Soviet economy, see Carolyn McGiffert Ekedahl and Melvin A. Goodman, *The Wars of Eduard Shevardnadze* (University Park: Pennsylvania State University Press, 1997), p. 30.

[13] On Shevardnadze's background and convictions, see also William E. Odom, *The Collapse of the Soviet Military* (New Haven, Conn.: Yale University Press, 1998), pp. 99–102.

chief economic advisers is uncertain, but the fact that he promoted liberal economists within his own staff at a time when such ideas were considered by many to be unacceptably radical is an important signal.

It cannot be said, however, that economic liberals governed Georgia upon Shevardnadze's return in 1992. Indeed it is a stretch to suggest that Shevardnadze himself governed Georgia in the first two years after his arrival in Tbilisi. At best, he served as a mediator (at worst, a figurehead) for a government that rested upon an unstable coalition of the three paramilitary leaders that had brought him back to the republic – Jaba Ioseliani, Tengiz Kitovani, and Tengiz Sigua. From June 1992, when Shevardnadze and the paramilitary groups successfully fought off an attempted coup by Gamsakhurdia's forces, to the unsuccessful assassination attempt on Shevardnadze in 1995, the country was marked by chaos, civil war, and political violence. During this period, the government had a wartime economy with no coherent economic policy.

It was only in 1995, when Shevardnadze arrested Kitovani and Ioseliani and disbanded their paramilitary groups and his Civic Union party won a major electoral victory in the parliamentary elections, that Shevardnadze consolidated his power and economic policy began to be driven by something other than paying off supporters or printing money to cover the costs of the ongoing violence. Civic Union professed liberal economic ideas and through a combination of coercion, patronage, and rigged elections managed to stay in power through 2000. With the near absence of an indigenous liberal economic elite, the primary responsibility for charting economic policy was often delegated to foreign economists, but the liberal bent of the government remained relatively constant from November 1995 to the end of 2000.

As with interviews conducted in Armenia, interviews reveal that the economic crisis was acutely experienced in Georgia. Indeed, during 1997 when the interviews were conducted, Georgia was still experiencing a severe crisis. There was no natural gas or hot water, electricity was sporadic, and most regions were without heat in the winter. In contrast with Armenia, however, the crisis was not seen by officialdom as the result of the breakup of the USSR. Several officials interviewed attributed the crisis to Russian interference and an effort to punish Georgia for its independence.[14] Such mercantilist arguments were particularly notable in the Ministry of

---

[14] As a point of reference, Western economists and other officials working in the country also noted this mode of thinking about the causes of the economic crisis but provided alternative (internal) explanations for the causes of the failure of the economy. Interviews G14, G19.

Foreign Affairs, where the Russian government was blamed for the country's maladies.[15]

The chief economic officials both in the presidential administration and in the parliament explained the crisis as a result of the Soviet legacy, however, and liberalism dominated the top economic elite even as they relied on the IMF to provide concrete policy advice.[16] Integralism survived in a few pockets of the government that were directly tied to the old industrial-planning complex. Integralist ideas were also reflected in interviews with the chairman of the Branch Economies Committee of the Georgian Parliament, who nonetheless explicitly noted that he and "his generation" were best to let the younger liberal economists decide matters. Integralist explanations were also prevalent in interviews with officials in the Ministry of Economy.[17] According to most sources, however, the Ministry of Economy, the vestige of the old Georgian Gosplan, was completely marginalized from both policymaking and implementation.[18] On the whole, however, the Georgian government exhibited liberal ideas, or at least liberal inclinations – with the concrete ideas often supplied by the IMF and U.S. economic advisers.[19]

Institutional and Policy Choice

Georgian economic policies follow closely the shifts in the ideas of the leadership, which were themselves the product of a highly contingent political struggle for control of the country.

In terms of its foreign economic policy and institutional membership, Georgian policy appears to follow directly from the economic ideas of the elite. Under Gamsakhurdia, the country pursued an autarkic path. The country practically ended shipments of goods to Russia and other post-Soviet

---

[15] In part, this was an example of a general cultural phenomenon of scapegoating Russia. Even officials as low in the hierarchy as deputy department heads attempted to convince the interviewer that Russian representatives in the CIS had contracted to have them killed because of their anti-CIS stance. Interview G10.

[16] Interviews with Temur Basilia, chief economic adviser to President Eduard Shevardnadze, 13 June 1997. Interview with David Onoprishvili (chairman of the Committee for Economic Policy and Reform, Parliament of Georgia), 20 June 1997.

[17] Interviews G7, G1, G25.

[18] Interview G22.

[19] Economic policy in Georgia was heavily dominated by the resident representative of the IMF. One top-level economic official noted, with wry humor, that the IMF had basically assumed the role once played by the Gosplan offices in Moscow: the IMF gave the government a plan or checklist of policies to implement, for which the country would receive resources in return. Many other respondents confirmed that the IMF effectively drafted Georgia's economic policy. Interviews G3, G5, G21.

countries through interstate contracts. Georgia, like the three Baltic states, initially refused to join the Commonwealth of Independent States and did not participate in its meetings or economic agreements. When Georgia finally did join the CIS in 1993, under Shevardnadze, it was not primarily for economic reasons. CIS membership was part of a deal that gave Shevardnadze's government the support of Russian-commanded CIS troops in the civil war he was fighting with Gamsakhurdia's forces and secured a ceasefire with the Abkhazian separatists. In short, the government's motivations in joining the CIS were to preserve the survival of the regime. Indeed, of the 12 states that joined the CIS Georgia was second only to Turkmenistan in its resistance to signing economic agreements during the 1990s, and the country had the worst record of implementing agreements that it had signed of all CIS members. The Georgian government has been a vocal opponent of the CIS Customs Union, the Eurasian Union, and the economic documents and agreements put forward by the IEC (see Chapter 10). Georgia has essentially remained a CIS member in name only, and its sole enduring concern has been in the CIS's role in stabilizing the situation in Abkhazia.

At the same time, immediately after liberal Civic Union representatives consolidated their control in November 1995, Georgia moved rapidly toward membership in the WTO. Georgia first submitted its application for membership in the WTO on 3 July 1996; that membership was approved only three years later in October 1999. The exceptional rapidity of the process stemmed from the fact that Georgia was quick to liberalize its trade, locked in very low tariffs, and engaged in a flurry of negotiations in 1998 and 1999. All of this is consistent with predictions based on the adoption of liberal ideas in the Georgian government. Georgian programs under President Zviad Gamsakhurdia and under the first three years of President Eduard Shevardnadze were characterized by few coherent economic policies. Consistently with the mercantilist ideal-type, the government of Zviad Gamsakhurdia gave massive subsidies to domestic producers. The Georgian government ran enormous budget deficits throughout the early 1990s. This forced the government to print money to meet its obligations, leaving the country with the highest rates of inflation of any post-Soviet state for several years. Unlike in Uzbekistan or Turkmenistan, however, these credits were not directed toward the formation of new industries to substitute for imports, and state control of existing industries was due more to the fact that the near-constant warfare and political violence in the country prevented any coherent programs from being carried out. State ownership was simply continuity of the past.

In 1995, after four postindependence years of economic collapse, hyper-inflation, and civil war, the Georgian government's shift to a reliance on liberal ideas for its economic policymaking was immediately evident in all areas except privatization. Few of the key large-scale enterprises were privatized, and most land still remained under state ownership.[20] In energy policy, the Georgian government pursued a rapid restructuring and privatization scheme beginning in 1995 that culminated in the privatization of the state electricity distributor (Telasi) and gas distribution system (Tbilgazi) to international bidders. In addition, the government established a set of market rules for the supply and sale of energy, and from 1997 the state role was limited to an independent regulatory body that seeks to maintain adherence to such rules. The Georgian government also pursued transit arrangements for an oil export pipeline linking Baku to the Georgian port of Supsa, allowing multiple sources of supply, and a much longer pipeline linking Baku to the Turkish port of Ceyhan.

Since 1995, macroeconomic policy has been liberal as well. In 1995, the Georgian government cut spending and stopped printing money to cover its obligations, ended bread and energy subsidies, and reduced inflation from 15,602% in 1994 to 163% in 1998. Georgia continued the liberal program of macroeconomic stabilization after the November 1995 elections gave Shevardnadze's Civic Union party a majority in parliament. A currency reform in September 1995 introduced a new currency (the lari), which the government has maintained with the support of international credits that have primarily been channeled through the IMF.

AZERBAIJAN

In the case of Azerbaijan, the information on the thinking of government officials is too thin for adequate coding in most years. The broad outlines are relatively discernable, but those ideas do not conform well to the typology of the book. In part, this is because toward the latter half of the 1990s, there appeared to be less focus on the problem of achieving general economic growth in the government, so that the basic premise that different ideas about how to achieve growth would explain policy appears to be inadequate for explaining Azerbaijani policy. Most specifically, the government, under the tight control of Haidar Aliev, has been primarily concerned with extracting resources from the economy for personal enrichment. While this

---

[20] However, farms are private and unlike in other parts of the USSR were not subject to collectivization.

is an element of government policy in all post-Soviet countries, it essentially eclipsed other motivations for economic policymaking in the case of Azerbaijan. In 1999, the EBRD ranked Azerbaijan as the most corrupt country in the world.[21]

Economic Ideas

This was not always the case, however, and we do see some critical variation in economic ideas playing an important role in the early 1990s – as the failure to deal with the interethnic violence in the republic and war with Armenia drove several changes in leadership. As in Armenia and Georgia, the changes in political leadership in the country were violent, highly contingent events that had little to do with either economic conditions or economic ideas. In Azerbaijan, as in Armenia, the changes in leadership were almost entirely driven by the government's management of relations between Armenians and Azeris and the Karabakh question. In this case, the selection of ideas of the governing elite was almost entirely exogenous to economic structures or policy concerns. But the outcomes of the leadership selection process had significant impact on the economic ideas that shaped government policy.

Azerbaijan followed a different trajectory than its two Caucasian neighbors, where the 1990 Supreme Soviet elections had brought non-Communist opposition groups into power. In Azerbaijan, Moscow-appointed elites governed the republic until the latter half of 1992. After the outbreak of violence between Azeris and Armenians in Nagornyi Karabakh and the massacre at Sumgait, the Soviet leadership imposed martial law in Azerbaijan in January 1990 and Gorbachev appointed Ayaz Mutalibov as leader of the republic. Mutalibov, a loyal political unionist and economic integralist, remained in power through the collapse of the USSR, but he was politically much weakened by his support for the Moscow coup plotters in August 1991. As Mutalibov's hold on power waned, the breach was filled by the opposition Azerbaijani Popular Front – a nationalist coalition of economic liberals and mercantilists headed by the dissident nationalist academic Abulfaz Elchibey. This left the country with an ideationally mixed and largely paralyzed government until the massacre of Azeris at Khodjali by Armenian forces finally led Mutalibov to resign and flee to Moscow in May 1992.

In June 1992, Elchibey was elected president in free elections. Elchibey's personal views on the economy were vaguely liberal, but because the

[21] European Bank of Reconstruction and Development, *Transition Report*, 1999.

coalition that supported him included some nationalist factions with mercantilist ideas the government retained strong mercantilist influences. The government's views on the economy mattered relatively little, however, as its attention was consumed with the task of fighting the war with Armenia. The Popular Front government's poor prosecution of the war and its embarrassing losses set the stage for its brief tenure in office, which was cut short by a coup d'etat in June 1993 led by Suret Huseinov that put the old Communist Party boss Haidar Aliev back in power in the republic.

Much like Shevardnadze, Aliev had made his career in the KGB and had ruled the republic as first secretary under Brezhnev from 1969 to 1982, when the republic had a reputation for corruption in the Soviet Union. Aliev reportedly continued to rule the republic through a chosen successor from 1982 to 1987, after Aliev himself was called to Moscow to serve in the Politburo of the All-Union government. Unlike Shevardnadze, however, Aliev was a bitter rival of Gorbachev and his reform program. In 1987, as Gorbachev consolidated power, Aliev was forced to resign from the Politburo and to return to the Nakhichevan province of Azerbaijan. Gorbachev then appointed Abdulrahman Vezirov, a party official from outside the Azerbaijan Republic, as first secretary of the Azerbaijani Communist Party. Because Aliev had controlled the powerful Communist Party patronage system in the republic for nearly 20 years, however, virtually every official in the republic owed his or her place to him. Thus, Aliev's return to power in 1993 was relatively unproblematic and he was quickly able to reactivate his Brezhnev-era networks and eliminate rivals. Since 1993, all potential challengers to Aliev have been arrested, exiled, or executed.

From 1993 to 2000, the economic ideas expressed by Aliev and his government were a mix of different types, which perhaps suggests a degree of opportunism and a lack of any genuine convictions. At certain times, Aliev expressed clear integralist sentiments and lamented the destruction of Soviet-era economic ties. At others, he expressed vaguely liberal views, although never with a detailed focus on the virtues of competition or other liberal tenets. Aliev, unlike Shevardnadze, had been called to Moscow by Gorbachev's KGB predecessor, Yuri Andropov. He never warmed to liberal ideas and never sought a place among Gorbachev's reform coalition. There were no liberal economists among Aliev's advisers and he had no discernable economic team. Indeed, according to most accounts he took direct responsibility for most matters in the republic.[22]

[22] Bank of Finland.

In terms of its foreign economic relations and institutional membership, Azerbaijan initially eschewed membership in international economic institutions and has primarily pursued a form of autarky based on the exploitation and corrupt distribution of its oil wealth. Consistently with expectations from a liberal-mercantilist Popular Front government, Azerbaijan initially refused to join the CIS, joining only in September 1993 after Aliev took control of the country. For the next three years Azerbaijan actually took an active role in CIS agreements and pursued a fair amount of interstate trade with other post-Soviet republics. But Azerbaijan has consistently opposed more active forms of CIS cooperation and integration. It opposed legislation that empowered the IEC and rejected membership in the Customs Union and its successor institutions. In terms of its general trade policy after the early 1990s, the country had no tariffs to speak of, but licenses, excise taxes, and state ownership allowed the state to exert a great deal of control over trade, and the most important commodities, oil and petroleum products, were strictly controlled by the state. Azerbaijan was one of the last of the Soviet republics to submit its application to the WTO, on 30 June 1997, and the government did not send the memorandum on foreign trade that would begin the actual accession process until April 1999.

CONCLUSIONS: OUT OF BOUNDS?

To the extent that an examination of three impoverished war-torn countries can provide useful insights about the sources of membership in international economic institutions, the Caucasus states provide some further support for the argument. An interesting and fruitful comparison can be drawn between Georgia and Azerbaijan, where despite the fact that both countries saw the resurrection of their long-standing First Secretaries, the differences between the views of Shevardnadze and Aliev appear to have been critical in determining the subsequent policies of the two states. The liberalism of the Armenian government also, eventually, bore fruit in the country's membership in the WTO.

But the Caucasian states are also useful for the way that they highlight the boundary conditions of the theoretical claims made in this book, as at several points the countries of the region fall outside those boundaries. The theoretical argument, as presented in Chapter 2, rests on the assumption that governments actually have the freedom to choose their trade institutions. To some extent this assumption holds necessarily – i.e. it is an intrinsic feature of sovereign states. But as we can see in the Caucasus, and most clearly in the case of Armenia, there can be international environments in which institutional choice is more highly constrained as a result of the actions of neighboring states.

At the same time, it is important to recognize that the international environment is not exactly exogenous. The constrained trade environment that Armenia found itself in was partly of the government's own making. But this, too, reveals another important assumption of the specific application of the theory in this case, i.e. that governments place a premium on achieving economic growth or development and choose their institutions accordingly. Economic ideas may be necessary to link institutional means with economic ends, but they are only politically relevant if government leaders are indeed pursuing economic ends. Although this is generally a reasonable assumption to make about the post-Soviet states during this period, it clearly does not hold universally. The government of Armenia cared a great deal more about securing Karabakh than it did about growing the economy – and indeed the economy was mercilessly sacrificed to pursue the war. It was only insofar as fighting subsided and economic growth came to be seen as a prerequisite for sustaining the military power needed to defend Karabakh that ideas about the institutions necessary to achieve growth began to play an important role in Armenian politics. But once economic growth reemerged as a goal, liberal ideas clearly played an important role in the country's decisions.

Similarly, one can argue that in Azerbaijan, the notion that the government was responsible for improving national economic conditions was so vestigial under Aliev that the pursuit of personal wealth became the primary goal. As a result, it becomes difficult to think about the set of economic ideas motivating policy. In this sense, the significance and explanatory power of economic ideas are a function of the salience of economic growth as a goal of political leaders. To the extent that the salience of economic goals varied in the Caucasus, we must recognize that there are key political choices that economic ideas will not explain.

8

Central Asia

In Central Asia, we see a much stronger case and one squarely consistent with the theory. For one, the separation between the selection of leaders and the selection of economic ideas is starker than anywhere else in the former Soviet Union. This is true for the simple reason that four of the five leaders were appointed while the Soviet Union was still in existence. Yet despite the fact that these leaders were not selected for their economic views, the ideas of those individual leaders came to be of particular importance because the extent of personal control over the state apparatus was so considerable. As a result, if the chapter tends more toward Kremlinology, drawing on the attributes of individual leaders, it is with good reason. The supreme power of the executive office in these countries renders the ideas, personal background, experience, and patronage ties of these leaders an important element of the explanation.

To capture this contingency, I describe how each leader came to power in order to make the case that the principles of selection had little to do with economic views. I then identify changes in the leaders' economic ideas over time and show the extent to which these ideas manifest in international institutional choice and economic policy.

UZBEKISTAN

Uzbekistan exhibits no changes in leadership and only one major shift in economic ideas during the decade, a turn from integralism to a form of mercantilism that occurs approximately at the end of 1993. As a result, Uzbekistan shifted from being one of the strongest advocates of regional institutions to one of their major detractors, and the country took progressive moves toward autarky as the decade wore on.

Attention to the economic ideas of the elite in the case of Uzbekistan naturally draws one to the person of the president. Since the collapse of the Soviet Union, Uzbekistan has been firmly under the control of Islam Karimov and economic policy in particular has been almost entirely conducted under Karimov's direction. Because of the supreme role of Presidential rule in Uzbekistan, Karimov's personal background is important. Two elements of Karimov's background are particularly critical. First, even though he was not first secretary under Brezhnev, Karimov, like Aliev in Azerbaijan and Shevardnadze in Georgia, was the beneficiary of the corrupt party patronage networks developed in the republic during the Brezhnev years – as a result he entered office with a ready-made network of cadres to draw on for sustaining control within the republic without having to undergo the trials and compromise of free and fair elections. Second, he was a trained Soviet economist who had served as the head of the State Planning Commission and minister of finance in the republic – he had his own economic convictions and took an active interest in economic theory.

To understand the influence of Karimov and, by extension, his ideas, it is useful to begin with the fate of his predecessor, Rafik Nishanov. Nishanov had been installed by Gorbachev's team as part of a general strategy to root out the corrupt patronage network of Sharaf Rashidov, who ruled the republic from 1959 until his death in 1983. In a five-year purge that came to be known as "the Uzbek cotton affair," Rashidov was portrayed as a criminal and his appointed loyalists were replaced by new cadres selected by Gorbachev's team.[1] One of those purged was Islam Karimov, who was demoted from his post as minister of finance to serve as the first party secretary in the "distant and dismal terrain" of Kashka-Daria oblast.[2] When the ethnic riots in the Fergana valley in June 1989 apparently led Moscow to be more concerned about securing stability in the republic than rooting out corruption, Nishanov was sacked and Karimov, with the support of key Rashidov-era power brokers, was appointed as first secretary by Gorbachev.[3] In short order the newly appointed Gorbachev cadres were removed, the anticorruption campaign was repudiated, and Rashidov's legacy and cadres were rehabilitated. Karimov has held power in the country ever since.

---

[1] Donald S. Carlisle, "Islam Karimov and Uzbekistan: Back to the Future?" in *Patterns of Post-Soviet Leadership*, ed. Timothy J. Colton and Robert C. Tucker, (Boulder, Colo.: Westview Press, 1995), p. 195.

[2] Ibid., p. 196.

[3] Karimov was from the same region of the country as Rashidov. Pauline Jones Luong, *Institutional Change and Political Continuity in Post-Soviet Central Asia: Power, Perceptions, and Pacts* (Cambridge: Cambridge University Press, 2002), p. 89.

And Karimov has not simply held power, he has held sway. In interviews and public statements, government officials constantly refer to him, his statements, and his economic views. He is the sole locus of intellectual as well as political authority. No one contradicts him. There is no diversity of views, or, rather, if such diversity exists it remains personal and private; alternative views play no role in political or public life.

Karimov's own economic views appear to have evolved over time. Having been a Soviet economic technocrat, he initially held decidedly integralist views. In 1992, Karimov decried the romanticism of the notion that the republic could create an economy that was separate from that of the USSR and consistently expressed integralist ideas. But in the early 1990s his ideas clearly began to evolve in light of the experiences of the Soviet collapse. The precise causes of Karimov's change of mind are not certain, but by the end of 1993 he had published an economic tract, "Uzbekistan: Its Own Model of a Transition to a Market Economy," that contained some core mercantilist ideas.[4]

In developing his own economic "model," Karimov appears to have transposed several Soviet economic conceptions, such as the need for the Soviet economy to be self-sufficient in the face of capitalist encirclement and the identification of economic progress with industrialization, to form a new view of Uzbekistan's role in the Soviet system. Because the economy of the Uzbek SSR had been primarily agricultural rather than industrial, Karimov argued – similarly to arguments that Soviet economists made about the Third World – that they had been deliberately underdeveloped and exploited by Moscow. The key to Uzbekistan's development, according to Karimov, was to achieve self-sufficiency through the rapid development of industry and reliance on their own resources. This view became the guiding theme of economic policy in the Uzbek government during 1994.[5] In interviews I conducted in Uzbekistan in 1997, it was stated explicitly that the government's overall economic program was designed to undo the interdependence of their economy with the rest of the CIS states and to make the country as economically independent, or autarkic, as possible. According to Karimov's main economic confidante, Uzbekistan was seeking "economic independence and

---

[4] The adoption of a new set of economic policy ideas was surely accelerated by the costly failure of Uzbekistan's efforts to cooperate with the Russian Federation in the formation of a new ruble zone at the end of 1993, which led the republic to be flooded with old ruble notes after Russia introduced its new currency. The end of the ruble zone also caused the end of "technical credits" from Russia, which amounted to 180 billion rubles (approximately $180 million) between January and July 1993. EIU third quarter 1993, 72.

[5] Jones-Luong, *Institutional Change*, pp. 133–134.

a closed cycle of production in certain products with no reliance on outside production."[6] After 1994, public statements and interviews with officials reflect the deep entrenchment of mercantilist ideas.

Institutional and Policy Choice

In terms of foreign economic policy and institutional membership, we see a clear shift after 1994 from active participation in regional economic institutions toward autarky, although with a significant lag. In 1992 and 1993, Uzbekistan signed and implemented all CIS economic agreements and the country continued to have one of the strongest records of participation in CIS economic agreements in 1994 and 1995. Beginning in 1996 this began to decline and by 1997 Uzbekistan had become one of the least active participants in CIS institutions.

Uzbekistan has never taken much interest in membership in the WTO. It applied for membership in December 1994 but neglected to send the memorandum on its foreign trade regime until October 1998 and had to refile it in 2000. As of the end of 2001, its Working Party had never met. Rather, the Uzbek government has continued to control foreign trade and foreign exchange. The creation of a Ministry of Foreign Economic Relations shortly after the country became independent allowed the state to control trade through a complex system of licenses and state contracts.[7] In the very early 1990s this extensive state control was used to manage trade with Uzbekistan's former Soviet partners, but by 1995 the ministry was essentially a vehicle for limiting imports and directing foreign exchange to strategic industrial sectors.

In terms of its domestic economic policies, after 1995 Uzbekistan closely approximates the autarkic ideal-type. Its industrial program was aimed directly at import substitution. This included joint ventures with Daewoo and Daimler-Benz to give Uzbekistan full domestic production in cars, trucks, and busses; a program to switch the agricultural system from its traditional cotton crop to the production of grain to secure independence in foodstuffs; and a successful program to gain total energy independence by developing the country's own resources.[8] The Uzbek government was also looking to gain a few niche production markets "as part of the international

---

[6] Author's interview with Uz2 (Rafik Saifulin), 27 November, 1997.
[7] Jones-Luong, *Institutional Change*, p. 134.
[8] Notably, the domestically produced Uzbek gasoline is more expensive and of lower quality than that which was previously imported from Kazakhstan. Interview Uz2.

distribution of labor," but even as late as 1997 these markets had not yet been defined by the government.[9] Establishing national self-sufficiency was the first priority.

Since the early 1990s, Uzbekistan's energy policy has been geared toward full self-sufficiency. Under the Soviet division of labor, Uzbekistan imported oil from Kazakhstan and its own oil was refined at Kazakh refineries. Since independence, however, Uzbekistan has increased its oil production, ended imports, and built a new refinery in Bukhara that produces gasoline of lower quality and higher cost than the country previously obtained from a refinery across the border in Kazakhstan. Uzbekistan continues to import electricity from Kyrgyzstan but will pay only the highly subsidized domestic Uzbek price for what it uses. Meanwhile, the government exported natural gas to Kyrgyzstan and charged world prices.

In privatization, the Uzbek government has undertaken some faux privatization auctions in which state-owned firms were transferred to state-owned banks or to family members of top officials in an attempt to fool international lenders into thinking that the country was moving forward on liberal reforms. In this way, the state has retained control of the key industries. The same has been true for agriculture. Cotton production, which makes up 75% of the country's export earnings, remains under state control. The state also controls the distribution of credit and has used subsidies and price controls to structure the economy in a way that reduces the country's dependence on other states and favors the development of heavy industries in which the country has not traditionally been strong. The result of this expansionist monetary policy has been a steady decline in the value of the Uzbek sum, which, given that the government set an artificially high rate, led to a system of dual exchange rates that persisted throughout the 1990s.

TURKMENISTAN

Turkmenistan is remarkably similar to Uzbekistan, in its political structure, the prevalence of mercantilist ideas, and the near-total closure of its economy.

The focus for the ideas behind policy in Turkmenistan naturally rests on Saparmurat Niyazov, who maintained tight control over the republic since he was appointed first secretary of the Central Committee of the Turkmen Communist Party by Gorbachev in December 1985 until his death in 2006. A reportedly unremarkable man trained as a power engineer in Leningrad,

---

[9] Ibid.

Niyazov was cultivated by the Soviet leadership beginning in 1984 because of one quality that was particularly useful to Moscow in a republic where there was concern about the influence of clan ties: Niyazov was raised in an orphanage and had no profound family ties with any of the dominant Turkmen tribes.[10] To his credit, however, Niyazov managed simultaneously to sustain close enough ties to Gorbachev to prevent his replacement and to establish himself well enough within the republic to secure 98% of the vote in his bid for the presidency of the republic in October 1990. After winning another presidential "election" in 1992 with 99.5% of the vote and postponing a subsequent election through a 1994 referendum, Niyazov was made president for life in 1999. As a supreme leader who appointed each member of the government and who in 1999 disbanded the country's Academy of Sciences, Niyazov was the primary source of the economic ideas and motivations relevant to economic policy.

Beginning in 1992, Niyazov took a very clear line on the republic's development: the path to prosperity essentially lay through the use of the republic's energy resources to fund a massive industrialization program geared toward self-sufficiency and to provide free goods to its citizens. Viewing imports as a drain on the country's resources, Niyazov had the stated goal of producing everything "in house." Reflecting on the agenda in an interview with a Russian newspaper in 1995, Niyazov noted:

Although Turkmenistan's economy experienced in full measure the burdens of the transitional period and the consequences of the disintegrated economic ties among the former union republics, its population felt confident and protected. We set the lowest, virtually symbolic prices for bread and flour and introduced free use of water, gas, and electricity. No, this was not populism. It was a sober calculation, and time has shown that it was right. Having ensured social guarantees for the population, the government prepared conditions for actions directly relating to a market reorientation: Carefully and pragmatically, without excitement, it drew up a program of reforms whose strategy was determined by the choice of an evolutionary path of development, while the tactic included structural restructuring, the formation of a mixed economy, and state regulation of economic processes. Briefly, its essence is characterized by the two most important, main directions: self-sufficiency in food and the rational, efficient utilization of our own resources. I shall cite just a few data. Turkmenistan today is a state with a deficit-free budget. A traditional supplier of raw materials for many years, it is rapidly turning into a producer of finished output. In accordance with the adopted three-year plan, approximately 700 enterprises,

---

[10] Almaty *Karavan* in Russian, 12 January 1996, no. 2, p. 9, AFS number: 964F0872A Citysource: Almaty *Karavan* Language: Russian Article Type: CSO Subslug: [Article by political scientist Allaberen Khadzhiyev: "Last Camel in the Caravan"] [FBIS Translated Text].

primarily with a processing profile, will be built in the country with a population of 5 million, mainly with internal investments.... Foreign trade turnover is growing at a high rate, and exports significantly exceed imports. You ask about successes. It seems to me that we have good reason to talk about them.[11]

Niyazov rarely expressed anti-Russian or anti-Soviet views and stressed the foreign sale of natural resources much more in his vision of how growth should be achieved, but his views were otherwise ideal-typical mercantilism.

Institutional and Policy Choice

These ideas have been manifested clearly in the government's institutional and policy choices. The stated policy of the Turkmen government is to achieve *full* import substitution,[12] and in its foreign economic relations and institutional membership, Turkmenistan's policies have consistently favored closure. The trade regime, while tariff-free, is entirely state-controlled. And while Turkmenistan did become a member of the CIS, it is a member in name only. It has signed fewer economic agreements than any other member-state and has implemented few of these. Beginning in 1997, Niyazov ceased to attend regularly the meetings of the CIS Council of Heads of State and Turkmenistan does not send representatives to other CIS bodies. Its record with respect to liberal international institutions is even worse: Turkmenistan has never applied for membership in the World Trade Organization and does not even hold observer status.

Turkmenistan's domestic economic policies have been almost identical to those pursued in Uzbekistan, only more extreme. In energy, the state has retained control of the natural gas monopoly, which provides the main source of export earnings. Moreover, the government has pursued the development of multiple outlets to gas markets[13] so as not to rely on the pipeline system operated by Russia's Gazprom. The government has also contracted with foreign oil corporations to develop its oil reserves, but many companies backed out after the government unilaterally changed the terms in its favor.

In privatization, government figures claimed that more than 70% of enterprises had been privatized by 1999. In actuality, however, as in Uzbekistan,

---

[11] Moscow *Rossiyskaya Gazeta*, in Russian, first ed., 5 May 1995 pp. 9, 11: [Interview with President Saparmurat Niyazov by unidentified correspondent; place, date not given: "Saparmurat Niyazov: The Sands of the Karakum Will Not Divide Us. The President of Turkmenistan Answers *Rossiyskaya Gazeta*'s Questions"] [FBIS Translated Text].

[12] This was initially to be achieved by 2000, but the deadline was not met.

[13] To Iran, and via Iran and Azerbaijan to Turkey.

"privatization" has generally meant the transfer of enterprises to state-owned banks. There have been no privatization of large enterprises and no transfer of shares to enterprises or ministries in other post-Soviet states.

The country's macroeconomic policy is also one of near-total autarky. Consumer goods and utilities are heavily subsidized, and utilities are slated in the country's 10-year plan to become completely free of charge. Prices were never fully liberalized and agricultural prices are still set by the state. Until 1996, state-set interest rates were considerably below the rate of inflation, effectively allowing the state-controlled banks to target subsidies to favored enterprises and sectors. Before 1997 the government interfered heavily in monetary policy and the state bank printed money to cover the outflow of government subsidies to agriculture and industry. The government has also pursued a massive import-substituting industrialization policy designed to end reliance on the union-wide division of labor by channeling export earnings from the sale of natural gas into the development of new industrial sectors. Money channeled into the economy was 37.2% of the state budget in 1996, with more funding reportedly originating outside the budget.[14] The government has maintained the traditional sectors of gas, oil, and cotton but has pushed for the development of machine-building and metallurgy – despite the fact that there is already oversupply in these sectors in the post-Soviet space. Turkish contractors have constructed new cellulose and steel plants, which are protected from foreign competition by the dual exchange rate system for the Turkmenistani Manat.

KAZAKHSTAN

Despite the fact the Kazakhstan, like Uzbekistan and Turkmenistan, is an energy- and resource-rich country surrounded by powerful (or warring) neighbors, the contrast with those countries in terms of institutional choice could not be more striking. Under Nazarbaev the government has consistently supported integralist ideas and has been one of the most active supporters of regional economic institutions of all types. Although in the middle of the decade there was a significant group of liberal officials tied to the prime minister, Kazakhstan has generally remained a bastion of integralist ideas.

While not as extreme as in neighboring Uzbekistan and Turkmenistan, most formal authority over matters of policy in Kazakhstan lies in the office of the president, who appoints the government and has the authority to remove any official. The parliament has very limited powers and has acted

[14] EIU Country Report 1999.

primarily as a rubber stamp for governmental proposals in the few areas where it has a role. There is no strong or well-organized opposition in the country. For this reason, any focus on the ideas behind policymaking is appropriately directed toward the ideas of the president and of the government officials appointed by him. In Kazakhstan, this task is greatly simplified. The country has had the same leader, Nursultan Nazarbaev, since he was appointed by Gorbachev in June 1989.

Nazarbaev's interviews and many published books testify to the long history of his integralist conception of the relationships among the post-Soviet republics.[15] Regarding the causes of the economic crisis facing Kazakhstan and the other post-Soviet states, Nazarbaev's position is unambiguous:

Let us say once again where our troubles stem from. You remember what I was fighting for when the USSR was disintegrating, don't you? I was against the demolition of the single economic space, *but this living organism was broken up nonetheless; this is where the cause of all our problems lies.*[16]

Even as many other republican leaders began to adopt nationalist agendas in 1990 and 1991, Nazarbaev clung to the idea that the USSR was an inseparable economic whole, the destruction of which would prove disastrous. As Olcott points out, "Nazarbaev spent the years 1989 to 1991 repeating his conviction that, whatever the injustices and stupidities of the present system, the economies of the Soviet republics were too tightly interwoven to permit the republics to go it alone."[17] As leader of the Kazakh SSR and a member of the Soviet Politburo, Nazarbaev was the chief non-Russian ally

---

[15] For those interested in investigating Nazarbaev's thinking further, the following sources for Nazarbaev's writings, speeches, and interviews may be of use: Nazarbaev, "Ideya Kotoroi Prinadlezhit Budushchee"; *Panorama* (Almaty) 22 October 1994, p. 11; *Interfax* (Moscow) in English 15:15 GMT 23 February 1995; *Kazakhstansaia Pravda* (Almaty), 14 April 1995 pp. 1, 2; Almaty Kazakh Television First Program Network (in Kazakh, FBIS Translation) 1500 GMT 27 April 1995; *Interfax* (Moscow) in English 1410 GMT 6 May 1995; *NTV* (Moscow), 1635 GMT 19 January 1996; *Delovoi Mir* (Moscow), 23 March 1996 pp. 1, 4; *Rossiyskaia Gazeta* (Moscow), 29 March 1996 Weekend Edition p. 2; *NTV* (Moscow), 1535 GMT 17 May 1996.

[16] Interview with President Nursultan Nazarbaev. *Kazakhstanskaia Pravda* (Almaty) 14 April 1995 pp. 1, 2. FBIS translation.

[17] Martha Brill Olcott, *The Kazakhs*, 2nd ed. (Stanford, Calif.: Hoover Institution Press, 1995), p. 265. Although this is in contradiction with some of the conclusions that she draws later in the text, Olcott, too, appears to suggest that the Nazarbaev's support for the union was motivated by a form of integralist reasoning (268): "Convinced that independence would be economic suicide for the Republics in general and Kazakhstan in particular, Nazarbaev continued to support Gorbachev and, indeed, emerged as the leading proponent of continued union."

of Gorbachev in his efforts to bind the republics in a new union treaty that would have preserved the common economic space.[18]

Throughout the 1990s, Nazarbaev consistently argued that the key to solving the economic crisis in each country was to draw on the "powerful unified potential formed over the decades" and to enter world markets "on the basis of collective strengths."[19] Nazarbaev remarked that those countries that try to "'realize themselves,' to reorient themselves to what would appear to be more profitable far-off partners, as a rule suffer failure."[20] He continually stressed that the crisis of the post-Soviet states was a collective predicament, to which only collective solutions could be applied with any hope of success.[21] Those countries that believed they could succeed on their own were, according to Nazarbaev in one interview, trying to violate the "inherent universal laws of the market."[22] Reflecting the Soviet planning documents cited in Chapter 4, Nazarbaev suggests that to ignore these laws is "to fall into economic romanticism and voluntarism," which he saw as the primary reason for the failure of the post-Soviet economies since their efforts to pursue independence. Nazarbaev suggested that "with common efforts we can exit this protracted crisis which the republics of the former USSR are in."[23] Even when criticizing CIS institutions, Nazarbaev merely chastises the organizations for their inability "to create a common economic space, repair the intersectoral cooperation, to form an effective system of interregional division of labor" – i.e. for not doing enough to pursue integralist goals.[24]

These statements do not imply that Nazarbaev is opposed to any reform or favors a return to the command economy. To the contrary, among Soviet

---

[18] Olcott, *The Kazakhs*, p. 268. There were even rumors that Nazarbaev would become head of the new union.

[19] Nursultan A. Nazarbaev, "Ideya Kotoroi Prinadlezhit Budushchee," *Evrazia. Narody. Kultury. Religii* (1995): 6.

[20] Ibid.

[21] Nazarbaev maintains that "young sovereign states, in my opinion, cannot allow themselves the luxury to solve separately each of these emerging problems, which are, in essence, constitutive parts of a common crisis." Nazarbaev, "Ideya Kotoroi Prinadlezhit Budushchee," p. 6. This is a prevalent theme in each interview. For other particularly explicit references, see the interview published in Almaty *Panorama* in Russian 22 October 1994, p. 11; also (ironically) Nazarbaev's Independence Day speech of 16 December 1995, "Ukreplenie nezavisimosti – cherez ustoychivoe razvitie" in Nursultan A. Nazarbaev, *Evraziiskii Soiuz: Idei, Praktika, Perspektivy, 1994–1997* (Moscow: Fond Sodeistvia razvitiiu sotsial'nykh i politicheskikh nauk, 1997), pp. 238–252.

[22] Nazarbaev, "Ideya Kotoroi," p. 6.

[23] Ibid.

[24] Ibid., p. 7.

officials in office prior to the breakup of the union, Nazarbaev was a reformer advocating a transition to a "market economy" and integration with the world economy, along with Leonid Abalkin, Bogomolov, and others in the Gorbachev camp. Like other post-Soviet integralists, however, he appears to believe that this task can only be accomplished collectively, and that it is best accomplished on the basis of the existing economic strength of the Soviet-era specialization, the regional division of labor, and joint scientific potential.[25] Also, like other integralists, he appeared to assume that the Soviet economic system could simply be reconstituted on a voluntary contractual basis while maintaining essentially the same relationships between enterprises forged as part of the command economy, i.e. that a common market could be created "on the basis of those ties which not long ago existed inside the single national-economic complex."[26]

Given the extensive control that Nazarbaev has over political life in Kazakhstan, his own views have had the most decisive influence on policy, but some of his subordinate officials were considerably more liberal in their thinking about economic matters.[27]

The liberals in the government were led by Akezhan Kazhegeldin, Kazakhstan's prime minister from 1994 to 1997. We may speak of Kazhegeldin's market liberalism not because he waved the banner of "market reforms" – this would not distinguish him from most other CIS politicians – but because of the subtle and apparently nondeliberate ways in which the core tenets of market liberalism were repeatedly employed in his justification of the government's policy.[28] Criticizing the demands made by manufacturing enterprises for trade protection, for example, Kazhegeldin noted:

---

[25] Independence Day speech "Ukreplenie Nezavisimosti" in Nazarbaev, *Evraziiskii Soiuz*, pp. 238–252.

[26] *ENKhK*, "Edinyi Narodno-Khoziaistvennyi Kompleks"; Nazarbaev, *Evraziiskii Soiuz*, 239. Nazarbaev even directly questions whether it makes sense, given that they are trying to create "inter-regional cooperation and division of labor, a common market for goods, services, and labor," to "destroy all of that, in order to later create it all over again"? (Nazarbaev 1997, 239) He clearly thinks that the old ties can be shifted from plan to market and does not think that the latter requires a wholly different logic of organizing enterprise relationships than the former. Note also, however, Nazarbaev's repeated claims that he does not seek a return to the Soviet Union, for example: "Zhelanie vosstanovit' SSSR – vredno i opasno" in Nazarbaev, *Evraziiskii Soiuz*, pp. 255–257.

[27] Or at least felt the need continually to proclaim their support publicly, and their subsequent actions reflect that integration was an important policy priority.

[28] It is worth noting that Kazhegeldin did not enter the government by moving up the ranks of the old nomenklatura (a fact that some Kazakh government officials interviewed initially found offputting). He was a successful businessman (and former KGB agent serving abroad) brought into the government by Nazarbaev. Interview Kz7.

If we give in to their pressure, Kazakhstan's finished product will still for a long time to come be inferior in quality to its overseas counterparts. Competition should be preserved and even intensified here.... I reply [to the managers]: No, go and find a sales market and solvent partners yourselves. I would like to emphasize this: The degree of probability of bankruptcy is nine-tenths dependent on the economic transactor itself and its position and behavior in the coming weeks and months.[29]

Basic liberal notions such as the importance of competition and the idea that the success of enterprises rests on actions taken by their individual managers rather than government support or the organization of the "system as a whole" are prevalent themes in Kazhegeldin's interviews.[30]

Aside from Kazhegeldin, the liberals in the government were predominantly housed in the National Bank, the antimonopoly commission under Piotr Svoik,[31] the National Securities Commission under Grigory Marchenko, as well as in some agencies under the Ministry of Economics, e.g. the National Agency for Foreign Investment.[32]

Still, integralist sentiments predominated in the decision-making centers concerned with foreign economic policy. Both in published interviews and on

[29] Interview with Akezhan Kazhegeldin in Andrey Zhdanov, "The Economy Is Forcing Politicians to Adopt More Rational Decisions," *Kazakhstanskaia Pravda (Almaty)* 19 August 1994, pp. 1, 3.

[30] See also the liberal economic discussion in Kazhegeldin's book (Kazhegeldin, *Kazakhstan*, pp. 25–42).

[31] Note the essential liberal logic employed by Svoik: "If there is price competition, decontrolled prices stabilize, and the quality of goods improves. If there is competition between goods – production gets modernized, and the resources of enterprises that go bankrupt shift into the hands of more effective ones. When competition is present in the banking sector, the currency is not devalued and investment resources 'work' for expanded reproduction and modernization. When political competition is present, the authority works for the society." *Kazakhstansaia Pravda* (Almaty) 24 August 1994, pp. 1–2. Interview with P. Svoik, chairman of the State Committee for Price and Antitrust Policy, by unidentified *Kazakhstanskaia Pravda* correspondent; place and date not given: "We Cannot Stop the Prices Until We Stop Monopolism,"

[32] The categorization is based on field interviews as well as a published interview in *Panorama* (Almaty) No. 36, 17 September 1994, pp. 11, 13. Interview with Musipaly Utebayev, first deputy chairman of the National Agency for Foreign Investment under the Ministry of Economics, by Nurlan Makhmudov; place and date not given: "A Score of Projects Guaranteed by the Government Turned Out Ineffective." *Panorama* (Almaty) No. 40, 15 October 1994, p. 13. Report on interview with Daulet Sembayev, chairman of the National Bank, by *Panorama* correspondents Karlygash Yezhenova and Andrey Kukushkin in Madrid; date not given: "Daulet Sembayev: It Is Feasible to Reduce Inflation to 1–2 Percent per Month by Next May. Then, Possibly, a Fixed Foreign Currency Exchange Rate Might Be Introduced"; Finance Minister Pavlov's views were mixed, as he was willing to support soft credits for some key industries. *Sovety Kazakhstana* (Almaty) 25 January 1995, p. 3 [Interview with Finance Minister Aleksandr Pavlov by unidentified correspondent; place and date not given; "From Pulling at the Budget Blanket to Precise Forecasts"].

interviews conducted in autumn 1997, integralist sentiments were pervasive in the Ministry of Economy and Trade and the Ministry of Foreign Affairs, among the deputy prime ministers in charge of the economy,[33] and in the presidential administration.[34] Even the minister of finance,[35] who is commonly somewhat liberal in most countries that hope to receive IMF funds, expressed integralist ideas about the economic situation. Minister Pavlov, for example, advocated the need for a whole range of development banks and funds to "organize a new integral system that will regulate the activities of enterprises, ensuring their normal functioning in today's complex conditions and protecting them from bankruptcy." This interventionist sentiment surely would not have won favor with Kazhegeldin or the other liberals in the government, but Nazarbaev's integralism ensured that officials with such attitudes would be promoted rather than punished. It is also noteworthy that integralist sentiments were so prevalent in the Ministry of Foreign Affairs given that under a more integrated system this ministry would give more and more of its competence over to supranational bodies and a Eurasian Union would likely have little use for a separate Kazakh Ministry of Foreign Affairs. In this respect, Kazakhstan, like Belarus, is striking in the extent to which the ideas expressed by ministry officials are often not what one might deduce to be the bureaucratic interests of those ministries.

In 1997, Kazhegeldin was forced from office and the influence of liberal ideas within the government was greatly diminished, although Kazhegeldin's removal was more likely due to his political ambitions than his economic policies or views. The critical sequence of events began in March 1997, when the critical Ministry of Oil and Gas was transformed into a state-owned company, Kazakhoil, and two proposed oil privatizations were scrapped. Then in September 1997, Kazhegeldin suddenly departed the country to receive emergency medical treatment, later claiming that there had been an

---

[33] Notably First Deputy Prime Minister Isingarin – who was chosen in 1996 to head the Integration Commission of the Union of the Four.

[34] Integralist sentiments also appear to be prevalent in the security ministries. Note the comments of the secretary of the Security Council: *Almaty Delovaia Nedelia* in Russian, 22 March 1996. Interview with Baltash Moldabayevich Tursumbayev, secretary of Kazakhstan's Security Council, by Aygul Abdysalimova; place and date not given: "The Security Council Has Looked Into Privatization": [Abdysalimova] What is Kazakhstan's place in the system of collective security of the CIS countries in the light of its geopolitical location? [Tursumbayev]. The reality is such that the former states of the Soviet Union are so organically interlinked that a joint system of security has to be developed. Kazakhstan, being at the center of the Eurasian continent, has experienced this most keenly and has consistently insisted on the need for the coordination of efforts for a solution of the economic crisis in which we have found ourselves.

[35] Pavlov was minister of finance until 1997.

attempt on his life. On 10 October, 1997 President Nazarbaev delivered a scathing attack on Kazhegeldin's liberal economic reforms and demanded Kazhegeldin's resignation. Four days later, the liberal economist Grigory Marchenko – whom EIU describes as "Kazakhstan's leading economic reformer" – resigned his post as the head of the National Securities Commission.[36]

The "deliberalization" of the government was completed with the appointment of Nurlan Balgimbaev as the new prime minister. Balgimbaev's economic views prior to his appointment are not on record, but he immediately put a stop to further privatization and was considered first and foremost to be a loyal subordinate to Nazarbaev.

In interviews I conducted in Kazakhstan in November and December 1997, all officials, without exception, were integralist in their explanation of the origins of the country's economic crisis.[37] For all of the officials, coordination of policy with other post-Soviet states through the CIS councils and commissions was an important part of the policymaking process of their ministries, and their knowledge of CIS institutions and procedures was extensive. In several cases, rather than stressing the need to reestablish production links that previously existed in the planned economy, greater emphasis was placed on the role of Russia as a market for Kazakhstan's goods.[38] On the whole, however, integralism was accepted as truth among Kazakh officials.

The financial crisis of 1998–1999 led to another shift in government, but one that again reflected Nazarbaev's predilection for integralist views. After the Kazakh currency, the tenge, lost over half of its value, Balgimbaev provided a convenient scapegoat. In October 1999, Balgimbaev was forced to resign from the post of prime minister and replaced by Kasymzhomart Tokaev, the foreign minister. Tokaev had previously served in the Foreign Ministry of the USSR and his ministry had remained a stronghold of integralism in the government.

Institutional and Policy Choice

Institutional choices by the Kazakh government over the decade consistently reflect the enduring dominance of integralist ideas among the country's elite.

---

[36] EIU Country Profile 2000/2001.
[37] The Central Bank was reputed to be the primary institutional core of Kazakh liberals; however, it was not possible to arrange interviews with bank officials.
[38] Interview Kz4.

In terms of its international institutional membership, Kazakhstan has consistently been one of the most active participants in CIS regional institutions. By Nazarbaev's own account, "All the integration initiatives in the CIS, right up to the Eurasian Union . . . all came from Kazakhstan."[39] While this statement is not strictly true, it captures the general advocacy role that Kazakhstan has held with respect to the CIS.

Indeed, were it not for the efforts of the government of Kazakhstan, particularly the efforts of Nazarbaev, it is entirely possible that the CIS itself would not exist in its current form. There was no certainty that a new regional organization would be formed after the destruction of the Soviet Union, or that a new union would include all of the post-Soviet states that wished to join. The decision of the leaders of Russia, Ukraine, and Belarus to disband the USSR took place at a private meeting on 8 December 1991 and the "Commonwealth of Independent States" that was established there only included the three Slavic states.[40] It was Nazarbaev who convinced Yeltsin, Kravchuk, and Shushkevich to expand their agreement to include the non-Slavic republics and to allow all states to join the Commonwealth on an equal basis.[41] A new CIS founding agreement (the one that created the CIS as it stood until a formal charter was drafted in 1993) was signed at a meeting of the 10 founding member-states in Almaty on 21 December 1991 only after continued pressure from Kazakhstan.[42] To an extent exceeding that of any other CIS politician, Nazarbaev acted to ensure the preservation of some form of regional union (with a common ruble zone and collective command of the armed forces).[43]

In sum, Nazarbaev's government actively resisted the breakup of the Soviet Union and the unified Soviet economy. Even when Kazakhstan was forced out of the ruble zone in 1993 (see Chapter 10), the government continued to lobby for the creation of a new ruble zone or unified CIS

---

[39] Interview with President Nursultan Nazarbaev. *Kazakhstanskaia Pravda* (Almaty), 14 April 1995, pp. 1, 2.

[40] Nazarbaev was in Moscow to finalize a new union treaty when the destruction of the USSR was presented to him as a fait accompli; he was reportedly taken entirely by surprise. Martha Brill Olcott, *The Kazakhs*, 2nd ed. (Stanford, Calif.: Hoover Institution Press, 1995), p. 270.

[41] Olcott, *The Kazakhs*, p. 270; Henry Ewing Hale, "Statehood at Stake: Democratization, Secession and the Collapse of the USSR" (Ph.D. Dissertation, Harvard University, January 1998, p. 381).

[42] Hale, *Statehood*, pp. 381–382.

[43] As one example of Kazakhstan's bargaining tactics: at the time of the Almaty meeting, Ukraine and Belarus used the opportunity to declare their intentions to become nuclear-free states. Nazarbaev, the leader of the fourth nuclear republic, did not follow suit. Hale notes that Nazarbaev sought to retain nuclear weapons on Kazakhstan's territory in the hope that this would force some type of political-military union to be preserved.

payments system. Nazarbaev was one of the architects of the 1993 Treaty on Economic Union and its most public advocate. The Kazakh government supported the formation of the IEC and consistently lobbied to give the body greater supranational authority. Upon hearing of the formation of a Customs Union between Russia and Belarus, Nazarbaev immediately flew to Moscow to ensure that Kazakhstan was included. As discussed in Chapter 10, Nazarbaev's government was one of the main driving forces behind the Treaty on Deepening Integration (the "4-ka") and the Eurasian Union was based on an idea advanced by Nazarbaev in 1996. Kazakhstan's record of signing and implementing CIS agreements is consistently strong, although not quite as strong as that of Belarus or Tajikistan. In short, Kazakhstan under Nazarbaev's leadership has been a pillar of support for CIS regional institutions.

Regarding participation in the WTO process, Kazakhstan's efforts were limited. The government applied for membership in the WTO late, submitting its application only in 1996, under Kazhegeldin's premiership. For a short time, Kazakhstan did appear to be pursuing active membership in the institution, but as discussed later, this stemmed in part from a lack of understanding of the organization and the consequences of WTO membership for its relations with other CIS countries. After 1997, Kazakhstan's strategy was to enter the WTO only with other members of the Customs Union and meetings of Kazakhstan's WTO Working Group ceased in 1998.

In economic policy, a focus on maintaining the Soviet production complexes and building new relationships with prior Soviet partners was combined with efforts to establish limited conditions of private ownership. Kazakhstan only underwent extensive privatization while Kazhegeldin was prime minister and liberals played a significant role in the government. Initially, the government resisted the sale of the primary large-scale enterprises and conducted a mass voucher privatization of medium-large sized enterprises (200–5,000 employees).[44] The government retained a 39% share in each of these enterprises, however, that ensured that state influence over privatized firms remained significant.

Even as far as privatization went forward, it was conducted in such a way as to ensure the preservation of Soviet-era ties. The Kazakh government gave the Russian government the first option to buy enterprises in key industries

---

[44] EIU 1996 notes that these enterprises had very low turnover and the whole privatization earned only $19 million. This program was a copy of the Russian mass privatization program and began in April 1994. EIU notes that Kazakhstan copies a large portion of Russian legislation.

like metals, mining, oil and gas, and defense before putting them up for auction or sale on a case-by-case basis in an effort to reestablish links to the Soviet complexes. Prior to the privatization of Kazakhstan's state-owned enterprises, the Kazakh government made several attempts to encourage Russian investors to purchase the assets coming up for sale.[45] In several cases, Russian investors were given the first opportunity to purchase the assets prior to a general auction. Interviews suggest that the sale of enterprise shares, particularly of military–industrial enterprises, to Russian partners was seen as a way to facilitate the maintenance of the common economic ties. Both government officials and industrialists firmly believed that the ties with enterprises in Russia were what made those enterprises viable.[46]

Prior to the privatization of military enterprises,[47] Russia was consulted before bids were opened up to third parties.[48] Prime Minister Kazhegeldin and Sarybay Kalmurzayev, the chairman of the State Property Commission, prepared a list of the enterprises to come up for sale, which they delivered to Russia through diplomatic channels, giving Russia the right to buy prior to the general auctions. The reason for doing so, Kalmurzayev claimed, was to preclude the possibility that in the future, if the enterprises were sold to foreign firms, there might be claims that the new owner was threatening "our security" if the enterprises were not kept in Russian or Kazakh hands.[49]

The same practice was carried out in other vital economic sectors as well. Separate sources both in Moscow and in Almaty noted that prior to the privatization of Kazakhstan's key mining industries, which the Economist Intelligence Unit describes as "the single most important industry in

---

[45] Here, I am speaking of "Stage 2" and "Stage 3" of Kazakhstan's privatization program, not the privatization of small (primarily retail) enterprises. For a discussion of the "formal" process of Kazakhstan's privatization – which differed substantially from the actual practices – see Marat Rysbekov, "Privatization in Kazakhstan," *Comparative Economic Studies*, 37 (1995): 1–10.

[46] Author's interview with Vetoshkin, Industrialists and Entrepreneurs; interviews Kz5, Kz7; Kz4.

[47] Examples include the Khimvolokno Association in Kustanai, Stepnyak, and the Stepnogorsk Plant in Akmola oblast.

[48] Note the comment by Sarybay Sultanovich Kalmurzaev, the chairman of the State Property Committee of Kazakhstan, in Ivan Dimov, "The Process of Integration with Russia Has Been Difficult, but There Is No Other Choice..." *Delovoi Mir*, Moscow, 16 December 1994, p. 5.

[49] "It is possible that Russian capital and the Russian military-industrial complex might take an interest in them and that we could reach an agreement on this before we sell any of the facilities to a third country. I want to stress that this is not only my own personal opinion, but also the position of my government." Ibid.

Kazakhstan,"[50] Prime Minister Kazhegeldin made a special trip to Moscow and reportedly pleaded with Russian investors to purchase the assets.[51] At the time, however, Russian investors were earning exceptionally high short-term returns on government bonds and could not be convinced to put their cash into assets in Kazakhstan. Although the ultimate result was that Kazakhstan's mining enterprises were often sold to foreign buyers for hard currency, it is quite clear that the Kazakh government went to great lengths to try to put their strategic assets into Russian hands or, more accurately, to establish transnational joint-stock companies in which the Kazakh government and Russian investors held shares. Moreover, the Kazakh government facilitated the sale of shares of other privatized enterprises to Russians by allowing payment in rubles rather than hard currency or Kazakh tenge.[52] All of these efforts were designed to facilitate the creation of cross-national joint-stock companies between Russia and Kazakhstan. And Olcott, on the basis of interviews that she conducted in 1993, argued that Russian companies were "buying significant positions in other Kazakhstan companies, as well as setting up joint ventures."[53] More general statistical evidence is not available, but the Kazakh government evidently sought to sustain regional ties and had a favorable attitude toward Russian investment.[54]

Kazakhstan also kept the regional ties alive by subsidizing its regionally linked industrial enterprises. When these enterprises proved unable to compete on an open market, the government did not let them fail and fall into bankruptcy, despite Kazhegeldin's claims that they should not be supported and should fend for themselves. As did many other governments in the region, Kazakhstan continued to give so-called soft credits to industry, usually by lending money at a rate below the rate of inflation or without the expectation of repayment or by repayment through barter schemes that allow firms to discount the costs. Such subsidization is quite opaque and

---

[50] Economist Intelligence Unit, *Country Profile: Kazakhstan 1996–97*.

[51] Interviews Kz8, R18, R26.

[52] Dimov, *Sarbay Kalmurzazaev*, p. 5.

[53] Olcott, *Kazakhstan*, p. 562.

[54] When asked about the increased presence of Russian banks in Kazakhstan, for example, something that several Ukrainian commentators noted with alarm with respect to their own country, Kazakh prime minister Akezhan Kazhegeldin noted that "the emergence of Russians' objective interest in our financial market is encouraging. This means a prospect of the pooling of capital, joint investment projects, and a resolution of the problem of reciprocal payments. *And, most important, the interpenetration once again of tangible interests.*" *Kazakhstanskaia Pravda* (Almaty) 19 August 1994, pp. 1, 3. Interview with Akezhan Kazhegeldin by Andrey Zhdanov; place and date not given: "The Economy Is Forcing Politicians to Adopt More Rational Decisions" [FBIS Translation].

difficult to trace, but Kazakhstan retained a relatively larger share of its industrial capacity after the collapse of the USSR.[55]

The case-by-case large-scale privatization has not moved quickly, however. In general, the extent of privatization is difficult to track, and according to some estimates, only 43% of so-called privatized firms in 1996 had a majority of their stock owned by the private sector.[56] In addition to the state's share, the equity was often held by workers and managers in the firms themselves, a system that tended to militate against changes away from Soviet-era practices and trade links.

When Kazhegeldin was removed and Balgimbaev took office in October 1997, all privatizations were initially called to a halt.[57] During the years of Balgimbaev's premiership, majority stakes were sold in only two enterprises, a bank and a copper chemical plant. In 2000, after Tokaev took office, the government initially stated its intention to privatize 10 major firms, but only Mangistaumunaigaz was sold. The rest were granted temporary exclusions or were postponed.

In short, privatization moved forward only when liberals were in the government and was conducted in such a way that the state and existing managers retained a significant amount of control.[58] An IMF report in April 2002 summarizes the results of the decade:

Although by 2001 Kazakhstan had privatized thousands of enterprises, several large important enterprises still remain in majority state ownership. Though few in number, these large and very large enterprises dominate the economy. According to the Statistical Office, less than half of the large and very large enterprises are fully privatized, i.e. private investors own more than 50 percent of the shares. The state is still the only owner of 333 of these enterprises, which account for about a third of GDP. Many of these large and very large enterprises have been transferred by the State Property Committee to "trust management," in which existing managers or regional administrators have control over the enterprises.... The pace of privatization has slowed down since its peak in 1997, when 6,777 enterprises were privatized.[59]

Kazakhstan's privatization policy has also been coupled with efforts to maintain Soviet-era ties by providing these union-linked enterprises with continued subsidies and tax and debt deferrals and by not enforcing

---

[55] Measured as a percentage of GDP.

[56] Kazakhstan Economic Trends cited in EIU 1996.

[57] EIU 1999.

[58] Kazakhstan's privatization essentially reinforced the status quo, in terms of both political power (regional leaders controlled the process) and economic management (the firms went to existing management). See also Jones Luong, *Institutional Change*, p. 149.

[59] IMF 2002, Appendix.

bankruptcy laws that would have forced many of these enterprises to be liquidated. Under the liberal Prime Minister Akezhan Kazhegeldin, the government had tighter credit policies from 1994 to 1997 and pursued an IMF macroeconomic stabilization program, but it also allowed unpaid wages, taxes, and interenterprise arrears to build up as a means of keeping uncompetitive Soviet-era enterprises afloat and preserving the union-linked industrial sector.

Kazakhstan's energy policies have similarly reflected the government's integralist ideas. At a time when many other post-Soviet countries sought to limit their dependence on Russia for energy sources or transit, Kazakhstan, consistently with expectations of an integralist elite, has enhanced its Soviet era ties both by exporting more oil through existing Russian pipelines and by choosing to lay new export pipelines through Russia rather than other potential routes.[60]

As an exporter of oil, Kazakhstan traditionally relied on a Soviet-era pipeline running via Russia and ultimately through the "Druzhba" trunk pipeline through Ukraine and Eastern Europe. As oil export revenues grew in importance both for Kazakhstan and for Russia during the 1990s, there was increasing friction over the quotas each country would be allotted for export.[61] Initially, this conflict of interests was resolved by maintaining the Soviet-era pipeline quotas.[62] However, as a result of the expected increase in supply from Kazakhstan's Tenghiz fields and the continued collapse of CIS industrial production, output was guaranteed to be in excess of existing pipeline capacity. Even in 1991, it was clear that Kazakhstan would be forced to search for alternatives to existing Soviet lines.[63]

Consistent with our expectations based on the country's integralist elite, Kazakhstan's first choice was to expand its ties to Russia rather than seek alternatives. The first new pipeline approved by the independent Kazakh government was the Caspian Pipeline (CPC) running from northwestern Kazakhstan through Russia to the Black Sea port of Novorossiisk.

---

[60] Energy policy is an area of particular interest for Kazakhstan. The country has substantial oil and gas reserves, which are expected to be exploited for export within the next decade and to provide the bulk of the national income in the coming years. The government is reported to aspire to become the world's sixth largest oil producer by 2010, producing 3.4 million barrels per day. "Kazakhs and Azeris to Lay Pipeline across Caspian Sea," *Alexander's Oil and Gas Connections* 3, no. 18, 26 June 1997.

[61] The quotas were determined by the Russian state-owned company Transneft.

[62] Interviews Kz12, Kz4.

[63] These are precisely the terms in which the matter is put by Kazakh officials. They claim that issues of independence or other political concerns play no role in the search for alternatives. It is simply a technical matter of excess supply; interviews Kz12, Kz4.

In the mid-1990s as oil began to flow from the Kazakh (Chevron) Tenghiz fields and CPC was not yet operational, political pressure mounted from the Kazakh side for their export quota to be increased, at the expense of Russian oil producers. On several occasions, Nazarbaev made direct requests to the Russian president, Yeltsin, and Kazakhstan's quota was increased, but the oil being produced in Kazakhstan was still in excess of the export quota.[64] As a result, the government has given consideration (and occasionally backing) to alternative pipeline routes through Iran[65] or China,[66] or across the Caspian, Azerbaijan, Georgia, and Turkey to the Mediterranean port of Ceyhan, and sent oil out by rail across Uzbekistan and Turkmenistan.

But it is clear that these alternative routes were considered by the Kazakh government as a last resort, rather than a means to enhance Kazakh independence from Russia.[67] Indeed, Nazarbaev explicitly stated that the only reason that Kazakhstan is considering participation in other pipelines is that the current Russian export options were simply too small to meet Kazakhstan's needs.[68] He implied that, if Russia so desired, it could increase the Kazakh quota and Kazakhstan would ship the bulk of its oil via Russia.[69] Nazarbaev has even suggested that if Russia increased Kazakhstan's quota, insufficient volumes of oil would be available for the alternative pipeline routes circumventing Russia – and hence destroy Western efforts to create a Eurasian transit corridor.[70] Whether Kazakh oil is necessary to the viability of these alternative routes or not, the Russians have not chosen to pursue the option of increasing the quotas to the levels that Kazakhstan desires.[71] Thus the Kazakhs have been forced to seek alternatives.

---

[64] Interview Kz12.

[65] Henry Ewing Hale, "Statehood at Stake: Democratization, Secession and the Collapse of the USSR" (Ph.D. Dissertation, Harvard University, p. 357).

[66] In 1997, the government signed a $3 billion deal with China to construct a pipeline running east from the Uzen oilfield to the Pacific Ocean. The entire funding of the project will be covered by China, but it is becoming increasingly likely that the pipeline will not be built; interviews Kz8, Kz12.

[67] Utetleuova stated quite plainly and convincingly that this was purely a technical matter, interview Kz12.

[68] See the interview of Nazarbaev on Moscow NTV in Russian, 1635 GMT, 19 January 1996 ["Hero of the Day": Interview with Kazakh President Nazarbayev at the Kazakh Embassy in Moscow by Leonid Parfenov – recorded] [FBIS Translated Text].

[69] Ibid. This position was also expressed to me by Utetleuova, Kz12.

[70] Nazarbaev in the NTV interview: "Incidentally, these pipelines will not operate through a Caucasus corridor or through Turkey unless Kazakhstan's oil is piped along them.... There will not be anything to fill [them] up with."

[71] Actually, according to an agreement signed by Nazarbaev and Primakov in April 1999, Russia agreed to double Kazakhstan's export quota. It is not clear whether this will be a permanent measure, or whether this was simply a way to help Kazakhstan export its way out of the economic/currency crisis that hit the country in January 1999.

Kazakhstan has also retained close energy relations with other CIS part-ners wherever it has been within the government's power to do so. The Soviet-era joint electricity grid linking southern Kazakhstan, Kyrgyzstan, and Uzbekistan was still being jointly managed and maintained by an inde-pendent regional organization in Tashkent at the end of 1997.[72] This form of cooperation stands in sharp contrast to the Baltic states, which have proven unable to reach the agreement necessary to maintain an equivalent Soviet-era institution linking the energy grids of their states.[73]

As Uzbekistan has moved toward autarky, however, tensions have grown between Kazakhstan and Uzbekistan in energy relations. Kazakhstan, in the Soviet period, received gas from Uzbekistan and Turkmenistan, and Uzbek oil was refined at the major Kazakh refinery in Chimkent. In a three-way barter arrangement, Kazakhstan provided the region with its coal supplies, Uzbekistan supplied natural gas and food, and Kyrgyzstan supplied water and electricity.[74] The Uzbeks have largely broken these ties in their effort to destroy regional specialization and become self-sufficient in fuel supplies. This has precluded the development of "organic" ties with Uzbekistan and, to a considerable extent, in the region as a whole.

KYRGYZSTAN

Although the extent to which liberal ideas were held by members of the Kyrgyz government in the 1990s has often been exaggerated by Western observers seeking bright spots in an illiberal region, it is true that Kyr-gyzstan has been more influenced by liberal ideas than its neighbors. In contrast to Kazakhstan, Uzbekistan, and Turkmenistan, where the Com-munist Party first Secretaries each retained their post, Askar Akaev was a relatively insignificant figure when he was selected by the Kyrgyz Supreme

---

[72] Under this system, electricity producers in each of the countries power a common grid for common usage. Payment is arranged through a central office in an ad hoc manner based on verbal commitment, barter, and other arrangements between energy producers and consumers. Author's interview with Aleksandr Alekseevich Pridatkin, director of the United Controlling Center of Energy Systems of Central Asia UCC "Energia" (hereafter "Pridatkin interview"); author's interview with Talantbek Kazymbekov, head of the External Affairs Department of the Join-Stock Holding Energy Company of the Kyrgyz Republic; author's interview with Bakhytzhan Mukhambetkalievich Dzhaksaliev, head of the Department of Analysis and Strategic Planning of the Ministry of Electricity, Industry, and Trade of the Republic of Kazakhstan.

[73] Personal communication, Teresa Sabonis, Harvard Institute for International Development, November 1997. Sabonis is a nuclear energy specialist who worked extensively on electricity provision in the Baltic region.

[74] Author's interview with head of Department of CIS Affairs, Ministry of Economy, Kaza-khstan.

Soviet to be president in 1990.[75] Most historical accounts attribute Akaev's rise to power to historical accident – he was a compromise figure selected because the most powerful politicians from the North (Absamat Masaliev) and the South (Apas Jumagulov) were too threatening to interests outside their region to secure majority support in the Supreme Soviet.[76] Few believed that he would hold his post for long, but once handed the considerable tools of executive power in Kyrgyzstan he used them effectively to repress or accommodate rivals.

Economic Ideas

As a professor of physics, the USSR's most dissident discipline, who studied in Leningrad, the RSFSR's most dissident city, Akaev was perhaps more inclined to be receptive to liberal economic ideas than his other Central Asian counterparts. And, indeed, he demonstrated an early preference for liberal economics – although the paucity of liberal economists in the republic meant that he largely had to rely on foreign advice. The country's leadership was an awkward hybrid of liberals and integralists throughout the 1990s, leading often to inconsistent positions on the country's choice of international institutions. But on the whole, the liberals retained the upper hand and the country was the first of the post-Soviet states to secure membership in the WTO.

In 1991 and 1992, with Akaev as president and Felix Kulov as vice president, liberal ideas dominated at the highest echelon of decision making in the republic.[77] But the economy went into free-fall as liberal ideas began to be implemented in government policy. And the combination of revived political opposition from the Communist Party and doubt regarding the validity of liberal ideas among government officials themselves opened the door for integralist ideas to gain influence. Between 1991 and 1993, Kazakh GDP (with its avowedly integralist government) declined by approximately 15% and Uzbek GDP by 18%, whereas per capita GDP in the Kyrgyz Republic declined by nearly 30%. The disparities in the quality of life between Kyrgyzstan and the other two countries became painfully obvious. The contrast was made particularly salient by the fact that the Kazakh capital of Almaty

---

[75] Akaev was serving as the president of the Kyrgyz Academy of Sciences when he was tapped for the presidency.

[76] Sadji (pseudonym), "Kyrgyzstan's President Askar Akaev: A Political Portrait," *Jamestown Foundation Prism*, 4, no. 11 (26 May 1998). On the historical origins of the cleavage between North and South in Kyrgyzstan, see Jones Luong, *Institutional Change*, pp. 74–82.

[77] See also Jones Luong, *Institutional Change*, pp. 114–115.

was only a four-hour drive from the Kyrgyz capital of Bishkek. Even in 1997, interviews conducted in the republic among both officials and common Kyrgyz reflected an acute awareness of such differences and the belief that they were linked to the principles behind the policies in the three countries.

By the end of 1993 popular and elite disillusionment with liberal ideas combined with a scandal surrounding the embezzlement of national gold reserves nearly brought down Akaev. Prime Minister Chyngyshev and Vice President Kulov both resigned. The Communist Party, led by two former Soviet-era first secretaries, had returned as a powerful force in parliament and was calling for Akaev's removal. Akaev remained in office but in December 1993 was forced to bring the head of the Communist Party into the government as first deputy prime minister and to name the former chairman of the Kyrgyz SSR Council of Ministers, Apas Jumagulov, as prime minister. Both were integralists. The combination of an integralist administration with a liberal presidency led local commentators to refer to the government, appropriately, as a "bureaucratic centaur."[78]

Akaev retained his liberal economic orientation, however, and his efforts to put liberal ideas into practice within the republic were helped along by the country's superpresidential constitution and a considerable amount of foreign aid. Foreign aid, much of it from the United States, rose from $5 per capita in 1992 to $25 in 1993, to $38 in 1994 – or 67% of government expenditure.[79] This allowed Akaev to buy off some of his illiberal enemies and to gain the upper hand over regionally based rivals like Jumagulov and Masaliev. But the split between liberals and integralists within the government remained a salient feature throughout the 1990s until Jumagulov was finally ousted in March 1998.

Interviews conducted in fall 1997 identified a notable division between top officials who were liberal-oriented and lower-level ministerial officials who viewed the economy in integralist terms. This was particularly notable in interviews in the Ministry of Finance, where the lower-level integralist officials were often engaged in debates with their superiors about the utility of joining the WTO and about the costs and benefits of maintaining an open economy.[80] Similar debates and battles were conducted in the Ministry of Industry and Trade, where the minister, who was close to President Akaev, drew on a younger cadre of economists to argue on behalf of economic openness and the need for smaller industrial enterprises to replace Soviet

---

[78] This expression was widely used in interviews.
[79] World Bank, World Development Indicators, in constant 1995 dollars.
[80] Interviews K2, K3, K4, K9.

behemoths whose production processes were no longer viewed as competitive or of the appropriate scale.[81] Such theoretical discussions took place within the Customs Commission as well.[82] In general, within individual ministries, Kyrgyz officials were divided, and very often personally conflicted, about the best way to organize their economy and escape the crisis. Across ministries, one could note that integralist ideas were more prevalent in the Ministry of Foreign Affairs, the Ministry of CIS Cooperation, the National Energy Company, and the Association of Industrialists and Entrepreneurs.[83] Liberalism was predominant in the National Bank, although there, too, there was active discussion concerning the proper economic course and whether a strong, stable currency was necessary.[84]

Institutional and Policy Choice

In terms of its foreign economic policy and institutional membership, Kyrgyzstan presents something of a puzzling picture. The country has been one of the most active participants of the post-Soviet countries in CIS economic agreements. In 1996, Kyrgyzstan signed the Treaty on Deepening Economic Cooperation with Russia, Kazakhstan, and Belarus and joined the Customs Union. In 2000, Kyrgyzstan joined the same four countries and Tajikistan in forming the Eurasian Union. At the same time, however, Kyrgyzstan was the first post-Soviet country to become a member of the World Trade Organization, securing its membership in 1998 after first submitting its application only in 1996.

Several points are worthy of note, however. First, Kyrgyzstan's rapid move toward WTO entry happened through a tremendous push of activity – an unprecedented five meetings of the Working Group – in 1998 after Jumagulov was ousted and Akaev was in complete control of the government. The activities toward CIS membership took place while Jumagulov was still in the government and then again after the political fallout from the August 1998 financial crisis led Akaev's government again to turn away from liberalism. Second, as explained in Chapter 10, the Kyrgyz government primarily participated in the Customs Union as a way of securing unrestricted trade with Russia and Kazakhstan – its two main trading partners. The country never actually implemented the common external tariff and retained a very

---

[81] Interviews K5, K10, K18.
[82] Interviews K1, K15.
[83] Interviews K7, K8, K11, K12.
[84] Interview K5.

liberal trade regime. Hence, Kyrgyz policy was more consistently liberal than it would appear. At the same time, however, the hybrid or "centaur"-like quality of the government was clearly reflected in the mix of Kyrgyz policy and institutional choices.

After the liberal reforms of 1991 and 1992 such as price liberalization and the privatization of land, Kyrgyzstan's domestic economic policies have actually followed closely along the lines of those in Kazakhstan. In energy policy, Kyrgyzstan is an importer of oil and gas and continues to receive supplies from its traditional sources in Uzbekistan and Turkmenistan. Kyrgyzstan is a net exporter of electricity from its hydroelectric plants and continued to supply the Central Asian electrical grid with electricity at below-market rates throughout the 1990s – in effect providing a subsidy to enterprises in neighboring Uzbekistan and Kazakhstan. As of 2000, there had been no privatization of the energy sector, although there were plans for the development of an independent oil refinery so as not to rely on neighboring states. Large-scale privatization was relatively limited, and with few exceptions large enterprises either remained under state ownership or were transferred to company collectives. Both strategies have facilitated the maintenance of prior inter-enterprise ties with other post-Soviet states. And as in Kazakhstan, the Kyrgyz government made an effort to transfer state shares of key union-linked enterprises, primarily military industries, to the Russian government ministries that control the enterprises that were once part of their Soviet complexes. In macroeconomic policy, Kyrgyzstan has been largely liberal. The country conducted price liberalization in 1992 and followed with an IMF stabilization package shortly thereafter. State orders were no longer made after 1994, but the government continued to give loans to industry that were not collected.

TAJIKISTAN

In Tajikistan, the government was fighting a civil war for most of the years between 1991 and 1998. The government in Dushanbe nonetheless did sustain a foreign economic policy during that time and established clear institutional commitments. Since November 1992, the government has been led by Emomali Rakhmonov, but heavily influenced by Russian policymakers. On the basis of the composition of the elite – an unreformed Communist Party – and the close ties to integralist factions in Russia, it seems reasonable to view Tajikistan as integralist, although the direct evidence of the economic beliefs of Tajik leadership is scarce and public statements vague and contradictory.

The government's record on institutional and policy choice is a bit clearer and more straightforward. In its foreign economic policy and institutional commitments Tajikistan has consistently worked to integrate within the CIS. Tajikistan signed all CIS economic agreements between 1992 and 1998 and had one of the best records of subsequent ratification and implementation of the agreements. The country consistently tried to gain access to the CIS Customs Union, but because of the ongoing civil war its two Central Asian neighbors opposed its admission. Finally, with an agreement to end the civil war in place, Tajikistan was allowed to join the Customs Union and subsequently took on membership in the Eurasian Union as well. True to the integralist type, Tajikistan has made essentially no progress toward WTO membership. The country took on observer status in July 2001 but did not follow with an application.

On the whole, the Tajik government pursued economic policies that followed integralist tenets and tried as much as possible to maintain ties with the other CIS states. The Tajik government fiercely resisted the collapse of the ruble zone and made a special arrangement with Russia whereby Tajikistan was allowed to use the new Russian ruble. This arrangement was maintained until May 1995, when the Tajik ruble was introduced after the Russian Central Bank ceased to supply the country with fresh Russian rubles.

In energy policy, Tajikistan made no effort to diversify supply away from previous partners or to privatize, but with limited resources with which to pay for imports of oil and natural gas it also had trouble maintaining supplies from Uzbekistan, its traditional supplier. Half of the country's electricity needs are supplied by domestic hydroelectric plants. One could say that Tajikistan's energy policy is as much a function of inertia as design, but it is consistent with integralist tenets.

Likewise, the government had not pursued a privatization program by the end of the 1990s, but the civil war limited the extent to which its enterprises have been able to maintain ties with their Soviet-era partners. Some spontaneous privatization took place during the civil war, as different armed factions seized factories, but this was clearly not indicative of any government policy. In 1994, the Council of Ministers created Soyuz, a transnational financial–industrial group with Russian backing, the purpose of which was "to restore disrupted economic ties and develop the country's construction industry and agro-industrial complex."[85]

---

[85] *Dushanbe Radio Dushanbe Network, FBIS-SOV-94-235, 6 December 1994.zzz*

In macroeconomic policy, consumer goods prices were freed in 1995, but the government still required that a significant portion of production be given to the state. Inflation has been rampant as the government has subsidized industries and farms, but as in Georgia, this most likely simply reflects the efforts of the Rakhmonov government to buy political support during the civil war.

CONCLUSIONS

Central Asia presents a useful set of cases for comparison and yields important confirmation for the role of economic ideas. Turkmenistan, Uzbekistan, and Kazakhstan were all rich in energy resources and exportable goods. All three countries had leaders who previously served as the first secretary of the Communist Party in the republic and managed to transition comfortably into the role of authoritarian leader of an independent state after the USSR was dismantled (despite their best efforts to preserve it). The region as a whole was one of the least developed industrially and nationalism was weaker in these five states than in any others.[86] Each of the five countries faced the potential security threat posed by the civil war in Afghanistan and the interests of foreign powers in a strategically important region. But despite these similarities, the region bears the starkest variation in the institutional choices made by its governments. Kyrgyzstan was the first of the post-Soviet states to join the World Trade Organization. Kazakhstan and Tajikistan were two of the strongest advocates of regional institutions, and Turkmenistan and Uzbekistan grew into models of economic and institutional autarky after 1994.

The Central Asian states also show us the importance of the economic views of leaders and, in this case, often the ideas of a single individual. The differences between a liberal professor (Akaev in Kyrgyzstan), a former industrial manager steeped in Soviet integralism (Nazarbaev in Kazakhstan), and a Soviet-trained economist who, spurned by Russia's liberals, converted typical Marxist arguments about colonialism into a mercantilist model exalting economic self-sufficiency (Karimov in Uzbekistan), became exceptionally important when independence gave those individuals supreme power and discretion over policy. Through both their direct decisions and the enormous power they wielded in selecting economic officials, the differences in the economic ideas of the Central Asian presidents were central in determining the international trajectories of the countries they ruled.

[86] Darden, "Scholastic Revolution"; Jones Luong, "Politics in the Periphery."

PART THREE

COMPARING CASES

9

Alternative Explanations and Statistical Tests

We now turn directly to the challenge of rival explanations. The purpose of this chapter is to test the argument that economic ideas drive institutional choice against the dominant alternative explanations for variation in support for international trade institutions. Drawing on both qualitative evidence and a novel cross-national time-series dataset covering the post-Soviet states from 1991 to 2000, this chapter finds little support for realist and liberal arguments and partial support for nationalism/identity-based arguments and finds that the estimated role of economic ideas on institutional choice is substantively significant, statistically significant, and robust. To make this case, I first assess the existing alternative explanations theoretically and methodologically, formulate their claims as testable hypotheses, and evaluate them using qualitative comparison where appropriate. Then, moving to a discussion of the statistical tests, I describe the relevant variables used to test these approaches and detail the methods used to identify the economic ideas of the governing elite. Finally, I present and interpret the statistical results.

EXISTING EXPLANATIONS: NATIONALISM AND IDENTITY

The increasing importance of national identity in constructivist theories of international relations has naturally led some scholars to ascribe the variation in the behavior of the post-Soviet states to differences in the strength or type of nationalist sentiment.[1] When applied to Russia, these approaches

---

[1] Several scholars have cited a lingering "imperial culture" and different levels of national identity as an explanation of the variation in state behavior in the region. See Mark R. Beissinger, "The Persisting Ambiguity of Empire," *Post-Soviet Affairs* 11 (1995): 149–194;

suggest that Russia carries an imperial identity that leads it to push for the creation of regional institutions to reestablish its empire. On these accounts, being "masters of the empire" is central to Russian national identity and Russians view the 14 other republics as their Eurasian patrimony. Authors making this case contend that Russia is unwilling to abandon its perceived role as "the Third Rome" and will use all forms of economic leverage or military pressure to bring the other post-Soviet states back under its control within CIS institutions.

Regarding the remaining 14 post-Soviet states, authors have suggested that it is the strength of national identity that explains the variation in institutional membership. Hence, countries with a stronger national identity are more likely to be able to resist Russian pressure. A widely assumed corollary to this argument claims that post-Soviet states with ethnically divided populations or lacking a prior history of independent statehood will have weaker national identities and be less able to resist Russian imperialism. Abdelal, drawing on the work of Friedrich List, has made a related argument that it is only countries with an uncontested national identity that will be willing to endure the short-term costs of liberalizing their economies and redirecting their trade to partners outside of the Soviet sphere.[2]

A related argument suggests that it is not the "strength" but the type or content of the national identity that best explains state choice. Abdelal, Tsygankov, Shulman, and others have all argued that national identity can pull states toward as well as away from particular partners and institutions.[3] These authors suggest that because the Baltic states, for example, had

Ronald Grigor Suny, "Ambiguous Categories: States, Empires, and Nations," *Post-Soviet Affairs* 11 (1995): 185–196; Roman Solchanyk, "Russia, Ukraine, and the Imperial Legacy," *Post-Soviet Affairs* 9 (1993): 337–365; Dawisha, "Constructing and Deconstructing"; Frederick S. Starr, "Introduction," in *The Legacy of History in Russia and the New States of Eurasia*, ed. Frederick S. Starr (New York: M. E. Sharpe, 1994); Roman Szporluk, "Introduction," in *National Identity and Ethnicity in Russia and the New States of Eurasia*, ed. Roman Szporluk (New York: M. E. Sharpe, 1994); Zbigniew Brzezinski, "Introduction: Last Gasp or Renewal?" in *Russia and the Commonwealth of Independent States*, ed. Zbigniew Brzezinski and Paige Sullivan (New York: M. E. Sharpe, 1997); Martha Brill Olcott, Anders Aslund, and Sherman W. Garnett, *Getting It Wrong: Regional Cooperation and the Commonwealth of Independent States* (Washington, D.C.: The Carnegie Endowment for International Peace, 1999).

[2] Abdelal, *National Purpose*, pp. 27–29.

[3] A. P. Tsygankov, "Defining State Interests after Empire: National Identity, Domestic Structures, and Foreign Trade Policies of Latvia and Belarus," *Review of International Political Economy* 7 (2000): 101–137; A. P. Tsygankov, *Pathways after Empire: National Identity and Foreign Economic Policy in the Post-Soviet World* (Lanham, Md.: Rowman & Littlefield, 2001); Abdelal, *National Purpose*; Ilya Prizel, *National Identity and Foreign Policy: Nationalism and Leadership in Poland, Russia, and Ukraine* (Cambridge: Cambridge University

a "European" identity, they were drawn toward the trade institutions that were considered to be consistent with that identity and away from the USSR. As Abdelal notes, "The directionality inherent in national identity engenders a direction for foreign economic policy. Nationalisms favor economic policies that emphasize separateness and autonomy from specific states in the international system; protectionism in trade is therefore a common consequence of nationalism.... Nationalism results in discord with specific states, and it may even lead to cooperation with other specific states."[4] In short, the main outcome that we should expect from nationalism is a consistent pattern of trade discrimination favoring some states and punishing others. In extending this argument to international institutions, we might expect that nationalism in states other than Russia should generate resistance to participation in CIS institutions but push states to move more rapidly into Western liberal institutions.

From the identity approaches, we may draw the following hypotheses, not all of which will be shared by all theorists in this group:

H1.1: States with stronger and more consensual national identities should erect barriers to trade with Russia (and/or other states identified as historical enemies or "others").

H1.2: More ethnically homogeneous states or states with stronger national identities should be less active participants in CIS institutions and move rapidly into Western liberal institutions.

H1.3: Russia should be a strong and consistent advocate of stronger regional institutions.

There are several difficulties with the nationalist or identity-based accounts, both theoretical–methodological and empirical. On the theoretical side, the relationship between national identity and specific policies is not carefully specified. "Who we are" may be a prior question to "what we want,"[5] but how identity determines or bounds the range of legitimate policies remains somewhat unclear; the theoretical account lacks a causal mechanism.

In terms of method, these accounts suffer from poorly specified measures for national identity and biases in case selection. In most of this work, there is insufficient evidence of the independent origins of nationalism or a good

---

Press, 1998); Steven Shulman, "Nationalist Sources of International Economic Integration," *International Studies Quarterly* 44 (2000): 365–390.

[4] Abdelal, *National Purpose*, p. 32.

[5] Wendt, *Social Purpose*; Abdelal, *National Purpose*, p. 1.

enough measure of it to test for its effects or ameliorate concerns about endogeneity. Indeed the implicit measures are often not clearly distinguished from the policies that they are intended to explain; hence liberalization and/or the redirection of trade away from Russia is used both as the primary evidence of "nationalism" and as the outcome that national identity is to account for. Moreover, all of the existing analyses share a similar bias in the cases that they have selected – each rests on a comparison between Ukraine and Belarus, and a Baltic state (Latvia or Lithuania). There are, however, a variety of factors that distinguish the Baltic states from Belarus and Ukraine that are not controlled for here but that potentially bias the analysis. Moreover, the choice also raises questions about the omission of countries like Moldova, which had a strong nationalist movement in 1990 but then participated actively in the CIS in the mid-1990s, or Kyrgyzstan, which has no history of anti-Russian nationalism yet was the first country in the region to enter the WTO. I attempt to resolve both of these problems in the statistical analysis that follows, by introducing a new instrument for measuring anti-Russian nationalism and by expanding the range of observations to include all 15 countries over 10 years.

The most important empirical limitation of the argument is that it does not mobilize any evidence in favor of the core hypothesis: i.e. that the more nationalistic Baltic countries took policy measures to discriminate against Russia in their trade relations (H1.1). And indeed, the evidence presented in Chapter 5 suggests precisely the opposite – i.e. that the Baltic governments went to considerable effort to try to expand rather than curtail their economic ties with Russia and other post-Soviet countries. Nor is it clear that the shift in trade flows from East to West occurred by government design or that it resulted from national sentiment rather than from the collapse of economies to the East and the opening of the Western frontier after the collapse of the USSR.

Indeed, there is some suggestion that a significant portion of this apparent shift in trade in the 1990s may also be the result of measurement error. Because the borders with Russia and other post-Soviet states were only legal fictions in the 1990s, much of the trade that crossed those boundaries went unmeasured. In contrast, the Western border was a "hard" border complete with customs posts, and hence this trade was more accurately recorded.[6]

---

[6] It is well known that the Baltic countries served as a corridor for evading Russian export tariffs in the early 1990s. Russian-produced goods would be shipped (illegally) through Latvia, Lithuania, and Estonia to be sold abroad. It is worth noting that, throughout the

The hypotheses about ethnic homogeneity, identity, and participation in the CIS and the WTO are tested using statistical methods below.

REALISM

Arguments drawing on realist or neorealist theories of international relations have stressed the power imbalances embodied in international institutions and the coercion required to establish and maintain them.[7] Writing in this vein, several scholars have suggested that Russia has pressured the other post-Soviet states to participate in CIS economic institutions such as the Customs Union because such institutions primarily serve Russian economic interests or provide important security externalities.[8] They contend that the variation in support for the regional economic institutions reflects differences in the capacity to resist Russia, and that military weakness, dependence on Russia for trade or energy resources, or dependence on Russia to help

1990s, the leading Western exports of the three Baltic countries were goods that were not produced within the country; much of their export is reexport.

[7] On the role of a hegemonic state in establishing a particular institutional order (liberal or otherwise) to serve its interests, see, among others, Albert O. Hirschman, *National Power and the Structure of Foreign Trade* (Berkeley: University of California Press, 1945); Stephen D. Krasner, "State Power and the Structure of International Trade," *World Politics* 28 (1976): 317–347; Robert Gilpin, *War and Change in World Politics* (Cambridge: Cambridge University Press, 1987); David A. Lake, *Power, Protection, and Free Trade* (Ithaca, N.Y.: Cornell University Press, 1988); David A. Lake, "Anarchy, Hierarchy, and the Variety of International Relations," *International Organization* 50 (1996): 1–33; Joanne Gowa, *Allies, Adversaries, and International Trade* (Princeton, N.J.: Princeton University Press, 1993). On the specific application of an approach that uses realist assumptions regarding Russian motivations, see Daniel W. Drezner, *The Sanctions Paradox: Economic Statecraft and International Relations* (Cambridge: Cambridge University Press, 1999).

[8] Examples of work that stresses the geopolitical, power-maximizing, or security concerns as explanatory factors for the behavior of states in the region are Barry R. Posen, "The Security Dilemma and Ethnic Conflict," *Survival* 35 (1993): 27–41; William E. Odom and Robert Dujarric, *Commonwealth or Empire? Russia, Central Asia, and the Transcaucasus* (Indianapolis: Hudson Institute, 1995); Abraham Becker, *Survival*, 38 (1996/1997): 117–136; Brzezinski and Sullivan, *Russia and the Commonwealth of Independent States*; Olcott, Aslund, and Garnett, *Getting It Wrong*; Hendrik Spruyt, "The Prospects for Neo-Imperial and Non-Imperial Outcomes in the Former Soviet Space," in *The End of Empire? The Transformation of the USSR in Comparative Perspective*, ed. Karen Dawisha and Bruce Parrott, 315–337 (New York: M. E. Sharpe, 1997) uses realism to explain the behavior of some states. Realist elements come into the discussion of Mark Webber, *CIS Integration Trends: Russia and the Former Soviet South.* (London: Royal Institute of International Affairs, 1997); Philip G. Roeder, *Red Sunset: The Failure of Soviet Politics*, (Princeton, N.J.: Princeton University Press, 1993). Some basic realist assumptions about preferences go into Lake, "Anarchy, Hierarchy."

counter internal or external security threats would make states more easily coerced into joining the union.[9] And consistently with the realist claim that all states seek to maximize their security and autonomy, the states in the region should work to achieve independent supply of energy, food, and other vital goods. Where possible, states should resist specialization.[10] The realist approach yields the following hypotheses:

H2.1: States with greater independent military capability will be less likely to participate actively in CIS institutions

H2.2: States that are more dependent on Russia for their external trade will be more likely to participate in CIS institutions and less likely to pursue membership in the WTO.

H2.3: States more dependent on Russia for their supply of oil or natural gas should be more likely to participate in CIS institutions.

H2.4: States that face internal or external threats to their security should be more likely to participate in CIS institutions.

H2.5: Russia, as regional hegemon, should be a strong and consistent supporter of CIS institutions.

There are some important empirical problems with the realist account. First and foremost, the actions of the Russian government, particularly in the early 1990s, are inconsistent with the realist account of how the hegemon should behave. If we look at the period from 1991 to 1993, when economic liberals were in control of the Russian government, Russia did not act to preserve its "empire" in the wake of the formal collapse of the Soviet Union in 1991. Indeed, the Russian leadership acted to expedite and ensure the

---

[9] Lake, "Anarchy, Hierarchy."

[10] Kenneth N. Waltz, *Theory of International Politics* (San Francisco: McGraw-Hill, 1979). Gowa, Mansfield, and others have pointed to the alternative possibility that security-conscious states will engage in specialized trade with alliance partners because such trade strengthens their partners (i.e. it generates security externalities). This would seem to be inconsistent with core (neo)realist assumptions, however, in which alliances are viewed as fluid marriages of convenience. As today's ally could be tomorrow's enemy, and states re-form alliances as suits them, the creation of interdependent ties with specific partners could threaten state autonomy and security. States should be concerned about relative gains even among their allies and bloc members. Joseph Grieco, "Systemic Sources of Variation in Regional Institutionalization in Western Europe, East Asia, and the Americas," in *The Political Economy of Regionalism*, ed. Edward D. Mansfield and Helen V. Milner (New York: Columbia University Press, 1997), pp. 164–187; Gowa, *Allies, Adversaries*; Edward D. Mansfield and Rachel Bronson, "The Political Economy of Major-Power Trade Flows," in *The Political Economy of Regionalism*, ed. Edward D. Mansfield and Helen V. Milner (New York: Columbia University Press, 1997), pp. 188–208.

collapse of union-level institutions (hence contradicting **H2.5**). And in both military and economic relations the Russian government scuttled any early efforts to create strong CIS institutions in the wake of the Soviet collapse.

In security matters, Russia quickly pressed all states other than those engaged in civil war to adopt separate, sovereign control over Soviet military forces on their territories.[11] In nuclear matters, several agreements were signed to transfer all tactical and strategic nuclear weapons to Russia – thus removing the need for joint control structures and common institutions. Indeed, the government of Kazakhstan, correctly interpreting the step as a move toward state sovereignty, initially resisted the removal of nuclear weapons from its territory as a way of ensuring that some sort of common security architecture would be maintained.[12]

We see a similar push by the Russian government toward the sovereignization of conventional forces. Despite the Russian government's early rhetoric about maintaining unified command of a CIS Joint Armed Forces, conventional forces were rapidly put into the sole control of sovereign states as well. Here, too, the process was spearheaded, rather than resisted, by Russia. Russia formed its own armed forces in 1992, assumed control of the Soviet troops in the Baltic states in January 1992, and in spring 1992 took command of former Soviet units in Poland, Germany, Mongolia, and Cuba as well as in the Transcaucasus and Moldova. Russia simultaneously assumed control of the Soviet Air Force and Navy and announced the formation of its own Ministry of Defense, which was made up mostly of officers of the CIS High Command.[13] In the rest of the post-Soviet states, Soviet army units and equipment on the territory of the former republics fell under the national control of those republics.

Following the establishment of the principle of sovereign control, the Russian government worked actively to limit the development of a unified security architecture under the CIS. A plan drafted by CIS Commander-in-Chief Evgenii Shaposhnikov in May 1993 outlined a North Atlantic Treaty Organization (NATO)-style arrangement with a permanent CIS force and consensus decision making. The proposal was supported by Armenia, Kazakhstan, Kyrgyzstan, and Tajikistan but became a dead letter as a result of

---

[11] For a remarkably detailed and informed account of the politics surrounding this decision, see William E. Odom, *The Collapse of the Soviet Military* (New Haven, Conn.: Yale University Press, 1998), chap. 16.

[12] Henry Ewing Hale, "Russia's Fiscal Veto on CIS Integration," *PONARS Policy Memo* 15 (1997): 382.

[13] The navy and air force were subsequently divided up among the successor republics as well.

opposition from the Russian military.[14] Instead, a Russian military proposal adopted in June 1993 abolished the CIS High Command and replaced it with a tiny "Staff for Military Cooperation and Coordination." This led Shaposhnikov to declare that "the Commonwealth's Joint Armed Forces have not been and will not be created."[15] This was the end of joint military command.

In sum, the Russian government worked to divide the Soviet security architecture into sovereign units and blocked any efforts to build strong CIS institutions. Such actions are inconsistent with the notion that CIS institutions are an expression of Russian imperial ambition and that Russia has fought to retain them. Even in the military sphere, where this argument seems most appropriately applied, the realist and identity arguments fail to explain the key role that Russia played in destroying, not supporting, the institutions of the CIS. Had the Russian leadership not been so committed to the sovereignization of the Soviet security architecture, it is unlikely that the "empire" would have broken up. And we see a similar pattern in economic matters, particularly in Russia's role in the destruction of the ruble zone, described in detail in the next chapter.

And indeed, there is little to support the claim that the most active participants in the regional institutions have done so because they were subject to coercion. Indeed, it has been states other than Russia – most notably Belarus and Kazakhstan – that have pushed most strongly for the formation of strong regional institutions. In fact, Kazakhstan forced its way into what was originally intended to be a customs union between Russia and Belarus. President Nursultan Nazarbaev of Kazakhstan has also consistently been the strongest advocate for the creation of supranational institutions. In the case of the Customs Union, for example, it was Kazakhstan that pushed for supranational institutions against Russia's initial opposition (see Chapter 10). Initiatives for stronger supranational institutions have often met with opposition from the Russian side, depending on who is governing the country at the time.

The pro-CIS position taken by several post-Soviet states was not a unique personal attribute of individual leaders like Nazarbaev, the Belarusian president Aleksandr Lukashenko, or others. Nor, in contrast to an argument advanced by Philip Roeder, does it appear that self-interested leaders turn

[14] The proposal was resoundingly crushed by the Russian Ministry of Defense: Odom, *The Collapse*, pp. 375–387; Mark Webber and Richard Sakwa, "The Commonwealth of Independent States, 1991–1998: Stagnation and Survival," *Europe-Asia Studies* 51 (1999): 383.

[15] Webber and Sakwa, *The Commonwealth*, 384.

to the CIS because they need Russia's help to stay in power and allay the threats of a hostile population.[16] Surveys and referenda indicate that broad popular support for economic union exists in many post-Soviet countries.[17] Even in Ukraine, a state that is well below the mean in its support for CIS institutions, a poll conducted in July 1995 by Socis-Gallup showed that only 44% of the population preferred an independent Ukrainian state: 56% of the population favored either a CIS federated state or direct unification with Russia.[18] In states that participate more actively in CIS integration, such as Belarus and Kazakhstan, support has been even stronger.[19]

To test the hypothesis that states facing internal or external security threats will be more likely to participate in the regional institutions (H2.4), we can examine Table 9.1.

According to the realist approach, any one of these security threats might lead a state to be drawn into Russia's "orbit." As is clear from Table 9.1, however, states that face any one of these potential threats are no more likely to support CIS institutions than those that do not. Aside from Armenia, which faced a clear threat from Azerbaijan and Turkey, the only countries that faced a direct military threat were the four Central Asian states that are in proximity to Afghanistan. And of these four states, two rank among the strongest supporters of CIS economic institutions, and two rank among the opponents. Likewise, of the seven states that face direct threats to their internal security through insurrection or separatist movements, only two, Kyrgyzstan and Tajikistan, have shown a strong inclination toward CIS institutions. If we assume that any one of these threats would be sufficient to lead a state to support CIS institutions, then, as shown in the final column, only half of the states conform to the expectations of the theory. Moreover, the state with the strongest commitment to CIS institutions, Belarus, faces none of these security concerns, whereas Ukraine, which is afflicted with two out of the three, has proved resistant. Thus, upon closer examination we find that the states that might be expected to rely on Russia for security reasons are some of the strongest opponents of CIS integration, and states that

---

[16] Philip G. Roeder, "From Hierarchy to Hegemony: The Post-Soviet Security Complex," in *Regional Orders*, ed. David A. Lake and Patrick M. Morgan (University Park: Pennsylvania State University Press, 1997), pp. 235–239.

[17] This has been documented extensively in U.S. State Department surveys. See Regina Faranda, "Ties That Bind, Opinions That Divide: How Neighboring Countries Have Viewed Russia, 1991–2001," *Office of Research, U.S. Department of State, May 21* (2001): R-2-01.

[18] Statistical error +/- 3%. *Kiev Demokratychna* Ukrayina, in Ukrainian, 17 June 1995, p. 1 (FBIS-SOV-95-131-S, 10 July 1995, p. 63).

[19] In a referendum conducted in Belarus in May 1995, more than 80% of the population supported union with Russia.

TABLE 9.1. *Potential Security Threats Faced by Post-Soviet States[a]*

	Large Russian population (more than 20% of total)	Internal Threat Due to Separatist Region or Insurrection	Russia Needed as a Balancing Partner against External Threat?	Institutional Membership (2002)[b]	Confirms Hypothesis?
Armenia	No	No	Yes	None (WTO)	No
Azerbaijan	No	Yes	No	None	No
Belarus	No	No	No	Eurasian Union	No
Estonia	Yes	No	No	WTO	No
Georgia	No	Yes	No	WTO	No
Kazakhstan	Yes	No	No	Eurasian Union	Yes
Kyrgyzstan	Yes	Yes	(Yes)	EAU/WTO	Yes/No
Latvia	Yes	No	No	WTO	No
Lithuania	No	No	No	WTO	Yes
Moldova	Yes	Yes	No	None (WTO)	No
Tajikistan	No	Yes	(Yes)	Eurasian Union	Yes
Turkmenistan	No	No	(Yes)	None	Yes (No)
Ukraine	Yes	Yes	No	None	No
Uzbekistan	No	Yes	(Yes)	None	No

[a] I consider states to face an internal security threat if they have suffered either an insurrectionary movement or regional separatism. States with external security threats are those that border on powers that either have made territorial claims on their territory, have a recent history of bellicose behavior, or otherwise appear threatening. As some scholars have suggested that a large Russian population is also a potential internal security threat, we will also include this in the analysis.

[b] Subsequent members of the WTO are noted "(WTO)."

face none of these security threats are among the most active proponents of stronger regional institutions. On the whole, the hypothesis performs worse than a coin toss – no systematic relationship is evident along the lines hypothesized.

It has become common for scholars to argue that the separatist conflicts that broke out in Nagornyi Karabakh in Azerbaijan, in Abkhazia and South Ossetia in Georgia, and in the Transdniestr region in Moldova were all fostered by the Russian government as a way of weakening these post-Soviet states and forcing their entry into the CIS.[20] There is good reason to question

---

[20] Olcott, Aslund, and Garnett, *Getting it Wrong*, p. 14, imply that states that sought independence of the CIS faced Russian-sponsored separatist movements as a result.

the conventional wisdom here. Of the six states that chose not to join the CIS, three confronted violent separatist movements, but three (the Baltic states) did not – despite the existence of a significant Russian minority in two of the states. If it were the Russian government's policy to secure membership of all 15 post-Soviet states in the CIS with force, one would have expected a more uniform response to efforts to achieve independence. Moreover, in one of the three separatist conflicts, Nagornyi Karabakh, violence broke out prior to the collapse of the Soviet Union and enjoyed considerable support from neighboring Armenia. In the case of Nagornyi Karabakh, it appears to have been the weakening of Soviet control over the region that led to the eruption of violence, not (at least not initially) the provocative actions of Soviet or Russian forces. In the other two cases, Transdniestr and Abkhazia, the conflicts began when the central governments deprived minorities of the status or privileges they previously enjoyed under the Soviet Union. Abkhazia was stripped of its autonomous status under Zviad Gamsakhurdia's rule and Transdniestr faced a pro-Romanian central government that was pursuing language policies that would have deprived the majority of the population of political and economic rights. In short, there were perfectly reasonable local reasons for the conflict. At the very least, one need not assume that the existence of separatist violence necessarily reflects the involvement of Moscow. Indeed, it is worth recalling that Russia itself has faced separatist violence in Chechnya.

Likewise, there is no evidence that states that are more dependent on Russia in trade or for the supply of vital resources have been more inclined toward CIS institutions (H2.2, H2.3), as one would expect if states joined CIS economic institutions as a result of Russian pressure. In fact, several of the countries in the region that are most dependent on Russia for their trade and energy resources have been the most resistant to moves to form stronger regional institutions.

First, we may note that only a minority of countries in the region supporting CIS integration are even dependent on Russia for their primary energy supply. In 1994, at the time of the creation of the IEC and shortly before the formation of the Customs Union, the energy trade of the post-Soviet states was as shown in Table 9.2.[21]

As shown in the table, Russia was the primary supplier of natural gas only for Belarus, Ukraine, and the Baltic states.[22] Of these states, only Belarus has chosen to take an active role in the regional economic institutions. Thus,

---

[21] Data compiled from CIS Statistical Commission (1994).

[22] The left column is the more significant one in the post-Soviet context. Gas is used to heat most homes and to run most of the region's nonnuclear power plants. The volume and

TABLE 9.2. *Oil and Gas Trade among the Post-Soviet States*

	Natural Gas Suppliers			Oil and Gas Condensate Suppliers		
	Russia	Turkmenistan	Uzbekistan	Russia	Kazakhstan	Uzbekistan
Armenia		X		X		
Azerbaijan		X				
Belarus	X			X		
Estonia	X			X		
Georgia		X		X		
Kazakhstan						
Kyrgyzstan	X (third)	X (first)	X (second)			
Latvia	X			X		
Lithuania	X			X		
Moldova		X		Supplied by Romania in 1994		
Russia						
Tajikistan			X			
Turkmen.				X (third)	X (second)	X (first)
Ukraine	X (first)	X (second)		X (first)	X (second)	X (third)
Uzbekistan						

even though it is commonly stated that Belarusian energy dependence is the cause of its prointegration stance, this claim for causation collapses given that all of the other countries facing the same conditions of dependency do not support CIS institutions.

The same criticism holds with respect to oil supplies. Those states that favor integration and those that resist it number equally among the oil exporters and oil suppliers in the region. Clearly, Russia either lacks the ability to use oil dependence as a means of political leverage or simply chooses not to do so. Once again, the resistance of energy-dependent Ukraine and the Baltic states to integration, and the fact that many states not dependent on Russia for energy resources, such as Kazakhstan and Kyrgyzstan, have been among the strongest advocates of further integration, suggests that this hypothesis should be rejected.[23]

Although most post-Soviet states are partially dependent on Russian pipelines for energy transit, the Russian firm Gazprom has only very rarely, and for very brief periods, shut off gas supplies as a means to force countries

significance of the oil trade are lower. Note: after 1994, Moldova made arrangements to import Russian gas as well.

[23] In terms of food products, it should be noted that Russia is a primary importer of agricultural products. Russia is dependent upon the other CIS states for food supplies and cannot exert leverage in this area except by applying import tariffs and quotas on exports from CIS states (but this probably does more harm to Russia than it does to the trading partners in question).

to deal with payment arrears. Given the size of their arrears, and the rarity of interruptions in delivery, there is no reason to suspect strategic intent on Russia's part. It is important to keep in mind that no paying customer has ever had the gas shut off, and Russia has been extremely flexible in rescheduling its neighbors' debts. In fact, Turkmenistan, which is the primary gas supplier for as many states as Russia, has been much more aggressive in interrupting supply as a means for exacting payment, and much less flexible in negotiating terms. As objective behavior, the interruptions in gas delivery by Russia and Turkmenistan are the same, and there is no good reason to interpret them differently. There is no reason to assume that the occasional interruptions in gas shipments to Ukraine or Belarus involve anything more than an effort to secure more timely payment. Russia has also been flexible with respect to transit. In most cases, Russia has increased the transit quotas available to countries seeking to export oil or gas to Europe.

If Russia were using its role as an energy supplier to leverage its geopolitical agenda, one would expect that the states such as Latvia, Lithuania, Estonia, and Ukraine, which are most vulnerable to such pressure, would be the most closely integrated into CIS structures. Their continued opposition, and the support for integration among countries independent of Russia for energy, do not support this hypothesis.

In sum, if Russia were preying on the weaknesses of its post-Soviet neighbors to draw them into regional economic institutions, this is not the pattern of participation that we would expect.

Economic Determinism: Endogenous Policy Theories, Commercial Liberalism

A third set of arguments points to the lobbying efforts of domestic commercial interests to explain a state's choice of institutional membership.[24]

---

[24] Andrew Moravcsik, "Taking Preferences Seriously: A Liberal Theory of International Politics," *International Organization* 51 (1997): 513–553; Helen V. Milner, *Interests, Institutions, and Information: Domestic Politics and International Relations* (Princeton, N.J.: Princeton University Press, 1997a). Much of this work has focused on the effects of an exogenous increase or decrease in the internationalization of capital flows or trade flows on domestic policy preferences and coalitions. See Peter Gourevitch, *Politics in Hard Times* (Ithaca, N.Y.: Cornell University Press, 1986); Ronald Rogowski, *Commerce and Coalitions* (Princeton, N.J.: Princeton University Press, 1989); Jeffry A. Frieden, "Invested Interests: The Politics of National Economic Policies in a World of Global Finance," *International Organization* 45 (1991): 425–451; Jeffry Frieden and Ronald Rogowski, "The Impact of the International Economy on National Policies: An Analytical Overview," in *Internationalization*, ed. Robert O. Keohane and Helen V. Milner (Cambridge: Cambridge University Press,

Referred to as endogenous policy theory, commercial liberalism, or more generically as political economy approaches, these accounts explain state behavior by pointing to the different distributional consequences of a policy as viewed by domestic commercial interests. As stated by Milner, "In any international negotiation the groups who stand to gain or lose economically from the policies are the ones who will become politically involved. Those who stand to lose should block or try to alter any international agreement, whereas those who may profit from it should push for its ratification."[25] This argument is most often applied to trade liberalization: less competitive enterprises with specific assets and high adjustment costs will seek to block liberalization; more competitive enterprises with mobile assets and strong international ties will push for openness. When applied to the formation of a customs union, the argument holds that a customs union will result if the enterprises or sectors that are competitive within the customs union but uncompetitive outside it politically outweigh those that benefit from either international openness or national protection.[26]

Applying this approach and testing it empirically can be difficult insofar as different theorists identify different logics of preference formation, as well as different societal actors (firms, sectors, and economic factors) that

---

1996), pp. 25–47. The logic can be reversed, however, as both Milner, *Interests, Institutions, and Information*, and Moravcsik, "Taking Preferences Seriously" have done, to argue that the policies of economic openness or closure are due to the relative balance of commercial interests favoring (or opposing) greater internationalization. The most well-developed literature of this type is endogenous tariff theory: Timothy J. McKeown, "Hegemonic Stability Theory and 19th Century Tariff Levels in Europe," *International Organization* 37 (1983): 73–91; Helen V. Milner, *Resisting Protectionism* (Princeton, N.J.: Princeton University Press, 1988); Stephen Magee, William Brock, and Leslie Young, *Black Hole Tariffs and Endogenous Policy Theory* (Cambridge: Cambridge University Press, 1989); Cheryl Schonhardt-Bailey, "Lessons for Lobbying for Free Trade in 19th Century Britain," *American Political Science Review* 85 (1991): 37–58; Daniel Trefler, "Trade Liberalization and the Theory of Endogenous Protection," *Journal of Political Economy* 101 (1993): 138–160; Gene Grossman and Elhanan Helpman, "Protection for Sale," *American Economic Review* 84 (1994): 833–850; Gene Grossman and Elhanan Helpman, "The Politics of Free Trade Agreements," *American Economic Review* 85 (1995): 667–690.

[25] Milner, *Interests*, p. 63.

[26] As applied to the formation of the European customs union, see Moravcsik, *Taking Preferences*, chap. 2. Milner makes a more sophisticated argument about increasing returns to scale in specific sectors that lead them to have a preference for a customs union over either a smaller national market or an open market in which they might be driven out by more competitive foreign producers. See Helen V. Milner, "Industries, Governments, and the Creation of Regional Trade Blocs," in *The Political Economy of Regionalism*, ed. Edward D. Mansfield and Helen V. Milner (New York: Columbia University Press, 1997), pp. 77–108. See also Robert Z. Lawrence, *Regionalism, Multilateralism, and Deeper Integration* (Washington, D.C.: Brookings Institution, 1996).

determine policy. As Douglas Nelson notes in his critique of the endogenous tariff literature, "None of [the works in this literature] develop any justification for their assumptions as to which of the theoretically possible groups do, and do not, engage in politics. One of the most serious flaws of the endogenous tariff literature is its failure to go beyond asserting one or another axis of conflict on the basis of the economic effects of a tariff to asking the question: What determines which, of the several possible, conflicts that *in fact* becomes politicized?"[27] More recent work by Kenneth Scheve and Matthew Slaughter has made considerable progress in resolving this problem, but for a study of the post-Soviet states the problem is less acute.[28] Since virtually all manufactured goods in post-Soviet countries are uncompetitive on international markets, it is relatively easy to identify the "losers" of trade liberalization and we can reasonably hypothesize that states with the highest concentration of Soviet-era industry would be the strongest supporters of closure.[29] Countries with strong natural-resource sectors should be inclined to maintain open trade without import restrictions and to resist regional bloc formation, as these sectors would not face significant competition under conditions of trade liberalization and would benefit from lower prices on imported goods.

[27] Douglas Nelson, "Endogenous Tariff Theory: A Critical Survey," *American Journal of Political Science* 32 (1988): 806. Emphasis in original.

[28] Kenneth F, Scheve and Matthew J. Slaughter, "What Determines Individual Trade Policy Preferences?" *Journal of International Economics* 54, 2 (2001): 267–292.

[29] With the possible exception of the arms market, there are not yet any significant markets for post-Soviet manufactured goods outside the post-Soviet space. Even within the post-Soviet space, the market for Soviet manufactured products has nearly disappeared. One can still purchase new post-Soviet automobiles, but televisions and refrigerators produced domestically are scarce. Domestic textiles are a rarity. Most manufactured consumer goods are purchased from countries outside the CIS. There are a few enterprises in the region that are exceptions to this rule, but on the whole, post-Soviet manufacturers find it nearly impossible to compete. To quote a recent U.S. government source: "'Free fall' is a term some used to describe industrial output immediately following the breakup of the Soviet Union. According to the Russian State Statistics Committee (Goskomstat), industrial production has fallen 53.8 percent since 1990; larger declines are suggested by other sources" (Bisnis, www.bisnis.doc.gov). In other republics the decline has been steeper. Manufacturing enterprises also lack the access to credit that would allow them to restructure in order to become competitive, even if their managers chose to take on the costs of adjustment. This grim assessment of economic competitiveness is not limited to manufacturing. Agriculture, too, arguably falls into this category, as there are few markets for post-Soviet food products outside the post-Soviet space, and domestic producers face increasing competition from Poland, Bulgaria, the United States, and the EU. Some agricultural products, like Uzbekistan's cotton crop, are exportable and therefore exceptions to this rule. These exceptions are few, however. Even with respect to metal exports, the case is not so simple, as steel and aluminum exporters have had difficulty entering foreign markets because of antidumping restrictions.

Looking at the post-Soviet republics, an informed political-economy account might also want to take into consideration other factors peculiar to the economies in question. As described in Chapter 4, many producers in the Soviet economy were linked in highly specialized cross-regional chains of production called "complexes," which led to a high degree of interenterprise specialization and intrasectoral "trade" within the region. As a result, many Soviet industrial assets were "transaction-specific" assets: i.e. they were tied to their place in the Soviet chain of production and of little use on their own.[30] Given the high level of asset specificity, the enterprises should seek to reestablish a formal "hierarchy" in their relations as subsidized regional financial–industrial groups or conglomerates.[31] Countries with a larger number of such union-level or specialized enterprises should therefore be more inclined toward economic integration and regional cooperation.

Thus, on the basis of the assumptions that Soviet-era manufacturing industries and collective farms are uncompetitive internationally and would face substantial and probably insurmountable adjustment costs under liberal market conditions, and that natural resources can be profitably exploited for export, the following hypotheses may be derived on the basis of the liberal or commercial approach:

> H3.1: States with a higher percentage of their production in industry and manufacturing should, ceteris paribus, show more support for CIS economic institutions and move less actively toward WTO membership.
>
> H3.2: States with a high percentage of their economy linked historically to union-wide production networks should show more support for CIS economic institutions and move less actively toward WTO membership.
>
> H3.3: States rich in natural resources and primary commodities should show less support for CIS economic institutions and move rapidly toward WTO membership.

These hypotheses are best tested with statistical methods, as we have good quantitative measures of the key explanatory variables and a variety of controls.

---

[30] Oliver E. Williamson, *The Mechanisms of Governance*, chap. 4.

[31] Indeed, this type of regional liberalization is on the agenda of every national industrial association that I visited in 1997 and is arguably the foremost guiding principle of the confederation of post-Soviet national industrial associations.

Economic Ideas

Finally, let us formally state the ideational hypotheses. If economic ideas have a role in the formation of states' preferences for different international institutions, then we would expect the following:

H4.1: States in which the government is integralist should participate actively in CIS regional institutions.

H4.2: States in which the government is mercantilist should not participate actively in any international trade institutions.

H4.3: States in which market-liberals are dominant in the government should support rapid entry into liberal multilateral institutions like the WTO and not participate actively in the CIS regional institutions.

STATISTICAL ANALYSIS

We can further test these arguments by examining the 15 post-Soviet countries over the past decade as a panel dataset and estimate the effects of the variables favored by each of these explanations on support for different international institutions. To do this, I have divided up the region into a 10-year cross-sectional time-series and coded the following variables:

Dependent Variables: *CISratify, WTO1, WTO2, (ratavg)*

As an indicator of support for the regional economic institutions, I look at the number of CIS economic agreements that countries ratified or implemented each year, for which data are available through the end of 1998. Not all CIS agreements required ratification or the passage of additional national legislation to demonstrate the implementation of the agreement, but it is reasonable to assume that the rate of ratification or implementation within this subset of agreements is a good proximate measure of the extent to which a country adhered to CIS agreements more generally. Moreover, because a country's decision to ratify or implement an agreement does not require the actions of other states, this variable, labeled *CISratify*, is more consistent with the statistical assumption that our observations are independent.

Because the overall number of agreements available for ratification changes over time, from 2 in 1991 to more than 100 by the end of 1998, and we do not wish to mistake an annual increase or decrease in the overall level of activity in CIS institutions for an increase or decrease in a specific country's level of support relative to other states, we need to control for such general shifts. Following Franzese (1999), who faced a similar problem in efforts to explain individual countries' inflation rates, I control for such yearly effects with a variable, labeled *ratavg*, that is calculated specifically for each country and for each year by averaging the number of CIS agreements ratified by the other 14 countries within that year. Put simply, *ratavg* gives us a benchmark of what would be the "normal" number of agreements for a country to ratify in any year, so that it is easier to determine variation in the relative participation rate of each country with respect to one another and across time.

To measure progress toward membership in the WTO, I use *WTO2*. As described in Chapter 3, *WTO2* counts the number of WTO-related events within a given year, with events defined as Working Group meetings and major document submissions. *WTO2* gives the best representation of annual levels of involvement, and it is not cumulative; hence each year's observation is independent. Moreover, it does not measure success, which to a great extent is determined not by the will of the applicant but by the interests of the existing members. Thus, for time-series analyses it is the best available measure.

Independent Variables

Economic Ideas: integgov, libgov, mercgov. I code the economic ideas for each country for every six-month period from the beginning of 1991 to the end of 2000 using content analysis of public statements by government officials using a coding scheme described in Chapter 4. The goal was to assess the relative strength of integralist, liberal, and mercantilist ideas (an "other" category was also used if ideas fell outside the typology) within the government within a six-month period. To arrive at this assessment, I researched the economic views of top government officials by analyzing the content of their official statements, and, where possible, the views associated with the political parties or academic institutes with which they are affiliated. After coding the officials according to their views, the relative weight of Soviet integralists, liberals, mercantilists, or "other" sets of ideas within the government was calculated by weighting the ideas held by a person by his position within the government.

To minimize the possibility for bias in the selection of officials' statements and to reduce the resources required for coding, I relied primarily on the highest echelon of government officials for the coding: the president, prime minister, first deputy prime minister, and where applicable, the leaders of governing parties in parliament. The weighting of these officials worked as follows: in countries with superpresidential systems, where the president's views held the most direct sway and appointed the government, the economic ideas of the president were given majority weight (.6) in the coding. The prime minister, the first deputy prime minister, and the economic ministers within the government are collectively given the remainder – with preference generally given to the prime minister if information on other ministers' views was sparse – as was generally the case. The exception to this general rule was coding in the Russian case, where there was a consensus among the secondary literature that President Yeltsin held no strong economic convictions and was not directly involved in any economic policy-making – and a rather large amount of primary materials on government officials. In the Russian case, the primary weight was given to the prime minister (.6) and secondary weight to the first deputy prime minister and the economic ministries. So, for example, in the first six months of 1995, when the integralist Victor Chernomyrdin was prime minister and the liberal Anatoly Chubais was first deputy prime minister and presided over a predominantly liberal set of economic ministers, Russia's integralist coding was .6, its liberal coding was .4, and its mercantilist coding was o.

In parliamentary systems, such as Latvia and Estonia, or where parliaments retained significant authority to direct economic policy, as in Moldova, the views of the parliamentary majority were coded. In Latvia and Estonia, the weights were calculated by evaluating the relative shares of different parties in the ruling coalition, with privilege being given to the prime minister (the ideas of the prime minister's party were given .6). In most cases, it is reasonable to assume that it was the relative weight of the parties in the ruling coalition that led to the selection of ministers. In Moldova and Lithuania, the president retained the majority weight (.6), with the remainder (.4) divided between the prime minister and the leading parties in parliament. To achieve the annual data needed to make the ideas indicators compatible with the rest of the panel dataset, scores for each country were averaged for each year.

The result were three ideational variables that measured the proportion of decision makers holding Soviet integralist, liberal, and mercantilist beliefs, labeled *integgov*, *libgov*, and *mercgov*, respectively. Each of the three economic ideology variables amounts to an estimate of the share of power within the government by individuals who hold that set of economic views. As a result, each variable is identified as a percentage and together with a residual "other" category they sum up to 1. Because of their obvious interdependence they are never included in the same model. But we must also recognize that error in any one measure is likely to be high, and to use as many means as are available to confirm the coding.

Economic-structural Indicators: lgdp, industempl9o, sovspec1, sovspec2, sovspec3, vpk85. To test the argument that some aspect of basic economic conditions could more easily predict a country's support for international institutions, I use a variety of structural or economic variables. The first is (logged) GDP per capita (*lgdp*), as many have argued that economic decline leads to pressure for trade protection and economic closure. It may also be the case that economic closure leads to collapsing GDP, however, so there is some concern with endogeneity in this measure.

I use several measures to try to get at the production profiles of each of the countries. Here, endogeneity is potentially an even more severe problem, since we are quite certain that the institutional choices made by states significantly affected the distribution of productive assets in the country. In countries that entirely opened their markets, domestic manufacturing industries could no longer compete and were effectively wiped out in the 1990s. In early liberalizing countries like Estonia, Georgia, and Kyrgyzstan, industrial production declined dramatically and industrial personnel as a share of the workforce more than halved. Hence, by the end of the 1990s we certainly find that institutionally liberal countries tend to be those with production profiles weighted less toward heavy industry and manufacturing and more toward commodities and services, but this is a product of liberalization rather than its cause.

To get around the problem that any postindependence changes are likely to be endogenous, I use data from 1990. This is not ideal, but is nonetheless a fair test. If traditional political economy theories argue that the structure of the economy at the outset of the period is a good predictor of the institutional choices the country will make during the period (particularly for as short a time frame as ours), then we should expect 1990 data to be fair predictors of institution choices made in the 1990s. Fortunately, we also have reliable, standardized data for all of the Soviet republics in 1990. This cannot be said for the subsequent decade, when methods for collecting statistical data underwent profound and varying changes across the former USSR.

In addition to collecting data on the percentage of the workforce employed in industry (*industempl9o*), I recorded the percentage of the population employed in military production (*vpk85*) at the time of the Soviet collapse, as well as three measures of the extent to which a republic's economy was linked to union-wide production networks: the production controlled by the union level as a percentage of the total production volume in the republic (*sovspec1*), the personnel in union-controlled enterprises as a percentage of total industrial personnel in the republic (*sovspec2*), and the production controlled at the union level as a percentage of total fixed assets for industrial production in the republic (*sovspec3*). We would expect each one of these variables to be positively associated with support for regional institutions and to be negatively associated with progress toward WTO membership.

Nationalism: pct_titular, presov_school. I draw on two different indicators to test for the role of nationalism. The first is the percentage of the population in the republic that is of the titular nationality (*pct_titular*), as some have argued that ethnic homogeneity leads also to more coherent national identities. But given that most arguments regarding nationalism view it as a set of beliefs that is not derived from "ethnic" attributes or necessarily captured in census data, I employ another measure for strength of nationalist sentiments, a dummy variable for regions that achieved mass literacy prior to their incorporation into the USSR (*presov_school*). According to Darden (2003), the formation of widespread nationalist sentiments in some regions of the USSR was caused by the inculcation of nationalist ideas into the population at the onset of mass schooling. Those areas where mass schooling was instituted prior to incorporation into the USSR exhibit nationalist movements throughout the twentieth century. Because the timing of mass literacy is clearly exogenous to international institutional choice in the 1990s, this variable provides a more reliable test of the nationalist hypothesis that regions with enduring anti-Russian and anti-Soviet sentiment would be less willing to join regional institutions and, according to Abdelal, more likely to move rapidly into liberal multilateral institutions. For countries such as Ukraine, for which only certain regions had developed national identities prior to their incorporation in the USSR, I take the population of those regions as a percentage of the country as a whole.

Realism: military, pctrusimp90, pctrusexp90. To test the realist hypotheses further, I first look at the number of military personnel in each country (*military*) and military personnel as a share of the population (*milpct*) – which is perhaps a better measure of mobilization and ability to defend territory. Here, the argument would be that the larger the number of military personnel, the more able the country would be to defend itself, and the less likely it would be to succumb to Russian pressure or to rely on Russian support to face internal or external threats. I also look at the share of a country's trade with Russia in 1990 (*rusimp90, rusexp90*) as a measure of a country's vulnerability to economic pressure. Here again, 1990 was chosen because trade data after 1991 are certain to be affected directly by international trade institutions.

Population Size: lpop. Finally, I use population size as a control variable, as there is an argument that smaller countries will be inclined toward liberal international trade institutions because they have no alternative to openness.[32] With limited resources and heavy reliance on both imports and exports to serve their economic needs, small countries – the argument goes – are unable to close their markets to trade. Here, the hypothesis would be that smaller country size would lead countries to be more active in international institutions of all types, but especially in the WTO.

Estimation

To estimate the effects of these variables, I rely primarily on a generalized least squares (GLS) random effects estimator. Given the problems identified in many IR analyses that use pooled OLS or random effects estimation,[33] this decision requires careful justification and I demonstrate the appropriateness of my use of random effects estimation using the relevant statistical tests for each of the regressions later. But there is also a basic intuitive reason why random rather than fixed effects estimation is appropriate for the post-Soviet data: random effects lead to biased estimates only if there are likely to be unobserved effects that would vary across countries, but remain stable over time; such country variation in culture, institutions, or other unobserved factors is not characteristic of our data. The countries that we are working with were selected precisely because we would expect the unobserved variables *not* to vary systematically. Indeed, because all 15 countries were parts of the homogenized environment of the USSR and share a common Soviet legacy, we can be relatively confident that most variables that are fixed and unobservable in these data do not vary much across the cases and therefore that fixed effects are, with rare exceptions, an inefficient estimation procedure. So long as we are able to identify the relevant variables, measure them, and include them in the specification of the model, the remaining disturbance term should simply be random noise[34] in our case – just the

---

[32] Peter J. Katzenstein, *Small States in World Markets* (Ithaca, N.Y.: Cornell University Press, 1985); Simmons, *Who Adjusts?* (Princeton, NJ: Princeton University Press, 1997), pp. 174–216.

[33] Donald P. Green, Soo Yeon Kim, and David H. Yoon, "Dirty Pool," *International Organization* 55, no. 2 (Spring 2001): 441–468.

[34] Or rather, to have an error term with a constant distribution unrelated to the *x*'s.

distorting effects of coups, dissolved parliaments, wars, assassination attempts, crises, and other forms of political instability that place inherent limits on our capacity to predict the behavior of governments with great precision.[35] Indeed, for most of the regressions, the model is sufficiently well specified so that there is no variation in country effects when using the GLS random effects estimator and, as a result, it simply reduces to a pooled OLS.

REGIONAL INSTITUTIONS

Let us start by modeling the sources of support for the CIS institutions, for which we have ratification data from December 1991 to January 1999. In examining the results, we find that the evidence is strongly consistent with the argument that economic ideas play a significant role in determining the extent to which countries participate actively in CIS economic institutions.

As shown in Table 9.3, when we regress *integgov* with *ratavg* added as a control, we find that integralist ideas have the predicted effect on support for CIS institutions, that the coefficient is substantial, and that the finding is highly significant statistically. Moreover, the finding is extremely robust; there is no combination of variables that renders *integgov* insignificant within a 99% confidence interval or substantially reduces the size of the coefficient.

We see similar results for *libgov*, although they are not quite as strong (Table 9.4). Model 9, a simple regression of *libgov* on *CISratify* using *ratavg* as a control, could not be estimated with random effects (LM = .03), but we find that *libgov* is robustly significant at the 95% confidence level across all other specifications. Additional tests also give us confidence that random effects estimation is not producing biased coefficients in these regressions.[36]

---

[35] Indeed, this instability leads to variable and sometimes long lags between when a change in government takes place and the implementation of policy or institutional choice. In a region where many countries faced exogenous shocks it is hard to define a fixed and rigid time lag between a shift in ideology and a shift in institutional support, and this increases the error term on the within-case explanation.

[36] To demonstrate that we cannot reject the null hypothesis that variation in country-specific effects is 0, I have included the Breusch and Pagan Lagrange multiplier test for fixed effects – and the chi-squared is quite low for most model specifications. Indeed, rho, the fraction of the variance that is due to u_i (the portion of the error term accounted for by fixed effects) is precisely 0 in most models involving *integgov*. This precludes the need for a Hausman test and is consistent with our informed assumption that there should be no systematic, unobserved variables in the error term given our model specifications. Hence, as discussed previously, the use of random effects does not bias our estimates and there is no need to use fixed effects. Indeed, because rho was 0, these regressions simply reduced to pooled OLS. To confirm this finding, I ran country dummies using pooled OLS and found them all to be insignificant. These results also held when using robust standard errors. The findings

TABLE 9.3. *CISratify: GLS Random Effects Estimation (integgov)*

	1	2	3	4	5	6	7	8
ratavg	.79***	.79***	.75***	.74***	.79***	.77***	.79***	.75***
	(.19)	(.18)	(.18)	(.18)	(.19)	(.19)	(.18)	(.18)
integgov	4.47***	3.28***	3.26***	3.86***	4.36***	3.60***	3.26***	3.26***
	(.98)	(1.05)	(1.04)	(.98)	(.99)	(1.14)	(1.11)	(1.11)
lgdp			−.97	−1.45***				
			(.62)	(.54)				
Industemploy90					−.059			
					(.053)			
sovspec1							−.040	−.012
							(.050)	(.051)
presov_school		−2.44***	−1.65[a]			−1.88*	−2.24**	−3.02***
		(.91)	(1.03)			(1.05)	(1.02)	(1.02)
pct_titular							.0043	−.019
							(.031)	(.031)
mil						18.20		
						(107.34)		
lpop						.59	.43	.53
						(.49)	(.51)	(.51)
Constant	−1.02	.19	6.81	9.46**	.43	−9.28	−5.32	−5.17
	(.82)	(.91)	(4.30)	(4.00)	(1.53)	(7.89)	(7.43)	(7.12)
r-sq within	.16	.18	.19	.18	.16	.17	.18	.22
between	.66	.71	.72	.71	.67	.80	.72	.42
overall	.28	.33	.35	.33	.29	.36	.34	.27
Rho	0	0	0	0	0	0	0	0
Hausman								
Breusch and Pagan Lagrange multiplier	.91	.38	.19	.36	.89	.20	.29	.15
n	95	95	95	95	95	87	95	95

[a] *Presovschool* and *lgdp* are jointly significant to a 99% confidence level.
* significant to the .1 level; ** significant to the .01 level; *** significant to the .001 level.

TABLE 9.4. *CISratify: GLS Random Effects Estimation (libgov)*

	9	10	11	12	13	14
Ratavg	.83***	.85***	.77***	.82***	.83***	.79
	(.18)	(.18)	(.18)	(.18)	(.18)	(.18)
Libgov	−3.40***	−2.53**	−2.90**	−2.53**	−2.51**	
	(1.23)	(1.52)	(1.22)	(1.19)	(1.23)	
Lgdp			−1.59**			
			(.72)			
Industempl90		−.02				
		(.09)				
sovspec1					.0065	−.01
					(.043)	(.05)
presov_school1				−2.78**	−2.71**	−3.02***
				(1.09)	(1.22)	(.96)
Titular		−.0028				−.019
		(.045)				(.031)
Lpop		.26				.53
		(.54)				(.51)
Constant	1.74**	−7.80	12.77**	2.31***	1.98	−5.17
	(.89)	(8.61)	(5.09)	(.84)	(2.16)	(7.52)
r-sq within	.22	.23	.24	.23	.23	.22
Between	.28	.33	.39	.49	.49	.42
Overall	.23	.25	.29	.31	.31	.27
Rho	.14		.13	.08	.11	0
Hausman	.27	.73	.36	.41	.47	
Breusch and Pagan Lagrange multiplier	.03	.06	.21	.62	.62	.15
N	95	95	95	95	95	105

* significant to the .1 level; ** significant to the .01 level; *** significant to the .001 level.

Inconsistent with the ideational argument, however, we also find that mercantilist ideas neither were significant nor carried the right sign (Model 3). This may reflect the smaller number of mercantilist observations, or is

also satisfy the tests for serial correlation and endogeneity. To check for serial correlation, I repeated the previous procedures and (1) added a lagged dependent variable to the regressors (the variables remained significant; (2) saved the residuals from the OLS regression as a new variable, created a new variable of lagged residuals, and regressed these with the original variables (the coefficient on the lagged residuals was not significant); and (3) ran the regression using Prais-Winston GLS estimation with autocorrelation. The variables retained their significance, rho was very close to 0 (.001), and the Durbin-Watson statistic was 1.9.

perhaps indication that mercantilists may use international institutions as it suits them – primarily as a means for enhancing exports.

Consistently with the view that the economic collapse led the countries in the region to increase their support for regional economic institutions, we find that per capita GDP is statistically significant (Models 3 – jointly with *presov_school*, 4, and 11). *Lgdp* simply improves the coverage of the model. As shown in Models 4 and 11, *integgov* and *libgov* remain both statistically and substantively significant with the inclusion of *lgdp*.

Perhaps the most striking finding is that structural conditions of a country's economy, such as the percentage of the population employed in industry, military production, or the extent to which the country was linked into union-wide production complexes, appear to have no influence on participation in regional institutions. Indeed, aside from GDP, the role of which is not particularly well-theorized and that we have reason to believe may be endogenous, only ideational factors (either nationalism or economic beliefs) appear to have a significant effect on institutional choice.

We also find relatively consistent support for the hypothesis that countries with strong nationlist sentiment will be more likely to reject participation in the Commonwealth of Independent States. Ethnic homogeneity appears to have no effect on CIS participation, but nationalism measured by *presov_school* is significant across most model specifications. Hence, our statistical analysis confirms the findings in qualitative work by Abdelal and others. Indeed the model performs significantly better when both economic ideas and nationalism are taken into account, and one suspects that this is the proper specification. The inclusion of both variables adds substantially to the explanatory power of the model (Models 2, 12), although the economic ideas variables are substantively more significant.

Testing the robustness of the nationalism finding is complicated by the correlation of *presov_school* (and other measures of nationalism that I have used) with GDP (.53), *sovspec3* (−.69), and the percentage of the population employed in industry in 1990 (.48), and the percentage of imports and exports going to Russia (.37 and .52, respectively).[37] For this reason, I regress these variables separately, but when included together with *presov_school* in

---

[37] The high correlation stems from the fact that the western areas of the USSR were considerably wealthier than the East and South, and all of the areas with pre-Soviet schooling were, for historical reasons, along the western edge of the Soviet Union. Elsewhere, see Darden, "Scholastic Revolution." I have used Ukrainian data to show that pre-Soviet schooling rather than wealth is the more likely cause of nationalist and secessionist sentiments in the USSR, so we need not be concerned that the two variables are causally related. But the high correlation between wealth and nationalism does not allow us to distinguish the relative significance of the two variables as causes for low levels of support for CIS institutions.

the model, *presov_school* either retains its significance or is jointly significant with these variables.

Presov_school is also somewhat negatively correlated with *integgov* ($-.43$). In part, this may be because nationalism is slightly negatively correlated with the presence of integralism in the government. Here, it is reasonable to assume that the relationship between the two variables may be causal, i.e. that countries with strong nationalist movements saw the USSR as an unnatural entity and rejected economic ideas grounded in the assumption that the USSR was an integral whole akin to a living organism. We can think of this as a two-stage process, where strong nationalist movements censored the selection of economic ideas in certain countries, but that economic ideas then provide a better explanation for the selection of international institutions across the region and over time. Indeed, if we leave out *integgov*, *presov_school* is significant to the .01 level even with the additional controls.

THE WTO

To explain support for the WTO, we can draw on panel data for all countries from the beginning of 1992 to the end of 2000. Because *WTO2*, the annual number of WTO-related events in a country, is count data, I use Poisson regression with robust standard errors adjusted for clustering on country. I initially attempted to use Poisson random effects, but the model could not be estimated with these data. Because there are some country cases with a smaller number of observations (Azerbaijan is the primary problem), the model was explaining those cases perfectly and biasing the results because it was overexplained when the key variables were included. Using Poisson regression on pooled data, while clustering by country to reduce the possible bias from pooling, appears to have been the best solution to this problem.

The resultant findings in Tables 9.5 and 9.6 are fully consistent with the hypothesis that governments in which liberal economic thinkers have a strong presence make greater progress toward WTO entry, regardless of how the model is specified. We also find that mercantilist ideas have the predicted effect; mercantilist presence in the government is negatively associated with WTO progress and remains significant across most specifications. Integralist ideas appear to have no statistically significant effect on progress toward WTO membership, but across all model specifications the coefficient is negative.

As with the CIS data, we find that the extent to which a country's economy was embedded in union-wide production during the Soviet period (*sovspec1*, *sovspec2*, *sovspec3*) or the percentage of its population employed in Soviet military production (*vpk85*) does not have a significant effect on WTO

TABLE 9.5. *Poisson Regression on WTO2 with Robust Standard Errors Adjusted for Clustering on Country*

	15	16	17	18	19	20	21	22	23
libgov	1.17***	1.66***	1.33***	1.39***	1.19***	1.21***	1.13***	1.19***	1.00**
	(.37)	(.40)	(.39)	(.41)	(.37)	(.40)	(.37)	(.38)	(.40)
lgdp				.0085		.042		.093	
				(.12)		(.16)		(.15)	
Industempl90									.045*
									(.025)
sovspec1				.013		.011			
				(.014)		(.008)			
presov_school		.49					.13		
		(.32)					(.16)		
pct_titular				-.014**	-.0071		-.0061		
				(.006)	(.0056)		(.0064)		
Military		28.00							
		(19.54)							
lpop		.35***	.13**	.063					.092*
		(.14)	(.06)	(.085)					(.048)
Constant	-.85	-6.91***	-2.91***	-1.63	-.38	-1.62	-.46	-1.48	-3.39***
	(.29)	(2.46)	(1.12)	(1.29)	(.32)	(1.09)	(.37)	(1.03)	(1.03)
Log pseudo-likelihood	-131.99	-106.67	-130.86	-129.46	-131.56	-131.04	-131.42	-131.79	-128.03
Wald prob	.001	.0000	.002	.007	.005	.007	.009	.002	.0001
n	119	99	119	119	119	119	119	119	119

* significant to the .1 level; ** significant to the .01 level; *** significant to the .001 level.

TABLE 9.6. *Poisson Regression on WTO2 with Robust Standard Errors Adjusted for Clustering on Country*

	24	25	26	27	28	29
integgov	−.46 (.45)					
mercgov		−1.10* (.58)	−1.33*** (.47)	−1.25** (.52)	−1.10* (.61)	−1.09*** (.40)
lgdp					.29 (.19)	
Industempl9o						.050 (.031)
sovspec1					−.0028 (.022)	
presov_school			.89* (.48)	.61** (.25)		.35 (.47)
pct_titular					−.0021 (.010)	
Military			39.87 (36.03)			−12.68 (32.08)
lpop			.12 (.18)		.014 (.16)	.044 (.14)
Constant		−.094 (.18)	−2.42 (3.17)	−.30 (.23)	−2.47 (2.09)	−2.10 (2.65)
Log pseudolikelihood	−140.54	−137.02	−110.99	−133.34	−135.24	−109.63
Wald prob	.32	.057	.0006	.0013	.17	.0000
n	119	119	99	119	119	99

* significant to the .1 level; ** significant to the .01 level; *** significant to the .001 level.

259

participation. In one specification, the coefficient for the percentage of the workforce employed in industry in 1990 approaches significance, but it has the opposite sign from that predicted by traditional political economy arguments that would have expected countries saddled with uncompetitive Soviet-era industry to push for greater restrictions on trade. I suspect that this near-finding is probably just capturing some distinct features of the Baltic states – which were heavily industrialized and also moved rather rapidly into the WTO.

Another notable finding was the relatively poor performance of the nationalist hypothesis in explaining progress toward entering the WTO. A central claim of existing arguments about nationalism was that countries with stronger nationalist movements would be more inclined to accept the short-term costs of liberalization and to reorient their trade and institutional affiliations to Western institutions. But we find no significant relationship between nationalism – regardless of how we measure it – and progress toward WTO membership. Indeed, we find in one specification that countries with more ethnically *heterogeneous* populations are significantly more likely to pursue WTO entry actively, although this is most likely a chance finding. Overall, it seems that nationalism acted primarily to censor and limit support for all ideas and institutions associated with the Soviet Union, but that nationalism does not itself directly affect support for liberal or Western trade institutions.

CONCLUSION

On the whole, the statistical findings conform closely to what we would predict on the basis of the theory that economic ideas drive institutional choice. Traditional explanations have suggested that states are primarily concerned with maximizing their power or security, that state interests are directly derived from the preferences of the country's commercial holdings, or that national identity defines national interests. But these arguments do not appear to hold empirically. Both the statistical findings and the case studies of the previous four chapters provide evidence for an alternative approach, one that stresses the ways that elite economic ideas shape the formulation of state interests, and, in particular, determine the type of international institutions chosen for managing trade relations with other nations. The economic ideas of the elite are certainly not the only factor affecting state choice, but the evidence presented previously on the post-Soviet states suggests that they were decisive.

10

Smoking Guns

A Causal History of Institutional Choice

> One extraneous movement is sufficient to smash the vase into thousands of
> pieces.
> Colossal efforts are needed to glue it back together.
>
> Nigmatzhan Isingarin, first deputy prime minister of Kazakhstan[1]

The evidence presented in the previous chapter demonstrates that there is
a strong association between economic ideas and institutional choices that
is very unlikely to have occurred by chance. But as important as it is to
demonstrate that ideas and institutions are closely associated, it is vital to
demonstrate precisely how they are tied, and to show that the economic ideas
did not merely coincide with the institutions, but were directly implicated
in the decisions of leading government officials to create, join, or reject
different international economic institutions. To do this, we need to deepen
our investigation – to identify the key actors, demonstrate their motivations
and intentions, and draw on subtle patterns in the timing and sequence of
events to show causation.

    The purpose of this chapter is to draw on a broad range of data sources –
wherever possible relying on internal government documents and direct
interviews with officials – to reconstruct the process by which institutional
choices were made across the decade as a whole. In a region where most
governments still place a premium on secrecy, it is no small task to trace
the process by which critical decisions were made. The vagaries of the data
and the fortuitous ways in which they were acquired do not always allow
a systematic presentation – and indeed some countries will be neglected

---

[1] Almaty, *Novoe Pokolenie*, in Russian, 19 January 1996, p. 3 [interview with Nigmatzhan
Isingarin, first deputy premier of the Republic of Kazakhstan, by Yuriy Kirinitsiyanov; place
and date not given: "Rivals? Allies? Partners?"].

here since their decision-making processes were simply impenetrable to the outsider. The goal here is to provide the best possible account of the process of institutional formation from 1991 to the end of 2000.

To do this, the chapter is organized around the analysis of five key episodes, or what I call institutional "choice points": the destruction of the ruble zone (1992–1993), the signing of the Treaty on Economic Union and the creation of the Interstate Economic Commission (1994), the formation of the Customs Union (1995), the signing of the Treaty on Deepening Integration (1996), and the creation of the Eurasian Union (2000). At each of these points, a major new regional initiative was put on the table and garnered the support of some of the post-Soviet states. Because each episode tracks a major initiative that each government was aware of and took an official position on, the episodes provide a convenient avenue for unearthing the different motivations of the different states. To provide a sense of historical flow, the episodes are linked by brief discussions of key shifts in the ideational landscape in the intervening years between agreements.

CHOICE POINT I: THE SCUTTLING OF THE RUBLE ZONE

By the time that the Soviet Union broke apart, not much remained of centralized union-wide economic management.[2] Planning and centralized allocation of materials had ceased under Gorbachev. The sovereign republics had the right to set, or free, prices as they chose. Trade among republics was decentralized to contracts between enterprises or managed through bilateral interstate agreements. The only economic authority that remained at a union level at the end of 1991 was the management of the common currency of the 15 states, the Soviet ruble. Whether to preserve, destroy, or remake this common currency zone was the first major decision regarding international economic and trade institutions by the newly independent states.

Some have argued that nationalism is what killed the ruble zone, and this is certainly a part of the explanation.[3] The three Baltic states and Ukraine each introduced their own currencies within the first year of independence and the view that national banknotes are a critical attribute of statehood clearly was an important impetus. But it was the liberal economists governing Russia who really drove the stake into the heart of the ruble zone and their motivations were first and foremost economic; they were driven

[2] For an account of the collapse of this system prior to December 1991, see Ellman and Kontorovich, *The Destruction*.

[3] Rawi Abdelal, *National Purpose in the World Economy: Post-Soviet States in Comparative Perspective* (Ithaca, N.Y.: Cornell University Press, 2001).

by monetarist ideas about how to control inflation and believed that they needed full control of the currency to enact them.

To appreciate the pivotal role of Russia, and in particular of the liberal forces within Russia, in this critical episode, let us look back at the governments of the 15 countries at the time of the Soviet breakup. At that time, Moldova, Georgia, and the three Baltic states, all of which were governed by separatist parties after the 1990 Supreme Soviet elections, were already treating their years as Soviet republics as no more than an illegitimate interlude and were working actively to destroy any ties to the former union.[4] By June 1992, these countries were joined by Azerbaijan (although less than a year later Azerbaijan's Popular Front government was overthrown in a coup). Ukraine's Communist elite had already conveniently remade themselves as nationalists and had begun to seek national control over all aspects of economic governance. In part out of a desire to pursue a national economic agenda – of either a mercantilist or liberal stripe – and in part out of a basic desire of the nationalists for a critical attribute of statehood, these countries took steps to abandon the Soviet ruble and, beginning with Estonia in June 1992, began to introduce national currencies.

But the ruble zone could have survived easily without these states, and several states retained integralist governments through the Soviet collapse and worked to sustain a common currency for the region. Kazakhstan's President Nazarbaev, who had tried fruitlessly to preserve the USSR itself, was committed to any institutions that would preserve Soviet economic ties and three of the remaining four Central Asian states (Kyrgyzstan excepted) were also committed to building a new set of regional economic institutions with supranational authority. These states retained their Soviet-era leadership and were, at this time, a stronghold of integralist economic ideas. These countries were joined by Belarus, which even under the leadership of Stanislav Shushkevich hoped for the preservation of a common economic system. All five of these states looked to Russia in their efforts to form a new union.

The supporters of the ruble zone turned to Russia not only because of the country's size and geographical location, but because of the Russian government's appropriation of Soviet monetary institutions. The Russian parliament had voted in November 1991 to have the Central Bank of Russia (CBR) assume control of the State Bank of the USSR, and it did so on 1 January 1992. And given that all currency-printing facilities were located

---

[4] The governments of Latvia, Lithuania, and Estonia each established their states as the legitimate continuity of the independent states established after World War I.

on the territory of the Russian Federation, this put Russia in a privileged position with respect to decisions regarding the preservation of the common currency. Each republican bank had the capacity to issue credits, which most did with abandon after independence, but the common currency could not exist without Russian support.

The position of Russia was thus decisive. But the Russian government at this time was under liberal control and opposed the preservation or reestablishment of common regional economic institutions. Yegor Gaidar and his team of liberal economists viewed the residual union-level institutions as antithetical to the free market and "macroeconomic stability" and set out to destroy them.[5] Gaidar's administration delivered its first blow to the existing regional economic institutions in January 1992 when it unilaterally liberalized prices and thus destroyed the artificial price structure that had served as the basis for intra-Soviet exchange.[6] Given that at world prices the vast majority of interrepublican exchange made no economic sense, the sudden shift to market prices brought much of this trade to a halt.

This first blow to the regional economic institutions predicated the second. In addition to crippling interrepublican trade, the freeing of prices led almost immediately to hyperinflation and the Russian liberals demanded early introduction of a Russian ruble as a first step to reduce the money supply and limit inflation.[7] But by this time the liberals' hold over the government was already beginning to be contested from within. Integralist forces within the Russian government and parliament – joined by the IMF and the international community – pushed for the preservation of the ruble zone.[8] These proponents of the ruble zone nearly succeeded in May 1992, as delegations from Russia, Armenia, Belarus, Uzbekistan, Turkmenistan, Kazakhstan, Kyrgyzstan, and Tajikistan were wrapping up negotiations in Tashkent to create a new ruble zone. But as the plans were being finalized, Grigory Matiukhin, the chairman of the Russian Central Bank, supporter of the ruble zone, and leader of the Russian delegation, was fired by Gaidar and immediately recalled to Moscow. Matiukhin was replaced by Sergei Ignatiev,

---

[5] See Yegor Gaidar, *Days of Defeat and Victory*, trans. Jane Ann Mille (Seattle: University of Washington Press, 1999), pp. 121–125, 154; Aslund, *How Russia Became*, chap. 4.

[6] See Clifford G. Gaddy, *The Price of the Past: Russia's Struggle with the Legacy of a Militarized Economy* (Washington, D.C.: Brookings Institution, 1996), chap. 4.

[7] John Odling-Smee and Gonzalo Pastor, "The IMF and the Ruble Area, 1991–1993," *IMF Working Paper* WP01/01 (2001).

[8] The IMF's motivations in preserving the ruble zone were complicated and largely political. At the time, U.S. policymakers were concerned that the USSR would go the way of Yugoslavia and were committed to keeping the country together. See Odling-Smee and Pastor, "The IMF."

a liberal economist and close friend of Gaidar's from Leningrad.[9] Ignatiev immediately proceeded to sabotage the ruble agreement through additional Russian demands that brought the negotiations to a halt,[10] and shortly after the Tashkent meeting, the Russian government took a unilateral decision to create a new Russian ruble.[11] With the switch in personnel marking such a clear turning point, it is hard to imagine a sharper demonstration of the critical effect of economic ideas.

And despite continued battles over the ruble, the Russian liberals continued to beat down any efforts to revive the common currency. When the Soviet ruble finally ceased to be legal tender in Russia on 26 July 1993, the integralist Viktor Chernomyrdin held the post of prime minister, and the Russian government claimed that other states would, in principle, be allowed to join the new ruble zone. But liberals – in particular First Deputy Prime Minister and Minister of Economy Yegor Gaidar and Deputy Prime Minister and Finance Minister Boris Fedorov – still held the critical economic posts. Hence, as a condition for entry to a new ruble zone, entrants had to agree to subordinate their fiscal, monetary, and trade policies to Russia – essentially giving the Russian government full control over their economic policy.[12] It was an offer the Russian liberals thought the other republics would be sure to refuse, but when, on 7 September 1993, Armenia, Belarus, Kazakhstan, Tajikistan, and Uzbekistan agreed to the strict terms, the bluff was called and the Russian government balked.[13] In Kazakh President

---

[9] Gaidar, *Days of Defeat*, p. 27.

[10] According to an IMF source present, "The Tashkent meeting was the turning point. Mr. Matiukhin, leader of the Russian delegation, appeared to favor the multilateral approach but on the second day of the meeting he flew back to Moscow amid reports that he was being 'retired,' while [Sergei] Ignatiev, who was close to those who favored a Russian ruble, assumed the leadership of the Russian delegation." Odling-Smee and Pastor, "The IMF," p. 7, fn 7.

[11] Other countries were invited to join a "new ruble zone" with the Central Bank of Russia as the only emission point by 1 October 1992, but Russia stalled in these negotiations. Moreover, the Russian government began simultaneously to limit the supply of existing Soviet ruble banknotes to the other republics and shortages of ruble banknotes became more acute. At this time, Belarus (May), Moldova (June), and Azerbaijan (August) compensated by introducing coupons that circulated as currency alongside the Soviet rubles and Kyrgyzstan introduced its own currency as sole legal tender in May 1993.

[12] As a result, Georgia, Azerbaijan, Turkmenistan, and Moldova announced their intent to leave the ruble zone. See Hale, "Russia's Fiscal Veto."

[13] Not only did these countries agree to give up the right to emit credit; they also agreed to back all ruble shipments with gold and hard currency reserves to be kept in Moscow. As a result, Belarus, Armenia, Kazakhstan, Turkmenistan, Uzbekistan, and Azerbaijan made national currencies the sole legal tender in the subsequent months. Tajikistan was the only country to receive a train load of new Russian rubles but ultimately introduced its own currency in May 1995.

Nursultan Nazarbaev's personal reflection on the episode, which he describes as being "forced out of the ruble zone," he notes the following:[14]

I firmly stood for keeping Kazakhstan in the ruble zone, while Shokhin and Fedorov[15] thought that extra weight should be dropped off. Here Kazakhstan was ready to meet all Russia's requirements and surrender its financial sovereignty. What does financial sovereignty mean? Everything! For days on end I had to persuade the parliament to give up sovereignty and ratify the document on keeping the ruble zone. And when I reached the impossible, Shokhin came and said: "Why do you need that for, Mr. Nazarbaev? The Russian train is going down, do you want to jump into the last car to crash with us? Kazakhstan with its powerful potential will survive better alone." I said: "You must be joking." So Shokhin says: "I deeply respect you and that is why I came here to tell you this." After that we had to hastily carry out the plan of introducing our own currency.[16]

At this point, it became clear that the liberal economists in the Russian government had the upper hand and had no intention of establishing a new ruble zone. They had simply raised the bar in the hope that the other republics would exit voluntarily – a politically more palatable solution as popular anger within Russia itself about the destruction of the USSR was growing and the liberals were under attack.

As a result of the actions taken by the Russian liberals, the 15 countries ceased to have a means of payment in their trade with one another and the last pillar sustaining the common economy of the USSR was removed. The critical role of economic ideas – particularly the liberal ideas of top officials in the Russian government – is clear. Table 10.1 shows the relationship between each government's economic ideas and the timing of its decision to introduce its own currency as sole legal tender.

As seen in the table, all of the mercantilist governments had early departures from the ruble zone, as did all of the liberal governments except for Azerbaijan and Armenia. But given that Armenia and Azerbaijan were at

---

[14] On Kazakhstan's efforts to preserve the ruble zone see Olcott, *The Kazakhs*, pp. 275–276; Olcott, *Kazakhstan*, p. 558; Henry Ewig Hale, "Statehood at Stake: Democratization, Secession and the Collapse of the USSR" (Ph.D. Dissertation, Harvard University 1998, pp. 390–396). Olcott provides a slightly different version of events, saying that Kazakhstan was prepared to give up economic sovereignty but balked at the prospect of having to leave the gold and hard currency reserves in Moscow. Hale's account cites local sources and for this reason is treated here as more authoritative.

[15] Alexander Shokhin and Boris Fedorov were both staunch liberals in the Russian government. Fedorov was first deputy prime minister and minister of finance. Shokhin was the deputy prime minister responsible for monetary issues and foreign economic relations.

[16] "Exclusive" report No. 8 (110) of 23 February 1995: "Vyacheslav Terekhov Interviews Nazarbayev at Commonwealth's Almaty Summit," Interfax (Moscow) in English, 15:15 GMT 23 Febuary 1995.

TABLE 10.1. *Economic Ideas and the Timing of Departure from the Ruble Zone*[a]

	Economic Ideas 1992–1993	Departed before August 1993 (before Russia)	Departed after August 1993 (after Russia)
Latvia	Mercantilist	July 1992	
Ukraine	Mercantilist	Nov. 1992	
Moldova	Mercantilist (.6)	July 1993	
Estonia	Liberal	June 1992	
Lithuania	Liberal	Oct. 1992	
Kyrgyzstan	Liberal	May 1993	
Russia	Liberal	July 1993	
Armenia	Liberal		Nov. 1993
Azerbaijan	Liberal (.6)[b]		Dec. 1993
Belarus	Integralist		Sept. 1993
Kazakhstan	Integralist		Nov. 1993
Turkmenistan	Integralist		Nov. 1993
Uzbekistan	Integralist		Nov. 1993
Tajikistan	Integralist		May 1995
Georgia	n.a.	July 1993	

[a] Date of departure from the ruble zone indicates the date upon which a national currency became the sole legal means of tender within the country.

[b] Integralist at time of departure. But the war with Armenia also clearly delayed introduction of the currency.

war with one another during this period and Azerbaijan experienced a coup d'etat in June 1993, we would expect them to have some delay in the introduction of their currencies. Moreover, we can see that each of the integralist governments held out until the bitter end, abandoning the ruble zone only after Russia itself no longer accepted the Soviet currency and refused to extend its currency to its post-Soviet neighbors.

THE ENSUING ECONOMIC CRISIS AS A SOURCE OF IDEATIONAL CHANGE

Perhaps the CIS would have remained a moribund shadow of the USSR and all regional initiatives would have met the same fate as the ruble zone if the Soviet collapse had coincided with the onset of prolonged economic growth and stability, but 1992 and 1993 were not good years in the former Soviet Union. In January 1992, civil wars broke out in Georgia and Moldova. The violent struggle between Armenia and Azerbaijan for control of Karabakh escalated throughout the year. The government of Tajikistan rapidly descended into a civil war that began in earnest in May 1992. And even those countries that managed to escape the hardships of war went into economic free-fall. Thus, as mercantilist governments were tearing their countries away from the Soviet production system, and Gaidar's team of liberals was rapidly dismantling what remained of Soviet economic institutions, the countries of the region were facing economic catastrophe.

The scale and scope of the economic collapse experienced by the post-Soviet states after the breakup of the USSR are difficult to describe. Production statistics alone do not capture the extent to which virtually all features of normal life collapsed, but they present a striking picture nonetheless. Even by the most conservative estimate, the average drop in per capita GDP of the post-Soviet states between 1991 and 1994 was 39.3%.[17] By contrast, during the depression years of 1930, 1931, and 1932, European national product declined by only 0.54%, 3.34%, and .63%.[18] Even if we calculate an average rate of change in GDP using only the sharpest decline of individual European countries between 1929 and 1934, the fall in European national product during the Great Depression is only 12.3%.[19] In short, the Soviet economy disintegrated at an unprecedented rate.

The trauma and social dislocation were clearly enormous. Life expectancy, marriage rates, and birth rates declined dramatically in all post-Soviet countries. Crime and suicide rates rose. Use of illegal drugs and alcohol skyrocketed. The collapse of health care and immunizations produced epidemics and new strains of disease. The future became unpredictable, paths to personal success and stability uncertain, and skills that were previously valued often became a liability. In many countries, wage arrears of six months or more became the norm and vast swaths of society turned to the farming of garden plots to subsist through the hard times. The social and personal trauma was epic.

It was also wholly unanticipated by most people. Interviews suggest that most elites did not anticipate the severe economic hardship that ensued

---

[17] Author's calculations based on Economist Intelligence Unit data published in 1998. These GDP figures, based on World Bank and IMF data, were significantly revised downward between 1996 and 1998 with the justification that in Soviet times there were incentives to overstate production figures and that in the post-Soviet period there was a tendency to understate production figures to evade taxes. Thus, the scale of the post-Soviet economic collapse, as reflected in IMF and World Bank data, is smaller than in the 1996 data. I have presented the 1998 data here, but the crash may have been even larger.

[18] Gerold Ambrosius and William H. Hubbard, *A Social and Economic History of Twentieth-Century Europe* (Cambridge, Mass.: Harvard University Press), p. 140.

[19] Ibid. The decline in the industrialized countries of Western Europe using the same method, excluding England, was 18.2%.

in 1992 in the wake of the Soviet collapse, and that the economic ideas held by many at the time had led them to believe life would improve after the collapse of the USSR. According to the mercantilist arguments against the Soviet Union, the destruction of the union and the independence of the national economy should have produced economic revival. Once its goods were no longer being siphoned away by the exploitative "imperial" center, the national economy was expected to thrive. Liberals often had similarly rosy expectations. The transfer of assets and authority to private individuals was supposed to increase their efficient use. Price liberalization and privatization, after a brief period of adjustment, were expected to be a boon to the economy as people adjusted to the notion that the state would not take care of them and reward would only result from their own productive efforts. Thus, according to both mercantilist and liberal thinking, one would have expected economic growth after the collapse of the union.

When this did not occur, and all of the CIS states experienced a precipitous fall in GDP between 1992 and 1993, there was a dual crisis. On the one hand there was the economic crisis itself – experienced as food shortages, hyperinflation, and a virtual stoppage of domestic industrial production. But in many cases the unanticipated economic hardship also bred an ontological crisis. The ideas that people had been using to make sense of the world and define courses of action had failed – leading to a particularly terrifying and anxiety-inducing anomaly. In countries such as Armenia, Georgia, Moldova, and Tajikistan, the population was left without gas or electricity even in the capital cities and people made kerosene fires in their apartments to cook and keep warm. A postwar generation who had enjoyed at least a base level of comfort and security throughout their lives experienced cold and hunger for the first time. In other republics, where conditions were less severe, it was still miserable enough to make words like *market*, *reform*, and *democracy* pejoratives and cause disillusion with the notion of "national sovereignty."[20]

In several countries, this anomaly, the economic crisis, led to something analogous to a scientific paradigm shift among the elite or to their summary removal by a disillusioned populace, and the years 1992 and 1993 were marked by changes of mind as well as changes of leadership across much of the former USSR. In the Lithuanian elections of November 1992, the mercantilist Sajudis government was tossed out and the liberal leadership came to power. The elections to the Moldovan parliament in April 1994 gave the integralist Agrarian Democrats a resounding victory. And in Azerbaijan and

---

[20] See Michael Urban, "The Politics of Identity in Russia's Postcommunist Transition: The Nation against Itself," *Slavic Review* 53 (1994): 733–765.

Georgia, Haidar Aliev and Eduard Shevardnadze rose to power via coups d'etat and took with them a new elite that largely rejected the mercantilism of their predecessors. In Russia, Boris Yeltsin demoted Prime Minister Yegor Gaidar and replaced him with the integralist Viktor Chernomyrdin, and the Communist Party scored major gains in the December 1993 parliamentary elections. In Armenia, President Levon Ter-Petrosian and the elite loyal to him stayed in power, but interviews suggest that they underwent a significant change in economic thinking toward integralism in response to the crisis.[21] In Kyrgyzstan, Akaev named the integralist former Communist Party leader Apas Jumagulov as prime minister and reshuffled the government to include integralists but retained liberals in the top positions in the Ministry of Finance and the National Bank.

At the same time, three previously integralist governments remained so. In Belarus, the integralist position strengthened first with the rise of Viacheslav Kebich, and then with the election of Aleksandr Lukashenko in 1994. Moreover, all of the Central Asian elites held on to power. Toward the end of 1993, and perhaps because of disillusionment at the failure of the ruble zone, Islam Karimov's government in Uzbekistan and Saparmurat Niyazov in Turkmenistan began to adopt mercantilist ideas. Throughout the crisis, Nazarbaev's Kazakhstan and the Rakhmonov government in Tajikistan remained integralist.

As a result of these changes, by the end of 1993 there were considerably more governments in the region in which integralist economic ideas held sway. On some level, the shift toward integralism made perfect sense. Only the integralists had correctly foretold the severe economic crisis that followed the collapse of the USSR. In the integralist mode of reasoning, the crisis that ensued after the breakup of the union was completely comprehensible. If the Soviet Union was akin to an organism, each part of which was dependent on the others, then the economic crisis could be understood as the result of dividing this natural functional whole into units that were incapable of functioning independently. Rather than an ontological crisis, the economic crisis gave the integralists a profound sense of ontological conviction.

From the integralist perspective, the solution to the crisis was equally clear – reintegration. The drop in production, high inflation, and collapse in quality of life could only be remedied by putting the specialized parts of the Soviet production system back together. Kazakhstan's President Nursultan Nazarbaev, who unlike other leaders had never abandoned the integralist mode of reasoning, put the agenda simply: "Without the restoration of

<hr />

[21] Interviews A2, A5, A13. See also Chapter 7.

the broken ties, it is impossible for the states of the CIS to get out of the severe crisis in which they currently find themselves."[22] On the basis of this logic, the restoration of the Soviet economic ties, the reestablishment of regional specialization and division of labor, and the revitalization and reform of regional industrial production became the pillars of a new regional economic agenda – one that called for the creation of new central institutions and organs for its implementation. On this way of thinking, integration was an objective necessity.

CHOICE POINT II: THE ECONOMIC UNION AND THE FORMATION
OF THE INTERSTATE ECONOMIC COMMISSION

The groundswell of integralist thinking generated renewed interest in developing joint economic institutions at the regional level and culminated in the signing of the Treaty on Economic Union in September 1993. As shown in Table 10.2, all five of the integralist governments at the time – Belarus, Kazakhstan, Tajikistan, Russia, and Moldova[23] – signed and ratified the Treaty on Economic Union. And of the three states with significant integralist presence within the government, two – Armenia and Kyrgyzstan – also signed and ratified the agreement, although given that there was a liberal majority in these governments we should not consider them confirmatory cases. Aside from Uzbekistan, all of the remaining governments opposed or failed to ratify the agreement.

The Treaty on Economic Union was a framework document that laid out a broad vision rather than a specific set of legal acts for its realization. It was the Interstate Economic Commission (IEC), the first significant regional economic organization to be formed after the collapse of the USSR, that first required member governments to devote money, time, and personnel to the common management of regional economic affairs. Because a core group of states supported the institution at a time when resources were particularly scarce, it makes sense to examine the motivations and actions of governments regarding the IEC. It was, in many respects, a more critical and demanding choice for these governments than was the treaty itself. And looking at the motivations of the IEC's proponents and detractors, the ideas of the cadres who worked in the organization, as well as its organizational

---

[22] Nursultan Nazarbaev, September 1993. Cited in Ispolnitel'nyi Sekretariat SNG, *Sodruzhestvo Nezavisimykh Gosudarstv: portret na fone peremen* (Minsk: Pangraf, 1996), p. 55.
[23] Moldova signed and ratified the treaty in April 1994, after parliamentary elections brought the Agrarian Democrats a majority.

TABLE 10.2. *Economic Ideas and Variation in Support for the Treaty on Economic Union*

	Ideas on Date of Ratification	Date Ratified	Confirms?
Belarus	Integralist	18 Nov. 1993	Yes
Kazakhstan	Integralist	19 May 1994	Yes
Tajikistan	Integralist	21 Nov. 1994	Yes
Moldova	Integralist (.7)[a]	10 Apr. 1994	Yes
Russia	Integralist (.6)[b]	27 Feb. 1995	Yes
Ukraine	Mercantilist (.6)[c]	No	Yes
Turkmenistan	Mercantilist	No	Yes
Uzbekistan	Mercantilist	22 May 1994	No
Estonia	Liberal	No	Yes
Lithuania	Liberal	No	Yes
Armenia	Liberal (.6)[d]	26 July 1994	No
Kyrgyzstan	Liberal (.6)[e]	18 Jan. 1994	No
Latvia	Liberal (.6)[f]	No	Yes
Azerbaijan	n.a.	29 Sept. 1993	
Georgia	n.a.[g]	No	

[a] Mercantilist (.3).
[b] Liberal (.4).
[c] Integralist (.4).
[d] Integralist (.4)
[e] Integralist (.4).
[f] Mercantilist (.4).
[g] At the time, Georgia was still effectively ruled by a triumvirate of warlords and Shevardnadze had not yet established his authority. See Chapter 7.

structure and policies, it is clear that the IEC was founded because a core group of states believed that economic reintegration on the basis of the Soviet division of labor was essential to their economic survival.

Let us begin with an examination of the distribution of support for the IEC treaties, where we see a pattern similar to the general voting on the Economic Union Treaty (Table 10.3). As with the Economic Union Treaty, all of the integralist states supported the IEC, and the treaty occurred at a time when there was a confluence of integralist ideas across several governments in the region. The Russian government, the main sponsor of the agreement, was in a brief window in which the liberals were not in a strong position. In Ukraine, Leonid Kuchma had just been elected on a platform endorsing regional integration and the prime minister of the country was the Soviet economist Yevgenii Masol, although the government exempted itself from the articles of the treaties that recognized the independent authority of the IEC. Similarly, Moldova's ruling Agrarian Democrats were strong supporters

10.3. *Economic Ideas and Variation in Support for the Interstate Economic Commission*

	Ideas at Time of Signing	Signed	Confirms?
Belarus	Integralist	21 Oct. 1994	Yes
Russia	Integralist	21 Oct. 1994	Yes
Tajikistan	Integralist	21 Oct. 1994	Yes
Ukraine	Integralist	21 Oct. 1994*	Yes
Moldova	Integralist (.7)	21 Oct. 1994	Yes
Kazakhstan	Integralist (.6)	21 Oct. 1994	Yes
Turkmenistan	Mercantilist		Yes
Uzbekistan	Mercantilist	21 Oct. 1994*	No
Estonia	Liberal		Yes
Lithuania	Liberal		Yes
Armenia	Liberal (.6)	21 Oct. 1994	No
Kyrgyzstan	Liberal (.6)	21 Oct. 1994	No
Latvia	Liberal (.6)		Yes
Azerbaijan	n.a.	21 Oct. 1994*	
Georgia	n.a.[116]	21 Oct. 1994	

* Signed with amendments effectively voiding the IEC's authority.

of the IEC. The integralist governments of Kazakhstan and Tajikistan were characteristically enthusiastic. Indeed, of the 15 post-Soviet states, 8 signed the two agreements forming the IEC and establishing its authority – Russia, Belarus, Kazakhstan, Armenia, Georgia, Kyrgyzstan, Moldova, and Tajikistan – although Georgia never ratified the agreements. Uzbekistan, Azerbaijan, and Ukraine signed IEC agreement with formal "reservations" that stated that they did not recognize the IEC's authority and that all decisions were to be ratified at the national level, and even with these limitations Ukraine never ratified the agreement.

Not only did the integralist states sign and implement the agreements, but leaders expressed their reasons for doing so in integralist terms – and the shift in thinking due to the economic crisis and its connection to the revival of regional institutions was something that leaders remarked on explicitly. Reflecting upon the relationship between the shift in economic ideas in the region and support for regional institutions in an interview upon his return from the CIS summit at which the Interstate Economic Commission was formed, the Belarussian prime minister, Mikhail Chygyr, noted:

I have an impression that everyone has begun to understand: We must overcome the current situation together. Attempts to overcome the economic crisis separately have collapsed, and, as of today, none of the former USSR republics can claim positive economic results.... I think that there is no other way. To achieve something real, we need to unify into one mechanism that economic organism which we broke up some time ago.[24]

One hears similar integralist views from an address at a meeting of the IEC Kollegia by Aleksei Bol'shakov, the first deputy prime minister of Russia:

The sharp demand for integration above all else is determined by the technological interdependence of the national-economic complexes achieved in the preceding decades, which – and life convincingly proved this – have not adapted today to autonomous functioning.[25]

... We can criticize the past system of inter-republican division of labor as much as we want. But the in principle the point stands: The collapse and curtailment of the mutual economic ties lies in the core interests of not one of our countries.[26]

The Moldovan position, as recorded in the minutes of an early IEC meeting in which the authority of the institution was the subject of debate, reflects similar motivations:

Let us take a look at world experience. The European Union, which has been active for a time somewhat longer than our Commonwealth, is endowed with strong supranational organs, combining legislative and executive power. Those organs work on the basis of majority rule, and not mandatory consensus.... Decisions made are executed by all participants of the Union. The outcome – favorable results.[27]

Shpak, the Moldovan representative, goes on to say that it is necessary to make additions and changes to the Treaty of the Economic Union and that integration is about the provision of "favorable conditions for the dynamic and harmonious development of the states' economies and carrying out economic reforms in the interest of raising the standard of living of the population." Without the union, however, "we witness the trend of a fall in production, disorder in investment activity, worsening of the level of life of people and many other negative indications."[28] In all three examples, we see the assumption of a causal link between CIS integration and the functioning of the economies – an integralist causal connection "proved" by the crisis that followed the breakup of the union.

The IEC's organizational structure also reflected integralist priorities, and aspects of the organizational design were copied directly from Soviet planning institutions. As explained by a Russian negotiator involved in designing

---

[24] Belinform interview with Prime Minister Chygyr published in Minsk *Zvyazda* in Belarusian, 13 September 1994, p. 1.
[25] *MEK Biulleten'*, no. 3, 1996, p. 6.
[26] *MEK Biulleten'*, no. 3, 1996, p. 7.
[27] Stenograficheskii Otchet 1996, p. 25.
[28] *Stenograficheskii Otchet* 1996, p. 25.

the IEC's structure, the IEC was seen as a combination of three different political forms: the European Union – from which it took the principle of decision making by qualified majority voting; the Sovet Ekonomicheskoi Vzaimnopomoshchi, or SEV – the organization that managed economic relations among the countries of the the Council for Mutual Economic Assistance (COMECON); and Gosplan – the State Planning Commission of the USSR.[29] Gosplan was seen as its primary influence in terms of organizational structure, and the titles of the departments are an inventory of the Soviet production complexes: cooperation in the sectors of the fuel and energy complex and heavy industry, cooperation in the area of machine-building and the conversion of military production, cooperation in the area of transport and communications, cooperation in the agroindustrial complex, forestry, and light industry.[30]

Moreover, among the members of the IEC staff itself, integralist reasoning was the assumed economic truth and provided the staff with a clear sense of mission, i.e. to reestablish the Soviet division of labor.[31] Integralist ideas provided the guiding theme in documents produced by the organization for the public;[32] they appeared regularly in the contributions of IEC experts to the Data Medium magazine supplement of the publication *Delovoi Mir* (Business World); and they were expressed in virtually every interview with IEC staff. As a representative illustration, note the introduction to the Concept (*Kontseptsiya*) for the Development of Integration in the CIS, one of the most important documents developed by the IEC:

The states which created the Economic Union, orienting themselves towards entry into the world community, should try to use the advantage provided by the international division of labor, specialization and cooperationalization (*kooperirovanie*) of production in the achievement of their common and current interests.

---

[29] Vladimir Pokrovskii, *Teorii i Praktikii Upravlennii*; author's interview with Boris Vladimirov, deputy chairman of the Board of the IEC, 15 December 1996; author's interview with Vladimir Pokrovskii, the Russian negotiator who was the primary designer of the IEC, 24 March 1997; author's interviews with Sergei Kristal'nyi and Dmitry Mirichenko, IEC deputy department heads involved in drafting the original agreement, November 1996. But as Aleksei Bol'shakov (at the time the chairman of the Presidium and first vice premier of Russia) makes quite clear, the IEC is a departure from Gosplan in that it was not created by a single center that it is intended to serve. Rather, the staff is on a quota system from all of the members and itself has a great deal of independence and autonomy ("including from the country of its location," i.e. Russia); Aleksei Bol'shakov, *MEK Biulleten'* no. 1, 1996, p. 9.

[30] Note also that in the hierarchically organized schema of the IEC's structure, the latter department is on the bottom, indicating its lesser prestige.

[31] Research on the IEC included repeated interviews with the same officials from November 1996 to December 1997 and a brief participant observation in the Department of Currency and Financial Relations.

[32] Such as the *IEC Bulletin* and annual report.

The development of the new independent states of the Commonwealth is characterized by a high level of economic-technological, cultural, and spiritual commonality, the presence of many similar problems, formed as a part of a past unified (integrated) economic complex – interconnected in its structure, distribution of productive forces, use of technology, and principles of organization of production. In result, the rupture of mutual economic ties has inflicted great economic harm on all states of the community, causing a protracted fall in production.[33]

... The face of modern integration – it is manufacturing, communications, science and technology. For this reason the priorities of integration development lie in the sphere of extending economic cooperation in the area of improvement in the use of the existing scientific-technical potential, the fuel and energy complex, modern machine-building sectors, and the agro-industrial complex. In these complexes it is expedient to first create financial-industrial groups, which could become centers of mutually-beneficial cooperation.[34]

The policies pursued by the IEC reflect integralist concerns as well. The IEC undertook such diverse tasks as coordinating the provision of farm equipment to the agricultural complex, organizing the delivery of low-priced fuel and electricity to industry, establishing subsidized railway tariffs for intraregional trade, lowering value-added taxes for financial-industrial groups (FIGs), developing interstate health-care programs for veterans, passing a wide range of agreements developing a joint science and technology space, providing for the mutual recognition of university degrees and joint use of research facilities, and passing key legislation protecting the rights of investors in CIS countries so that CIS enterprises could purchase enterprises in other countries that were once part of the same Soviet complex without fear of having those assets nationalized.

The opposition to the IEC was similarly guided by principle and opponents took issue precisely with the integralist ideas that underpinned the institutions. A clear example of this is the Georgian government's criticism of the previously mentioned *Kontseptsiia* in private diplomatic correspondence submitted to the IEC by the Georgian Ministry of Foreign Affairs:

For successful integration to take place the traditions of a market economy in the member-states should be common to all, and at this time in the CIS they are highly contradictory.[35] Citing the argument that the system of inter-enterprise ties, specialization, cooperation and division of labor has been in existence for decades is in

---

[33] Reprinted in *MEK Biulleten'*, 3'97, 6.

[34] *MEK Biulleten'*, 3'97, 6–7.

[35] It is a common theme of the Georgian government that they have a long tradition of experience with the market economy (due to the fact that Georgian agriculture was not subject to a high degree of collectivization and to the size of the black market in Soviet Georgia). This may be what the reference to "traditions" here implies.

its essence an *anti-argument*, because it is precisely the backwards and non-market nature of that system that was a significant cause of the collapse of the USSR.[36]

Here the attack on the integralist argument is explicit and the letter goes on to criticize the *Kontseptsia* further on the basis of liberal arguments. It suggests that the *Kontseptsia*'s proposed customs union and unification of economic legislation "contradicts the economic interests of Georgia... as a state with an open economy." Using entirely inaccurate figures,[37] the document takes issue with the *Kontseptsia*'s contention that there has been a continued economic collapse since the collapse of the USSR. The Georgian government instead cites the reduction in inflation, the reduction in the budget deficit, and growth of foreign investment as evidence that the post-Soviet course taken by the government was economically correct.

In sum, in terms of the ideas of the governments that supported it, the structure of its organization, the convictions of its staff, and the policy agenda it pursued, the IEC reflected its origins in a shared set of integralist ideas. It emerged from an island of common integralist understanding that existed among several key governments.

CHOICE POINT III: THE CUSTOMS UNION

Because the coexistence of opposed viewpoints among the members of the broader CIS institutions often led to conflict and stagnation, a smaller group of countries more committed to regional integration started to move forward independently with the development of regional institutions. The first manifestation of this was the formation of the Customs Union in January 1995.

At the time the Customs Union was formed in 1995, the governments of Belarus and Tajikistan and the dominant forces in Kazakhstan, Moldova, and Russia were all integralist in their thinking. Top decision makers in Georgia, Kyrgyzstan, Latvia, Lithuania, Estonia, and Armenia had adopted liberal economic ideas. The Ukrainian, Uzbek, and Turkmen governments were mercantilist.

Consistent with what we would expect if economic ideas drove institutional choice, Belarus, Russia, and Kazakhstan were the initial members. In

---

[36] "O proekte kontseptsii ekonomicheskogo integratsionnogo razvitiia SNG," document submitted to IEC by Georgian Ministry of Foreign Affairs. Emphasis in original. Acquired by author from Georgian Ministry of Foreign Affairs in June 1997.

[37] The Georgian growth figures cited in the table for the years 1991 to 1996 were 128.2%, 722.5%, 183.3%, 5608.3%, 221.8%, 144.9%. It is not entirely clear how they generated these growth figures, but they may have simply used GDP in the coupon or the lari without factoring in the massive inflation.

TABLE 10.4. *Economic Ideas and Customs Union Membership, 1995*

Government	Ideas	Customs Union?	Confirms?
Belarus	Integralist	Jan. 1995	Yes
Tajikistan	Integralist	Denied entry	Yes
Moldova	Integralist (.6)		No
Kazakhstan	Integralist (.6)	Jan. 1995	Yes
Russia	Integralist (.6)	Jan. 1995	Yes
Turkmenistan	Mercantilist		Yes
Uzbekistan	Mercantilist		Yes
Ukraine	Mercantilist (.6)		Yes
Estonia	Liberal		Yes
Georgia	Liberal		Yes
Lithuania	Liberal		Yes
Armenia	Liberal (.6)		Yes
Kyrgyzstan	Liberal (.6)		Yes
Latvia	Liberal (.6)		Yes
Azerbaijan	n.a.		

the case of Tajikistan, the government requested membership in the Customs Union, but the requests were privately rejected by the Kazakh government.[38] At the time that the Customs Union was formed, Tajikistan was engaged in civil war. The Kazakhs were concerned that with Tajikistan in the Customs Union, the open border would simply serve as a means for unwanted arms, drugs, and radical ideas to spill over into surrounding Central Asian states.[39] It was only after the end of the Tajik civil war that Tajikistan's accession was permitted.

Moldova would appear to be an exception to the argument, but it is easily explained. The Moldovan government expressed interest in joining the Customs Union, but because the country is landlocked and did not share a border with any of the Customs Union members, they could be expected to reap few of the benefits of the Customs Union. Both Moldova and Armenia signed comprehensive free trade agreements with the Customs Union members, but without the entry of Ukraine, Moldova could not benefit from the open borders that provided much of the integralists' incentive to join the CU. As such, this exception does not call the logic of the argument into question. As shown in Table 10.4, all of the integralist states that shared a common boundary joined the Customs Union in 1995, and none of the remaining states initially sought membership.

[38] Interviews Kz4, Kz9.
[39] Ibid.

Although smoking guns are hard to come by, in a few cases there is also direct evidence of the calculations made by decision makers that shows that different modes of reasoning were applied in weighing the costs and benefits of forming a CU.

Internal documents acquired from the Kazakh economic ministries reveal that officials in Kazakhstan drew on integralist ideas in determining the costs and benefits of membership in the Customs Union. According to one internal memo, the Kazakh government calculated that there would be an annual loss of $85 million to the state budget due to the adoption of the common external tariff and the removal of tariffs in trade with Russia and Belarus as a result of Kazakhstan's entry into the Customs Union. But, consistent with integralist thinking, Kazakh officials reasoned that "the restoration of the broken ties with the enterprises of Russia and Belarus [would] bring the revival of the main sectors of the economy" and stop the collapse in production that the country had faced since 1991.[40] According to government models, the expected economic revival would increase revenues from income tax, profits tax, and value-added tax (VAT), more than making up for the losses to the budget due to the removal of customs duties in trade with Russia and Belarus.[41] In this way, the Kazakh government's calculations rested on the assumed synergistic effect of reintegration of the Soviet economic complexes – a central tenet of integralism. This same set of integralist causal linkages pervades the Kazakh files and appeared in other internal documents and in interviews with officials in Kazakhstan and other integralist states.[42]

We see similar integralist sentiments among the Russian officials who were behind the decision to form the Customs Union. The Russian government was divided between liberals and integralists at the time the union was formed in the mid-1990s. Consistent with our expectations, the economic ministries that were headed by liberal economists were resistant to the Customs Union. The liberals attacked the Customs Union on the grounds that its supposed benefits would not outweigh the losses to the budget, and they

---

[40] "O tamozhennykh Soyuzakh: Istoriia, praktika, perspektivy edinykh tamozhennykh territorii informatsionnyi material." From the files of the State Customs Commission, Kazakhstan.

[41] Ibid.

[42] *Sostoianie ekonomicheskikh sviazei so stranami SNG.* Kazakh Ministry of Economy internal report, October 1997; confidential sources in Ministry of Economy, Ministry of Finance, Customs Commission. Author's interview with Igor Pasko, head of Department of Multilateral Collaboration of the CIS in Ministry of Foreign Affairs (Pasko accompanies Kazakh president Nursultan Nazarbaev to all CIS meetings and is a close adviser), 8 November 1997.

raised the spectre of a return to the Soviet-era subsidization of the other republics by Russia. They felt that little was to be gained from access to the smaller CIS markets and were not willing to make any sacrifices to gain such access.[43] Two well-placed interview respondents noted independently that there was particular resistance to the Customs Union encountered from the Ministry of Foreign Economic Relations, the Ministry of Finance, and the Ministry of Economy.[44] All three ministries were headed by liberals.

Support for the Customs Union was largely from the then-prime minister Victor Chernomyrdin and several of his deputy prime ministers,[45] the Ministry of Foreign Affairs, the Ministry of CIS Affairs, and the State Customs Commission.[46] The primary logic behind the agreement, as conveyed by officials in the Ministry of Foreign Affairs in personal interviews, was that "the recreation of the single chain of production [*edinnaia proizvodstvennaia tsepochka*] was essential to the development of Russia."[47] We can also get a sense of the integralist calculus circulating inside the Russian government from a letter written to Konstantin Zatulin, the chairman of the Russian parliamentary (Duma) committee responsible for evaluating the customs legislation.[48] After listing the legislation that needed to be passed for the completion of the Customs Union, the letter stated that the purpose of the agreements, from the Russian perspective, was to remove the customs barriers,

to restore, on a new basis, the production ties between the member countries of the customs union... to make manufactured products less expensive [cut costs], raise their competitiveness, and provide for their sale in the traditional markets of the

---

[43] Interview R7; interview with Vladimir Pokrovskii, a Russian negotiator (himself an integralist, who later headed the Executive Commission of the Russia-Belarus Union), 17 April 1997.

[44] Deputy Minister Fradkov of the Russian Ministry of Foreign Economic Relations and Sergei A. Vasiliev (at the time in the Ministry of Economy) were particularly opposed according to a confidential memo prepared by a Russian economist working for the World Bank; author's interview with Vladimir Pokrovskii, 17 April 1997. This division was also noted in several articles in *Kommersant Daily*. Pokrovskii also noted that Dubinin, the head of the Russian Central Bank at the time, was in opposition.

[45] Including Valery Serov and Aleksei Bol'shakov, who also served, respectively, as the chairmen of the Kollegia of the IEC and the Presidium of the IEC.

[46] World Bank memos. The memos were written by two World Bank staffers with close ties to the Russian government who tried to ascertain who within the government was behind the Customs Union agreement after it was announced. The findings are corroborated by interviews that I later conducted with one of the advocates of the CU (Pokrovskii) and thus appear to be quite reliable about the divisions within the Russian government at the time. Pokrovskii interview, 17 April 1997.

[47] Interviews R22, R33, 7 April 1997.

[48] The letter was never intended to be made public.

former republics of the USSR, and to significantly reduce spending on the creation of customs controls on mutual trade, and in the long term...remove control on internal borders.[49]

Interviews with parliamentary figures from several major parties in the Duma in 1997, shortly after the implementation of the agreement, revealed a widespread sense that the Russian economy could only get on its feet again if the production ties between the post-Soviet states were revived and if these countries became markets for one another's goods.[50] The Customs Union was a means to this end. In response to the question of why the Customs Union was in Russia's interest, the Duma representative responsible for the position on CIS affairs of the "Our Home Is Russia" party responded there was "not just a Russian interest in the Customs Union," and that the pressures for integration resulted from "the model of territorial distribution of the economic production of the USSR."[51] The representative explained that because there was a single Soviet economic system,

when it all fell apart, it became difficult for everyone.... Some do not have resources, others have a great store of metals without the means to process them. For Russia this is much less of a problem. For other countries it is much worse since they cannot create all of the parts of the process from scratch.

In closing, he noted that "before, everything was together in a single complex. The goal of integration is to find that past productive strength."[52] It was believed that the Customs Union would facilitate this process, and the union was viewed as the first step toward economic union.

In Belarus, in 1995–1996 and continuing through to the present time, we find the same rational calculations based on integralist assumptions. Although no internal Belarusian documents pertaining to the formation of the Customs Union were made available, interviews reflected the same concern with the broken economic ties of the Soviet Union and the negative effect this condition was having on the Belarusian economy. But all of

---

[49] Undated letter to Konstantin Zatulin from the head of the Department of External Relations of the State Customs Commission of the Russian Federation (Fedosov).

[50] Our Home Is Russia, Yabloko, Communist Party, author's interview with Viacheslav Igrunov of Yabloko, 21 April 1997. Yabloko supported a customs union with a lower external tariff than the Russian tariff – a liberal customs union. Igrunov noted that no major Duma faction was opposed to the process of integration, but that there were differences of opinion about how it should be accomplished.

[51] Author's interview 21 May 1997 with A. A. Tiagunov of *Nash Dom Rossii*. At the time, Our Home Is Russia was referred to as the "Party of Power" (*Partiia Vlast'*) because of its ties to Prime Minister Chernomyrdin (a member of the party) and the Kremlin.

[52] All quotations from Tiagunov interview.

those interviewed stressed that they had no role in making the decision and that the decision on the Customs Union was made by President Aleksandr Lukashenko and his closest advisers without a broader discussion in the government.[53] All officials expressed that there was considerable political will behind the Customs Union from integralists in the office of the president.

THE CALCULATIONS OF THE OPPONENTS
OF THE CUSTOMS UNION

We have evidence of officials' calculations on the Customs Union in two of the states that chose not to join: Georgia and Uzbekistan.

Uzbekistan's position on the Customs Union at first appeared favorable. In 1995, Karimov made several statements reflecting a concern with enhancing Uzbekistan's economic ties with Russia and the other CIS states, and in July, the Uzbek government stated that it wished to accede to the Customs Union. Karimov, in preparation for a visit by Russian Prime Minister Chernomyrdin, noted that talks would be held

on removing and eliminating these customs barriers between us. . . . The reason is that many of our relations are connected mainly with Russia . . . if Russia's potential and authority assist our enterprises and promote all-round economic ties with us, many problems will be solved and our enterprises that are currently in a difficult position will certainly be resolved and made easier.[54]

Indeed, following the visit by Chernomyrdin, where several key bilateral agreements were also signed,[55] Karimov spoke in favor of "further deepening

---

[53] However, the industrialists and bankers stressed that they did not have influence over politics in Belarus. Both industrialists and bankers noted that the political actors significantly influenced economic conditions, but that economic actors did not influence political choices. (One top government official noted, in regard to a question on decision making, that "one man makes all the decisions. It is like under Stalin!"); interview B15.

[54] Tashkent *Radio Mashal* 1100 GMT 27 May 1995 [in Uzbek, FBIS Translated Excerpt].

[55] The agreements included the memorandum on the comprehensive development and expansion of cooperation between the Republic of Uzbekistan and the Russian Federation and the agreement between the government of the Republic of Uzbekistan and the government of the Russian Federation on the basic principles and main areas of economic cooperation in 1996–1997. At the intergovernmental level, the following agreements were signed involving the government of the Republic of Uzbekistan, the Central Bank of the Republic of Uzbekistan, the government of the Russian Federation, and the Central Bank of the Russian Federation: On measures to ensure the mutual convertibility and stabilization of the exchange rates of the Uzbek som and Russian ruble; To establish an international radioastronomical observatory in Sufa, Dzhizak Region; Agreement between the government of the Republic of Uzbekistan and the government of the Russian Federation on cooperation in higher education; Agreement between the government of the Republic of Uzbekistan and

trade and economic relationships, promoting integration processes, eliminating obstacles in bilateral trade, and creating a favorable legal regime for carrying out economic cooperation."[56] At the meeting, Uzbekistan had expressed its desire to accede to the Customs Union formed by Russia, Belarus, and Kazakhstan. A few months later, Uzbekistan called on other CIS states to join the Customs Union in a joint statement with Russia, Belarus, Kazakhstan, Kyrgyzstan, and Tajikistan in November 1995.

These public statements and apparent intentions were a ruse, however. In a private meeting between top-level Uzbek government officials and the head of the World Bank (Wolfensohn), the Uzbek officials noted "difficult issues concerning Russia's requirements under the Customs Union," including "the arrangements for protecting Uzbekistan's border with Russia; 50% manning by Russian customs officials of customs posts in Uzbekistan; and maintaining customs records centrally in Moscow."[57] However, at the meeting, Deputy Prime Minister and Minister of Finance Hamidov "stressed that customs duties have been eliminated [by the Uzbeks] on paper only; in practical terms, they still exist."[58] Hence, the Uzbeks were not adhering to the agreements that they had signed with Russia, which had been authorized to negotiate the Uzbek accession to the CU, and they did not intend to in the future. Moreover, subsequent interviews with Uzbek officials closely involved in these processes revealed that the government was primarily seeking to use Customs Union "membership" to facilitate the development of a corridor for the transport of its goods via Russia.[59] They were not concerned with maintaining or expanding the interdependent production ties with the CU members,[60] they were opposed to the creation of a customs space with borders that were collectively protected,[61] and they had

---

the government of the Russian Federation on cooperation in fighting crime and in other fields to guarantee public security; An agreement between the government of the Republic of Uzbekistan and the government of the Russian Federation on setting up a Russian-Uzbek textile holding company.

[56] Ibid.

[57] 8 November 1995 World Bank Office Memorandum from Ziad Alahdad, EC3TA [Tashkent] to Veeyen Rajagopalan [Washington] Subject: Mr. Wolfensohn's visit: Meeting with DPMs on 31 October. On the actual tenets of the agreement see Chapter 11.

[58] Ibid.

[59] Interview Uz4. Uzbek officials noted that as a "double-landlocked state," i.e. a state with two or more countries lying between its borders and a usable port, Uzbekistan was particularly concerned with transport issues. This concern was heightened by the government's mercantilist stress on exports and the desire to diversify its markets so as not to be dependent on CIS countries.

[60] Interview Uz2.

[61] Interviews Uz2, Uz4.

no intention of adopting a common external tariff regime that differed from their own.[62] In short, they had no intention of following through on the commitment to form the Customs Union and did not base their policy on integralist calculations. The government hoped, primarily, to facilitate their exports by having restrictions removed on transport and communications links through Russia.

By January 1996, Karimov was stating this position openly. While noting that "we are for joining the customs union," Karimov added the condition that "accession to the customs union must have absolutely no impact on our foreign and economic policy – in the sense that what it is profitable for us to export and what we have to import should not be subject to influence and *diktat* from outside."[63] Given the inherent restrictions of a Customs Union on a state's right to engage in an independent foreign economic policy, Karimov's "conditions" effectively precluded membership. Over time, Karimov's attacks on the Customs Union, particularly on its subsequent supranational decision-making institutions, increased in venom. In public speeches, he referred to standard integralist arguments as "a deliberate attempt to mislead people as to the true reasons for the crisis which has shaken the whole post-Soviet space" and stated that integration will only give Uzbekistan "the role of a raw-materials supplier" and that "such unions and communities [as the CU and Belarussian–Russian Community] are categorically unacceptable to Uzbekistan."[64] By June 1996, Karimov proclaimed, "We will never enter the customs union."[65] This has indeed been the case.

In the Georgian case, we have a reliable record of the analytical work that the government drew on in its assessment of how membership in the Customs Union would affect Georgian interests. According to an interview with Shevardnadze's chief economic adviser, Temur Basilia,[66] the decision

[62] Ibid. In most respects, the Uzbek tariff was higher than the common external tariff of the Customs Union.

[63] Tashkent *Uzbekistan Television* [in Russian, FBIS Translated Excerpt] 1430 GMT, 20 January 1996. Karimov also noted, "We cannot agree to any linkage between the customs union being set up and our borders being defended by Russian Border Troops." It is my understanding that the CU was not linked to the agreements on border troops, and Karimov may be simply embellishing here (given that joint control of the borders *by the customs services* was part of the agreement).

[64] Address by Uzbek president Islam Karimov to the diplomatic corps and journalists, "The People of Uzbekistan Will Not Turn from Their Chosen Path," 12 April 1996, published in *Narodnoe Slovo* (Tashkent) 13 April 1996, pp. 1–2. [FBIS translation].

[65] Elmira Akhundova, "Aliev and Karimov Do Not Long for the USSR and They Are Not Inspired by the 'Pact of the Four,'" *Literaturnaia Gazeta*, 5 June 1996, no. 23, p. 2.

[66] Basilia's official title was "President's Aide in the Issues of Economic Reforms," but he handled all economic issues for Shevardnadze.

not to join the Customs Union was based on a commissioned study, which concluded that Georgia's membership in the CU would cost it $600 million to $700 million.[67] The study was done by an American economist at the Center for Economic Policy and Reform (CEPAR) in Tbilisi under contract from USAID. Beginning with the false assumption that "all Georgian trade with CIS countries is duty-free,"[68] it employed a standard comparative static analysis to show how Georgia would be hurt by increased protection due to the adoption of the Customs Union's common external tariff, resulting in a "net welfare loss."[69] The conclusions and policy recommendations of the report were as follows:

1. The present case of Georgia joining the CIS CU is not the standard case of FTA (Free Trade Area) or CU analysis. First of all, Georgia and the CIS countries already have an FTA through the Commonwealth of Independent States Agreement. Thus, all Georgian trade with CIS countries is duty-free. Secondly, that which has been proposed under the CIS CU is the adoption of an external tariff (i.e. the Russian

---

[67] Author's interview with Temur Basilia, 13 June 1997. Basilia actually noted that there were two parallel studies done. One study was done by "young experts" in the Georgian government itself, as part of a small commission established for the purpose of determining whether the CU was in Georgia's interests. The second study was done by the Center for Economic Policy and Reform (CEPAR) under contract from USAID. Basilia claimed that the Georgian analysis had been done first, but that both reached the same conclusion independently. No one else in the Georgian government whom I spoke to had ever heard of the independent Georgian study. Several were very familiar with the CEPAR study (most notably, David Onoprishvili, head of the Economics and Finance Committee in the Georgian Parliament, and Irakli Svanidze of the Ministry of Foreign Affairs, who had the CEPAR paper on file and showed it to me). The staff at CEPAR had never heard of an independent Georgian study. Basilia denied my request to examine the independent Georgian study, and I suspect that there was only the CEPAR study. One Western adviser noted to me that CEPAR had made its study available to the press; that had caused a rift in relations with Basilia as the report created a scandal among parliamentarians and forced Basilia's hand somewhat in making the decision on the CU (nationalist parliamentarians were opposed to closer ties with Russia, and the CEPAR report was an important weapon for them).

[68] The CIS Free Trade Agreement had an ever-expanding appendix of exemptions on trade in the goods between specific countries. Russia and Georgia did not have a free trade regime. Russia had quotas and duties on imports of Georgian alcohol and other goods and Georgia was subject to Russian export taxes. The CEPAR economist should have been aware of these duties (as it was public knowledge and the Georgian government was quite upset about the restrictions). CEPAR received its data from the Georgian government.

[69] Although crafted by Ph.D. economists, the logic of these analyses is the standard defense of free trade of the type one encounters in first-year economics (and generally the same as the calculation by which a neoclassical economist demonstrates that *any* government intervention reduces welfare). Most notably, these analyses leave out any possible dynamic effects of the CU – i.e. precisely those factors that are of significance to the integralists.

Federation import tariff schedule) by all CU members. This would mean an average tariff of 14%, with a range between zero and 50% (and some 100% spikes), a regime which contrasts with Georgia's current uniform import tariff of 12%.

2. Based upon these preliminary results, if Georgia joins the CIS CU, it is likely to suffer a net welfare loss of as much as 8.6% compared to total imports, while import tariff revenues may or will be reduced by as much as 36%.

3. By joining the CIS CU, the imposition of the Russian import tariff structure would introduce distortions in Georgia's relative prices, leading Georgian economic agents to misallocate resources (i.e. labor, land, and capital).

4. Applying a general equilibrium approach (shifting analysis), we conclude that joining the CIS CU may reduce Georgian exports by as much as 2%.

5. Joining the CIS CU may produce a reduction in Georgian imports from Non-CIS countries. This may affect long-run economic growth perspectives for the economy since it is well-known that imports of inputs and capital goods from Non-CIS countries for both manufacturing and agricultural activities can be a major engine of technological progress.

6. Since total Georgian imports (sum of CIS and Non-CIS) and exports are not necessarily affected in the short-run by joining the CIS CU, the net effect on Georgia's balance of payments may be insignificant. However, considering the argument above (#5), we conclude that in the long-run, exports of Georgian goods could be negatively affected under the CIS CU proposal.

7. According to both short-run quantitative results and long-run quantitative analysis, joining the CIS CU would be a mistake from a purely economic point of view. Georgia should promote policies that integrate it into the world economy, especially with developed countries, while continuing to enjoy the benefits from the CIS FTA.

Here, we see a close reflection of the ideal-typical liberal logic.[70] It is not clear how much the liberal economic logic of these arguments was understood by national officials, but the general conclusions and the dollar amount placed

---

[70] Trade diversion not trade creation, increased cost to consumers and loss of welfare, misallocation of resources, increased cost of technology transfer, etc.

by the analysts on the cost of joining the CU were clearly influential.[71] In this sense, although not an indigenous product of the Georgian officials, a liberal mode of reasoning was employed in the government's calculations over whether to join the CU.

The CU was opposed by liberal international organizations and Western governments. The IMF and World Bank both directly opposed the Customs Union on the grounds that it was an illiberal institution that would lead to "trade diversion."[72] These organizations exerted pressure on CU member states to abandon the Customs Union and pursue immediate entry into the WTO. The Bretton Woods institutions were aided by the USAID, which in each CIS state had a well-funded program devoted to securing rapid WTO entry with the lowest possible tariff levels.

CHOICE POINT IV: THE EVOLUTION OF THE CUSTOMS UNION AND THE FORMATION OF THE TREATY ON DEEPENING INTEGRATION

Despite strong international opposition and the rejection of the agreement by most governments in the region, the remaining integralist governments worked actively to deepen the Customs Union and to transform it into a broader economic union. The moves to expand the Customs Union began, paradoxically, with conflict between the states over the decision-making processes within the union. For despite their effective compliance with the tenets of the agreement, the Belarusian and Kazakh governments clearly began to chafe at the one-sided nature of the Customs Union by the end of 1995. Both governments viewed their membership in the Customs Union as necessary but would also have preferred that, within the union, their interests were given greater weight. They were happy with the immediate benefits of the union – a substantial increase in mutual trade, the revival of interenterprise links, access to oil and gas at Russian domestic prices, and privileged access to the large Russian market – but they both sought to influence the foreign economic regime of the union in a way that they felt better served their interests.

The dissatisfaction with the Customs Union's decision-making apparatus was greatly exacerbated by a Russian presidential decree that reduced the list of goods subject to export tariffs. This action was taken by Yeltsin

---

[71] The study (which had a duplicate version distributed in Georgian) was noted in several interviews and received press coverage when it was released. See fn 76.

[72] World Bank Memo.

unilaterally, only a month after the other two countries had taken on the Russian preference system.[73] Not only were Belarus and Kazakhstan not consulted about the change, but the two governments were not even informed of what had taken place. As Kazakhstan had already removed some of its export restrictions upon entry into the Customs Union, this appeared to be another affront in what had become a long series of violations of trust in Russian–Kazakh relations.[74] In general, the action seemed to portend that the Russian leadership would not treat the Customs Union as a forum for collective decision making and common policy, but as an extension of Russian authority over the two other states.[75]

The unhappiness of Kazakh officials with the existing state of affairs, while initially quite muted, is clearly present in an internal government review of the progress on the Customs Union conducted in 1995:

> For the majority of tariff levels the parties came to the opinion on the expediency of taking the Russian customs tariff. Nonetheless, there remains disagreement on this position. For example, the countries of the EU, in the acceptance of a unified customs tariff, agreed on an arithmetic mean value of the national levels of import and export duties. The experts did not follow world experience on this matter.[76]

Here, we begin to see a growing unwillingness to accept the Russian system whole cloth, as well as an awareness of alternative arrangements that might incorporate the interests of each member-state more equally.

At the same time, Kazakhstan remained firmly committed to the idea of economic union. In another internal report on the progress in realizing the Agreement on the Customs Union, this one prepared by Kazakhstan's

73 The fact that the change in the list of goods subject to export tariff was established by presidential decree rather than by a Postanovlenie of the government of the Russian Federation (as is customary) indicated that it was probably done against the wishes of the Chernomyrdin government – which had been the primary force behind the CU agreement. As the removal of export restrictions was one of the key planks in the liberal platform (and one of the primary goals of the IMF in their negotiations with Russia), it is likely that the liberal faction bypassed the government and took the issue directly to Yeltsin, who was probably not aware of the rules of the Customs Union and, regardless, appeared to recognize no constraints on his personal authority – legal or otherwise.

74 Beginning with the breakup of the Soviet Union and the destruction of the ruble zone.

75 As noted in the previous chapter, the Kazakh customs commission initially received laws from the Russian customs commission that were stamped "for implementation."

76 Customs Commission of Kazakhstan, "O tamozhennykh Soiuzakh: Istoriia Praktika, perspektivny edinykh tamozhennykh territorii. Informatsionnyi material." In fact, the EU case was somewhat more complicated. It is true that the initial external tariff was determined by the mean of the tariff levels of the members, but a list of goods covering approximately 20% of the European Community's imports by value were kept out of this system and subject to further negotiation (the so-called List G).

State Commission on Cooperation with CIS Countries, the dual attitude toward the union is represented quite clearly.[77] After presenting a detailed list of the areas of legislation that had been unified, the report comments, in typical integralist fashion, that "the unification of the normative-legal base, the formation of an identical mechanism for the regulation of the economy is stimulating the creation of collective enterprises, financial-industrial groups, and the development of other coordinated ties. At the current time 5 Kazakhstani-Belarussian and 61 Kazakhstani-Russian enterprises have been created and are active." Moreover, the trade results of the first phase of the customs union seemed only to confirm the causal tenets of the logic behind joining:

The results of this step [the removal of barriers] expressed themselves in the data on the trade balance between Russia and Kazakhstan. The analysis of statistical records for [illegible but probably 3] months of 1995 showed an increase in the volume of trade ties with Russia. Trade volume with Russia expanded in comparison with the same period in 1994 by 11% with exports increasing by 38%. The volume of the main exports also increased.[78]

These developments were viewed very positively by the authors of the Kazakh documents. From the integralist standpoint, the favored causes, i.e. regional economic institutions, were leading to their anticipated effects – the enhancement of the vital interrepublican productive ties. The Customs Union was working according to their expectations.[79]

Unflinching support for the Customs Union in general, but discontent with the decision-making arrangement in the union in particular became the

[77] "Spravka o khode realizatsii Soglasheniia o TS v chasti unifikatsii normativnoi bazy po tamozhennomu delu," 18 April 1995. Goskomsotrudnichestvo (State Commission on Cooperation with the CIS States), RK.

[78] "O Tamozhennykh Soiuzakh: Istoriia, praktika, perspektivy edinykh tamozhennykh territorii (informatsionnyi material)," State Customs Commission of Kazakhstan (undated). Other analyses have suggested that the statistical increase in trade volumes was due primarily to an increase in the prices of the goods traded. In actuality there was a continued decrease in the quantity of goods traded.

[79] Here, the case is presented in such a way as to suggest that the data reflect that the causal relationship between the formation of a customs union, the reestablishment of internal ties, and the health and increased productivity of the main production sectors certainly holds. Indeed, as stated in the conclusion of the report: "World practice in the formation of customs unions bears witness to the length of this process. However, the present and significant success in this, and in particular, the success of the development of the European Common Market, which occasioned the unification of countries on the principle of common borders, interconnected economies, single external and internal economic policy, is quite convincing."

position taken by both Kazakhstan and Belarus one year into the agreement. The Kazakh report goes on to note that

the practice/experience of work in the formation of the Customs Union shows that the absence of an executive organ and mechanism for taking decisions on matters pertaining to the regulation of foreign economic activity in the countries of the union frequently leads automatically to the acceptance of the Russian version, which does not always take into account the economic interests of all member-states, and with time might bring harm to their economies. This was the case, for example, when the Russian party changed the level of export duties.[80]

The report then proposes the next steps to push forward with the union – suggesting that the Kazakh government viewed the solution to the problem as a higher degree of integration, not an abandonment of the process. Indeed, the subsequent creation of a new set of decision-making organs to manage conflicts and set policy within the Customs Union would be interpreted correctly as a drive by the Kazakh and Belarusian governments to have an institution that would mediate and control the course of legislation and foreign economic policy.[81] They had come to see that without such institutions, this role would be performed by the Russian government.

When the discontent with the existing intergovernmental decision-making arrangement was aired at the fifth meeting of the Joint Commission of Belarus, Russia, and Kazakhstan – the loosely organized council that managed the Customs Union – the participants initially decided that the appropriate solution would be to transfer authority permanently to the IEC for the management of the Customs Union.[82] Toward this end, the prime ministers of the three countries agreed in January 1996 "to focus in the IEC the task of coordinating activity between ministries and departments, monitor the implementation of stage II [the economic union], and expand the three states to include new members; to put the most important strategic issues [regarding the CU] in the hands of the three representatives of Kazakhstan, Belarus, and Russia in the IEC presidium and organize daily practical work . . . in the IEC Kollegia."[83] It was also agreed that the representatives

---

[80] "O Tamozhennykh Soiuzakh: Istoriia, praktika, perspektivy edinykh tamozhennykh territorii (informatsionnyi material)."

[81] "O tamozhennykh Soiuzakh: Istoriia Praktika, perspektivny edinykh tamozhennykh territorii. Informatsionnyi material."

[82] Which is probably the reason that the Russian Ministry of Foreign Economic Relations was always opposed to the creation of supranational organs for the Customs Union.

[83] "Protokol rabochoi soveshchaniia ruk . . . ," 18 January 1996. Heads of delegations were Miasnikovich-Belarus, Isingarin-Kazakhstan, Bol'shakov-Russia. As with all matters handled in the higher intergovernmental bodies, the tenets of the agreement were worked out

of the three states in the IEC presidium would, within two weeks, draft and ratify a system for organizing the interaction of different ministries and agencies for the realization of these goals. In essence, the IEC would be relied upon to preserve the CU agreement, to ensure its further implementation, and to define strategic goals of the Customs Union.

This attempt to create a new decision-making system for the CU was unsuccessful, however. The other countries in the IEC voiced their opposition to the use of IEC's resources for a separate agreement to which that they were not parties.[84] And in essence, the changes called for were little more than a way of repackaging the same decision-making arrangement that had existed previously. The countries' representatives in the IEC presidium were the first deputy prime ministers – precisely the same officials who were meeting quarterly as part of the Joint Commission. There were no provisions made to have policy proposals worked through by the IEC staff, which presumably would have meant that this influential role, as previously, would have been taken on by the Russian ministries. This was precisely the condition that the transfer of policymaking to joint institutions was designed to prevent.

In particular, this arrangement did not satisfy the government of Kazakhstan. The matter came to a head at the beginning of 1996 when Kazakhstan made unilateral changes in its external tariff.[85] Unlike the surprise unilateral decision taken by Russia, the changes in the Kazakh tariff were technically within the CU agreement, which stipulated that if one country made a proposal for changes in the external tariff that was not addressed by the other members within a period of six weeks, then that government was permitted to take unilateral action. More than six weeks prior to taking action, the Kazakh government had sent a proposal to reexamine the tariff levels on a group of goods that Kazakhstan did not produce.[86] Kazakh

---

long before the meeting in working groups of lower-level officials. The decisions taken at meetings were generally orchestrated in advance.

[84] "Reshenie glav pravitel'stv RB, RK, i RF as gosudarsva-uchastniki TS," 19 January 1996.

[85] Interview with IEC customs, 28 May 1997.

[86] The Kazakh government's decision removed tariffs (in trade with non-CU members) on those goods that were not produced in the republic, goods purchased with international credits, and goods that were used for production for export, i.e. raw materials for the chemicals and metals industry. It also lowered the tariff on cars to 2% of the customs value and increased tariffs to protect the domestic production of salt, meat preserves, and metal tailings (*otkhody metallov*) to 30%. In a second government act, however, Kazakhstan removed export duties on all goods with the exception of wheat – aligning the regime with the prior unilateral actions taken by Russia, but also pleasing international donor organizations. Postanovlenie Pravitelstva Kazakhstana 12 March 1996 #810.

officials had also submitted the grounds or justification for their proposal several times to the Russian government, but to no effect. According to an internal Kazakh document, "because within the framework of the CU a single option was not achieved, it was necessary for the Republic of Kazakhstan to temporarily, until the acceptance of a common agreement, introduce partial changes in the level of the import customs tariff."[87] But the decision also reflected a deeper frustration with Russia's unilateral actions, the inadequacy of the collective decision-making arrangement, and the lack of success in trying to persuade Russia to change some levels of the external tariff.

In response to Kazakhstan's defection from the common external tariff, the Russian government did not attempt to punish Kazakhstan by reimposing tariffs on trade between the two countries. Rather, the moves taken by Kazakhstan appear to have been received precisely as they were intended to be: as a signal to the Russian government that it needed to take the interests of its partners more seriously, and that changes in the common external tariff would have to be the subject of negotiation, not just unilateral Russian action. The actions of Kazakhstan were an impetus to conduct a more substantial overhaul of the Customs Union's decision-making structures. Russia responded favorably to this pressure and the preparation of an expanded decision-making apparatus devoted to the Customs Union began to intensify. These efforts culminated in the Treaty on Deepening Integration in Economic and Humanitarian Spheres and the formation of the Interstate Council, the Integration Commission, and an expansion of the agenda of the Customs Union to attempt a broader economic union of Russia, Belarus, Kazakhstan, Kyrgyzstan, and, by 1999, Tajikistan.

The history of the treaty is illuminating. The original draft was developed by the same group of negotiators who were responsible for the initiatives to form the IEC, and who had been involved actively in efforts to draft a new union treaty for the USSR during fall 1991.[88] And the draft certainly bore the marks of its Soviet designers. Provisionally entitled "Treaty on All-Round Convergence and Deepening of Integration . . . " (ellipsis in original), the new treaty initially called for the creation of very strong supranational institutions.[89] The treaty would have created a Higher Soviet (Vysshiy Sovet)

---

[87] Tariffs were changed on pharmaceuticals, cars, equipment, and electronics.

[88] Postanovlenie Pravitelstva, 3 March 1996 #300. June 1996 "Spravka o khode vypolneniia Soglashenii i Dogorov s stranami SNG" (Prepared by the Department of Foreign Economic Relations of the Customs Commission of the Republic of Kazakhstan).

[89] Pokrovskii interview, 10 April 1997. Other members of this group included Vasili Ivanovich Sheladonov of Belarus, a deputy minister of economy of Ukraine, and Victor Dmitrevich Gladov (also of Ukraine).

made up of the presidents and prime ministers of the member-states. The treaty also called for the establishment of a permanent institution to govern the new union, the Integration Commission. Both the Higher Soviet and the Integration Commission would be endowed with the authority to take decisions "of a mandatory character," i.e. "for immediate implementation by the national organs of state power."[90] The Integration Commission would also work out the overall budget for integration and develop concrete integrative programs.

The scope of the treaty also went well beyond the management of the Customs Union and other economic affairs. The treaty included plans to introduce a new payments system in the region; accounts between states would be in a single currency and the Central Bank of Russia would perform the functions of a reserve system.[91] The completion of the "first stage" of the treaty would also involve the formation of a Parliamentary Congress with parity in the number of seats for each member-state. It called for the creation of "unified sectoral organs of government," i.e. Ministries of Customs, Transport, Defense of State Borders, and Foreign Economic Relations. The completion of the "second stage" demanded the creation of a Unified Command of the Armed Forces of all the member countries, and the initiation of direct elections to the Parliamentary Congress. In short, the draft was a new manifestation of the union treaty that its drafters had been seeking to implement since the Soviet Union began to fall apart in 1991.

But there was a sizable gap between intentions of those who drafted the treaty and those of the national leaders who were expected to sign it. The latter seemed primarily to want the regional institutions to have sufficient authority so that collective decisions on economic affairs could be implemented, but were not particularly keen on a new union that might ultimately take their authority away from them involuntarily.[92]

---

[90] Draft "Dogovor o vsestoronnem sblizhenii i uglublenii integratsii…" dated 18 March 1996. Version as delivered to the government of the Republic of Kyrgyzstan (in Russian).

[91] Article 11.

[92] In an interview conducted in 1996 with Arkadii Volskii, he noted that many of the CIS leaders, because of their history of infighting as members of the same Politburo, are particularly wary of one another's intentions and fear that supranational institutions may be captured by one leader or another (threatening the position of all others). These fears, whether they are the product of membership in the Politburo or simply due to the fact that leaders like to hold on to their positions of power and fear the creation of an alternative center, certainly appear to be present among the leaders of the CU members. Although Article 18 of the draft treaty noted, "The tenets [*polozheniia*] of this treaty do not harm the international subjectness of each of the Parties, or their participation in international treaties, organizations and other forums," it is likely that leaders did not feel secure in these legal guarantees. Given that reintegration was quite popular among the general populations of all of these countries,

Indeed, there were clearly some misgivings about the draft treaty among some of the member governments. We know, for example, that the Kyrgyz, who had been involved in the negotiations since declaring their desire to join the Customs Union in November 1995, reacted negatively to aspects of the draft treaty that raised the possibility of an unsanctioned expansion of the union's powers at the expense of the member-states.[93] The internal memo of a top Kyrgyz economic official assigned to assess the implications of the new treaty noted:

1. The Title of the Treaty does not conform to the content of the articles. If what is being talked about is the convergence of deepening of integration of sovereign states in all aspects, then the Treaty should fundamentally contain measures for the attainment of these purposes (economic, legal, social, etc.) without raising the issue of the creation of supranational political organs with the symptoms (signs) of a state structure and international legal subjecthood. In reality, the text speaks of a Treaty on the creation of a new Union state.
2. In the case of concluding the treaty, it is necessary to specifically and clearly lay out the principles of relations between the members of this union as well as the process of its creation, also in the long-term functioning of the new state institution. It is especially necessary to firmly define the borders of the limitation of the sovereignty of the member-states to the benefit of Union organs. In the treaty there should not be articles, allowing the possibility for those organs to expand their authority without control (article 9).[94]

In the Kyrgyz version of the treaty, submitted along with a general commentary that included these notes, the sections that give the Integration Commission mandatory authority have all been crossed out. All references to decisions being "for immediate implementation by the organs of state power" are also stricken.

The Kyrgyz and Kazakh governments both expressed reservations, and as a result the negotiations moved onto two separate tracks. The first track was the creation in April 1996 of the Belarusian-Russian Community Treaty (also known as the *dvoika*, or twosome), which retained much of the content

---

there was reason to fear that popular resistance to the "involuntary" or illegal formation of a new union state would not be forthcoming.

[93] It should be remembered that the signing of this treaty took place only a few months after the Russian Duma passed a law declaring the breakup of the Soviet Union invalid – an act that sent a chill through leaders throughout the region.

[94] Zamechanie of 1st Zam Minekon E. Omuraliev to Government of the Kyrgyz Republic on the Draft Treaty on Vsestoronnom Sblizhenii i uglublenii integratsii, 22 March 1996.

and spirit of the original draft. A second track involved all four governments (the *chetverka*, or foursome), Belarus, Russia, Kazakhstan, and Kyrgyzstan, in signing of a final draft of a revised agreement on 29 March 1996. In the final agreement, many of the elements of the treaty giving authority to the joint regional institutions were removed, as were most explicit references to matters not directly related to the management of the economy, e.g. the Unified Command of Armed Forces. Indeed, the final treaty reflected many of the revisions called for by the Kyrgyz officials. In the end, the Higher Council was created, but with the more conservative title of the "Interstate Council" and the Integration Commission was not initially given supranational authority.[95]

THE INCREASING INFLUENCE OF LIBERAL IDEAS IN THE LATER 1990S AND THE RISE OF THE WTO

By the mid-1990s, liberal ideas such as those drawn on in the Georgian decision on the Customs Union had made significant inroads into the region as a result of efforts of a variety of governmental and nongovernmental international actors. Country-specific liberal policy research, such as the CEPAR paper on the Customs Union, was funded not only by USAID, but by the Soros Foundation, the EU program on Technical Assistance to the Commonwealth of Independent States (TACIS), the World Bank, the IMF, and many smaller organizations. These organizations also used a variety of other means for disseminating liberal economic ideas. Top officials in the Ministries of Finance and in the Central Bank were whisked abroad for training in liberal ideas and IMF country representatives generally taught economics courses at the main national university as part of an effort to cultivate a new liberal post-Soviet elite. Significantly, economics departments at most universities throughout the region began to use translated Western textbooks and Soviet economic theory was no longer taught. As a result, the traditional institutional mechanisms that sustained integralist thought in the region for many decades began to lay the foundations for a new generation of liberal elites. The result, as we can see in Figure 10.1, was a secular trend toward liberalism and a decline in the influence of integralist ideas in the region beginning in mid-1994.

This trend toward liberal ideas across the region was also manifested in more rapid progress toward WTO entry among the liberal governments

---

[95] The role and functions of the Interstate Council are established in the "Polozhenie o Mezhgo-sudarstvennom Sovete Respubliki Belarus," Respubliki Kazakhstan, Kyrgyzskoy Respubliki i Rossiyskoy Federatsii," ratified by decision of Interstate Council of RB, RK, KR, and RF, 16 May 1996, no. 2. Bulletin 96/1, p. 18.

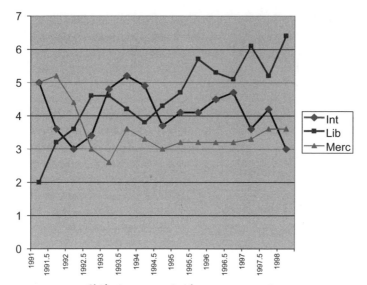

FIGURE 10.1. Shifts in economic ideas, 1991–1998

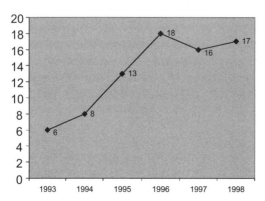

FIGURE 10.2. Number of WTO accession events, 1993–1998 (sum of all 15 post-Soviet states).

of the region. Indeed, we can see a sharp increase in the number of WTO accession–related events in the region between 1994 and 1996, and a high level of sustained activity between 1996 and 1998 (Figure 10.2), culminating in the approval of the first two post-Soviet countries, Kyrgyzstan and Latvia, for membership in the WTO in October 1998.[96]

---

[96] Meetings of the Working Group or submission of key accession documents by a country are coded as WTO Accession–related events.

TABLE 10.5. *The Relationship between Economic Ideas and the Trade Institutions of the Post-Soviet States in 1996*

	Economic Ideas 1996	Trade Institutions[a]	Confirms Hypothesis?
Belarus	Integralist	Customs Union/Treaty of the 4 (4-ka)/Belorussian-Russian Union Treaty (2-ka)	Yes
Russia	Integralist	Customs Union/4-ka/2-ka	Yes
Tajikistan	Integralist	Customs Union (1998)/4-ka[b]	Yes
Kazakhstan	Integralist (.6)	Customs Union/4-ka	Yes
Moldova	Integralist (.6)	Liberal (FTA with CU)	No
Turkmenistan	Mercantilist	Autarky[c]	Yes
Uzbekistan	Mercantilist	Autarky[d]	Yes
Ukraine	Mercantilist (.6)	Autarky[e]	Yes
Estonia	Liberal	Liberal	Yes
Georgia	Liberal	Liberal	Yes
Lithuania	Liberal	Liberal	Yes
Armenia	Liberal (.6)	Liberal (FTA with CU)	Yes
Kyrgyzstan	Liberal (.6)	Customs Union/4-ka*	No
Latvia	Liberal (.6)	Liberal	Yes
Azerbaijan	n.a.	Autarky[f]	n.a.

[a] Here, as noted previously, a "liberal" regime denotes a regime with no tariffs above 15% (and usually an average weighted tariff of considerably less than 15%). The data here have been culled from ministry sources of the countries in which I conducted research but are now conveniently available on the Web site of the U.S. Commerce Department's Business Information Service for the Newly Independent States (Bisnis, www.bisnis.doc.gov).

[b] Prior to joining the CU, Tajikistan had a liberal regime with no tariffs higher than 15%. Bisnis.

[c] Turkmenistan has no tariffs on imports but has currency restrictions and other state regulations that effectively allow the state to control trade.

[d] Uzbekistan has high tariffs on all domestically produced goods (including a 100% tariff on cars) as well as in strategic areas where it seeks to develop domestic capacity or restrict imports.

[e] Ukraine has high tariffs on most goods, especially manufactured goods produced domestically, and on agricultural products. Effective 28 November 1997, there was a significant reduction in agricultural duties, but these still generally fall in the range of 20%–50% with some 100% spikes. Bisnis.

[f] Azerbaijan, consistently with the resource-extractionist logic, also has a 70% export tariff on oil and a number of petroleum-related products. Bisnis.

Thus, in 1996, with the moves of some states toward WTO entry and others toward closer economic union within the region, we can see a clear relationship between the economic ideas and institutional choice across the region (Table 10.5). Of the five integralist states, four – Russia, Belarus, Kazakhstan, and Tajikistan – moved forward with the closer economic union called for in the Treaty on Deepening Integration. Moldova, for the reasons outlined with respect to the Customs Union, remains an unsurprising exception. The three mercantilist governments, Turkmenistan, Uzbekistan, and Ukraine, all eschewed membership in the new economic union and continued to sustain their autarkic foreign economic regimes. Of the six liberal governments at the time, all worked toward rapid entry into the WTO and sustained a liberal trade regime. Kyrgyzstan, however, chose to sign the Treaty on Deepening Integration and, at least formally, to pursue integration with its prior Soviet partners.

Kyrgyzstan would appear to run against the argument that economic ideas drive institutional choice and to complicate our assumption that the WTO and regional institutions were mutually exclusive choices at this time. But upon closer scrutiny, we can see that the Kyrgyz government's decision to sign the treaty was consistent with liberal ideas; it was a guileful strategy to gain restriction-free access to Russian and Kazakh markets – not the product of a genuine preference for the creation of a customs or economic union. For a while the Kyrgyz government did implement a large number of agreements, its persistent avoidance of the common external tariff and subsequent unilateral decision in 1998 to enter into the World Trade Organization revealed that the government's primary commitment was to liberal international institutions.

Kyrgyzstan had adopted a liberal trade policy following independence and never abandoned it. By March 1997, Kyrgyzstan had already passed the first stage of WTO negotiations, presenting its existing import tariffs (ranging from 0% to 10%) as well as a tariff schedule that it proposed to use to protect the domestic market. The former were considerably lower than any conceivable common external tariff for the Customs Union, and an internal government memo from the Kyrgyz Ministry of Finance to the Ministry of CIS Cooperation noted:

> At the current time, the IK [Integration Commission] proposes to coordinate work on agreement upon a common customs tariff and has submitted a number of measures on this issue, which will take quite a long time to work out, and in our opinion, makes the process of WTO entry more complicated/difficult. . . . For this reason, the Ministry of Finance of the Republic considers the task of agreeing on a common customs tariff as an intermediate step on the road to a full unification of customs and full unification of the customs territory to be premature.[97]

---

[97] Ministry of Finance zamechanie sent to Minsotrud on the materials for the Fifth Meeting of the IK, 29 May 1997.

And indeed, by their second meeting with the WTO Working Group in July 1997, the Kyrgyz government secretly took an official decision to negotiate tariff concessions with the WTO "independently, without conducting additional consultation with the member-states of the Customs Union."[98] While making no public declarations to this effect, in every possible instance Kyrgyzstan chose conformity with the WTO requirements over its treaty commitments to the Customs Union.[99] Given that the government of Kyrgyzstan was aware that its WTO-negotiated tariffs could never be accepted as the common external tariff for the Customs Union, its behavior with respect to the CU is best viewed as a way of securing free trade with its two main partners, Russia and Kazakhstan, rather than a commitment to closed regional economic institutions.[100] Consistently with the liberal ideas that were predominant in the upper echelons of the government, Kyrgyzstan's commitment to free trade was clear, and its support for the external tariff of the Customs Union was simply an empty formality.

This type of duplicity was not practiced by the other signatories to the treaty. Although it was not initially clear to Belarus, Kazakhstan, and Russia that entry into the WTO would be incompatible with their plans for economic union, they ultimately chose the Customs Union over the WTO. At the third meeting of the Integration Commission (IK), on 19 December 1996, a protocol was discussed that pointed out that because the second stage of the economic union, the harmonization of taxes and general economic policies, would take a long time, in the meantime member-states should formulate documents for entry into the WTO independently. The member-states agreed to take into account their obligations based on prior customs union treaties and to "coordinate work, exchange information, consult with one another on strategy and tactics, and exchange experience on the resolution of problems" in the negotiation process for WTO entry "with the purpose of creating favorable conditions for the formation and

[98] Postanovlenie Pravitelstva #384, "O merakh po podgotovke vtorogo zasedaniia Rabochei Gruppy VTO," point 2.

[99] Kyrgyzstan did ultimately send on the tariff schedule that it used for negotations with the WTO members but did not seek to involve its CU partners in any way. 4 July 1997. MinFin's Biialinov sent customs levels to MinFin Kazakhstan, MFER RB, Gabunia at MVES RF, and the IK.

[100] Oddly, the economic ministries continued to go through the motions, often involving considerable administrative work, of preparing for agreement on a common external tariff for the Customs Union, even though such efforts were pointless if Kyrgyzstan were to enter the WTO on its own with tariff levels locked in below 10%.

functioning of the Customs Union."[101] The IK was charged with the task of coordinating these efforts, and with arranging for the specialists from each country working on WTO entry to meet at least twice per year. The proposal for independent entry had been put forward first by the Russian Ministry for Foreign Economic Relations, as Russia had already started entry procedures into GATT in 1992.

Shortly thereafter, however, the different member-states began to discover that the requirements for WTO entry might conflict with the agreements of the Customs Union. Upon discovery of this, the Kazakh government chose not to sacrifice the Customs Union or its institutions for the purpose of gaining entry into the WTO. In an internal memo from the Kazakh customs commission to the Ministry of Finance, it was noted that

> the Foundations of the customs legislation, signed by the heads of state on February 10, 1995 in Almaty and ratified by the Presidential Decree of July 3, 1995 #2357 are in contradiction to separate demands for entry to the WTO. In accordance with article 4 number 3 of the Constitution of the Republic of Kazakhstan, international treaties ratified by the republic [e.g. the Customs Union Treaty] have priority before the republic's laws, and in article 6 of the Decree "On Customs Matters in the Republic of Kazakhstan" we find the same principle. In connection with this, the introduction of changes in the customs legislation of the RK in accordance with demands of the GATT/WTO will be impossible without corresponding changes in the Foundations. We regard it as necessary to send this to the IK [Integration Commission] for discussion, and also to send a proposal on the necessity of continuing the comparative analysis.[102]

Here, in contrast to the Kyrgyz choice, we see a firm commitment to honor the existing Customs Union legislation; this ultimately became the Kazakh government's position with respect to the WTO.[103]

At a meeting of the Integration Commission on 5 June 1997, Russia, Belarus, and Kazakhstan took a decision jointly to delay their entry into the WTO. At the meeting, the IK staff distributed a comprehensive assessment

---

[101] "Proekt Protokol o mezhdunarodnykh torgovykh peregovorakh gosudarstv-uchastnikov TS pri vstuplenii v VTO," Appendix 4 to Protokol of the Third Meeting of the IK, 19 December 1996. Protokol was passed at the fourth meeting of the IK on 25 February 1997.

[102] Zamechanie on "Predlozheniia po povestke 4-ogo zasedaniia IK" sent from GTK Kazakhstan to MinFin Kazakhstan, 8 February 1997.

[103] It should be noted that there were significant countervailing pressures on the government. Enclosed with the memo was a "List of differences between the customs legislation of the RK and the GATT/WTO agreement" that had been prepared by USAID – and the Western aid organizations were very active in trying to influence Kazakhstan and the other member-states to choose the WTO over the CU.

of the requirements of WTO entry, explained the threat that this posed to the Customs Union, and outlined a strategy for preserving the union in the face of countervailing pressures generated by WTO requirements. The document opened by outlining Russia's five years of experience with the WTO process, stating that the Russian government was currently reluctant to move forward in its negotiations with the WTO, because of "the worsening conditions for joining," which primarily amounted to the fact that Russia would not be given the "trade-political status like that enjoyed by the developed member-states of the organization." It then outlined all of the difficulties associated with not being a WTO member, first and foremost being the lack of protection from "antidumping" measures imposed unilaterally and without consultation as well as restrictive quotas on Russian exports.[104] The document then encouraged each of the member-states to take advantage of all possible grace periods allowed under the WTO to "soften the unavoidable difficulties of taking on the corresponding obligations." The document then raised an entirely new set of issues, and it is worth quoting at length:

For states entering into the Customs Union, the issue of joining the WTO is extraordinarily difficult. Belarus, Kazakhstan, and Kyrgyzstan have already begun this work. In accordance with the decision of the IK [etc.] . . . we are consulting one another on this issue. Previously, consultation was conducted for the most part on the preparation of the memoranda on the foreign trade regime and answers to the questions that member-states of the WTO might ask.

Together with this, it has now become completely obvious that many member countries of the WTO propose to use their influence over individual countries in Customs Union to secure our economic estrangement and the destruction of the integration structures we have created by imposing separate conditions for entry into the WTO. All of this may in the long term create insurmountable difficulties for unifying the conditions needed for cooperation, and makes the formation of a customs union impossible.

One of the key aspects of the process of joining, which will either have decisive significance for strengthening a common regime with third countries for countries of the Customs Union, or in effect make it impossible to unify [*sostykovat'*], will be the final stage of the negotiations between member states of the WTO and Customs Union member states entering the WTO on the so-called *tariff concessions*. [emphasis in original]

For example, the Russian import tariff for industrial goods from third countries on average is 14%; at the same time in WTO countries it is 6%, and in the long term this will be lowered to 3.9%.

In order not to make serious mistakes, which could bring entry into the WTO on truly discriminatory conditions significantly different for separate countries, that in

---

[104] Aluminum to the EU, mineral fertilizer to the United States, etc.

result make integration more difficult, we propose that it would be useful to discuss the following issues:

- not to give out materials for information in the first stage and not to take on obligations;
- not to present information on matters with no relation to the WTO (for example, privatization), stipulating that this is not an accepted obligation;
- discuss the consistency of the rules of the Customs Union with the norms of the WTO not during the joining period [of the Customs Union], but after it in the framework of a special organ;
- at the first stage abstain from time periods for beginning negotiations on market access and from the establishment of percent share of the customs tariff, or lowering duties on separate goods;
- limit the extent of the negotiations with active legislation (or existing legislation).

In order to resolve these issues, it would be useful for the countries entering the Customs Union, in the interests of all and of each country individually, to work out an agreed-upon external-trade policy, including tariff and non-tariff regulation, in order to avoid concessions that establish different tariffs for similar (analogical) goods from third countries.[105]

In sum, the IK suggested that Western governments were using their influence in the WTO to divide the members for the purpose of making the formation of a Customs Union impossible. In response, the IK proposed that members discuss the possibility of employing deliberate stalling tactics, not take on any obligations that might hinder the formation of the Customs Union, and develop a common tariff for negotiations with the WTO Working Group. Consistently with this agenda, the Russians proposed that member-states individually present a common tariff for negotiations with the WTO, worked out by the member-states in the IK. Toward this end, the governments would present proposals for the common external tariff and conduct another meeting in less than a month to work out a common tariff policy for the CU. The Kazakh, Belarusian, and Russian parties supported the proposal and expressed their preparedness to present proposals for a common tariff to other member-states. The Kyrgyz agreed to present their WTO tariff proposal only as information for other CU members, without working out a common position on tariff issues for WTO entry.[106]

True to their word, the other states submitted tariff proposals in short order. Consistently with the idea of creating a protective tariff wall to foster production within the region, the proposed tariffs were generally quite

---

[105] "K voprosu o prisoedinenii GUTS k VTO (k soveshchaniiu ekspertov 5 June 1997)."

[106] Letter from Minister of Finance Biialinov to Presidential Apparat of KR, "Information on the meeting-consultation of experts on the problems of member-states of the Customs Union joining the WTO," 17 June 1997.

high. Most notably, the proposed tariffs of individual countries included relatively high tariffs on goods they themselves did not produce, an indication of willingness to accept some sacrifices and to bargain on behalf of their partners for the good of the union. The intent to construct a linked tariff that would benefit the Customs Union as a whole was reflected in the letter accompanying the Kazakh schedule:

This document takes into account the conditions for the development of industry and agricultural production in the republic. Insofar as the decision is to be taken for the future [but] in conditions of uncertainty, the proposed levels also take into account factors that support domestic goods production, the stimulation of production of end-use goods, and the fulfillment of the budget. The document also takes into account the priorities of the industrial and agricultural development of the member states of the Customs Union.[107]

CHOICE POINT V: THE 1998 FINANCIAL CRISIS AND THE CREATION OF THE EURASIAN UNION

In 1997 and 1998, however, the development of regional institutions slowly ground to a halt as Russia's government grew progressively more liberal. In March 1997, the integralist first deputy prime minister, Alexei Bolshakov, was removed and liberals Anatoly Chubais and Boris Nemtsov were appointed jointly to replace him. But the most decisive shift occurred in March 1998, when Chernomyrdin was sacked and Sergei Kirienko was appointed as prime minister of Russia. This was the first time since Gaidar's dismissal in December 1992 that liberals had held the prime minister's post and integralists were virtually excluded from the new government. Whereas progressively more ambitious regional initiatives had been put forward every year since Chernomyrdin took office in 1993, the years 1997 and 1998 were marked by an absence of new moves toward integration.

Matters changed in August 1998, when Russia entered a severe financial crisis, leading the government to default on its debt and to the summary dismissal of Kirienko as prime minister. Within the subsequent two months, integralists were appointed to the top posts in the Russian government and liberals were incrementally purged. As discussed in Chapter 6, the appointment of the foreign minister and Soviet economist Yevgeny Primakov as prime minister and former Gosplan head Yuri Masliukov as first deputy prime minister revealed a sharp shift toward integralism. The resurgence

---

[107] Letter from Vice-Minister of the Economy of Kazakhstan to Biialinov (Minister of Finance of Kyrgyzstan). June 27, 1997.

of integralist economic ideas as reflected in the content analysis of Russian government officials interviewed in the press is quite stark, rising from 7.5% of public statements in the first quarter of 1998, to 73% in the last quarter of 1998. And with integralist governments in Belarus, Kazakhstan, and Tajikistan, this shift in the Russian position again laid the basis for new regional initiatives.

As in 1993, the economic crisis that ensued was regionwide, and the crisis initially wreaked havoc on the trade arrangements of the Customs Union. In the first two weeks of September, the Russian ruble lost more than 70% of its value and took most of the currencies of the region down with it – with the exception of the Kazakh tenge. Nazarbaev's reasons for sustaining the tenge were purely political – he scheduled an early presidential election for 10 January 1999 and could not afford to suffer the rampant inflation and financial crisis that were hitting Russia and his other post-Soviet neighbors. At the same time, the radical drop in the currencies of the other Customs Union members meant that goods would be sucked out of the markets of these countries and flood Kazakhstan as cheap imports. To carry Nazarbaev through a sensitive electoral period Russia and Kazakhstan agreed to several temporary trade restrictions. On 11 January, Kazakhstan imposed a six-month ban on the import from Russia of a list of goods that included mainly food supplies, and on 5 February Kazakhstan imposed 200% duties on a similar list of goods from both Kyrgyzstan and Uzbekistan. These remained in place until the government finally devalued the tenge in April 1999 when Nazarbaev's political control was more secure.

These measures and the financial crisis itself temporarily disrupted trade among the Customs Union members but did not mark the end of the regional institutions. In the midst of the crisis, Russia, Kazakhstan, Belarus, Tajikistan, and Kyrgyzstan reaffirmed their commitment by signing the Treaty on the Customs Union and the Single Economic Space, an extensive treaty of more than 70 articles that laid out in more specific detail the steps toward economic union. While this may have seemed a strange course to pursue at the height of a severe economic crisis, it is wholly consistent with the integralist view that the true source of the crisis was the neglect of the "real economy," i.e. the interlinked industrial sectors of the USSR, by successive liberal governments.

In October 2000, the five countries signed a treaty forming the Eurasian Union – which essentially amounted to no more than a retooling of the decision-making structure of the union. Thus, by the end of the decade, we can see clear distinctions in the institutional trajectories of the post-Soviet states (Table 10.6). Although the ideas of the leadership do not match up

TABLE 10.6. *Economic Ideas and Institutional Membership at the End of 2000*

	Economic Ideas July–Dec. 2000	Eurasian Union Membership	WTO Membership	Confirms?
Belarus	Integralist	11 Oct. 2000		Yes
Kazakhstan	Integralist	11 Oct. 2000		Yes
Tajikistan	Integralist	11 Oct. 2000		Yes
Turkmenistan	Mercantilist			Yes
Uzbekistan	Mercantilist			Yes
Russia	Liberal	11 Oct. 2000		No
Latvia	Liberal		14 Oct. 1998	Yes
Estonia	Liberal		21 May 1999	Yes
Georgia	Liberal		6 Oct. 1999	Yes
Armenia	Liberal		10 Dec. 2002	Yes
Kyrgyzstan	Liberal (.6)	11 Oct. 2000	14 Oct. 98	Mixed
Moldova	Liberal (.6)		8 May 2001	Yes
Lithuania	Liberal (.6)		8 Dec. 2000	Yes
Ukraine	Liberal (.6)			(No)
Azerbaijan				

precisely with institutional membership, in part because the membership decisions were the result of many steps taken earlier under different government leadership and that history is not reflected in this snapshot, the linkage between the two is striking.

In sum, this chapter has mapped the evolution in economic ideas and the effect of those ideas on institutional choices at five key points across the decade: whether or not to preserve the common regional currency, to sign the Economic Union Treaty and participate in the formation of the Interstate Economic Commission, to participate in the Customs Union, the Treaty on Deepening Integration, and/or the Eurasian Union. Whether we take the broad overview, looking at how different states lined up at the time each of these key regional initiatives was being considered, or whether we examine a state's decision closely using internal documents and interviews, it is hard to escape the conclusion that the way the leaders of these states understood the economy heavily influenced the type of international trade institutions that they preferred and the choices that they made.

Conclusions and Implications of the Analysis

> It is evident, that all the sciences have a relation, greater or less, to human nature; and that however wide any of them may seem to run from it, they still return back by one passage or another.
>
> David Hume, *A Treatise of Human Nature*[1]

This book has run a long course, charting the politics of 15 states across a decade; let us now return to the larger questions that lie at its core.

Let us begin by answering the empirical question that we started with: why did the 15 post-Soviet states, which were so similar upon achieving independence in 1991, choose such different international institutions to manage their economic relations with other states? The evidence presented in the previous chapters suggests that a government's decision to pursue membership in international trade institutions was rooted in its economic ideas. Different economic ideas led government officials to different views on the policies needed to achieve economic efficiency and growth and, as a result, to prefer different international institutions. Ultimately, the three institutional trajectories we find among the post-Soviet states can be traced to differences in the economic ideas of government officials.

To make this case we first identified the main economic ideologies in the region using traditional interpretive methods – involving more than 200 interviews with post-Soviet officials and a study of Soviet economic texts. From this analysis, three sets of economic ideas stood in sharp relief, each with clear implications for institutional choice. Integralist ideas stressing the virtues of specialized, monopolistic cooperation led officials to view their

---

[1] Hume, *An Enquiry Concerning.*

national economy as an integral part of a larger regional division of labor and to see regional economic institutions as necessary to economic growth. Liberal ideas championing market competition led officials to discount the old Soviet division of labor, considered an artificial and inefficient product of state planning, and to prefer integration into global multilateral liberal institutions like the WTO. Mercantilist ideas led government officials to see international economic exchange as exploitative. Mercantilists viewed international institutions as a threat to national economic autonomy and an effort by other states to impose an economic regime serving their own interests.

To demonstrate the independent and systematic effects of these ideas on institutional choice, we took several key steps. First, using public statements, we identified and coded the economic ideas of top government officials in each of the 15 countries during their first decade of independence. Next, in each individual case we mapped out the contingent or idiosyncratic reasons that led those ideas to prevail within a country's government and showed the systematic effects of those ideas on institutional and policy choices. Finally, we estimated the effect of economic ideas on institutional participation while controlling for other variables using a new cross-sectional dataset and, where possible, traced the governments' decisions on key agreements using internal government documents, interviews, and memoirs. The results of these investigations were encouraging.

We found that governments in which officials with integralist ideas prevailed became active participants in the regional economic institutions crafted under the CIS. Such efforts began with the endeavor to preserve the ruble zone and continued with the signing of the Treaty on Economic Union (1993), continued with the creation of the Interstate Economic Commission of the CIS (1994), and culminated in the formation of the Customs Union (1995), the Treaty on Deepening Integration (1996), and the Eurasian Union (2000). The countries where integralists persistently controlled the government across the decade – Kazakhstan, Belarus, and Tajikistan – were the drivers in this process, but many countries had an integralist faction in power for some period during the decade. The Russian government, in particular, played a critical role in the 1990s, but only when integralists held the top posts. An examination of internal documents pertaining to the decisions that these governments took on joining these key institutions showed that the link between integralism and support for the institutions was more than coincidence. Integralist ideas were reflected in the actual, documented calculations made by these governments concerning the economic costs and benefits of creating these institutions.

The effect of integralist economic ideas was manifest in domestic economic policies as well. Integralist governments chose to maintain or increase their dependence on energy supplies and pipeline routes from their prior Soviet partners, to encourage the formation of ownership ties between national enterprises and their prior Soviet partners by giving post-Soviet enterprises a privileged role in privatization or by establishing special regional joint-stock companies, and to sustain enterprises closely tied to production networks with other post-Soviet states by providing state subsidies. In interviews, public statements, and internal documents, decision makers in these countries predominantly relied on integralist ideas to explain their choices.

Governments in which liberal economic ideas prevailed made swift moves toward freer trade and entry into multilateral liberal institutions. We found that critical steps to WTO membership such as the submission of an application, the completion of the Memorandum on Foreign Trade, and regular meetings with the Working Group to identify the adjustments needed to secure membership tended to be taken when liberals were in power. And, indeed, it is the countries with protracted periods of liberal governance that have secured WTO membership. Kyrgyzstan (1998), Latvia (1999), Estonia (1999), Georgia (2000), Lithuania (2001), and Moldova (2001) secured membership in the first decade of independence, and Armenia (2003) has joined since the end of the study. Each one of these governments took the key steps toward membership while liberals were in the government and stalled in their progress when liberals were out of power.

Liberal governments were also much more resistant to participation in the regional economic institutions of the CIS. Estonia, Latvia, and Lithuania never joined the CIS and have not participated in any post-Soviet regional institutions. Georgia is a member in name only, with a poor record of signing and implementing agreements second only to Turkmenistan's. Kyrgyzstan and Moldova have been more active participants, but this can be attributed to the fact that integralists prevailed in Moldova for half of the decade and Kyrgyzstan's geographic isolation meant that freer trade often had to be pursued through closer relations with its post-Soviet partners. When Kyrgyzstan faced a choice between the freer trade requirements for WTO membership and the common external tariff of the Customs Union, it chose the former.

As with integralism, the effect of liberal ideas was not limited to trade institutions. Government officials with liberal ideas broke up national energy monopolies and privatized their constituent parts, privatized large-scale industries through auctions open to national and international bidders, cut off subsidies to enterprises, pegged their currencies to the U.S. dollar or the German mark, and ran balanced budgets.

Although mercantilism has been less prevalent in the region – it lacked both a history of direct Soviet promotion and contemporary international support – several countries, particularly in the early 1990s, adopted mercantilist ideas. When they achieved independence, the governments of Ukraine, Moldova, Latvia, Lithuania, and Georgia each were governed by mercantilist leaders. Turkmenistan and Uzbekistan have subsequently become the standard bearers of mercantilism in the region. And when mercantilists prevailed, governments pursued an autarkic international strategy. They rejected active participation in CIS regional economic institutions, eschewed membership in multilateral liberal institutions like the WTO, and developed myriad ways of closing their markets to imports and controlling international exchange.

Mercantilist ideas also translated into a distinct set of preferences in domestic economic policy. States governed by officials with mercantilist ideas pushed for centralized state control over national energy monopolies and for domestic sources of supply, even when import substitution came at a higher cost, and made efforts to diversify their sources of supply or avenues of distribution so as not to remain dependent on any one partner. They resisted privatization, kept industries under national control rather than merge enterprises with their former partners in other states, and used government subsidies and state-controlled banks to finance a policy of import substitution to extract the country from its reliance on the division of labor constructed during the Soviet period.

In sum, we find that the economic ideas of high-level government officials induced their preference for international institutions and economic policy, and that, with few exceptions, these preferences translated directly into government choice.

IMPLICATIONS FOR THE STUDY OF INTERNATIONAL ORDER

Although the empirical scope of this book is limited to the contemporary politics of post-Soviet Eurasia, these findings have implications well beyond the empirical terrain of the former USSR. Post-Soviet Eurasia is only the most recent field of engagement in a struggle between the advocates of economic liberalism and their rivals that began in Western Europe in the late eighteenth century, and the international politics of the region are rightly viewed as a microcosm of this broad historical rivalry.

A broader look at the choices made by the countries of the world in the past 200 years reveals a pattern similar to the one we find within the region.

In the latter half of the nineteenth century, the choice by many countries of the world to follow liberal England's lead by shedding their restrictions on imports and by adopting international economic institutions that facilitated open international exchange generated the rise of the liberal trading order, the first wave of "globalization." Similarly, the choice of many of those same states, including England, to close their markets in the 1920s and 1930s produced the general autarky of the interwar period. The decades following World War II saw the emergence of multiple competing international economic orders, quite similar to those we find in the post-Soviet space: a revived liberal trade regime based on the Bretton Woods institutions (now the WTO); a specialized, monopolistic system of state trading in the Communist bloc; and the national autarky that characterized many countries of Latin America, Africa, and Asia. In short, many of the choices made by the post-Soviet states are familiar ones; they have characterized the variety and the main shifts in international order of the past two centuries.

Such broad historical changes in international order – the rules that govern relations among states – have generally been attributed to factors other than ideas: to the reshuffling of domestic coalitions, the emergence of new social classes, or the rise of newly hegemonic states,[2] as teleological progress toward increased economic efficiency or as shifts in the "culture of anarchy" brought about by changes in the density of international transactions.[3] While major changes in economic structure and political power are undeniably a critical part of these changes in international order, some essential features of the politics of the past two centuries are lost in such accounts.

This book examines changes in international order through a different theoretical lens. First, it views international order as the aggregate result of choices made by individual states about institutional membership and seeks an explanation of change and stability by looking at the reasons for choice at the unit level. It suggests that international institutions exist only so long as their members choose to respect their rule, and individual countries, no matter how small or weak, have always been at liberty to choose their own institutional path. To explain international order, we must therefore explain why different states choose to support or reject a set of common institutional arrangements.

Second, the findings presented in this book suggest that countries choose to create and abide by institutions because of a shared set of economic

---

[2] Charles P. Kindleberger, *The World in Depression: 1929–1939* (Berkeley: University of California Press, 1973); Gilpin, *War and Change*; John G. Ikenberry, *After Victory*.

[3] Wendt, *Social Theory*, chap. 7.

ideas that leads their governments to prefer one set of trade rules over another. It suggests that we may be misled by an effort to read preferences, or interests, off a balance sheet of a country's economic or military attributes. We must know something of how officials think, and its conclusions direct our attention to government cadres rather than to geopolitical or economic conditions for an explanation of state behavior. Moreover, it suggests that not all ideas that officials hold matter equally in explaining state behavior. The findings of this book suggest that actors' ideas about who they are (*identity*) are less determinative of their institutional choices than their ideas about how the world works (*causation*).[4]

The post-Soviet states are uniquely suited to test these claims. The remarkable historical commonalities within post-Soviet Eurasia allow us to run something akin to a controlled experiment, in a laboratory that one could never hope to construct for all of the countries of the world over a 200-year period. This controlled, measurable, empirical setting allows us to parse out the effects of economic ideas and other difficult-to-measure factors on the creation of national and international economic institutions.

The result of this experiment – the empirical finding that causal ideas, of which the economic ideas under study here are one type, structure institutional preferences – is a robust one. It stands up well against the dominant alternatives. The different elite ideas that we found in the region could not simply be reduced to the underlying structural conditions favored by traditional IR theorists, and traditional explanations for the formation of international institutions did not fare well in our efforts to make sense of the evidence we find among the post-Soviet states. Realist theories instructed us to look for Russian coercion to explain why several post-Soviet states joined regional economic institutions rather than pursuing unilateralism or membership in the WTO. Instead, we found that several non-Russian states were quite eager and enterprising in their efforts to bind Russia and the other post-Soviet economies into collective institutions – far more eager, at times, than the government of Russia itself. Moreover, the states that took steps to relinquish some of their autonomy were no more vulnerable to Russian pressure, either through resource dependence or crippling security threats, than those that rejected participation in the CIS institutions. Even more unsettling for the realists is the paucity of evidence of Russian coercion against the countries that took an active role in the CIS. The empirical record does

---

[4] The contention here is not that identity does not matter, but that identity appears to matter much more in constituting the relevant political actors (states, churches, etc.) than it does in determining how those actors will behave.

not square well with the general theory that international institutions are imposed by strong states on the weak.

Nor did we find much support for the contention that a country's economic structure or situation determines its institutional choice. According to such an approach, states saddled with industries that were less competitive on international markets would more likely be in favor of closing off their economies to international markets through some form of regional bloc. States with a high percentage of enterprises linked in common production networks with enterprises in other post-Soviet republics would support common institutions to preserve such ties. What we found, however, was that the economies of states most committed to the regional institutions or to WTO entry were no different from the economies of states that opposed them. If the economic factors identified by these theorists determined states' preferences for institutional arrangements, one would have expected structurally identical countries like Ukraine and Belarus to behave quite similarly. They did not, and the fact that similar countries have behaved so differently raises important questions about the foundations of the theory.

The failure of these traditional explanations may hint at a larger problem with the structuralist ideas that underpin both neorealist and liberal theories of international politics. For if actors are essentially simple beings who respond directly to objective incentives and constraints in their environment, then actors facing similar constraints – in this case because they are similarly dependent on Russia for natural resources, or because their industries are similarly uncompetitive on international markets – should behave similarly. When they behave differently, as we found in this study, we begin to suspect a problem.

The problem may simply lie in the inadequacy of existing models and data. Traditional structural theories may simply have misidentified, mismeasured, or poorly estimated the objective factors that genuinely motivate human behavior. If this were the case, then specifying new structural variables or improving the characterization of economic processes with better models and estimation procedures might be all that is required. In this spirit, social scientists have been revising their models and generating new structural variables, measures, and data for more than a century – and surely should continue to do so. But the results so far have been modest when ideational variables are not employed, especially when we compare them with the physical sciences, where simple assumptions about particles and the way they respond to environmental forces and stimuli have yielded much more impressive results.

This book suggests that the problem with traditional approaches may lie deeper than questions of operationalization. It may lie in the fact that human actors are not simple beings whose interests are defined by an environment objectively given and understood in the same way by all. Rather, we find that actors understand the world differently and that, as do social scientists, they infer or impute causation to phenomena in different ways. This fundamentally shapes what they want and how they go about attaining it.

THE INDEPENDENCE OF IDEAS

But can we really treat ideas as first movers, as an independent cause? This book makes a strong claim that we can. It has based its case for independence, in part, on a novel theoretical position that the process by which ideas come to be held by top government officials is sufficiently contingent and resistant to systematic explanation that officials' ideas, in most cases, can be treated as independent and exogenous. And rather than simply take this as a theoretical assumption, we have worked to demonstrate the contingency of selection, to prove the idiosyncrasy of the origins of dominant ideas on a case-by-case basis.

In taking this path, the book runs against two disciplinary instincts in political science. One is the tendency to assume that everything is conducive to systematic explanation, perhaps even to prediction, and to assume that the only true explanation is one that identifies the relevant lawlike, systematic relationship.[5] This is an instinct that, when taken to its extreme, leads to the complete denial of human agency and runs against our commonsense understanding that we act intentionally, that we, as political actors, make things happen.[6] In contrast, the science of this book lies not in finding systematic explanations for ideas, but in recognizing and, indeed, seeking out the unsystematic origins of official ideas in order to demonstrate better their independent, systematic effects.

The other disciplinary instinct of which this book runs afoul is the tendency to reject culture or ideas as a cause, to assume that there must be something deeper, some unseen or hidden interest or mechanism that selects both the behavior and the ideas actors use to justify it. As a result, there is a tendency to view ideational explanations as simply incomplete explanations –

---

[5] Following Carl G. Hempel, "The Function of General Laws in History," *Journal of Philosophy*, 39 (1942): 35–48.
[6] See Searle, *Intentionality*, chap. 4, on intentional causation.

a deep resistance to the view that ideas are not derived directly from structures. This is the long intellectual shadow of materialism, and this book tackles it directly.

For if there is one general theoretical point that this book has tried to establish, it is that the notion of a prior or objective interest distinct from one's ideas about the world is a chimera. Causal ideas tell us why we want something as well as the best strategy for getting it. Without them, interests, particularly the type of interests we speak of in the study of politics, would not exist. Lacking some causal sense of how we benefit from a rule, law, or policy, we would not have a preference for it any more than we can have preferences for circles over squares. For something to have utility, we must understand its use, and to a great extent those subjective understandings vary across individuals and groups.

To argue, as we have, that actors' choices are rooted in their ideas does not mean that actors are irrational. Indeed, the analysis of this book undermines the traditional contradiction assumed between rational action and action motivated by ideas. The available evidence suggests that the behavior of each of the post-Soviet states was motivated by a set of economic ideas. But the actors we have examined in this study were certainly rational in their selection of courses of action. In all cases where internal government documents were made available, we found that the governments conducted cost–benefit analyses of the value of joining international institutions. But the way in which costs and benefits were conceived, and the ideas about the economy that lay behind those calculations, differed significantly across countries in the region, and this is what explains variation in support for the different international institutions. In sum, actors are rational, but the reasoning that they employ is rooted in their ideas linking cause and effect.

Nor do I wish to imply, despite the critique of materialism, that actors are not motivated by material interests such as the desire for economic gain. If the argument presented in this book is sound, then the debate over whether states are motivated primarily by material interests or by ideas and ideals rests on a false contradiction. If an actor's interest ultimately rests on the causal idea that links concrete means to a desired end and a set of understandings that lead one to believe that the end is desirable, then material interests, too, are best thought of as a type of idea. And in this sense, idealism and materialism are equally flawed, as the question of whether actors are motivated by their ideas or by their interests loses all meaning. And to explain why individuals, states, or other organized collectivities behave as they do, it falls upon us to identify the set of causal ideas that underpins the way they conceive of their interests. This book offers one example of how this might be done.

In sum, the book is a study of the central role of economic ideas in the decisions of governments to participate in international economic institutions. Its findings lend empirical support to the theoretical position that material interests are also ideas, that ideas are not determined by material structures, and that the definition of economic interests is an ideational process based on an actor's thinking about economic causation. The revision of, and struggle over, these ideas and the human institutions based on them are a never-ending dynamic process, and a central feature of political life. The contest between actors with different ideas has always been a central cleavage of international and domestic politics. We can have little doubt but that this will continue to be so.

Appendix A

Measurement and Coding of Economic Ideas – Additional Tests

As a way of checking the ideational coding, as well as experimenting with alternative means for coding ideas, I created another set of indicators in addition to *libgov*, *integgov*, and *mercgov*. These indicators were based on a coding of all causal statements by economic officials in the U.S. Government's Foreign Broadcast Information Service (FBIS) database of translated newspaper articles, radio broadcasts, and television broadcasts in 1992, 1994, 1996, and 1998. There are several sources of bias in the FBIS database that could affect the analysis. First, FBIS does not select all articles or broadcasts for all countries in the period. It often selects articles on the basis of requests of the U.S. government agencies and contractors that it serves. As a result, the principles of article selection are not explicit and conversations with FBIS staff suggest that the selection criteria for articles have varied over time. Second, country coverage was not even and the FBIS articles heavily favor Russia and Ukraine. Indeed, it was not even possible to code Tajikistan because there were virtually no causal statements by Tajik economic officials recorded in the FBIS dataset. Finally, because all of the statements have appeared in the country's media, the editorial policies of national media also have an important influence on the range of ideas expressed in the sample. Because the media in these countries were generally more liberal than officialdom and because the U.S. government agencies were interested in the adoption of liberal reforms, we would expect there to be a liberal bias in the FBIS dataset. By targeting officials rather than the frequency of causal statements, the government coding was less subject to bias, but it is important to have multiple measures.

To account for the fact that many of the officials in the FBIS dataset held minor offices and were not likely to be important decision makers, I

TABLE A.1. *Weights Accorded to Economic Statements by Officials Based upon Rank*

Rank	Weight
Head of state: president in presidential system, prime minister in parliamentary system	6
Head of government: prime minister in presidential system	5
First vice premier, chairman of parliament, head of presidential administration in superpresidential regimes	4
Ministers, deputy ministers, heads of state agencies and vice premiers, first deputy chairman of parliament in nonsuperpresidential system	3
Head of parliamentary faction with more than 10% of seats, parliamentary committee chairman, presidential spokesman	2
Advisers, parliamentarians, department heads	1

have also weighted the causal statements by the rank of the officials who made them, using the scheme shown in Table A.1. The value of one of the FBIS ideology variables is the share of (weighted) statements of that ideology out of the total of all (weighted) causal statements by government officials within that year. To calculate Kazakhstan's score for *libfbis* in 1995, for example, we would collect all of the liberal causal statements made by Kazakh officials during 1995, attribute to each one the value accorded to the rank of the speaker, sum them, and calculate that sum as a percentage of the total of all weighted statements (liberal, integralist, mercantilist, and other) in Kazakhstan in 1995.

The measure gives us some confidence that the patterns identified in the coding scheme hold. As shown in Table 9.5, the correlation between *mercgov* and *mercfbis* is .80, the correlation between *integgov* and *sovfbis* is .58, but the correlation between *libgov* and *libfbis* is a mere .29. This divergence between the measures for liberal ideas is expected, given the known biases of the FBIS dataset and our anticipation that it would likely be a less accurate measure of liberal ideas within the government, but this has a distorting effect on the other variables. If we look at the average difference between the values of the *gov* and *fbis* variables (Table 9.8), the convergence is somewhat less stark but still might lead us to question the use of FBIS as a primary measure.

As seen in Table A.2, the accuracy of the *fbis* measure varies significantly by country. For Belarus, Kazakhstan, Moldova, Turkmenistan, Ukraine, and Uzbekistan, the *gov* and *fbis* measures are very closely matched. In part, this may be due to the fact that these countries, with the exception of Moldova, have much less free press – hence the editorial policies of the media would

TABLE A.2. *Correlations between Ideas Indicators (fbis and gov)*

	Soviet Integralism	Liberalism	Mercantilism	Other
Armenia	.18	.68	.04	.38
Azerbaijan	.17	.42	.37	.00
Belarus	.20	.27	.03	.15
Estonia	.00	.38	.00	.13
Georgia	.61	.30	.05	.13
Kazakhstan	.20	.16	.00	.04
Kyrgyzstan	.51	.54	.00	.03
Latvia	.00	.33	.58	.00
Lithuania	.00	.62	.29	.08
Moldova	.26	.36	.20	.00
Russia	.53	.49	.06	.00
Tajikistan	.75	.50	.00	.00
Turkmenistan	.06	.04	.35	.25
Ukraine	.07	.31	.30	.04
Uzbekistan	.00	.00	.14	.14
All countries	.24	.36	.16	.09
Correlation between FBIS and GOV measures	.58	.29	.80	

more closely reflect the policies of the government. Belarus, Kazakhstan, and Ukraine were also heavily represented in the FBIS database, so the sample of causal statements from these countries was more likely to be representative. Indeed, the wide discrepancies in Tajikistan, Kyrgyzstan, Latvia, Lithuania, Estonia, Armenia, and Azerbaijan most likely reflect the fact that the data on these countries were limited, and therefore (especially in Tajikistan) the small sample of government officials quoted in articles was not representative.

For Russia and Georgia, the large discrepancy between *fbis* and *gov* cannot be attributed to the small sample size, since there was a relatively large amount of data from both countries. Moreover, Georgia is especially puzzling since the *fbis* measures for Georgia score the government as considerably more integralist than the *gov* measures in the mid-1990s, a score that goes against the general liberal bias of the *fbis* dataset as well as Shevardnadze's well-documented history of supporting liberal economic ideas. It appears, upon closer examination of the data, that this is perhaps because the preponderance of the Georgian data are from President Eduard Shevardnadze's weekly radio address, a more populist forum in which he may have been loath to express liberal ideas that were not generally popular among Georgian citizens. In Russia, the government is consistently coded as more liberal in the mid-1990s (by 1998, the two measures overlap perfectly), but this is relatively easy to understand. The major Russian newspapers were liberal in orientation and liberal officials were much more open to sharing their views with the press. Nonetheless, because of these concerns with the dataset, I use *integgov*, *libgov*, and *mercgov* as the primary measure for ideas.

Appendix B

Interviews Conducted by the Author

A1 Garnik Nanagoulian, Minister of Trade, 2 June 1997

A2 Newspaper Editor, 2 June 1997

A3 Electricity Ministry, 4 June 1997

A4 Ministry of Economy, 5 June 1997

A5 National Bank, 3 June 1997

A6 Ministry of Economy, section preparing for WTO accession, 6 June 1997

A7 Fuel Ministry, 6 June 1997

A8 Union of Armenian Manufacturers and Businessmen, 6 June 1997

A9 Ministry of Industry, 5 June 1997

A10 U.S. Embassy, 3 June 1997

A11 Union of Armenian Manufacturers and Businessmen, 3 June 1997

A12 Assistant to Minister, Ministry of Finance, 4 June 1997

A13 Businessman who was a close associate of President Levon Ter-Petrosian 27 May 1997, interview conducted in Moscow

A14 Ministry of Finance, 5 June 1997

A15 Confidential, 5 June 1997

A16 Arthur P. Manaserian, Ministry of Foreign Affairs, 3 June 1997

A17 Deputy Minister of Economy, 4 June 1997

A18 Fuel Ministry, 4 June 1997

A19 Head of Union of Journalists, 1 June 1997

A20 Deputy Minister of Trade, 1 June 1997

MINSK, BELARUS

B1 Piotr Prokopovich, Presidential Administration, 21 July 1997

B2 Ministry of Economy, 18 July 1997

B3 CIS Executive Secretariat, 23 July 1997

B4 CIS Executive Secretariat, 18 July 1997, 22 July 1997

B5 Chief Inspector, State Customs Committee (Multiple meetings)

B6 International Division of the State Customs Committee of the Republic of Belarus (Multiple meetings)

B7 Belarussian National Front Political Party, 22 July 1997

B8 Confidential, 21 July 1997

B9 Belarusian National Front Political Party, 17 July 1997

B10 Nikolai Averianovich Strel'tsov, Union of Industrialists, 21 July 1997

B11 Evgenii L'vovich Ivanov, Director of "Evro-Ural," 21 July 1997

B12 Factory Director, 24 July 1997

B13 CIS Executive Secretariat, 22 July 1997

B14 Association of Belarusian Bankers, 17 July 1997

B15 Deputy Minister of Finance, 18 July 1997

B16 Journalist, 15, 16 July 1997

TBILISI, GEORGIA

G1 Levan Totadze (Assistant to the Minister, Ministry of Economy), 17, 18 June 1997

G2 Temur Basilia (Presidential Administration, Chief Economic Adviser), 13 June 1997

G3 Deputy Minister of Finance, 16 June 1997

G4 Ministry of Finance, 16 June 1997

G5 David Onoprishvili (Chairman of the Committee for Economic Policy and Reform, Parliament of Georgia), 20 June 1997

G6 Merab Pachulia (Chairman of the Georgian Institute of Public Opinion), 13 June 1997

G7 Zurab Tskitishvili (Chairman of the Branch Economies Committee of Parliament of Georgia), 19 June 1997

G8 Michael Ukleba (First Deputy Minister of Foreign Affairs), 17 June 1997

G9 Ministry of Foreign Affairs, Department of International Economic Relations, 17 June 1997

G10 Ministry of Foreign Affairs, 11 June 1997

G11 Ministry of Foreign Affairs, 17 June 1997

G12 David Zubitashvili (Chairman of the National Energy Corporation), 23 June 1997

G13 Gela Nioradze (Deputy Minister of Trade and Foreign Economic Relations), 18 June 1997

G14 U.S. Embassy, 19 June 1997

G15 USAID officer, 20 June 1997

G16 Commission of the European Union, 16 June 1997

G17 World Bank, 19 June 1997

G18 Hunter Monroe (IMF Head of Mission), 16 June 1997

G19 Confidential (American citizen), 20 June 1997

G20 Presidential Administration, 23 June 1997

G21 Oliver Weeks (Editor of *Georgian Economic Trends*), 18 June 1997

G22 Deputy Minster of Economy, 13 June 1997

G23 U.S. Embassy, 18 June 1997

G24 Confidential (Georgian citizen), 11 June 1997

BISHKEK, KYRGYZSTAN

K1 Deputy Chief of State Customs Inspection, 12, 13, 14 November 1997

K2 Ministry of Finance, Head of Department (Multiple meetings)

K3 Ministry of Finance, Deputy Head of Department (Multiple meetings)

K4 Ministry of Finance (Multiple meetings)

K5 National Bank, Head of Department (Multiple meetings between 10 and 22 November 1997)

K6 Mirbek S. Eshaliev (Head of International Department, Presidential Administration of Kyrgyz Republic), 12 November 1997

K7 Kasym Isaovich Isaev (Deputy Minister of CIS Cooperation), 10 November 1997

K8 Union of Industrialists and Entrepreneursm, 11 November 1997

K9 Shailobek Musakojoev (Head of Institute of Economics under Ministry of Finance, the former Gosplan institute), 13 November 1997

K10 Deputy Minister of Foreign Trade and Industry, 16 November 1997

K11 Ministry of Foreign Affairs (Department head), 12 November 1997

K12 Ministry of Foreign Affairs, 12 November 1997

K13 Talantbek Kasymbekov (Head of the External Affairs Department of the Joint-Stock Holding Energy Company of the Kyrgyz Republic), 13 November 1997

K14 Ministry of Foreign Affairs, 12 November 1997

K15 Head of Department, State Customs Inspection (Multiple meetings)

K16 Bazarbay Estebesovich Mambetov (Deputy Chairman of the Executive Commission of the Interstate Council of the Republic of Kazakhstan, Kyrgyz Republic, and the Republic of Uzbekistan), 10 November 1997

K17 Ministry of Economy, 3 November 1997

K18 Ministry of Trade and Industry, 6 November 1997

K19 Ministry of Finance, 6 November, 1997

K20 Ministry of Fuel and Energy, 13 November 1997

ALMATY, KAZAKHSTAN

Kz1 Ministry of Finance, Department of Macroeconomics and Budget Policy, 15 October 1997

Kz2 Ministry of Finance, 15, 16 October 1997

Kz3 Bakhitzhan Mukhambetkalievich Dzhaksaliev (Head of the Department of Analysis and Strategic Planning of the Ministry of Energy, Industry, and Trade), 29 October 1997

Kz4 Igor Petrovich Pasko (Head of Department of Multilateral Cooperation in the CIS, Ministry of Foreign Affairs), 28 October 1997

Kz5 Union of Industrialists and Entrepreneurs, 22 October 1997

Kz6 Ministry of Finance, Department Head, 16 October 1997

Kz7 Ministry of Economy, Department Head, 24 October 1997

Kz8 Ministry of Economy, Deputy Head (of different department than Kz7), 22 October 1997

Kz9 State Customs Commission, high-level official, 27, 29, 30 October 1997; 4 November 1997 (Multiple meetings)

Kz10 U.S. Embassy, 20 October 1997

Kz11 World Bank, 27 October 1997

Kz12 Bakhit U. Utetleuova (Manager, Department of Oil and Gas Production and Transportation, Kazakhoil) 29 October 1997

Kz13 HIID, 23 October 1997

Kz14 Deputy Minister of Finance, 16 October 1997

Kz15 Ministry of Electricity, 17 October 1997

Kz16 HIID, 23 October 1997

Kz17 Batyr Apenovich Makhanbetazhiev (Department of Analysis of Monetary-Credit Policy of the Central Asian Bank of Cooperation and Development), 22 October 1997

Kz18 Ministry of CIS Affairs, 17 October 1997

MOSCOW AND ST. PETERSBURG, RUSSIA

R1 Arkady Volsky (Chairman of Confederation of Unions of Industrialists and Entrepreneurs), 14 November 1996

R2 Deputy Minister of Foreign Economic Relations, 2 July 1997

R3 Oleg B. Aleksandrov (Program Officer, Moscow Public Science Foundation), 18 April 1997

R4 Andrei Vadimovich Kortunov (President, Moscow Public Science Foundation), 18 April 1997

R5 Sergei Viktorovich Shilov (Director of the Department of Currency Operations and Foreign Economic Activity, Sberbank), 19 May 1997

R6 Konstantin M, Khasanov (Deputy Head of Emerging Markets Department, Head of CIS Markets Division of National Reserve Bank), 19 May 1997

R7 Vladimir Drebentsov (Economist, World Bank) 23 April 1997, 30 June 1997

R8 Aleksandr Konstantinovich Griznov (Council on Foreign and Security Policy), 30 June 1997

R9 Parliamentary Representative and member of CIS Committee of Russian Duma, 22 May 1997

R10 Grigory Ivanovich Tikhonov (Chairman of CIS Duma Committee), 22 May 1997

R11 Andrei Andreevich Piontkovsky (Director, Strategic Studies Center), 27 May 1997

R12 Viacheslav Vladimirovich Igrunov (Duma Deputy, Deputy Chairman of Committee on CIS Affairs and Relations with Compatriots, Deputy Chairman of the Yabloko Party), 21 April 1997.

R13 Andrei Vladimirovich Zagorskii (Rector of Moscow State Institute for International Relations (MGIMO), 12 March 1997

R14 Vladimir Anatolevich Pokrovskii (Executive Commission of the Bel-Rus Union), 24 March 1997; 7–8 April 1997; 17 April 1997

R15 U.S. Embassy, Economic officer, 25 March 1997

R16 U.S. Embassy, Political officer, 17 April 1997

R17 Boris Vladimirov (Deputy Chairman of the Kollegia of the IEC), 14 November 1996

R18 IEC Department Head, 7, 21, 22 April 1997; 31 June 1997 (Multiple interviews between November 1996 and December 1997, by date in text)

R19 Sviatoslav Nikolaevich Perfilov, Director of the Department of Trade and Economic Relations, IEC, 28 May 1997

R20 IEC Consultant, 14 November 1996

R21 IEC Department Head (Multiple interviews, by date in text)

R22 Head of Department, Ministry of Foreign Affairs, 1 July 1997

R23 Ministry of Foreign Affairs, Deputy Head of Department, 4 July 1997

R24 IEC Staff, 10 July 1997

R25 IEC Staff (Multiple meetings, by date in text)

R26 IEC Department Head, 2 July 1997 (Multiple interviews, by date in text)

R27 IEC Department Head, 19 November 1996

R28 IEC Staff, Central Asian (Multiple interviews by date in text)

R29 Ministry of Economy, Department Head, 19 August 1997

R30 U.S. Embassy, 17 April 1997

R31 Foreign Policy Adviser to President Boris Yeltsin, 18 April 1997

R32 Ministry of CIS Cooperation, Department Head, 30 June 1997

R33 Legal Scholar who works with CIS Interparliamentary Assembly, 18 July 1996; 2 August 1996.

R34 Pavel Valentinovich Onishenko, IEC Deputy Department Head, 2 December 1996

R35 Interstate Monetary Commission of the CIS (Multiple interviews between November 1996 and December 1997, by date in text)

R36 RAO Gazprom, Annual Shareholders Meeting 1997

KIEV, UKRAINE

U1 Presidential Administration, Economic adviser, 31 July 1997

U2 Parliamentary Representative, Parliamentary Commission on Foreign Affairs and CIS Matters, 31 July 1997; 5 August 1997

U3 Ministry of Foreign Affairs, Department Head, 6 August 1997

U4 Ministry of Finance, 29 July 1997

U5 Ministry of Finance, Department Head, 31 July 1997

U6 Ministry of Foreign Economic Relations, 30 July 1997

U7 Deputy Minister of Foreign Economic Relations, 30 July 1997

U8 Viktor Dmitrovich Gladushch, First Deputy Minister of Foreign Economic Relations, 30 July 1997

U9 Ministry of Energy, Department of External Relations, 5 August 1997

U10 Deputy Minister of Economy 31 July 1997; 8 August 1997

U11 U.S. Embassy, 30 July 1997

U12 State Committee of Oil and Gas and Oil Refining Industry of Ukraine, 6 August 1997

U13 Sergei A. Guridov (Secretary of the Kollegii of the State Committee of Oil and Gas and Oil Refining Industry of Ukraine – Derzhnaftogazprom), 6 August 1997

U14 Confidential, 28 July 1997

U15 HIID, 7 August 1997

U16 Deputy Minister of Industry, 6 August 1997

U17 Deputy Minister of Finance, 7 August 1997

U18 National Bank, 29 July 1997

U19 Ukrainian Union of Industrialists and Entrepreneurs, 28 July 1997

U20 U.S. Embassy, 1 July 1997

U21 Confidential, 7 August 1997

TASHKENT, UZBEKISTAN

Uz1 Deputy Minister of Foreign Economic Relations, 1 December 1997

Uz2 Economic Adviser to President Islam Karimov, 27 November 1997

Uz3 Ministry of Foreign Affairs, Deparment Head, 25 November 1997

Uz4 Aleksandr Alekseevich Pridatkin (Head of the United Controlling Center of the Energy Systems of Central Asia UCC Energia), 25 November 1997

Uz5 Ministry of Finance, 25 November 1997

Uz6 Confidential, 28 November 1997

Uz7 Ministry of Energy, 24 November 1997

Bibliography

Official Publications of CIS Institutions

Sodruzhestvo Nezavisimykh Gosudarstv, Mezhgosudarstvennyi Ekonomicheskii Komitet Ekonomicheskogo Soiuza. *Informatsionnyi Biulleten'*. [Commonwealth of Independent States, Interstate Economic Commission, *Informational Bulletin*.] Moscow. Published Quarterly beginning January 1996. Cited in text as *IEC Biulleten*.

Integratsionnyi Komitet. *Biulleten' Razvitiia Integratsiia*. [Integration Commission. *Bulletin of Integration Developments*]. Moscow. Published Quarterly beginning January 1996. Cited in text as *IK Biulleten*.

Vestnik Mezhparlamentskoi Assamblei. [*Bulletin of the Interparliamentary Assembly*]. St. Petersburg. Published semiannually beginning 1993. Cited in text as *Vestnik MPA*.

Sodruzhestvo Nezavisimykh Gosudarstv, Ispolnitelnyi Sekretariat, *Sodruzhestvo*. [Lists all agreements passed by the Council of Heads of State and Council of Heads of Government.] Published semiannually beginning 1992.

Secondary Sources

Abdelal, Rawi. *National Purpose in the World Economy: Post-Soviet States in Comparative Perspective*. Ithaca, N.Y.: Cornell University Press, 2001.

Adler, Emmanuel. *The Power of Ideology: The Quest for Technological Autonomy in Argentina and Brazil*. Berkeley: University of California Press, 1987.

Adler, Emmanuel and Peter M. Haas. "Conclusion: Epistemic Communities, World Order, and the Creation of a Reflective Research Program." In "Knowledge, Power, and International Policy Coordination," edited by Peter Haas. *International Organization* 46 (special issue 1992): 367–390.

Akaev, Askar. *On State Economic Policy in 1998*. Bishkek: Ichkun, 1997.

Ambrosius, Gerold and William H. Hubbard. *A Social and Economic History of Twentieth-Century Europe*. Cambridge, Mass.: Harvard University Press, 1989.

Appel, Hilary, "The Ideological Determinants of Liberal Economic Reform: The Case of Privatization." *World Politics* 52 (July 2000): 520–549.

A New Capitalist Order: Privatization and Ideology in Russia and Eastern Europe. Pittsburgh: University of Pittsburgh Press, 2004.

Aslund, Anders. *How Russia Became a Market Economy.* Washington, D.C.: Brookings Institution, 1995.

"Post-Soviet Free Trade." May 2003. Available at: http://www.ceip.org/files/Publications/aslund_ postsoviettrade.asp?from=pubdate.

Barkai, Avraham. *Nazi Economics: Ideology, Theory, and Policy.* New Haven, Conn.: Yale University Press, 1990.

Barnett, Michael N. "Institutions, Roles, and Disorder: The Case of the Arab States System." *International Studies Quarterly* 37, no. 3 (September 1993): 271–296.

Dialogues in Arab Politics: Negotiations in Regional Order. New York: Columbia University Press, 1998.

Becker, Abraham. "Russia and Economic Integration in the CIS." *Survival* 38 (1996/1997): 117–136.

Beissinger, Mark R. "The Persisting Ambiguity of Empire." *Post-Soviet Affairs* 11 (1995): 149–194.

Nationalist Mobilization and the Collapse of the Soviet State. Cambridge: Cambridge University Press, 2002.

Bentall, Richard. *Madness Explained.* London: Allen Lane, 2003.

Biersteker, Thomas J. and Cynthia Weber. "The Social Construction of State Sovereignty." In *State Sovereignty as Social Construct,* edited by Thomas J Biersteker and Cynthia Weber. Cambridge: Cambridge University Press, 1996.

Bisnis. U.S. Commerce Department's Business Information Service for the Newly Independent States. Available at: www.bisnis.doc.gov. Accessed on March 3, 2002.

Blyth, Mark. *Great Transformations: Economic Ideas and Institutional Change in the Twentieth Century.* Cambridge: Cambridge University Press, 2002.

Bor, Mikhail. *Aims and Methods of Soviet Planning.* London: Lawrence and Wishart, 1967.

Breslauer, George W. "Soviet Economic Reforms since Stalin: Ideology, Politics, and Learning." *Soviet Economy* 6 (1990): 252–280.

Gorbachev and Yeltsin as Leaders. Cambridge: Cambridge University Press, 2002.

Browning, Lynnley E. "Rebel Chechen Currency New Salvo to Moscow." *Reuters,* April 24, 1997.

Brzezinski, Zbigniew. "Introduction: Last Gasp or Renewal?" In *Russia and the Commonwealth of Independent States,* edited by Zbigniew Brzezinski and Paige Sullivan. New York: M. E. Sharpe, 1997.

Brzezinski, Zbigniew and Paige Sullivan, eds. *Russia and the Commonwealth of Independent States.* New York: M. E. Sharpe, 1997.

Bukharin, N. and E. Preobrazhensky. *The ABC of Communism: A Popular Explanation of the Program of the Communist Party of Russia.* Ann Arbor: University of Michigan Press, 1996.

Bukovansky, Mlada. "The Altered State and the State of Nature: The French Revolution and International Politics." *Review of International Studies* 25 (1999): 197–216.

Bull, Hedley. *The Anarchical Society: A Study of Order in World Politics.* London: Macmillan, 1977.

Bunce, Valerie. *Subversive Institutions: The Design and Destruction of Socialism and the State.* Ithaca, N.Y.: Cornell University Press, 1999.

Buzan, Barry. "The English School: An Underexploited Resource in IR." *Review of International Studies* 27, no. 3 (2001): 471–488.

Carlisle, Donald S. "Islam Karimov and Uzbekistan: Back to the Future?" In *Patterns of Post-Soviet Leadership*, edited by Timothy J. Colton and Robert C. Tucker, 191–216. Boulder, Colo.: Westview Press, 1995.

Carr, E. H. and R. W. Davies. *Foundations of a Planned Economy, 1926–1929*, Vol. 1, part 2. London: Macmillan, 1969.

Cohen, Stephen F. *Bukharin and the Bolshevik Revolution: A Political Biography 1888–1938*. New York: Oxford University Press, 1980.

Cooper, Richard N. "International Cooperation in Public Health as a Prologue to Macroeconomic Cooperation." In *Can Nations Agree? Issues in International Economic Cooperation*, edited by Richard N. Cooper et al. Washington, D.C.: Brookings Institution, 1989.

Corrales, Javier and Richard Feinberg. *International Studies Quarterly* 43 (1998): 1–36.

Crowther, William. "Moldova: Caught between Nation and Empire." In *New States, New Politics: Building the Post-Soviet Nations*, edited by Ian Bremmer and Ray Taras. Cambridge: Cambridge University Press, 1997.

Darden, Keith A. "The Origins of Economic Interests: Explaining Variation in Support for Regional Institutions among the Post-Soviet States." Ph.D. dissertation, University of California, Berkeley, 2000.

"The Dark Side of the State: Formal and Informal Mechanisms of State Supremacy." Paper presented at State-Building in Post-Communist States: Toward Comparative Analysis, Yale University, April 27–28 2001.

"The Scholastic Revolution: Explaining Nationalism in the USSR." Unpublished mimeo, 2003.

Content analysis of articles by government officials, *Finansy* 1994–2000. (Statistical Dataset), 2003a.

Dawisha, Karen. "Constructing and Deconstructing Empire in the Post-Soviet Space." In *The End of Empire? The Transformation of the USSR in Comparative Perspective*, edited by Karen Dawisha and Bruce Parrott. New York: M. E. Sharpe, 1997.

Dawisha, Karen and Bruce Parrott. *Russia and the New States of Eurasia: The Politcs of Upheaval.* Cambridge: Cambridge University Press, 1994.

Deudney, Daniel H. "The Philadelphian System: Sovereignty, Arms Control, and Balance of Power in the American States-Union, Circa 1787–1861." *International Organization* 49 (1995): 191–228.

Deutsch, Karl W. *The Nerves of Government: Models of Political Communication and Control.* New York: Free Press, 1966.

Diamond, Jared. *Guns, Germs, and Steel: The Fates of Human Societies.* New York: W. W. Norton, 1997.

Dimov, Ivan. "Sarybay Kalmurzazaev: 'The Process of Integration with Russia Has Been Difficult, but There Is No Other Choice...'" *Delovoi Mir* (Moscow). 16 December 1994, p. 5.

Dobbin, Frank. *Forging Industrial Policy: The United States, Britain, and France in the Railway Age*. Cambridge: Cambridge University Press, 1994.

Downs, Anthony. *An Economic Theory of Democracy*. New York: Harper Collins, 1957.

Drezner, Daniel W. *The Sanctions Paradox: Economic Statecraft and International Relations*. Cambridge: Cambridge University Press, 1999.

Dryzek, John. "How Far Is It from Virginia and Rochester to Frankfurt? Public Choice as Critical Theory." *British Journal of Political Science* 22 (1992): 397–417.

Economist Intelligence Unit. *Country Profile* [Various countries]. Online data source of Harvard University Libraries, 1996.

Economist Intelligence Unit. *Country Profile* [Various countries]. Online data source of Harvard University Libraries, 1999.

Ekedahl, Carolyn McGiffert and Melvin A. Goodman. *The Wars of Eduard Shevardnadze*. University Park: Pennsylvania State University Press, 1997.

Ellman, Michael and Vladimir Kontorovich, eds. *The Destruction of the Soviet Economic System: An Insiders' History*. New York: M. E. Sharpe, 1998.

[ENKhK]Akademiya obshchestvennykh nauk pri Tseka KPSS Kafedra ekonomiki i organizatsii proizvodstva. In *Edinyi Narodno-khozyaistvennyi Kompleks: Soderzhanie i zakonomernosti razvitiya*. Moscow: Mysl', 1985.

European Bank of Reconstruction and Development. *Transition Report*, 1999.

Evangelista, Matthew. *Unarmed Forces: The Transnational Movement to End the Cold War*. Ithaca, N.Y.: Cornell University Press, 1999.

Faranda, Regina. "Ties That Bind, Opinions That Divide: How Neighboring Countries Have Viewed Russia, 1991–2001." Office of Research, U.S. Department of State, 21 May 2001 R-2-01.

Finnemore, Martha. *National Interests in International Society*. Ithaca, N.Y.: Cornell University Press, 1996.

Finnemore, Martha and Kathryn Sikkink. "International Norm Dynamics and Political Change." *International Organization* 52 (1998): 887–917.

Freeland, Chrystia. "Rukh: The New Ukrainian Nationalism." Thesis (A.B. Honors in History and Literature), Harvard University, 1991.

Frieden, Jeffry A. "Invested Interests: The Politics of National Economic Policies in a World of Global Finance." *International Organization* 45 (1991): 425–451.

"Actors and Preferences in International Relations." In *Strategic Choice and International Relations*, edited by David E. Lake and Robert Powell. Princeton, N.J.: Princeton University Press, 1999.

Frieden, Jeffry A. and Ronald Rogowski. "The Impact of the International Economy on National Policies: An Analytical Overview." In *Internationalization and Domestic Politics*, edited by Robert O. Keohane and Helen V. Milner, 25–47. Cambridge: Cambridge University Press, 1996.

Furner, Mary and Barry Supple, eds. *The State and Economic Knowledge*. Cambridge: Cambridge University Press, 1990.

Gaddy, Clifford G. *The Price of the Past: Russia's Struggle with the Legacy of a Militarized Economy*. Washington, D.C.: Brookings Institution, 1996.

Gaidar, Yegor. *Days of Defeat and Victory*, translated by Jane Ann Miller. Seattle: University of Washington Press, 1999.

Gazprom, RAO. *Annual Report*, Moscow: Gazprom, 1996.

Geertz, Clifford E. *The Interpretation of Cultures*. New York: Basic Books, 1973.

Gill, Stephen. "Globalization, Market Civilization, and Disciplinary Neoliberalism." *Millennium: Journal of International Studies* 24 (1995): 399–424.

Gilpin, Robert. *War and Change in World Politics*. Cambridge: Cambridge University Press, 1981.

Goldgeier, James M. and Michael McFaul. "A Tale of Two Worlds: Core and Periphery in the Post–Cold War Era." *International Organization* 46 (1992): 467–491.

Goldstein, Judith. *Ideas, Interests, and American Trade Policy*. Ithaca, N.Y.: Cornell University Press, 1993.

Goldstein, Judith and Robert O. Keohane. "Ideas and Foreign Policy: An Analytical Framework." In *Ideas and Foreign Policy: Beliefs, Institutions, and Political Change*, edited by Judith Goldstein and Robert O. Keohane, 3–30. Ithaca, N.Y.: Cornell University Press, 1993.

Goltz, Thomas. *Azerbaijan Diary*. Armonk, N.Y.: M. E. Sharpe, 1998.

Gopnik, Allison, Andrew N. Meltzoff, and Patricia K. Kuhl. *The Scientist in the Crib: What Early Learning Tells Us about the Mind*. New York: Perennial, 2000.

Gosplan SSSR. *Metodicheskie Ukazaniya k Sostavleniyu Gosudarstvennogo Plana Razvitiya Narodnogo Khozyaistva SSSR*. Moscow: Ekonomika, 1969.

Gourevitch, Peter. *Politics in Hard Times*. Ithaca, N.Y.: Cornell University Press, 1986.

Gowa, Joanne. *Allies, Adversaries, and International Trade*. Princeton, N.J.: Princeton University Press, 1993.

Gray, Tim S. *The Political Philosophy of Herbert Spencer: Individualism and Organicism*. Brookfield, Vt.: Avebury, 1996.

Green, Donald P. and Alan S. Gerber. "Reclaiming the Experimental Tradition in Political Science." In *Political Science: The State of the Discipline*, 3rd ed., edited by Helen V. Milner and Ira Katznelson, 805–832. New York: W. W. Norton, 2002.

Green, Donald P., Soo Yeon Kim, and David H. Yoon. "Dirty Pool." *International Organization*, 55, no. 2 (Spring 2001): 441–468.

Grieco, Joseph. *Cooperation among Nations: Europe, America, and Non-Tariff Barriers to Trade*. Ithaca, N.Y.: Cornell University Press, 1990.

"Systemic Sources of Variation in Regional Institutionalization in Western Europe, East Asia, and the Americas." In *The Political Economy of Regionalism*, edited by Edward D. Mansfield and Helen V. Milner, 164–187. New York: Columbia University Press, 1997.

Grossman, Gene and Elhanan Helpman. "Protection for Sale." *American Economic Review* 84 (1994): 833–850.

"The Politics of Free Trade Agreements." *American Economic Review* 85 (1995): 667–690.

Grossman, Gregory. "The Solidary Society: A Philosophical Issue in Communist Economic Reforms." In *Essays in Socialism and Planning in Honor of Carl Landauer*, edited by Gregory Grossman. Englewood Cliffs, N.J.: Prentice-Hall, 1970.

"The Party as Manager and Entrepreneur." In *Entrepreneurship in Imperial Russia and the Soviet Union*, edited by Gregory Guroff and F. V. Carstensen. Princeton, N.J.: Princeton University Press, 1983.

Grzymala-Busse, Anna M. *Redeeming the Communist Past: The Regeneration of Communist Parties in East Central Europe.* Cambridge: Cambridge University Press, 2002.

Guelfat, Isaac. *Economic Thought in the Soviet Union, Concepts and Aspects: A Comparative Outline.* The Hague: Martinus Nijhoff, 1969.

Haas, Ernst B. *Beyond the Nation-State: Functionalism and International Organization.* Stanford, Calif.: Stanford University Press, 1964.

"Words Can Hurt You: Or, Who Said What to Whom about Regimes." In *International Regimes*, edited by Steven D. Krasner. Ithaca, N.Y.: Cornell University Press, 1983.

When Knowledge Is Power: Three Models of Change in International Organizations. Berkeley: University of California Press, 1990.

Nationalism, Liberalism, and Progress: The Rise and Decline of Nationalism. Ithaca, N.Y.: Cornell University Press, 1997.

Haas, Peter M., ed. "Knowledge, Power, and International Policy Coordination." *International Organization* 46 (special issue, 1992a): 289–322.

Haas, Peter M. "Introduction: Epistemic Communities and International Policy Coordination." In "Knowledge, Power, and International Policy Coordination," edited by Peter Haas. *International Organization* 46 (special issue, 1992b): 1–35.

Hale, Henry Ewing. "Russia's Fiscal Veto on CIS Integration." PONARS Policy Memo 15, 1997.

"Statehood at Stake: Democratization, Secession and the Collapse of the USSR." Ph.D. dissertation, Harvard University, 1998.

Hall, John A. "Ideas and the Social Sciences." In *Ideas and Foreign Policy: Beliefs, Institutions, and Political Change*, edited by Judith Goldstein and Robert Keohane, 31–56. Ithaca, N.Y.: Cornell University Press, 1993.

Hall, Peter A., ed. *The Political Power of Economic Ideas: Keynesianism across Nations.* Princeton, N.J.: Princeton University Press, 1989.

Governing the Economy: The Politics of State Intervention in Britain and France. New York: Oxford University Press, 1986.

"Policy Paradigms, Social Learning, and the State: The Case of Economic Policy-Making in Britain." *Comparative Politics* 25, no. 3 (April 1993): 275–296.

Hanson, Stephen E. *Time and Revolution: Marxism and the Design of Soviet Institutions.* Chapel Hill: University of North Carolina Press, 1997.

Hayek, F. A. von. "Scientism and the Study of Society." *Economica* 9, no. 35 (1943): 267–291.

Hempel, Carl G. "The Function of General Laws in History." *Journal of Philosophy* 39 (1942): 35–48.

Herrera, Yoshiko. *Imagined Economies: The Sources of Russian Regionalism.* New York: Cambridge University Press, 2005.

Hirschman, Albert O. *National Power and the Structure of Foreign Trade.* Berkeley: University of California Press, 1945.

"Ideologies of Economic Development in Latin America." In *Latin American Issues – Essays and Comments*, edited by A. O. Hirschman. New York: Twentieth Century Fund, 1961.

Shifting Involvements: Private Interest and Public Action. Princeton, N.J.: Princeton University Press, 1982.

Hopf, Ted. *Social Construction of International Politics: Identities and Foreign Policies, Moscow, 1955 and 1999.* Ithaca, N.Y.: Cornell University Press, 2002.

Hume, David. *A Treatise of Human Nature,* 1739.

An Enquiry Concerning Human Understanding, 2nd ed. Indianapolis: Hackett, 1993.

Ikenberry, G. John. "A World Economy Restored: Expert Consensus and the Anglo-American Postwar Settlement." In "Knowledge, Power, and International Policy Coordination," edited by Peter Haas. *International Organization* 46 (special issue, 1992): 1–35.

"Creating Yesterday's New World Order: Keynesian 'New Thinking' and the Anglo-American Postwar Settlement." In *Ideas and Foreign Policy: Beliefs, Institutions, and Political Change,* edited by Judith Goldstein and Robert Keohane, 57–86. Ithaca, N.Y.: Cornell University Press, 1993.

After Victory: Institutions, Strategic Restraint, and the Rebuilding of Order after Major Wars. Princeton, N.J.: Princeton University Press, 2003.

Ikenberry, G. John and Charles Kupchan. "Socialization and Hegemonic Power." *International Organization* 44, no. 3 (Summer 1990): 283–315.

International Monetary Fund. Country Report 02/64, April 2002. Republic of Kazakhstan, Selected Issues and Statistical Appendix, 2002.

Ispolnitel'nyi Sekretariat SNG. *Sodruzhestvo Nezavisimykh Gosudarstv: Portret na fone peremen.* Minsk: Pangraf, 1996.

Jackson, Robert H. *Quasi-States: Sovereignty, International Relations, and the Third World.* Cambridge: Cambridge University Press, 1990.

Jacobsen, John Kurt. "Much Ado about Ideas: The Cognitive Factor in Economic Policy." *World Politics* 47 (1995): 283–310.

Johnson, Juliet. "Russia's Emerging Financial-Industrial Groups." *Post-Soviet Affairs* 13 (1997): 333–365.

Johnston, Alastair Iain. *Cultural Realism: Strategic Culture and Grand Strategy in Chinese History.* Princeton, N.J.: Princeton University Press, 1995.

"Cultural Realism and Strategy in Maoist China." In *The Culture of National Security: Norms and Identity in World Politics,* edited by Peter Katzenstein. Princeton, N.J.: Princeton University Press, 1996.

Jones Luong, Pauline. *Institutional Change and Political Continuity in Post-Soviet Central Asia: Power, Perceptions, and Pacts.* Cambridge: Cambridge University Press, 2002.

"Politics in the Periphery: Competing Views of Central Asian States and Societies." In *The Transformation of Central Asia: States and Societies from Soviet Rule to Independence,* edited by Pauline Jones Luong. Ithaca, N.Y.: Cornell University Press, 2003.

Jowitt, Ken. *New World Disorder: The Leninist Extinction.* Berkeley: University of California Press, 1991.

Kahler, Miles. *International Institutions and the Political Economy of Integration.* Washington, D.C.: Brookings Institution, 1995.

Kant, Immanuel. *Critique of Pure Reason,* translated by Norman Kemp Smith. New York: St. Martin's Press, 1965.

Karimov, Islam. *Building the Future: Uzbekistan – Its Own Model for Transition to a Market Economy.* Tashkent: Uzbekiston, 1993.

Karl, Terry Lynn. *The Paradox of Plenty: Oil Booms and Petro-States.* Berkeley: University of California Press, 1997.

Katzenstein, Peter J. *Small States in World Markets.* Ithaca, N.Y.: Cornell University Press, 1985.

Kazhegeldin, Akezhan. *Kazakhstan: Meeting the Challenges Ahead.* Published by Author, 1998.

Keck, Margaret E. and Kathryn Sikkink. *Activists beyond Borders: Advocacy Networks in International Politics.* Ithaca, N.Y.: Cornell University Press, 1998.

Keohane, Robert O. *After Hegemony: Cooperation and Discord in the World Political Economy.* Princeton, N.J.: Princeton University Press, 1984.

Kharkhordin, Oleg. *The Collective and the Individual in Russia.* Berkeley: University of California Press, 1999.

Kier, Elizabeth. *Imagining War: French and British Military Doctrine between the Wars.* Princeton, N.J.: Princeton University Press, 1997.

Kindleberger, Charles P. *The World in Depression: 1929–1939.* Berkeley: University of California Press, 1973.

King, Gary, Robert O. Keohane, and Sidney Verba. *Designing Social Inquiry.* Princeton, N.J.: Princeton University Press, 1996.

Kirichenko, Olexiy. "Moving Forward into the Past." *The Ukrainian Panorama* 1 (1997): 2.

Knight, Jack. *Institutions and Social Conflict.* Cambridge: Cambridge University Press, 1992.

"Models, Interpretations, and Theories: Constructing Explanations of Institutional Emergence and Change." In *Explaining Social Institutions,* edited by Jack Knight and Itai Sened, 95–119. Ann Arbor: University of Michigan Press, 1995.

Knight, Jack and Itai Sened, eds. *Explaining Social Institutions.* Ann Arbor: University of Michigan Press, 1995.

Konovalov, Vladimir. "Russian Trade Policy." In *Trade in the New Independent States,* edited by Constantine Michalopolous and David G. Tarr, 29–51. Studies of Economies in Transformation No. 13. Washington, D.C.: World Bank, 1994.

Korotchenia, I. M. *Ekonomicheskii Soyuz Suverenniykh Gosudarstv: Strategiya i Taktika Stanovleniya.* St. Petersburg: Saint Petersburg University of Economics and Finance, 1995.

Kotkin, Stephen. *Magnetic Mountain: Stalinism as a Civilization.* Berkeley: University of California Press, 1995.

Kowert, Paul and Jeffrey Legro. "Norms, Identity, and Their Limits: A Theoretical Reprise." In *The Culture of National Security: Norms and Identity in World Politics,* edited by Peter J. Katzenstein, 451–497. New York: Columbia University Press, 1996.

Krasner, Stephen D. "State Power and the Structure of International Trade." *World Politics* 28 (1976): 317–347.

——. *Defending the National Interest: Raw Materials Investments and U.S. Foreign Policy*. Princeton, N.J.: Princeton University Press, 1978.

——. "Westphalia and All That." In *Ideas and Foreign Policy: Beliefs, Institutions, and Political Change*, edited by Judith Goldstein and Robert O. Keohane, 235–264. Ithaca, N.Y.: Cornell University Press, 1993.

Kreps, David M. *A Course in Microeconomic Theory*. Princeton, N.J.: Princeton University Press, 1990.

Kuhn, Thomas S. *The Structure of Scientific Revolutions*, 2nd ed. Chicago: University of Chicago Press, 1970.

Laitin, David D. *Identity in Formation: The Russian-Speaking Populations in the Near Abroad*. Ithaca, N.Y.: Cornell University Press, 1998.

Lake, David A. *Power, Protection, and Free Trade*. Ithaca, N.Y.: Cornell University Press, 1988.

——. "Anarchy, Hierarchy, and the Variety of International Relations." *International Organization* 50 (1996): 1–33.

——. "The Rise, Fall, and Future of the Russian Empire: A Theoretical Interpretation." In *The End of Empire? The Transformation of the USSR in Comparative Perspective*, edited by Karen Dawisha and Bruce Parrott, 30–63. New York: M. E. Sharpe, 1997.

Lawrence, Robert Z. *Regionalism, Multilateralism, and Deeper Integration*. Washington, D.C.: Brookings Institution, 1996.

LeGall, Francoise. "Ukraine: A Trade and Exchange System Still Seeking Direction." In *Trade in the New Independent States*, edited by Constantine Michalopolous and David G. Tarr, 65–81. Studies of Economies in Transformation No. 13. Washington, D.C.: World Bank, 1994.

Legro, Jeffrey W. "Which Norms Matter? Revisiting the 'Failure' of Internationalism." *International Organization* 51 (1997): 31–63.

——. "The Transformation of Policy Ideas." *American Journal of Political Science* 44, no. 3 (July 2000): 419–432.

Leontiev, A. and E. Khmelnitskaia. *Ocherki Perekhodnoi Ekonomiki*. Leningrad: Priboi, 1927.

Leontyev, Mikhail. "Couponization at a Faster Rate: The First Concept of Ukrainian Economic Reform," *Nezavisimaia Gazeta*, Moscow, 1 April 1992, p. 1. FBIS-USR-92-045.

Levy, Jack S. "Learning and Foreign Policy: Sweeping a Conceptual Minefield." *International Organization* 48 (1994): 279–312.

Lieven, Anatol. *The Baltic Revolution: Estonia, Latvia, Lithuania and the Path to Independence*. New Haven, Conn.: Yale University Press, 1993.

Lumsdaine, David Halloran. *Moral Vision: The Foreign Aid Regime, 1949–1989*. Princeton, N.J.: Princeton University Press, 1993.

Machiavelli, Niccolo. *The Discourses*, translated by Leslie J. Walker. New York: Penguin Books, 1970.

Magee, Stephen, William Brock, and Leslie Young. *Black Hole Tariffs and Endogenous Policy Theory*. Cambridge: Cambridge University Press, 1989.

Mannheim, Karl. *Ideology and Utopia: An Introduction to the Sociology of Knowledge*, translated by Louis Wirth and Edward Shils. New York: Harcourt, Brace and Company, 1936.

Mansfield, Edward D. "Effects of International Politics on International Trade." In *Regional Integration and the Global Trading System*, edited by Kym Anderson and Richard Blackhurst. London: Harvester Wheatsheaf, 1993.

Mansfield, Edward D. and Marc L. Busch. "The Political Economy of Non-Tariff Barriers: A Cross-National Analysis." *International Organization* 49, no. 4 (Autumn 1995): 723–749.

Mansfield, Edward D. and Rachel Bronson. "The Political Economy of Major-Power Trade Flows." In *The Political Economy of Regionalism*, edited by Edward D. Mansfield and Helen V. Milner, 188–208. New York: Columbia University Press, 1997.

Marx, Karl and Friedrich Engels. *The German Ideology*. New York: International, 1986.

Masol, Vitaliy. "What Has the 'New Policy' Brought Us? My View of the Socioeconomic and Political Processes in Ukraine." Article in five installments by Ukrainian Prime Minister Vitaliy Masol. *Silski Visti* 3, 7, 9, 10, 14 June 1994. [FBIS Translation]

Mattli, Walter. *Logic of Regional Integration: Europe and Beyond*. Cambridge: Cambridge University Press, 1999.

McFaul, Michael. *Russia's Unfinished Revolution: Political Change from Gorbachev to Putin*. Ithaca, N.Y.: Cornell University Press, 2001.

"The Fourth Wave of Democracy and Dictatorship: Noncooperative Transitions in the Post-Communist World." *World Politics* 54, no. 2 (January 2002): 212–244.

McKeown, Timothy J. "Hegemonic Stability Theory and 19th Century Tariff Levels in Europe." *International Organization* 37 (1983): 73–91.

"Decision Processes and Co-Operation in Foreign Policy." In *Choosing to Cooperate: How States Avoid Loss*, edited by Janice Gross Stein and Louis W. Pauly, 202–219. Baltimore: Johns Hopkins University Press, 1993.

McNamara, Kathleen R. *The Currency of Ideas: Monetary Politics in the European Union*. Ithaca, N.Y.: Cornell University Press, 1998.

Mearscheimer, John J. "The False Promise of International Institutions." *International Security* 19 (1994/1995): 5–49.

"A Realist Reply." *International Security* 20 (1995): 82–93.

Meyer, John W. and Brian Rowan. "Institutionalized Organizations: Formal Structure as Myth and Ceremony." In *The New Institutionalism in Organizational Analysis*, edited by Walter W. Powell and Paul J. DiMaggio. Chicago: University of Chicago Press, 1991.

Michalopoulos, Constantine and David Tarr. "The Economics of Customs Union in the Commonwealth of Independent States" *Post-Soviet Geography and Economics* 38 (1997): 125–143.

Milner, Helen V. *Resisting Protectionism*. Princeton, N.J.: Princeton University Press, 1988.

Interests, Institutions, and Information: Domestic Politics and International Relations. Princeton, N.J.: Princeton University Press, 1997a.

"Industries, Governments, and the Creation of Regional Trade Blocs." In *The Political Economy of Regionalism*, edited by Edward D. Mansfield and Helen V. Milner, 77–108. New York: Columbia University Press, 1997b.

Milner, Helen V. and Robert O. Keohane. "Internationalization and Domestic Politics: An Introduction." In *Internationalization and Domestic Politics*, edited by Robert O. Keohane and Helen V. Milner, 3–24. Cambridge: Cambridge University Press, 1996.

Moore, Barrington, Jr. *Soviet Politics — the Dilemma of Power: The Role of Ideas in Social Change*. New York: Harper & Row, 1950.

Moravcsik, Andrew. "Taking Preferences Seriously: A Liberal Theory of International Politics." *International Organization* 51 (1997): 513–553.

The Choice for Europe: Social Purpose and State Power from Messina to Maastricht. Ithaca, N.Y.: Cornell University Press, 1998.

Murillo, M. Victoria. "Political Bias in Policy Convergence. Privatization Choices in Latin America." *World Politics* 54 (2002): 462–493.

[*Narkhoz*] Gosudarstvennyi Komitet SSSR po Statistike. *Narodnoe Khoziastvo SSSR v 1990g*. Moscow: Finansy i Statistika, 1991.

Natsionalnyi Sostav Naseleniia SSSR, po dannym vsesoiuznoi perepisi naseleniia 1989. Moscow: Finansy i Statistika, 1991.

Nazarbaev, Nursultan A. "Ideya Kotoroi Prinadlezhit Budushchee," *Evrazia. Narody. Kultury. Religii*, 1995.

Evraziiskii Soiuz: Idei, Praktika, Perspektivy, 1994–1997. Moscow: Fond Sodeistvia razvitiiu sotsial'nykh i politicheskikh nauk, 1997.

Nelson, Douglas. "Endogenous Tariff Theory: A Critical Survey." *American Journal of Political Science* 32 (1988): 796–837.

Nettl, J. P. "The State as a Conceptual Variable." *World Politics* 20 (July 1968): 559–592.

Nietzsche, Friedrich. *The Will to Power*, translated by Walter Kaufmann and R. J. Hollingdale. New York: Vintage Books, 1968.

Nordlinger, Eric A. *On the Autonomy of the Democratic State*. Cambridge, Mass.: Harvard University Press, 1981.

Nove, Alex. *An Economic History of the U.S.S.R.* New York: Penguin Books, 1989.

Odell, John S. *U.S. International Monetary Policy: Markets, Power, and Ideas as Sources of Change*. Princeton, N.J.: Princeton University Press, 1982.

Odling-Smee, John, and Gonzalo Pastor. "The IMF and the Ruble Area, 1991–1993." *IMF Working Paper* WP01/01, 2001.

Odom, William E. *The Collapse of the Soviet Military*. New Haven, Conn.: Yale University Press, 1998.

Odom, William E. and Robert Dujarric. *Commonwealth or Empire? Russia, Central Asia, and the Transcaucasus*. Indianapolis: Hudson Institute, 1995.

Olcott, Martha Brill. *The Kazakhs*, 2nd ed. Stanford, Calif.: Hoover Institution Press, 1995.

"Kazakhstan: Pushing for Eurasia." In *New States, New Politics: Building the Post-Soviet Nations*, edited by Ian Bremmer and Ray Taras. Cambridge: Cambridge University Press, 1997.

Olcott, Martha Brill, Anders Aslund, and Sherman W. Garnett. *Getting It Wrong: Regional Cooperation and the Commonwealth of Independent States.* Washington, D.C.: Carnegie Endowment for International Peace, 1999.

Pocock, J.G.A. "On the Non-Revolutionary Character of Paradigms." In *Politics, Language, and Time: Essays on Political Thought and History,* 273–291. Chicago: University of Chicago Press, 1971.

Polanyi, Karl. *The Great Transformation: The Political and Economic Origins of Our Time.* Boston: Beacon Press, 1957.

Posen, Barry R. "The Security Dilemma and Ethnic Conflict." *Survival* 35 (1993): 27–41.

Powell, Robert. "Anarchy in International Relations Theory: The Neorealist–Neoliberal Debate." *International Organization* 48 (1994): 313–344.

Preobrazhensky, E. A. *New Economics.* English translation of *Novaia Ekonomika,* 2nd ed. Oxford: Clarendon Press, 1926.

PriceWaterhouseCoopers. "Final Report: Ukraine Mass Privatization Project." (PriceWaterhouseCoopers for United States Agency for International Development, 1998).

Prizel, Ilya. *National Identity and Foreign Policy: Nationalism and Leadership in Poland, Russia, and Ukraine.* Cambridge: Cambridge University Press, 1998.

Putnam, Robert D. "Diplomacy and Domestic Politics: The Logic of Two-Level Games." *International Organization* 42 (1988): 427–460.

Risse, Thomas. "'Let's Argue!': Communicative Action in International Politics." *International Organization* 54, no. 1 (Winter 2000): 1–39.

Risse, Thomas and Kathryn Sikkink. "The Socialization of International Human Rights Norms into Domestic Practices: Introduction." In *The Power of Human Rights: International Norms and Domestic Change,* edited by Thomas Risse, Stephen C. Ropp, and Kathryn Sikkink. Cambridge: Cambridge University Press, 1999.

Rizhinashvili, Constantine. "Further CIS Integration Does Not Make Economic Sense." *Russia and Commonwealth Business Law Report* 8, no. 14 (22 October 1997).

Roeder, Philip G. *Red Sunset: The Failure of Soviet Politics.* Princeton, N.J.: Princeton University Press, 1993.

"From Hierarchy to Hegemony: The Post-Soviet Security Complex." In *Regional Orders,* edited by David A. Lake and Patrick M. Morgan. University Park: Pennsylvania State University Press, 1997.

Rogowski, Ronald. *Commerce and Coalitions.* Princeton, N.J.: Princeton University Press, 1989.

Rohrlich, Paul Egon. "Economic Culture and Foreign Policy: The Cognitive Analysis of Economic Policy Making." *International Organization* 41 (1987): 61–92.

Ruggie, John Gerard. "International Regimes, Transactions and Change: Embedded Liberalism in the Postwar Economic Order." *International Organization* 36 (1982): 195–231.

"Continuity and Transformation in the World Polity: Toward a Neorealist Synthesis." In *Neorealism and Its Critics,* edited by Robert O. Keohane, 131–157. New York: Columbia University Press 1986.

"Territoriality and Beyond: Problematizing Modernity in International Relations." *International Organization* 47 (1993): 139–174.

Constructing the World Polity: Essays on International Institutionalization. New York: Routledge, 1999.

Rumer, Boris Z. *Soviet Steel: The Challenge of Industrial Modernization in the USSR.* Ithaca, N.Y.: Cornell University Press, 1989.

Rysbekov, Marat. "Privatization in Kazakhstan." *Comparative Economic Studies,* 37 (1995): 1–10.

Sachs, Jeffrey D. and A. Warner. "Economic Reform and the Process of Global Integration." *Brookings Papers on Economic Activity* 1 (1995): 1–118.

Sadji (pseudonym). "Kyrgyzstan's President Askar Akaev: A Political Portrait." *Jamestown Foundation Prism* 4, no. 11 (26 May 1998).

Sandholtz, Wayne and John Zysman. "1992: Recasting the European Bargain." *World Politics* 42, no. 1 (October 1989): 95–128.

Schelling, Thomas. *Micromotives and Macrobehavior.* New York: W. W. Norton, 1978.

Scheve, Kenneth F. and Matthew J. Slaughter. "What Determines Individual Trade Policy Preferences?" *Journal of International Economics* 54, no. 2 (August 2001): 267–292.

Schonhardt-Bailey, Cheryl. "Lessons for Lobbying for Free Trade in 19th Century Britain." *American Political Science Review* 85 (1991): 37–58.

Scott, James C. *Domination and the Arts of Resistance: Hidden Transcripts.* New Haven, Conn.: Yale University Press, 1990.

Seeing Like a State: How Certain Schemes to Improve the Human Condition Have Failed. New Haven, Conn.: Yale University Press, 1998.

Searle, John R. *Intentionality: An Essay in the Philosophy of Mind.* Cambridge: Cambridge University Press, 1983.

The Construction of Social Reality. New York: Free Press, 1995.

The Rediscovery of the Mind. Cambridge, MA: MIT Press, 1992.

Sen, Amartya. "Rational Fools: A Critique of the Behavioural Foundations of Economic Theory." *Philosophy and Public Affairs* 6 (1977): 317–344.

Senn, Alfred Erich. "Post-Soviet Political Leadership in Lithuania." In *Patterns of Post-Soviet Leadership,* edited by Timothy J. Colton and Robert C. Tucker, 123–140. Boulder, Colo.: Westview Press, 1995.

Serov, V. M. "Razumnoi al'ternativy integratsii ne sushchestvuyet." *MEK Biulleten'* 96 (1996): 4.

Shafer, D. Michael. *Deadly Paradigms: The Failure of U.S. Counterinsurgency Policy.* Princeton, N.J.: Princeton University Press, 1988.

Shen, Raphael. *Restructuring the Baltic Economies: Disengaging Fifty Years of Integration with the USSR.* Westport, Conn.: Praeger, 1994.

Shepsle, Kenneth A. "Comment on Derthick and Quirk." In *Regulatory Policy and the Social Sciences,* edited by Roger G. Noll. Berkeley: University of California Press, 1985.

Shleifer, Andrei and Daniel Treisman. *Without a Map: Political Tactics and Economic Reform in Russia.* Cambridge, Mass.: MIT Press, 2000.

Shulman, Steven. "Nationalist Sources of International Economic Integration." *International Studies Quarterly* 44 (2000): 365–390.

Sikkink, Kathryn. *Ideas and Institutions: Developmentalism in Brazil and Argentina.* Ithaca, N.Y.: Cornell University Press, 1991.

Simmons, Beth A. *Who Adjusts? Domestic Sources of Foreign Economic Policy During the Interwar Years.* Princeton, NJ: Princeton University Press, 1997.

Simon, Herbert. *Models of Man.* New York: John Wiley & Sons, 1956.

"The Architecture of Complexity." *Proceedings of the American Philosophical Society* 106 (1962): 467–482.

Administrative Behavior, 3rd ed. New York: Free Press, 1976.

Solchanyk, Roman. "Russia, Ukraine, and the Imperial Legacy." *Post-Soviet Affairs* 9 (1993): 337–365.

Sombart, Werner. *Deutscher Sozialismus.* Berlin: Buchholz and Weisswange, 1934.

Sorsa, Piritta. "Lithuania: Trade Issues in Transition." In *Trade in the New Independent States,* edited by Constantine Michalopolous and David G. Tarr, 157–170. Studies of Economies in Transformation No. 13. Washington, D.C.: World Bank, 1994.

"Latvia: Trade Issues in Transition." In *Trade in the New Independent States,* edited by Constantine Michalopolous and David G. Tarr, 141–156. Studies of Economies in Transformation No. 13. Washington, D.C.: World Bank, 1994.

Spann, Othmar. *Types of Economic Theory,* translated by Eden and Cedar Paul. London: George Allen and Unwin, 1930 [1910].

Spencer, Herbert. *Essays: Scientific, Political, and Speculative,* Vol. 1. London: Williams and Norgate, 1901.

Spruyt, Hendrik. *The Sovereign State and Its Competitors: An Analysis of Systems Change.* Princeton, N.J.: Princeton University Press, 1994.

"The Prospects for Neo-Imperial and Non-Imperial Outcomes in the Former Soviet Space." In *The End of Empire? The Transformation of the USSR in Comparative Perspective,* edited by Karen Dawisha and Bruce Parrott, 315–337. New York: M. E. Sharpe, 1997.

Starr, S. Frederick. "Introduction." In *The Legacy of History in Russia and the New States of Eurasia,* edited by S. Frederick Starr. New York: M. E. Sharpe, 1994.

Stein, Janice Gross. "International Co-Operation and Loss Avoidance: Framing the Problem." In *Choosing to Co-Operate: How States Avoid Loss,* edited by Janice Gross Stein and Louis W. Pauly, 2–34. Baltimore: Johns Hopkins University Press, 1993.

Stein, Janice Gross and Louis W. Pauly, eds. *Choosing to Co-Operate: How States Avoid Loss.* Baltimore: Johns Hopkins University Press, 1993.

"Stenograficheskii otchet zasedaniia kollegii MEKa po voprosu 'ob itogakh deiatel'nosti MEKa v 1995 – pervoi polovine 1996 gg in ego zadachakh na vtoruiu polovinu 1996–1997 gg.' August 30, 1996." *MEK Biulleten'* 1996, no. 3.

Sternhell, Zeev. *Birth of Fascist Ideology: From Cultural Rebellion to Political Revolution.* Princeton, N.J.: Princeton University Press, 1994.

Suny, Ronald Grigor. "Ambiguous Categories: States, Empires, and Nations." *Post-Soviet Affairs* 11 (1995): 185–196.

Swidler, Ann. "Culture in Action: Symbols and Strategies." *American Sociological Review* 51 (1986): 273–286.

Szporluk, Roman. "Introduction." In *National Identity and Ethnicity in Russia and the New States of Eurasia,* edited by Roman Szporluk. New York: M. E. Sharpe, 1994.

Trefler, Daniel. "Trade Liberalization and the Theory of Endogenous Protection." *Journal of Political Economy* 101 (1993): 138–160.

Tsygankov, A. P. "Defining State Interests after Empire: National Identity, Domestic Structures, and Foreign Trade Policies of Latvia and Belarus." *Review of International Political Economy* 7 (2000): 101–137.

Pathways after Empire. National Identity and Foreign Economic Policy in the Post-Soviet World. Lanham, Md.: Rowman & Littlfield, 2001.

Tucker, Robert C. *The Soviet Political Mind: Stalinism and Post-Stalin Change.* New York: W. W. Norton, 1971.

Urban, Michael. "The Politics of Identity in Russia's Postcommunist Transition: The Nation against Itself." *Slavic Review* 53 (1994): 733–765.

Urban, Michael with Vyacheslav Igrunov and Sergei Mitrokhin. *The Rebirth of Politics in Russia.* Cambridge: Cambridge University Press, 1997.

U.S. Department of State, *Country Reports on Economic Policy and Trade Practices: Ukraine*, 1997.

Ushakov, D. N., ed. *Tolkovyi Slovar' Russkogo Iazyka: Tom II.* Moscow: State Press for Foreign and National Dictionaries, 1938.

Van Arkadie, Brian and Mats Karlsson. *Economic Survey of the Baltic States: The Reform Process in Estonia, Latvia and Lithuania.* London: Pinter, 1992.

Van Selm, Bert. *The Economics of Soviet Break-Up.* New York: Routledge, 1997.

Viner, Jacob. "Power versus Plenty as Objectives of Foreign Policy in the Seventeenth and Eighteenth Centuries." *World Politics* 1 (1948): 1–29.

"Mercantilist Thought." In *Essays on the Intellectual History of Economics*, edited by Douglas A. Irwin. Princeton, N.J.: Princeton University Press, 1991.

Van Arkadie, Brian and Mats Karlsson, *Economic Survey of the Baltic States: The Reform Process in Estonia, Latvia and Lithuania.* London: Pinter, 1992.

Waltz, Kenneth N. *Man, the State and War.* New York: Columbia University Press, 1959.

Theory of International Politics. San Francisco: McGraw-Hill, 1979.

Webber, Mark. *CIS Integration Trends: Russia and the Former Soviet South.* London: Royal Institute of International Affairs, 1997.

Webber, Mark and Richard Sakwa. "The Commonwealth of Independent States, 1991–1998: Stagnation and Survival." *Europe-Asia Studies* 51 (1999): 379–415.

Weber, Max. *The Protestant Ethic and the Spirit of Capitalism*, translated by Talcott Parsons. New York: Charles Scribner's Sons, 1958.

Weir, Margaret. "Ideas and Politics: The Acceptance of Keynesianism in Britain and the United States." In *The Political Power of Economic Ideas: Keynesianism across Nations*, edited by Peter A. Hall, 53–86. Princeton, N.J.: Princeton University Press, 1989.

Wendt, Alexander. "Anarchy Is What States Make of It: The Social Construction of Power Politics." *International Organization* 46: 2.

Social Theory of International Politics. Cambridge: Cambridge University Press, 1999.

Wendt, Alexander and Daniel Friedheim. "Hierarchy under Anarchy: Informal Empire and the East German State." *International Organization* 49 (1995): 689–722.

Wight, Martin. *Systems of States.* Bristol, England: Leicester University Press, 1977.

Williamson, Oliver E., *Markets and Hierarchies: Analysis and Antitrust Implications.* New York: Free Press, 1975.

Williamson, Oliver E. "The Economics of Governance: Framework and Implications." *Journal of Theoretical Economics* 140 (1984): 195–223.

Williamson, Oliver E. The Mechanisms of Governance. New York: Oxford University Press, 1996.

Wilson, Andrew. *Ukrainian Nationalism in the 1990s: A Minority Faith.* Cambridge: Cambridge University Press, 1997.

Woods, Ngaire. "Economic Ideas and International Relations: Beyond Rational Neglect." *International Studies Quarterly* 39, no. 2 (June 1995): 161–180.

World Bank. *Statistical Handbook 1995: States of the Former USSR.* Studies of Economies in Transformation Paper No. 19. Washington, D.C.: World Bank, 1995.

Yee, Albert S. "The Causal Effects of Ideas on Policies." *International Organization* 50 (1996): 69–108.

Yeltsin, Boris N. *The Struggle for Russia*, translated by Catherine A. Fitzpatrick. New York: Times Books, 1994.

Young, Oran R. "The Politics of International Regime Formation: Managing Natural Resources and the Environment." *International Organization* 43 (1989): 349–375.

Zullow, H., G. Oettingen, C. Peterson, and M.E.P Seligman. "Pessimistic Explanatory Style in the Historical Record: Caving LBJ, Presidential Candidates and East versus West Berlin." *American Psychologist* 43 (1988): 673–682.

Index